Which? …ING GUIDE 1991

Which? BOOKS

Published by Consumers' Association,
publishers of *Which?* magazine,
and Hodder & Stoughton

Which? Buying Guide 1991 is a compilation of *Which?* test reports, researched by The Association for Consumer Research, that were first published between October 1989 and October 1990. This *Guide* is published by Consumers' Association, 2 Marylebone Road, London NW1 4DX and Hodder & Stoughton, 47 Bedford Square, London WC1B 3DP

First edition November 1990
Reprinted November 1990

British Library Cataloguing in Publication Data
Which? buying guide 1991.
1. Great Britain. Consumer goods. Selection
I. Consumers' Association
640.730941

ISBN 0-340-53857-0

Compiled by Simon Enticknap
Designed by Paul Saunders with Dick Vine
Cover photograph by Hilary Moore

Typeset by Rowland Phototypesetting Limited,
Bury St Edmunds, Suffolk
Printed and bound in Great Britain by
Richard Clay Ltd, Bungay, Suffolk

CONTENTS

IN THE KITCHEN

CLEANING AND LAUNDRY

SOUND AND VISION

ABOUT THE HOUSE AND GARDEN

ON THE ROAD

Welcome to *Which? Buying Guide*!

Every year we test thousands of products and report on them in *Which?*. This year, for the first time, we are reproducing a selection of key test reports in a handy paperback.

All the information in these test reports was as up-to-date as we could make it at the time of its publication in *Which?*. We've shown when that was at the top of each report. Some details – prices and product model numbers, names of some companies and other bodies or organisations, for instance – may have changed since then. We've left out full details on some models that we know have been discontinued (but see page 285 for the list of items we've excluded). You may find that other models have disappeared since then but, even so, there's still lots of useful advice on product features, and particular points to look for when you're out shopping. Most products should still be on the market, however, and, of course, if you're buying second-hand, the *Guide* should prove invaluable.

***Which?* – independent, unbiased, unique**

As with *Which?* magazine itself, all the information in *Which? Buying Guide* is totally objective. You may not realise quite what lengths we go to in order to give you the unbiased facts. Even some people who've known and trusted the information they got from *Which?* for years are still amazed to discover that we *buy* every single product that we test – and that includes cars and cookers as well as toasters and tyres.

Buying what we test means that there's no chance of our getting 'doctored' samples, and that manufacturers have no hold over us, as they might if we merely borrowed their products or were given free samples. We go out shopping just as you would – and we make sure no one knows we're shopping for *Which?*.

Which? has been doing all this, on behalf of its subscribers and other consumers, for over 30 years. And it does it without any financial support from Government or industry or anyone else – and without accepting any advertising or other form of sponsorship. What makes it possible is the fact that so many people want and need the information that only *Which?* can give them.

When you subscribe to *Which?*, you become a member of Consumers' Association. CA uses the income it gets from selling *Which?* magazines and books to carry on testing products and services – and to campaign on behalf of all consumers. Some of our campaigns have brought about changes in the law; others have persuaded manufacturers to improve safety standards.

If you're new to *Which?*, we hope you'll find enough in *Which? Buying Guide* to make you consider subscribing to the magazine itself – see page 287 for how to get three trial issues completely free. If you're already a subscriber, we think you'll find it useful to have 'the pick of *Which?*' all in one handy volume, particularly for checking out potential purchases in the high street.

Sue Leggate

Sue Leggate
Editor, *Which?*

About *Which?* test reports

Test reports in *Which?* provide two sorts of information:

• ***test results*** on a range of models, from which specific buying recommendations are made. Tests generally cover performance, convenience in use, safety and economy; where possible, durability is also assessed

• ***general advice*** about the products – types available, features to look for, typical buying and running costs, and so on. This is based on our tests over the years, together with surveys of owners' experiences, advice from independent experts, our research to find out the full ranges of products available in the shops, and price surveys.

Where possible, *Which?* reports aim to cover all the products available at the time the research was carried out. But in many cases this isn't possible because of the large number (over 200 models of washing machine and video recorder are available at any one time, for example), and because of rapid model changes. Where we have to choose a limited number from the models on the market, we take into account considerations such as readers' interest in different price ranges, availability of products across the UK, innovations in design, brand shares and advertising claims, to give as broad and useful a coverage of the market as we can without testing everything.

In this Guide, we've reprinted the original reports (which are the most recent on each product) as they appeared in *Which?*, except that the text has been slightly shortened where necessary; the date of the report's original publication is stated on each. We've also taken account of subsequent corrections printed in *Which?*, and of any new research completed in time to be included. Inevitably, there will have been some changes in models in the shops – the longer ago the original report was published, the more new models you may find on the market now. Bear in mind, too, that there tends to be much more rapid model change with 'high-tech' products (TV, video, cameras, audio, computing) than with domestic appliances or d-i-y and motoring equipment. Where some models have changed, the general guidance about what to look for and the value of particular features will still apply.

A few of the products featured in the original *Which?* reports have been removed from the Tables, as the manufacturers had told us they had ceased production ('discontinued' the model) by the time we first published the report. Since, even now, some of these models may be in the shops, or of interest if you're buying second-hand, we've listed them on page 285; the individual reports draw your attention to any models that featured in the original Buying Guides. If you would like full information on these deleted models, please consult the relevant issue of *Which?*. Back issues can be bought by subscribers to *Which?* (details on page 287), and are also available at most public libraries.

We generally give *target* prices for products we've tested. These are based on our own price surveys, and were prices people in most places should have been able to find with some shopping around when the *Which?* report was published. Prices in the Guide have not been updated, and some may have changed. Models which have been discontinued by the manufacturer are often sold off at reduced prices and may be very good value. Or you may be able to buy them second-hand.

Much of our testing of products is done in our own laboratory at Harpenden in Hertfordshire. When necessary, we commission testing from other specialist laboratories in the UK. Many products are tested jointly with consumer organisations from other European countries, sometimes in the laboratories they use, mostly in the Netherlands and Germany.

Many of the tests used to assess products are based on published Standards, some British, some international. But wherever necessary our technical staff devise their own tests and design and build the equipment needed to carry them out. We place particular emphasis on assessments by users to judge convenience/ease of use, to complement the technical measurement of performance.

Using *Which? Buying Guide*

Which? reports aim to be clear and concise, making test results, general advice and our recommendations instantly comprehensible. We use plain English and avoid 'technobabble'.

The introductory text of each report gives general information and advice, also covering safety issues and findings of surveys that *Which?* carries out. We feature a 'Green Guide' in some reports, detailing related environmental issues.

Other features of the reports concern the products on test; the test results are normally given in a Table.

BUYING GUIDE This panel summarises our findings and lists our recommended models.

BEST BUY The product or products which offered the best combination of price and performance in our tests. A *Which?* Best Buy is not necessarily the model with the best test results, nor the one with the most features; nor is it necessarily the cheapest. Occasionally, nothing performed well enough, or represented sufficient value for money, to be a Best Buy.

GOOD VALUE Performance and features don't match up to a Best Buy, but these models are good value for money.

Other models mentioned in the Buying Guides have particular strengths which may be better suited to your needs.

FACTS, FIGURES AND TEST RESULTS This section gives details of the products on test and contains the test results, including the Table.

1 2 3 These numbers link columns in the Table to explanatory notes.

► Recommended in the Buying Guide ◄

KEY TO RATINGS best ◩ > ◪ > □ > ◪ > ■ worst

Recommended models are indicated by arrows at each side of the Table.

Prices quoted in the Tables and the Buying Guides are the prices you should be able to find by shopping around. Prices in *italics* are manufacturers' estimates of typical high street prices. We have not updated the prices since they were published and they may have changed.

Similar models are products which we would expect to perform similarly to ones we have tested. They may look different (cosmetic differences) or have slightly more or fewer features. They may be better suited to your needs than the tested models.

IN THE KITCHEN

Cookers • Microwave Ovens • Fridges
Freezers • Fridge-Freezers • Food Processors
Toasters • Coffee Makers • Water Filters

COOKERS

Gas, Electric and Dual-fuel

From *Which?* October 1989 and March 1990

A new cooker could set you back anything from £150 to £900 or more – a costly mistake if it turns out to be inconvenient to use, or not to do everything you want. Our cooker tests give us the know-how to warn you about drawbacks to watch out for on any cooker you find, as well as helping us pick the ones most worth buying.

Built-in or not?

I'm having my kitchen refitted and can't decide between a free-standing cooker and a built-in oven and hob. What are the pros and cons?

Built-in appliances have the obvious advantage of looking streamlined, and they let you put your hob and oven in different parts of the kitchen. You can build in the oven at waist height, so you don't have to bend to see or tend food. You can mix one manufacturer's oven with another's hob if you want, and you have a much larger choice if you want to mix fuels for your hob, grill and oven than if you bought a dual-fuel free-standing cooker.

But built-ins can cost a lot more than a free-standing cooker, and there's the expense of an oven housing unit as well. Building in your oven at waist height means you lose more worktop space than if you go for a free-standing cooker. You could build in the oven under the hob, but then you lose the convenience of having the oven at a comfortable height.

You could compromise and choose a slot-in free-standing cooker. These are designed to slip neatly between kitchen units without a gap on either side, so they have the streamlined looks of a built-in.

Slot-in cookers are more likely than traditional free-standing cookers to have a low-level grill – and the low grill may make the oven too low for easy access, especially if anyone in your household is elderly or has a bad back. This report covers free-standing and slot-in cookers only.

Fit for your kitchen?

My new house has a fitted kitchen, with a gap for the cooker. Will any cooker fit?

It's best to check (see 'Feature-finder' Tables). Even among slot-ins, there are variations in dimensions. Be particularly careful if you're buying an ordinary free-standing cooker rather than a slot-in that there's enough room in your kitchen to leave the gap at each side recommended by the manufacturer.

Electric options

I've always cooked with gas, but my new house is all-electric. What should I look for?

In general, electric cookers are cheaper to buy than gas cookers with similar features. For about £300 you could buy an electric cooker with radiant rings and a single or double oven, or one with sealed hotplates and a single oven. If you're prepared to spend more, you could go for a ceramic or halogen hob. Electric cooker hob types vary in how long they take to warm up and cool down, and in how controllable they are.

Many more electric cookers than gas have double ovens and fan-assisted ovens. The ovens of some electric cookers have all kinds of fancy cooking options. Virtually all electric cookers have a low-level grill.

It's a gas

I've had my gas cooker for 20 years. I'm out of date on what's around.

You can buy a basic gas cooker for around £250 to £300. It will have a single oven, and is less likely to have a timer or other extra features than electric cookers for the same price. There are only a few gas cookers with double ovens or fan-assisted heat. All but one – the Moffat Discovery – have traditional gas burners and pan supports. The Discovery has gas-powered discs.

Alternative cooking

Are there any alternatives to conventional gas or electric cookers?

Some range-type cookers can run on oil or solid fuel. They cost between £650 and £3,000, and you may have to pay around £200 for installation on top. They can heat your hot water, and may also incorporate a boiler for your central heating. You need to allow more space to fit one in your kitchen, and you'll have to keep the cooker 'stoked up' for heat and hot water, even if you don't need to cook.

Going for the double

I do a lot of entertaining. Is a double oven really more useful than a single large oven?

A double oven is useful if you want to be able to cook several foods at the same time at widely different temperatures, and you can use the second oven to keep plates or food warm while food is cooking in the main oven.

If you do go for a double, check that the main oven is the right size and shape for the kind of food you're likely to cook. Check, too, that access to the lower main oven isn't too awkward.

How low must you go?

If I want a slot-in cooker, do I have to have a low-level grill?

It depends how fussy you are about other features: there are very few slot-ins with high-level grills. There are eight gas slot-ins on the market with a high-level grill. Apart from two slot-ins, all electric cookers have a low-level grill.

The main disadvantage of a low-level grill is that you can't see at a glance how the food is cooking, or whether a gas grill is lit. Access to the cooker controls on a splashback or to pans on the hob may be difficult if you have to lean across the open grill compartment door to reach them. A low-level grill may be too easily accessible to small children.

On the plus side, you can usually slide out the grill pan on to the open grill door and rest it there while you turn the food, and a low-level grill may be more convenient for people with some kinds of disability.

If you're buying a single-oven slot-in cooker with a low-level grill, remember that, if the grill is in the main oven rather than in a separate compartment, you can't use the oven and grill at the same time. You may need to leave the oven door ajar or fully open while the grill is in use, and you may have to fit a metal deflector plate to stop the controls from getting too hot. We've found that these deflector plates can get too hot.

Not child's play

I have two children, aged two and four, and I want to make sure I'm choosing a cooker they're not going to hurt themselves on. What should I look for?

Look for the cookers we've tested which have safe surface temperatures, so that your children won't hurt themselves if they touch the oven door front, say, when the cooker is in use.

Avoid cookers where the grill is in the main oven, if the instructions say you have to leave the oven door open while grilling. Children could easily trip over a fully open door, or they could trap their fingers or burn themselves on a partly open door. In addition, some cookers of this type have a metal deflector plate. Deflector plates can get too hot, and they're at just the height to be a hazard to young children.

A high-level grill which is out of reach is better than a low-level one; children could injure themselves on the open door of a low-level grill compartment. Controls situated on the splashback, instead of at the front, are out of reach of children. Controls requiring a push and turn action are less easy for children to fiddle with.

Shopping around

Where should I go to look at different types of cooker?

The message is: shop around. You can find big price differences. British Gas and Electricity Board showrooms, department stores, and multiples like Comet, Currys and Rumbelows sell a wide range of cookers. Mail-order catalogues concentrate on the cheaper end of the market, and specialist kitchen retailers tend to offer the more expensive (and built-in) models.

FEATURES WORTH WATCHING OUT FOR

Use this checklist to help you decide which of the features you may find matter to you. We also report on any convenience drawbacks we found in our tests (see 'General Drawbacks' under the 'Convenience' heading in the Tables). Some of these drawbacks will matter more to one cook than another; take a look at the ones we report on and check at the shop before you buy to see whether you can live with a cooker's disadvantages.

Convenient cooking

Check that:

- the oven has enough shelves for the kinds of cooking you normally do
- the grill pan is the right size for your cooking needs
- the grill pan and oven shelves are supported when partially withdrawn; this enables you to turn food with both hands
- the grill pan handle is comfortable to hold – if it's removable, check that it's stable in use
- the grill pan and oven shelves have effective stops to prevent you from pulling hot food out on top of you
- the hob is not too cramped and that the splashback does not obstruct large pans
- pan supports have enough struts to prevent small pans toppling over. Individual supports are easier to handle and clean but all-in-one supports may allow you to slide pans more easily from one burner to the next.

Controls

These should be:

- easy to reach, grasp and turn
- clearly marked (and maybe illuminated) so you can see settings at a glance

• removable for cleaning, or easy to clean on the cooker.

Timers

• Make sure the timer is easy to set
• A minute minder is like an alarm clock: you set it to go off at the end of the cooking time. It doesn't switch the oven on or off like an autotimer.
• An autotimer allows you to start and stop cooking at the times you set (sometimes just the beginning or end). Check how much delay you can set before cooking starts.
• Some have a digital clock, some the more traditional analogue type.

Ease of cleaning

Check for potential dirt traps, and look for:
• catalytic oven linings which vaporise splashes and help to keep the oven clean
• removable parts – control knobs, pan supports, etc. – for easy cleaning
• streamlined design and smooth surfaces.

Safe cooking

• If you're buying an electric cooker with a ceramic or halogen hob, choose one with a 'hob hot' light to show that the hob is too hot to touch, even though it may be switched off.
• If you buy a cooker with a fold-down hob cover, check that there's a safety cut-out which cuts off the gas or electricity to the hotplates if you accidentally lower the cover while the hob is still lit. On some cookers, the controls turn automatically to the off position; on others you have to press a reset button to restore the hob supply next time you raise the cover, so the hob can't come on accidentally.

COOKING FOR DISABLED PEOPLE

If anyone in your household is disabled or elderly, this checklist should help you buy a suitable cooker.

It's based on the work we've done in collaboration with the Handicapped Persons Research Unit at Newcastle Polytechnic, assessing the cookers we test for use by people with a variety of disabilities.

Findings on the first cookers we've assessed in this way appear as 'Special needs good features' or 'Special needs drawbacks' under the 'Convenience' heading in our Tables of tested cookers.

Blind or partially-sighted people

• Controls should enable the user to 'feel' the right setting – click-stop controls, for example. Digital timers can't be easily set.
• Cookers with sharp edges should be avoided. A blind or partially-sighted person could hurt themselves when cooking or cleaning the cooker.
• Any parts that a person could touch, other than the heat areas, should not get too hot when the cooker is in use.
• Audible signals may be useful in some cases – the click of control knobs or on-off controls, or the sound the burners make on a gas cooker when they light.

Wheelchair users

Built-in appliances give most flexibility for the wheelchair user. A built-in oven can be positioned at the most convenient height, for example.

For non-built-in cookers:
• controls need to be within easy reach at the front of the cooker, not on a splash-back at the rear

• low-level grills are best – high-level grills are inaccessible (but a low-level grill could make access to the oven difficult for a wheelchair user)
• a side opening door gives better access than a drop-down door, but a drop-down door on the grill compartment or second oven can be used for resting the grill pan on.

People with impaired mobility

People who have to use walking aids, or who have back trouble, tend to find bending very difficult. Built-in ovens at a comfortable height are better for them than the ovens on free-standing cookers. If a built-in oven isn't an option:
• go for a high-level grill, where the food can be seen and tended easily without bending (but remember that using the grill might mean leaning across hot areas on the hob)
• if you go for a low-level grill, make sure that it's easy to rest the grill pan on the drop-down door or that the pan is supported when wholly or partially withdrawn so there's no need to bend
• a drop-down oven door is also useful for resting dishes on.

People with reduced manual dexterity or general weakness

This includes elderly people and those who either have a weak grip or lack coordination.
• Avoid stiff controls, or those which need a dual action to operate – press and turn, for example.
• Avoid door handles which are shallow or otherwise difficult to grip.
• Grill pan handles should be easy to fit and take off if removable – make sure the grill pan is well balanced and not too heavy to lift comfortably.
• Make sure any hob cover is easy to lift, and pan supports and hinged hob tops aren't too heavy to lift for cleaning.
• Ceramic or halogen hobs may allow pans to be slid more easily (although be careful not to scratch the hob surface).

SAFETY ISSUES

Surface temperatures under scrutiny

It's a fact of life that cookers get hot. But while you might expect the working parts of the cooker – the bits that do the actual cooking and those very close to them – to get unavoidably hot, you might also reasonably expect areas that you have to touch, or are likely to touch, to stay fairly cool. Unfortunately this is often not the case.

In our tests, the grill pan handles on many of the cookers reached temperatures which we class as unsatisfactory or unacceptable. Grill pan handles on all tested electric cookers are detachable, but were not always easy to remove and replace for grilling.

We think manufacturers could and should do a lot more to keep surface temperatures within safe limits. And we are pressing for amendments to the relevant Standards to try to get cooker surface temperatures brought down to the safer limits suggested in the medical guidelines we use. The problem at the moment is that cookers can meet the British Standards and yet still get too hot – particularly on the fronts and sides. We hope our pressure will get this changed.

Reheating cook-chill foods

There has been increasing concern in the past year about how effectively cook-chill foods can be reheated.

BUYING GUIDE

ELECTRIC
Free-standing

GOOD VALUE

The **Tricity Radiant President 2558B/W** (£360) is one of very few free-standing electric cookers on the market. It's a reasonably-priced double-oven cooker – but make sure you can live with its convenience drawbacks.

The double-oven **Tricity Halogen Fanfare 2789** is very expensive at £660, but performs well and has a halogen hob.

Slot-in

GOOD VALUE

The **Tricity Princess Deluxe 1528A** (£340) is a reasonably-priced single-oven slot-in. It has radiant rings and a fold-down hob cover. The similar **Princess 1518** (£280) doesn't have a hob cover.

If you want a slot-in with a ceramic hob and double oven, the **Belling Forum 601C Ceramic** (£500) is reasonably priced.

The **Electra EFS500** (£420) has a double oven and sealed hotplates. It's available in some Electricity Board showrooms.

DUAL-FUEL

If you want a dual-fuel cooker (gas hob, electric grill and oven), the slot-in **Leisure 3000** (£500) with fold-down hob cover performed reasonably well and is convenient to use.

GAS
Slot-in

GOOD VALUE

The **Parkinson Cowan Strata** (£280) is a basic slot-in cooker with high-level grill. The **Pisces** (£290), the **Mink II** (£250) with more basic ignition and the **Strand** (£350) with more features, are similar.

The **New World Montage SBS** (£490) is a slot-in cooker with fold-down hob cover. The more basic **Insight SBS** (£400) is similar.

The **New World Royale 600 SBS** (£500) has similar features and performance to the Insight. The **Plan 6 SBS** (£550) is also similar.

We looked at how well some typical cookers could reheat three cook-chill foods to 70°C – the temperature recommended to kill any listeria bacteria that could be present in the food. The lasagne and curry presented virtually no problems, but there were variable results with a spare rib dish.

When you're cooking from scratch, it's usually easy to tell whether the food is done, but that may not be the case when you're reheating cook-chill foods, because the food may not change colour, or may be hidden by packaging. So accurate oven temperatures and full instructions on the food are vital.

It's essential that all ovens have controls which you can set accurately, and which reflect the actual temperature inside the oven, preferably at one standard point – in the centre of the oven.

We'd also like to see cook-chill food manufacturers telling you in cooking instructions which oven shelf to put food on – the same information you get in a recipe book when cooking from scratch.

Our advice

When you're reheating food in a conventional oven:

- pre-heat the oven (whether it's gas or electric) to the temperature recommended in the instructions
- put food on the middle shelf (unless the food or oven instructions say otherwise); remember that gas ovens can be cooler at the bottom
- a baking tray under the food will speed up the transfer of heat
- heat for the full time advised
- check before you eat: food that has been reheated to the right temperature – 70°C – should be too hot to eat immediately.

FACTS, FIGURES AND TEST RESULTS

For each type of cooker (Electric, Dual-Fuel and Gas) we present the information in a pair of Tables: detailed information on 'Cookers we have tested' specifically for this report and more general information about 'Cookers available in the shops', which *includes* information from the first Table. This is to give you as full a picture as possible without our being able to test every cooker every year.

ELECTRIC COOKERS

√ = has this feature — = does not

Any figures in *italics* are those given to us by manufacturers.

1 Type

We have separated out the slot-in cookers from the traditional free-standing ones.

2 Price

Prices in *italics* are manufacturers' guide prices. Other prices are what you should expect to pay in the shops if you shop around. Some models are sold in different colours, at different prices – in which case their model numbers may vary slightly from those in the Table.

3 Width/Dimensions

For slot-in models, the width given here is the size, within a few mm, of the gap you need in your kitchen; for free-standing cookers, check how much space to leave on either side. The 'Feature-finder' Table gives overall height, including splashback, high-level grill or hob cover (in brackets).

4 Main oven

All tested cookers would take a 9kg turkey. All but the Creda Horizon, Philips ACH587 and the Tricity Princess Deluxe and Radiant President had a fan oven. A fan can reduce cooking times slightly, and/or allow you to cook at a lower setting. All the main ovens had at least three oven runners and two oven shelves, except the Philips ACH587, which had only one shelf.

Door

D = drop-down V = reversible

L = hinged on the left

5 Second oven

All are under the hob, above the main oven and 45 litres or less in size.

6 Grill

All tested cookers except the Creda Horizon Program 600 and Tricity Princess Deluxe had a half grill: this allows you to heat part of the grill area to cook small amounts of food. Each grill pan came with wire grid or metal trivet and detachable handle(s).

Grill position

H = high-level L = low-level
M = in main oven S = in second oven

7 Hob

Electric cookers have four main types of hob, though within each type there can also be variations.

Radiant rings heat up and cool down quickly. They glow red on medium to high. A spillage tray under the rings, or a hinge-up hob top with a support, helps make hob easier to clean.

Sealed hotplates heat up slowly and cool down very slowly. They do not glow red, so it may be difficult to tell that they're switched on. The hotplates are easy to clean: they're sealed into the hob with no gaps for spills to fall through.

Ceramic heat areas have electric heating elements concealed beneath a special kind of glass surface; the elements glow red on medium to high settings. They heat up fairly slowly and cool down slowly. They're easy to clean, but you may need to use special ceramic hob cleaners recommended by the manufacturer. Be careful not to let sugary or acid spills burn on, as these can damage the surface.

Halogen heat areas have a similar ceramic surface, but use special tungsten halogen filament lamps as the heat source. They glow very brightly when switched on. Halogen heats up quickly but cools down slowly. Like ceramic hobs, hobs with halogen heat areas are easy to clean, but again, you need to be careful to mop up sugary or acid spills straight away.

Hob heat areas (number and type)

C = ceramic R = radiant rings
H = halogen S = sealed hotplates

Hob cover

G = glass M = metal

Hob safety features

C = electricity supply to hob cut off if hob cover lowered when a hob heat area is on
H = hob-hot light to show that the hob surface is still hot after it has been switched off.

8 Features

Accessories (tested cookers only)

All tested cookers except the Philips ACH587 had a roasting tin.

B = baking tray(s)
T = trivet for roasting tin

Timers

A = autotimer which controls main oven
B = autotimer which controls main and second oven
C = analogue clock D = digital clock
M = minute minder

Main oven (tested cookers only)

C = catalytic linings standard (we tell you how many are fitted)
(C) = catalytic linings optional extra
O = oven light
V = viewing panel in oven door
Z = defrost setting

Hob (tested cookers only)

D = dual element ring: you can use just the inner portion if required
T = thermostatically-controlled sealed hotplate: the power cuts in and out to maintain the pan at a set temperature

Storage/warning

√ = separate storage/warming compartment or drawer

Mobility (tested cookers only)

√ = has wheels or castors

9 Safety approvals

B = approved by British Electrotechnical Approvals Board (BEAB)

BC = BEAB via CCA (has BEAB approval via another European testing authority)

10 Performance (tested cookers only)

Oven baking

We assess evenness of heat distribution by baking trays of small cakes. Where ovens have fans, we test batch baking, cooking three or four trays of cakes at the same time. We also bake a fruit cake to test oven performance at low temperature over a long period of time. All the ovens we tested gave satisfactory baking results except the Creda Horizon, which was poor with fruit cake.

Oven heat-up time

How long it takes to reach about 200°C

◩ = 6 to 10 minutes

□ = 11 to 15 minutes

◪ = 16 to 20 minutes

■ = more than 21 minutes

Grill

Ratings are for full grills only. All grills but two would take six whole slices of bread from a large sliced loaf; the Creda Carefree Solarplus and Contour Solarglo Ceramic grills would take four.

ELECTRIC COOKERS TESTED BY US

	Price (2)	Width (3)	Main oven door (4)	Second oven / Shelves/runners (5)	Grill (6)	7 Hob: Heat areas	Cover	Safety features	8 Features: Accessories	Timers	Main oven	Hob	Storage/warming	Mobility	Safety approvals (9)
	£	cm													
1 FREE-STANDING															
▶ **1 Tricity Halogen Fanfare 2789** (UK)	660	55	L	1/3	S	3C1H	—	H	T	BDM	4COVZ	—	—	√	B
▶ **2 Tricity Radiant President 2558 B/W** (UK)	360	55	V	1/3	S	4R	—	—	T	C	2CO	1D	—	√	B
1 SLOT-IN															
3 Belling Format 6060C (UK)	770	60	D	2/4[2]	S	3C1H	—	H	—	BDM	1COV	1D	—	—	B
▶ **4 Belling Forum 501C Ceramic** (UK)[3]	*500*	50	D	1/1	S	4C	—	—	—	BCM	1CO	—	√	—	B
5 Creda Carefree Solarplus 49711L (UK)	630	60	V	1/3	S	4C	—	—	T	BDM	4COV	1D	—	√	B
6 Creda Contour Solarglo Ceramic 48413 (UK)	500	50	V	1/2	S	4C	—	—	T	BCM	3COV	1D	—	—	B
7 Creda Horizon Program 600 49604 (UK)	*420*	60	V	—	H	4R	—	—	—	ACM	4COV	1D	√	√	B
▶ **8 Electra EFS 500** (UK)[5]	420	50	D	1/1	S	4S	—	—	—	BCM	1CO	—	√	—	B
9 Hotpoint 6530 (UK)[6]	650	60	V	1/3	S	4C	—	H	T	BDM	3COVZ	—	—	—	B
10 Leisure 3020 (UK)	370	56	V	—	L	4S	G	C	T	ADM	2C(C)OV	IT	—	√	B
11 Philips ACH587 (Italy)	280	55	D	—	M	4S	M	—	—	A[7]	3COV	—	—	—	B
12 Toshiba TC400 (UK)[8]	600	56	L	1/3	S	4C	—	H	2BT	BDM	4COVZ	3D	—	√	B
▶ **13 Tricity Princess Deluxe 1528A** (UK)[9]	340	50	V	—	L	4R	G	C	—	A	2C	—	—	—	B
14 Valor Lite-Speed (UK)	570	56	V	1/3	S	2C2H	—	H	BT	BDM	4COVZ	1D	—	√	B
15 Zanussi HC5617 (UK)[10]	700	60	D	4/3[11]	S	2C2H	—	H	—	BDM	3COVZ	—	—	√	B

▶ Recommended in the Buying Guide ◀

KEY TO RATINGS best ◩ > ◩ > □ > ◪ > ■ **worst**

Evenness
How much of the grill pan area was effectively heated.
▨ = 90 to 100 per cent
◤ = 85 to 90 per cent
□ = 75 to 85 per cent

Speed
Time taken to cook a batch of toast, excluding pre-heat time (two to five minutes).
▨ = less than 2 minutes
◤ = 2 to 3 minutes
□ = 3 to 4 minutes

Height for large dishes
We use a 7cm high dish
◤ = plenty of room for browning (more than 14cm)
□ = adequate room (12 to 14cm)
◪ = barely enough room (10 to 12cm)
■ = not enough room (less than 10cm)

11 Convenience (tested cookers only)

General drawbacks
a = oven/grill too low for easy access
b = grill pan feels heavy or unbalanced or uncomfortable to hold
c = some controls small or awkward to grip
d = oven thermostat lights very difficult to distinguish between on and off
e = back panel restricts hob space
f = no front stops for main oven shelves/ stops ineffective
g = necessary to reach over hob to use controls on splashback
h = cramped hob
j = hob top heavy to lift for cleaning
k = markings on controls poor/controls awkward to set because of poor marking
l = shelf supporting grill pan difficult to remove and relocate
m = no front stop for grill pan or stops ineffective
p = storage area low and/or awkward to use
q = hob awkward to clean
r = grill in main oven; cannot use both at the same time

10 Performance: Oven heat-up time: Main	Second	Grill evenness	Grill speed	Grill height	11 Convenience: General drawbacks	Special needs good features	Special needs drawbacks	12 Surface temperatures[1]	
□	□	▨	◤	◤	afgh	★ABD	cefgjk	GH	1 ◀
◪	□	▨	□	◤	abcef gjx	★BG	efgjkl	GS	2 ◀
◪	◪	▨	□	◤	abcd	N/T	N/T	G	3
□	■	▨	□	□	ahpqz	N/T	N/T	(GH)	4 ◀
□	□	▨	◤	◤	aefgz	N/T	N/T	GH	5
◤	◤	▨	▨	◤	akmt uxz	★A	cdef gjkl	G	6
□[4]	—	▨	□	■	cfp	★AE	efgjk	G	7
□	■	▨	□	□	ahpq	N/T	N/T	(GH)	8 ◀
□	□	▨	□	◤	abcm	AE	bdhjk	B	9
□	—	□	□	◪	abchk	N/T	N/T	—	10
◪	—	◤	□	◤	abkmr	N/T	N/T	(BEGOP)	11
□	◪	▨	◤	◤	abcm	★A	cdjk	B	12
□	—	▨	◤	◤	abhk	N/T	N/T	(G)	13 ◀
□	◪	□	□	◤	abl	★ADJ	defjk	GH	14
◪	□	▨	◤	□	acty	★ABCJ	ejkl	BRG	15

[1] Method used for checking surface temperatures has changed slightly; results in brackets are not directly comparable with other results
[2] Main and second oven are the same size
[3] Similar model Belling Forum 501H (£530) has one halogen heat area
[4] Two samples had inaccurate thermostats; contact Credacare service agency if your oven is underperforming
[5] Exclusive to Electricity Boards, prices vary from Board to Board
[6] Similar model 6540 (£750) with two halogen heat areas
[7] Sets end of cooking time only
[8] Similar model TC500 (£650) with one halogen heat area and different timer
[9] Similar model 1518 (£270) without hob cover
[10] Similar model 9617 – colour difference only
[11] All four shelves are interchangeable between main and second ovens

FEATURE-FINDER: ELECTRIC COOKERS IN THE SHOPS

Main oven size
1 = up to 45 litres
2 = 46 to 70 litres
3 = 71 to 90 litres

	2 Price	3 Dimensions h × w × d (overall height)	4 Main oven			6 Grill		7 Hob			8 Features		9 Safety approvals
			Size	Fan	Door	Position	Half grill	Heat areas	Cover	Safety	Timers	Storage/warming	
	£	cm											
1 FREE-STANDING/SINGLE OVEN													
Radiant rings													
Belling Compact 431T/431N (UK)	290/240	92 × 47 × 53(132)	1	—	L	L	—	4R	—	—	ACM/-	√	B
Tricity Marquis 2587B (UK)	300	91 × 55 × 59(129)	2	—	V	L	—	4R	—	—	ACM	—	B
Tricity Tiara 1417B (UK)	250	92 × 46 × 59(126)	2	—	V	L	—	4R	—	—	—	—	B
Sealed hotplates													
Ariston E55 MO4M6GB (Italy)	180	*85 × 55 × 57(140)*	2	—	L	M	√	4S	M	—	—	√	—
1 FREE-STANDING/DOUBLE OVEN													
Ceramic hob													
Electra Fantasia EFC 90 (UK)[5]	540	*92 × 54 × 54(137)*	2	√	L	S	√	4C	—	—	BDM	—	B
Halogen hob													
Tricity Halogen Contessa 1689 (UK)	*550*	*91 × 46 × 59(125)*	2	√	V	S	√	3C1H	—	H	BCM	—	B
▶ **Tricity Halogen Fanfare 2789** (UK)	660	91 × 55 × 59(129)	2	√	V	S	√	3C1H	—	H	BDM	—	B ◀
Radiant rings													
Belling Classic 91 DL (UK)	400	92 × 53 × 53(137)	2	—	L	S	√	4R	—	—	ACM	—	B
Tricity Radiant Contessa 1659 (UK)	*350*	91 × 46 × 59(125)	2	√	V	S	√	4R	—	—	BCM	—	B
▶ **Tricity Radiant President 2558B/W** (UK)	360	92 × 55 × 59(129)	2	—	V	S	√	4R	—	—	C	—	B ◀
1 SLOT-IN/SINGLE OVEN													
Ceramic hob													
AEG FV64.1GL (W Germany)	580	*90 × 60 × 60(0)*	2	√	D	M	—	4C	—	H	ADM	√	—
Miele H868 (W Germany)	*1179*	*85 × 60 × 60(0)*	2	√	D	M	—	4C	—	H	ADM	√	—
Halogen hob													
Creda Concept Microwave Circulaire 48312 (UK)	*1100*	90 × 60 × 60(0)	2	√	V	M	√	2C2H	—	H	ADM	—	B
Zanussi HC9515/5515 (UK)	580	*90 × 50 × 60(0)*	2	√	D	L	√	3C1H	—	—	ADM	—	—
Radiant rings													
Creda Cavalier 49411 (UK)	300	*90 × 50 × 60(124)*	2	—	L	L	—	4R	—	—	ACM	—	B
Creda Commodore 49111 (UK)	230	*90 × 50 × 60(0)*	1	—	L	M	—	4R	—	—	—	—	B
Creda Concord 49421 (UK)	*350*	*90 × 50 × 60(140)*	2	—	L	L	—	4R	G	C	ACM	—	B
Creda Horizon Program 600 49604 (UK)	*420*	90 × 60 × 58(143)	2	—	V	H	—	4R	—	—	ACM	—	B
Creda Starlight 49211 (UK)	250	*90 × 50 × 60(124)*	2	—	L	L	—	4R	—	—	—	—	B
Creda Trimline 49311 (UK)	290	90 × 50 × 60(135)	2	—	L	H	—	4R	—	—	—	—	B
▶ **Tricity Princess Deluxe 1528A/1518** (UK)	340/280	90 × 50 × 60(146)	2	—	V	L	—	4R	G/—	C/—	A/M	—	B ◀
Sealed hotplates													
AEG FH64.1GD (W Germany)	420	*90 × 60 × 60(145)*	2	√	D	M	—	4S	M	—	ADM	√	—
Ariston 7E/Opal E (Italy)	*400/350*	*90 × 60 × 60(145)*	2	√	D	M	√	4S	G	C	ADM	√	B
Fagor FE4W (Spain)	*215*	*84 × 54 × 56(135)*	1	—	D	M	—	4S	M	—	—	√	—
Indesit 6044 (Italy)	280	87 × 60 × 60(145)	1	√	D	M	√	4S	G	—	AD	√	—
Leisure 3020 (UK)	370	90 × 56 × 60(140)	2	√	V	L	√	4S	G	C	ADM	—	B
Philips ACH 587 (Italy)	280	85 × 55 × 55(139)	2	—	D	M	√	4S	M	—	M	—	—
Philips ACH 984 (Italy)	430	*85 × 60 × 60(145)*	2	√	D	M	√	4S	M	—	ADM	√	—
Thor E54 (Yugoslavia)	*200*	*84 × 50 × 60(143)*	2	—	D	M	—	4S	M	—	—	√	BC
Thor E64 (Yugoslavia)	*230*	*84 × 60 × 60(143)*	2	—	D	M	—	4S	M	—	ACM	√	BC
Zanussi EC5614/9614 (Italy)	*400*	*90 × 60 × 59(150)*	2	√	D	M	—	4S	G	C	ADM	—	—
Zanussi EC9512 (UK)	400	*90 × 50 × 60(150)*	2	—	D	L	—	4S	G	C	ACM	—	—

	Price (2)	Dimensions h x w x d (overall height) (3)	(4) Main oven: Size	Fan	Door	(6) Grill: Position	Half grill	(7) Hob: Heat areas	Cover	Safety	(8) Features: Timers	Storage/warming	Safety approvals (9)	
	£	cm												
(1) SLOT-IN/DOUBLE OVEN														
Ceramic hob														
Belling Format 600XR (UK)	600	90 × 60 × 61(0)	2	√	V	S	√	4C	—	H	BDM	—	B	
► **Belling Forum 501C Ceramic** (UK)	*500*	91 × 50 × 50(0)	1	√	D	S	√	4C	—	—	BCM	√	B	◄
Creda Carefree Solarplus Ceramic 49711L (UK)	630	90 × 60 × 58(131)	2	√	V	S	√	4C	—	—	BDM	—	B	
Creda Concept Circulaire 48313 (UK)	*650*	*90 × 60 × 60(0)*	2	√	V	S	√	4C	—	—	BDM	—	B	
Creda Contour Solarglo Ceramic 48413 (UK)	500	90 × 50 × 59(0)	2	√	V	S	√	4C	—	—	BCM	—	B	
Hotpoint 6510 (UK)	*600*	*90 × 50 × 60(0)*	1	√	V	S	√	4C	—	—	BCM	—	B	
Hotpoint 6530 (UK)	650	90 × 60 × 60(0)	2	√	V	S	√	4C	—	H	BDM	—	B	
Toshiba TC400 (UK)	600	90 × 56 × 60(0)	2	√	L	S	√	4C	—	H	BDM	—	B	
Halogen hob														
Belling Format Halogen 4 600HR (UK)	800	*90 × 60 × 61(0)*	2	√	V	S	√	4H	—	H	BDM	—	B	
Belling Format 6060C (UK)	770	90 × 60 × 61(0)	1	√	D	S	√	3C1H	—	H	BDM	—	B	
Belling Forum 500H (UK)	530	91 × 50 × 50(0)	1	√	D	S	√	3CIH	—	—	BCM	√	B	
Creda Concept Solarplus 48317/48319 (UK)	740	*90 × 60 × 60(0)*	2	√	V	S	√	1C3H	—	H	BDM	—	B	
Electrolux Monet CF502 (UK)	*600*	*90 × 50 × 60(0)*	2	—	V	S	√	3C1H	—	H	BC	—	B	
Electrolux Picasso CF606 (UK)	750	*90 × 60 × 60(0)*	2	√	D	S	√	4H	—	H	BD	—	B	
Hotpoint 6540 (UK)	750	90 × 60 × 60(0)	2	√	V	S	√	2C2H	—	H	BDM	—	B	
Toshiba TC500 (UK)	650	90 × 56 × 60(0)	2	√	L	S	√	3C1H	—	H	BDM	—	B	
Tricity Halogen Princess 1588 (UK)	550	*90 × 50 × 60(0)*	2	√	V	S	√	3C1H	—	H	BDM	—	B	
Tricity Halogen Sovereign 4629 (UK)	680	*90 × 60 × 60(0)*	2	√	D	S	—	3C1H	—	H	BDM	—	B	
Tricity Halogen Sovereign 4638/4639 (UK)	680/770	90 × 60 × 60(0)	2	√	D	S	√	2C2H	—	H	ADM/ BDM	—	B	
Tricity Halogen Sovereign 4649 Limited Edition (UK)	*900*	*90 × 60 × 60(0)*	2	√	D	S	—	4H	—	H	BDM	—	B	
Valor Lite-Speed (UK)	570	90 × 56 × 60(0)	2	√	V	S	√	2C2H	—	H	BDM	√	B	
Zanussi HC5617 (UK)	700	90 × 60 × 60(0)	2	√	D	S	√	2C2H	—	H	BDM	—	B	
Radiant rings														
Creda Carefree Radiant 49708L (UK)	*480*	*90 × 60 × 58(131)*	2	√	V	S	√	4R	—	—	BDM	—	B	
Creda Contour Radiant 48424 (UK)	*400*	*90 × 50 × 60(140)*	2	—	L	S	√	4R	G	C	ACM	—	B	
Creda Hallmark 49511 (UK)	360	*90 × 50 × 60(124)*	2	—	V	S	√	4R	—	—	ACM	—	B	
Electrolux Renoir CF501 (UK)	*440*	*90 × 50 × 60(137)*	2	—	V	S	√	4R	G	C	BC	—	B	
Tricity Radiant Princess Double Oven 1568 (UK)	380	*90 × 50 × 60(0)*	2	√	V	S	√	4R	—	—	BCM	—	B	
Sealed hotplates														
Belling Format 600SR (UK)	580	90 × 60 × 61(0)	2	√	V	S	√	4S	—	—	ADM	—	B	
Belling Forum 500SR (UK)	430	91 × 50 × 50(0)	1	√	D	S	√	4S	—	—	BCM	√	B	
► **Electra EFS 500** (UK)[5]	420	91 × 50 × 50(0)	1	√	D	S	√	4S	—	—	BCM	√	B	◄
Electrolux Matisse CF604 (UK)	*600*	*90 × 60 × 60(0)*	2	√	D	S	√	4S	—	—	BD	—	B	

► Recommended in the Buying Guide ◄

t = grill compartment too deep for easy cleaning
u = oven door catch rather stiff to open
x = timer controls stiff to turn or awkward to use
y = no 'stop' between 'off' and 'high' on hob controls
z = no hob-hot light

Convenience for special needs

The results of our assessments for use of cookers by disabled and elderly people.

N/T = not tested for this report
⋆ = grill pan has one handle – good for some people, could be a problem for others

Special needs good features

A = pans can be easily pushed across the hob
B = minimum force needed to open/close grill door
C = grill pan handle easy to grip
D = heat sources on hob can be seen at all settings (halogen heat areas only)
E = oven door opens wide to the side
G = well shaped, easy-to-grip controls
J = as some controls rotate, can feel/hear some heat settings (as well as off and maximum)

Special needs drawbacks

b = some force needed to open/close grill door
c = grill door handle hard to grip
d = grill pan needs lifting to cooking position
e = grill pan handle(s) difficult to engage/disengage
f = some force needed to open/close oven door(s)
g = oven door handle hard to grip
h = oven shelves awkward to move
j = sharp edges on hob/grill/oven
k = some controls turn both ways from off position – could be confusing
l = fine control needed to set heat

12 Surface temperatures (tested cookers)

We tell you the areas of each cooker which got hot enough to cause you pain or discomfort if you touch them.

B = control panel
E = oven door centre
G = grill pan handle
H = front edge of hob
O = oven door handle
P = grill deflector plate
R = hob side trim
S = oven side panels

DUAL-FUEL COOKERS

Dual-fuel cookers have gas hob, electric grill and electric oven except the New World CKG 21027, which has a gas grill.

√ = has this feature — = does not
Manufacturers' figures are in *italics*.

1 Price

Prices not in *italics* are what you can expect to pay if you shop around. Some models are sold in different colours at different prices.

2 Width/Dimensions

The Leisure 3000 and Philips cookers have hob covers; the New World has a splashback.

3 Main oven

All tested cookers would take a 9kg turkey. All ovens had at least three runners, two shelves.

Size ('Feature-finder' Table)

1 = up to 45 litres 3 = 71 to 90 litres
2 = 46 to 70 litres

Door

D = drop-down V = reversible
L = hinged on the left

4 Grill

All grill pans come with wire grid or metal trivet.

Position

L = low-level   M = in main oven

5 Hob

Cover

G = glass   M = metal

Hob safety features

C = gas supply to hob cut off if hob cover lowered when a hob heat area is lit

R = as C, and the hob can't be re-lit until a reset button is pressed

6 Features

Accessories (tested cookers only)

B = baking tray(s)   T = trivet for roasting tin

R = roasting tin

Timers

A = autotimer which controls main oven

D = digital clock

M = minute minder

Ignition system

M = manual

S = automatic ignition – mains generated spark

X = mains ignition can be overridden manually in the event of a power failure (tested cookers only)

Main oven (tested cookers only)

C = catalytic linings standard

V = viewing panel in oven door

Z = defrost setting

U = oven light

Storage/warming (Feature-finder)

√ = separate storage-warming compartment/drawer

Of the tested cookers, only the Leisure 3000 had wheels/castors.

7 Safety approvals

BSI = approved by the British Standards Institution

√ = satisfactory in our tests

8 Performance (tested cookers only)

Oven baking

See 'Performance' on electric ovens. All ovens tested gave satisfactory results.

Oven heat-up time

How long it takes to reach about 200°C

□ = 11 to 15 minutes

◪ = 16 to 20 minutes

Grill

Ratings are for full grill only. All the grills would take six slices from a large sliced loaf, except the New World which would take three.

Evenness

◩ = 90 to 100 per cent

◤ = 85 to 90 per cent

□ = 75 to 85 per cent

Speed

Time taken to cook a batch of toast, excluding pre-heat time.

◤ = 2 to 3 minutes

□ = 3 to 4 minutes

Height for large dishes

◤ = plenty of room for browning (more than 14cm)

◪ = barely enough room (10–12cm)

9 Convenience

General drawbacks

See 'Electric cookers' for Key.

Convenience for special needs

N/T = not tested for this report

* = grill pan has one handle – good for some people, a problem for others

Special needs good features

B = easy to open/close grill door

D = lit burners can be seen at all settings

G = oven door handle easy to grip

J = as some controls rotate, can feel/hear some heat settings (as well as off and maximum)

L = controls easily identifiable

DUAL-FUEL COOKERS TESTED BY US

	Price (1)	Width (2)	Main oven door (3)	Grill (4)	Hob safety features (5)	Features (6): Accessories	Timers	Ignition system	Main oven	Safety approvals (7)	Oven heat-up time
	£	cm									
► 1 **Leisure 3000** (UK)	*500*	55	V	L	C	BRT	ADM	SX	4COV	BSI	□
2 **New World CKG 21027** (UK)[2]	280	50	L	L	—	BRT	—	SX	4CV	BSI	◪
3 **Philips ACH586** (Italy)	280	55	D	M	C	—	[3]	M	3COV	√	◪
4 **Philips ACH983** (Italy)[4]	430	60	D	M	C	—	ADM	SX	3COVZ	[5]	□

FEATURE-FINDER: DUAL-FUEL COOKERS IN THE SHOPS

(1)	Price (2)	Dimensions h x w x d (overall height)	Main oven (3): Size	Fan	Door	Grill (4): Position	Half-grill	Cover
	£	cm						
1 **Ariston 7M KL40EVES** (Italy)	350	*90 × 60 × 60(145)*	2	√	D	M	√	G
2 **Ariston Opal M KL40VES** (Italy)	*380*	*90 × 60 × 60(145)*	2	√	D	M	√	G
3 **Creda Contour 48405** (UK)	410	90 × 54 × 60(142)	2	—	L	L	√	G
4 **Fagor Brisa FD4WT** (Spain)	*250*	*84 × 54 × 56(135)*	1	√	D	M	—	M
5 **Indesit K6406VG** (Italy)	*250*	*85 × 60 × 60(145)*	2	—	D	M	√	G
6 **Indesit K6406WG** (Italy)	*260*	*85 × 60 × 60(145)*	2	—	D	M	—	G
► 7 **Leisure 3000** (UK)	*500*	*90 × 55 × 60(140)*	3	√	V	L	√	G
8 **New World CKG 21027/21028** (UK)	280	90 × 50 × 60(101)	3	√	L	L	—	—
9 **Philips ACH586** (Italy)	280	85 × 55 × 55(145)	2	—	D	M	√	G
10 **Philips ACH983** (Italy)	430	85 × 60 × 60(145)	2	√	D	M	√	G
11 **Smeg SP690** (Italy)	*600*	*85 × 60 × 60(149)*	2	√	D	M	√	G
12 **Tecnogas 6549** (Italy)	250	*90 × 60 × 60(150)*	2	—	D	M	—	G
13 **Zanussi MC5634/9634** (Italy)	420	*90 × 60 × 60(150)*	2	√	D	M	√	G

► Recommended in the Buying Guide ◄

KEY TO RATINGS best ◩ > ◩ > □ > ◪ > ■ worst

Special needs drawbacks

a = pans cannot be easily pushed across hob

d = grill pan needs lifting to cooking position

j = sharp edges on hob/grill/oven

k = some controls turn both ways from off position – could be confusing

(10) Surface temperatures

We tell you the areas of each cooker which get hot enough to cause you pain or discomfort.

B = control panel

E = oven door centre

G = grill pan handle

O = oven door handle

P = grill deflector plate

8 Performance: Grill evenness	Grill speed	Grill height	9 Convenience: General drawbacks	Special needs good features	Special needs drawbacks	10 Surface temperatures[1]		
□	◩	◪	a	N/T	N/T	N/T	1	◄
□	□	◪	acdkm	⋆BDJL	ajk	BE	2	
◩	□	◩	abfkr	N/T	N/T	(BEGOP)	3	
■	◩	◩	abcdfghpr	⋆DG	adjk	P	4	

5 Hob: Safety	6 Features: Timers	Ignition	Storage/warming	7 Safety approvals		
C	ADM	S	√	—	1	
C	ADM	S	√	—	2	
C	A	S	—	—	3	
—	—	S	√	—	4	
R	M	S	√	—	5	
R	M	S	√	—	6	
C	ADM	S	—	BSI	7	◄
—	—	S	—	BSI	8	
C	—	M		√	9	
C	ADM	S	—	[5]	10	
S	ADM	S	√	—	11	
C	M	S	√	—	12	
R	ADM	S	√	—	13	

[1] Method used for checking surface temperatures has changed slightly, results in brackets are not directly comparable with those for other cookers
[2] Similar model CKG 21028 (£280), white version
[3] Sets end of cooking time only
[4] Similar models ACH984 (£430), sealed hotplates rather than gas
[5] Not BSI approved. In our tests we found the glass hob cover falls to a closed position too quickly, because it is insufficiently 'damped'; could trap your (or your child's) fingers

See page 8 for how to use ***Which? Buying Guide***.

GAS COOKERS

√ = has this feature — = does not

Any figures in *italics* are those given to us by manufacturers.

1 Type

Slot-in cookers are separated out from other free-standing models in the Tables.

2 Price

Prices in *italics* are manufacturers' guide prices. Other prices are what you should expect to pay in the shops if you shop around. Some models are sold in different colours at different prices – in which case model numbers may vary slightly from those in the Table. We found some gas cookers mainly in Gas showrooms rather than in multiples or department stores. Prices varied from Board to Board, so for these cookers we've taken a mid-range price.

3 Width/Dimensions

See 'Feature-finder' Table for full dimensions. You need to allow space above for all the cookers tested as they all have either a fold-down hob cover, splashback or a high-level grill.

4 Main oven

All tested cookers would take a 9kg turkey, except the Valor Fresco, which would take a 6.8kg turkey. All the main ovens had at least two shelves and five runners. The Leisure 2040 and 3010, and Zanussi GCF9621/5621 are the only gas cookers we know of with a fan. A fan can reduce cooking times slightly, and/or allow you to cook at a lower setting.

Most UK gas cookers have a row of gas burners across the back of the oven floor. The oven is hotter at the top and cooler at the bottom, so you can cook foods needing different temperatures at the same time.

GAS COOKERS TESTED BY US

	Price (2)	Width (3)	Main oven door (4)	Second oven Shelves/runners (5)	Grill (6)	Hob safety features (7)	Accessories (8 Features)	Timers	Ignition system	Main oven	Storage/warming	Mobility	Safety approvals (9)
	£	cm											
1 FREE-STANDING													
1 Cannon Cambridge (UK)	425	54	L	—	H	—	—	—	FSTX	4CVX	√	—	BSI
2 Cannon Double Oven De Luxe (UK)	580	54	L	1/3	H[2]	—	—	ADM	FGST(X)	4CGOVX	—	√	BSI
3 Leisure 230 (UK)	415	55	L	—	H	—	T	M	BF	4CVX	√	√	BSI
1 SLOT-IN													
4 Cannon Canterbury (UK)	490	54	L	—	L	C	—	—	FSTX	4CGOVX	—	√	BSI
5 Leisure 2040 (UK)[3]	580	55	V	—	L	C	T	ADM	FST(X)	4COVX	—	√	BSI
6 Moffat Discovery (UK)	650	55	L	—	L	A	T	ADM	FST(X)[4]	4COVX	—	√	BSI
7 New World Apex CKS 21007/8 (UK)	355	50	L	—	H	—	—	—	BF	X	√	—	BSI
▶ **8 New World Montage SBS** (UK)[6]	490	51	L	—	L	S	T	—	FSTX	4COVX	—	—	BSI
9 New World Rapport CKS 21036/7 (UK)	460	51	L	—	L	S	T	—	BF	3CX	—	—	BSI
▶ **10 New World Royale 600 SBS** (UK)[7]	500	60	V	—	L	S	T	—	FSTX	4COVX	—	—	BSI
11 Parkinson Cowan Chique (UK)	370	51	L	—	L	R	—	—	BF	(C)VX	—	—	BSI
12 Parkinson Cowan Fiesta (UK)	335	50	L	—	L	—	—	—	BF	X	—	—	BSI
▶ **13 Parkinson Cowan Strata** (UK)[8]	280	50	L	—	H	—	—	—	BF	(C)X	√	—	BSI
14 Valor Fresco (UK)	345	49	L	—	L	C	—	—	BFX	(C)X	—	—	BSI

▶ Recommended in the Buying Guide ◀

KEY TO RATINGS best ◩ > ◪ > □ > ◪ > ■ worst

In Continental gas cookers, the oven burners are often in a different arrangement (in a line running front to back directly underneath the oven floor, for example), and the heat distribution pattern is quite different. This affects the cooking performance of the oven: foods are browned and crisped from underneath, which is ideal for some dishes (flans, say), but you may be disappointed in the way a fruit cake turns out, for example. Check carefully before you buy where the oven burners are, and whether this will make a difference for the sort of cooking you usually do.

Door

D = drop-down
L = hinged on the left
V = reversible

5 Second oven

All are 45 litres or less, and are under the hob, above the main oven, except for the Cannon Cordon Bleu where the second oven is alongside the main oven.

6 Grill

We tell you the grill position. None of the cookers we tested had a half-grill. The Leisure 2040 was the only cooker tested which had removable grill-pan handles, but all grill pans came with a wire grid or metal trivet.

H = high-level = low-level
M = in main oven

7 Hob

All the cookers tested had traditional burners, except the Moffat Discovery, which

10 Performance: Oven heat-up time – Main	Second	Grill evenness	Grill speed	Grill height	11 Convenience: General drawbacks	Special needs good features	Special needs drawbacks	12 Surface temperatures[1]	
◩	—	▣	▣	◪	p	DJ	fj	BGZ	1
□	□	□	◩	◩	a	N/T	N/T	(CT)	2
◩	—	□	□	■	k	N/T	N/T	DGH	3
□	—	□	□	◪	bcm	★DJ	fj	GHT	4
□	—	□	□	◪	abck	N/T	N/T	(BGH)	5
◩	—	□	□	◪	ckn	★BJ	adfj	GH	6
▣	—	□	□	■[5]	kp	CIJ	agj	DG	7
▣	—	◩	□	□	a	N/T	N/T	(T)	8◀
▣	—	□	□	□	atu	★BCJ	adghj	BDEG	9
▣	—	◩	□	□	a	N/T	N/T	(T)	10◀
◩	—	◩	□	◪	abc	N/T	N/T	(BGHST)	11
◩	—	◪	□	□	abckmt	★BGJ	adgj	BGS	12
▣	—	◩	□	◪	p	N/T	N/T	GH	13◀
▣	—	□	▣	■	ak	DIJ	acfj	BEGJS	14

[1] Method used for checking surface temperatures has changed slightly; results in brackets are not directly comparable with those for other cookers
[2] Grill folds away when not in use
[3] Similar model 3040 (£655), cosmetic differences
[4] Automatic re-ignition to hob and grill also
[5] For large dishes, manufacturer recommends removing grill pan and standing dish directly on shelf
[6] Similar model Insight SBS (£400), without illuminated control panel
[7] Similar model Plan 6 SBS (£550) with autotimer, minute minder and cosmetic differences
[8] Similar models Pisces (£290); Strand (£360), with autotimer, minute minder and mains ignition; Mink II (£250) with battery spark ignition to hob only

has gas-powered discs. With these, the flames emerge from around the edge of special ceramic discs, so the hob looks more streamlined than a traditional gas hob. All the tested slot-ins (except the New World Apex and Parkinson Cowan Fiesta and Strata) had a fold-down glass hob cover.

Safety features

A = as C, but ignition continues to spark, and when cover is lifted the burners ignite automatically

C = gas supply to burners is cut off if hob cover lowered while a burner is lit

R = as C, *and* the hob can't be re-lit once the hob cover is raised until a reset button is pressed.

S = as C, *and* the controls on the hob reset to 'off' as the hob cover is lowered

8 Cooker features

Accessories (tested cookers only)

All tested cookers came with a baking tray and roasting tin

T = trivet for roasting tin

Timers

A = autotimer which controls main oven

C = analogue clock

D = digital clock

M = minute minder

Ignition system

Ignition on a gas cooker can range from basic manual, where you use a match, taper or lighter to light the flame, to fully automatic, where a spark is generated when you turn the burner on. Check whether the cooker has a flame-failure device to shut off the gas supply to the burners if the flame is blown out.

Tested cookers Table:

B = automatic ignition – battery-generated spark

F = flame-failure device for oven

G = flame-failure device for hob and grill

S = automatic ignition – mains-generated spark

T = oven burners automatically re-light if blown out

X = mains spark ignition can be overridden if there is a power failure

(X) = X, but on hob and grill burners only

Feature-finder Table:

B = automatic ignition – battery-generated spark

M = manual (needs a match/taper/lighter)

FEATURE-FINDER: GAS COOKERS IN THE SHOPS

Main oven size
1 = up to 45 litres
2 = 46 to 70 litres
3 = 71 to 90 litres

Hob cover
G = glass
M = metal

	Price (2)	Dimensions (3) h × w × d (overall height)	Main oven (4): Size	Fan	Door	Grill position (6)	Hob (7): Cover	Safety	Timers	Ignition	Features (8): Storage/warming	Safety approvals (9)
	£	cm										
(1) FREE-STANDING/SINGLE OVEN												
Cannon Cambridge (UK)	425	90 × 54 × 61(147)	3	—	L	H	—	—	—	S	√	BSI
Leisure 100 (UK)	230	90 × 54 × 60(145)	3	—	L	H	—	—	—	B	√	BSI
Leisure 2000 Deluxe (UK)	400	90 × 54 × 63(145)	3	—	V	H	—	—	ADM	S	√	BSI
Leisure 200S (UK)	300	90 × 55 × 60(145)	3	—	L	H	—	—	—	B	√	BSI
Leisure 210 (UK)	290	90 × 54 × 60(145)	3	—	L	H	—	—	—	B	√	BSI
Leisure 220 (UK)	360	90 × 54 × 60(145)	3	—	V	H	—	—	M	B	√	BSI
Leisure 230 (UK)	415	90 × 55 × 60(145)	3	—	L	H	—	—	M	B	√	BSI
Valor Calypso (UK)	315	90 × 49 × 55(137)	2	—	L	H	—	—	—	B	√	BSI
Valor Freestyle (UK)	340	90 × 55 × 60(145)	3	—	L	H	—	—	—	B	√	BSI
Valor Revue (UK)	250	90 × 49 × 55(137)	2	—	L	H	—	—	—	P	√	BSI
Valor Valencia (UK)	460	90 × 56 × 60(145)	2	—	L	H	—	—	DM	S	√	BSI
(1) FREE-STANDING/DOUBLE OVEN												
Cannon Cordon Bleu Classique (UK)	1085	92 × 90 × 62(144)	2	—	L	H	—	—	ACM	S	√	BSI
Cannon Double Oven (UK)	550	91 × 54 × 60(148)	3	—	L	H	—	—	—	S	—	BSI
Cannon Double Oven Deluxe (UK)	580	91 × 54 × 60(148)	3	—	L	H	—	—	ADM	S	—	BSI

► Recommended in the Buying Guide ◄

P = piezo spark
S = automatic ignition – mains-generated spark

Main oven (tested cookers only)
C = catalytic linings standard (we tell you the number fitted)
(C) = catalytic linings optional
G = inner glass oven door
O = oven light
V = viewing panel in oven door
X = extra slow cooking setting

Storage/warming
√ = separate storage/warming compartment or drawer

Mobility (tested cookers)
√ = has wheels or castors

9 Safety approvals

All the tested cookers were approved by the British Standards Institution.

For cookers in the shops:
BSI = approved by the BSI

10 Performance (tested cookers only)

Oven baking

We assess evenness of heat distribution by baking trays of small cakes. Where an oven has a fan, we test batch baking, cooking three or four trays of cakes at the same time. We also bake a fruit cake to test oven performance at low temperature over a long period of time. All the ovens we tested gave satisfactory results.

Oven heat-up time

How long it takes to reach about 200°C.
■ = less than 6 minutes
◪ = 6 to 10 minutes □ = 11 to 15 minutes

Grill

All grills would take at least three whole slices of bread from a large sliced loaf.

	2 Price	3 Dimensions h × w × d (overall height)	4 Main oven: Size	Fan	Door	6 Grill position	Cover	Safety	7 Hob: Timers	Ignition	8 Features: Storage/warming	9 Safety approvals
	£	cm										
1 SLOT-IN/SINGLE OVEN												
Cannon Canterbury (UK)	490	90 × 54 × 60(143)	3	—	L	L	G	C	—	S	—	BSI
Cannon New Harvest (UK)	*330*	*91 × 54 × 60(111)*	3	—	L	L	—	—	—	B	—	BSI
Fagor Ambar F4GT (Spain)	*205*	*81 × 54 × 56(135)*	1	—	D	M	M	—	—	M	√	—
Fagor Nacar N40G (Spain)	*250*	*85 × 60 × 60(143)*	1	—	D	M	M	—	—	S	√	—
Indesit K6400VG (Italy)	*260*	*85 × 60 × 60(145)*	2	—	D	M	G	R	M	S	√	—
Indesit K6400WG (Italy)	*260*	*85 × 60 × 60(145)*	2	—	D	M	G	R	M	S	√	—
Leisure 2040 (UK)	580	90 × 55 × 60(150)	3	√	V	L	G	C	ADM	S	—	BSI
Leisure 3010 (UK)	500	*90 × 55 × 60(150)*	3	—	V	L	G	C	ADM	S	—	BSI
Leisure 3040 (UK)	655	90 × 55 × 60(150)	3	√	V	L	G	C	ADM	S	—	BSI
Leisure Profile (UK)	*595*	*90 × 55 × 60(150)*	3	—	V	L	G	C	ADM	S	—	BSI
Moffat 500TC (UK)	550	*87 × 51 × 60(144)*	3	—	L	L	G	R	ADM	S	—	BSI
Moffat 600TC (UK)	*670*	*87 × 60 × 60(144)*	3	—	L	L	G	R	ADM	S	—	BSI
Moffat Discovery (UK)	650	88 × 55 × 60(143)	3	—	L	L	G	A	ADM	S	—	BSI
New World Apex CKS 21007/8 (UK)	355	86 × 50 × 59(147)	3	—	L	H	—	—	—	B	√	BSI
New World Aspect SBS (UK)	350	90 × 51 × 60(149)	3	—	L	L	G	S	—	B	—	BSI
New World Asset (UK)	*350*	*90 × 51 × 60(149)*	3	—	L	L	G	S	—	B	—	BSI
New World CKG21025/21026 (UK)	280	*90 × 50 × 50(101)*	3	—	L	L	—	—	—	B	—	BSI
New World Debut (UK)	320	*90 × 50 × 63(101)*	3	—	L	L	—	—	—	S	—	BSI
New World Highlite 3 (UK)	*280*	*90 × 50 × 60(147)*	3	—	L	H	—	—	—	B	√	BSI
New World Insight SBS (UK)	400	*90 × 51 × 60(147)*	3	—	L	L	G	S	—	S	—	BSI
▶ **New World Montage SBS** (UK)	490	90 × 51 × 60(143)	3	—	L	L	G	S	—	S	—	BSI ◀
New World Phase 2 (UK)	400	*90 × 50 × 60(147)*	3	—	L	H	—	—	M	B	√	BSI
New World Plan 6 SBS (UK)	550	*90 × 60 × 60(148)*	3	—	L	L	G	S	ADM	S	—	BSI
New World Rapport CKS 21036/7 (UK)	460	90 × 51 × 60(143)	3	—	L	L	G	S	—	B	—	BSI
▶ **New World Royale 600 SBS** (UK)	500	90 × 60 × 60(148)	3	—	L	L	G	S	—	S	—	BSI ◀
Parkinson Cowan 4500D/L (UK)	435	90 × 50 × 60(145)	3	—	L	H	—	—	—	S	√	BSI
Parkinson Cowan Chique (UK)	370	90 × 51 × 60(148)	3	—	L	L	G	R	—	B	—	BSI
Parkinson Cowan Fiesta (UK)	335	*89 × 50 × 59(94)*	3	—	L	L	—	—	—	B	—	BSI
Parkinson Cowan Mink II (UK)	*250*	*90 × 50 × 60(146)*	3	—	L	H	—	—	—	BM	√	BSI
Parkinson Cowan Pisces (UK)	*290*	*90 × 50 × 60(146)*	3	—	L	H	—	—	—	B	√	BSI
Parkinson Cowan Prospect Sheerline (UK)	430	90 × 50 × 60(148)	3	—	L	L	G	R	—	S	—	BSI
Parkinson Cowan Strand (UK)	350	90 × 50 × 60(146)	3	—	L	H	—	—	ADM	S	√	BSI
▶ **Parkinson Cowan Strata** (UK)	280	90 × 50 × 60(146)	3	—	L	H	—	—	—	B	√	BSI ◀
Tecnogas 1129 (Italy)	150	*90 × 50 × 50(140)*	2	—	D	M	M	—	—	M	√	—
Tecnogas 1371/9 (Italy)	210	*90 × 50 × 50(140)*	2	—	D	M	G	C	M	S	√	—
Tecnogas 6571 (Italy)	280	*90 × 60 × 60(150)*	2	—	D	M	G	C	M	S	√	—
Valor Fresco (UK)	345	87 × 49 × 54(136)	2	—	L	L	G	C	—	B	—	BSI
Valor Vienna (UK)	510	*90 × 56 × 60(143)*	3	—	L	L	G	C	—	S	—	BSI
Zanussi GC5601/9601 (Italy)	*340*	*90 × 60 × 60(150)*	2	—	D	M	M	R	—	S	√	—
Zanussi GC9502 (UK)	460	*90 × 50 × 60(150)*	1	—	D	L	G	R	—	S	—	—
Zanussi GC9557/5557 (UK)	*570*	*90 × 55 × 60(150)*	1	—	D	L	G	R	AD	S	—	—
Zanussi GCF9621/5621 (Italy)	*450*	*90 × 60 × 60(150)*	2	√	D	M	G	R	C	S	√	—

Evenness
How much of the grill pan area was effectively heated.

◼ = 90 to 100 per cent
◩ = 85 to 90 per cent
□ = 75 to 85 per cent
◪ = less than 75 per cent

Speed
Time taken to cook a batch of toast.

◼ = less than 2 minutes
◩ = 2 to 3 minutes
□ = 3 to 4 minutes

Height for large dishes
We use a 7cm high dish

◩ = plenty of room for browning (more than 14cm)
□ = adequate room (12 to 14cm)
◪ = barely enough room (10 to 12cm)
■ = not enough room (less than 10cm)

11 Convenience (tested cookers)

a = oven/grill too low for easy access
b = grill pan feels heavy or unbalanced or uncomfortable to hold
c = some controls small or awkward to grip
k = markings on controls poor/controls awkward to set because of poor marking
m = no front stop for grill pan or stops ineffective
n = difficult to see size of gas flame below gas powered disc. Discs have to be unscrewed for cleaning
p = storage area low and/or awkward to use
t = grill compartment too deep for easy cleaning
u = oven door catch rather stiff to open

Convenience for special needs
The results of our assessments for use of cookers by disabled and elderly people.

N/T = not tested for this report
★ = grill pan has one handle – good for some people, a problem for others

Special needs good features

B = minimum force needed to open/close grill door
C = grill pan handle easy to grip
D = heat sources on hob can be seen at all settings
G = oven handle easy to grip
I = well shaped/easy to grip controls
J = as some controls rotate, can feel/hear some heat settings (as well as off and maximum)

Special needs drawbacks

a = pans cannot be easily pushed across hob
c = grill door handle hard to grip
d = grill pan needs lifting to cooking position
f = some force needed to open/close oven door(s)
g = fine control needed to set heat
h = oven shelves awkward to move
j = sharp edges on hob/grill/oven

12 Surface temperatures (tested cookers)

We tell you the areas of each cooker which got hot enough to cause you pain or discomfort if you touch them.

B = control panel
C = control knobs
D = top edge of oven door
E = hob side trim
G = grill pan handle
H = front edge of hob
J = grill door
S = oven side panels
T = control panel trim
Z = plate warming rack

*Subscribing to **Which?** will enable you to buy back numbers – see the advertisement on page 287 for how to subscribe.*

MICROWAVE OVENS

Microwave and Combination Ovens

From *Which?* April 1990

Microwave ovens, and in particular their ability or otherwise to reheat 'cook-chill' foods safely, have been very much in the news for the last 18 months or so. During that time, the biggest problem for consumers has been the lack of detailed information – about the potential risks of reheating cook-chill convenience foods in a microwave oven, and about how different models of oven compare in their effectiveness at reheating.

As soon as we at *Which?* realised how serious the problem might be, we set up our own research programme to try to answer these questions. We introduced new reheating tests with a range of cook-chill dishes, increased the number of temperature measurements in one of our cooking tests, and looked more closely at microwave power output. We also began retesting the microwave ovens we had recommended previously which were still available. Some of those ovens, we gathered, had not performed satisfactorily in the Government's own reheating tests – see the 'Reheating' section in the Table.

Probing the probes

Three of the microwave-only ovens we tested have their own temperature probe (programme 'T' under 'Features' in the Table). You put the probe into the food, and programme the oven to the final temperature you want. The probe is designed to monitor the temperature during cooking; once your pre-set temperature is reached, the oven should turn itself off automatically.

All three worked accurately at heating water to our pre-set temperature. So, in theory, they could be a way of checking that food is cooked or reheated to a safe temperature. To find out how useful temperature-probe heating is with cook-chill foods, we repeated the reheating test on these ovens, with the same foods, using the temperature probes.

On the whole, using the probes with cook-chill foods didn't give very good results. Final temperatures in the foods were generally much lower than in the normal reheating test. Also, reheating times didn't match those based on the instructions on the food packets.

Our verdict Based on these results, don't rely on temperature probes when reheating cook-chill foods.

Microwave oven thermometers

The safety advice is to make sure food is cooked or reheated to at least 70°C throughout. But how can you tell what temperature your food has reached? We tested five microwave oven thermometers (all the ones that were readily available when we did our shopping in November and December 1989).

Three of the thermometers were designed to be inserted into food during cooking, the other two to check the temperature of food when it comes out of the microwave.

All the thermometers were accurate, and we found them fairly helpful when cooking chickens and joints of lamb, but there were practical problems when using them with cook-chill foods.

- The cook-chill foods we tested (spare ribs, lasagne, curry) weren't deep enough to allow the three thermometers intended for use inside the ovens to stand up in the food during reheating. So we had to use them like the other two thermometers – at the end of the cooking time.
- To position the thermometers accurately (in pieces of meat, say), the microwave film over the food sometimes had to be removed. If the food needed further reheating because it wasn't hot enough, it tended to dry out without this film.
- Our main microwave oven tests have shown us how much temperature variation there can be in one cook-chill dish at the end of its cooking time. To measure the temperature in several positions with only one thermometer would mean waiting for the thermometer to register the temperature in one position before moving to the next.
- Several temperature measurements may mean visible holes in the food.

Our verdict A good idea in theory, and helpful with meat and poultry, but in practice too many problems for them to really help with many cook-chill foods.

To stand or not to stand?

Microwave cookery books often recommend letting food stand after it comes out of the oven – because, they say, food continues to cook, and temperature variations are evened out. We decided to test this on our cook-chill foods.

Our main reheating results for the three cook-chill foods are based on a one-minute standing time. But we also went on to record temperatures after two, three, four and five minutes.

Out of all the temperatures that we measured, only around a quarter were higher after five minutes than after a one-minute standing time. More than half had gone down; under a quarter were unchanged.

In general, we found that initially high temperatures tended to fall on standing, whereas lower temperatures tended to rise, so the overall effect was to even out temperatures. But even the largest rises, to areas initially well below 70°C, still left these areas below 70°C, which suggests that longer standing periods won't solve the problems of unacceptably low temperatures.

Our verdict Based on this information, we don't think you should rely on longer-than-recommended standing times to raise temperatures in cook-chill foods to a safe level. But with larger amounts of food, which are likely to retain heat for longer, temperatures may increase more on standing: check your instructions for information.

Combis as conventional ovens

None of the four combination ovens we tested for this report reheated our cook-chill foods completely satisfactorily on microwave power; all but the Toshiba gave quite poor results.

For anyone who has bought a combi as a substitute for a full-size conventional oven, we decided to reheat the same cook-chill foods (spare ribs, lasagne and curry), in the four combis using fan-assisted conventional heat. We also included a frozen fish pie and a chicken and tagliatelle dish, and reheated these from frozen using conventional heat.

BUYING GUIDE

Our tests for cooking and defrosting suggest that with most ovens you'll probably be able to achieve at least satisfactory results, although some trial and error may be needed. Any under-cooking or under-defrosting with the sorts of foods we use for these tests is likely to be obvious – because the sponge isn't firm to the touch or the strawberries and mince are still icy instead of properly thawed. So even the few poor results in these tests probably represent the real-life inconvenience of having to cook or defrost for a bit longer, rather than a potential risk to health.

With shop-bought cook-chill foods, thorough reheating to at least 70°C is essential. But it's very difficult to be sure that these foods have been reheated properly, because they may not change in appearance, and our tests have shown how some parts of the same dish can be steaming while others are too cool. Because of this, when you're reheating cook-chill foods, you rely very much on the instructions with the food – and on the performance of your oven – to give you a safe result.

Our reheating tests (with heating times based on instructions with the food) showed up big differences between ovens. We feel able to recommend only those ovens with the best results for reheating.

GOOD VALUE The **Bosch HMG 762B**, £295 (may not be widely available), and the **Panasonic Genius NN6808**, £270, gave at least satisfactory results in all our tests. In our original report we recommended the **Hitachi MR7950** as the Best Buy microwave oven – it is now discontinued (see page 285).

Of the combination ovens we tested, none got top marks for reheating, but the **Toshiba ER9630EW**, £300, did best overall. If you buy this oven, make sure you use the plastic rack for reheating.

The conventional heat settings on three of the combis generally gave very good results, with temperatures well over 70°C. With the Brother, we recorded one temperature out of 12 below 70°C for each food, when reheating spare ribs, curry and the frozen chicken and tagliatelle dish.

Based on these results, and following current food instructions, reheating cook-chill foods using a combi oven's conventional heat setting seems to be more reliable than microwave-only power, although conventional cooking obviously takes much longer.

FACTS, FIGURES AND TEST RESULTS

Key

√ = has this feature/was satisfactory in our tests

— = does not have this feature/not applicable

MICROWAVE OVENS

	2 Target price	3 External dimensions h x w x d	4 Oven space	Rectangular dish	5 Door hinge	6 Microwave power: Stated maximum power output	Recorded maximum power output	Power levels
	£	cm	litres			W	W	
1 MICROWAVE ONLY OVENS								
1 **Baucknecht MWE 732** (Sweden)[1]	*550*	41 x 54 x 43	32	√	D	725	710	8
▶ 2 **Bosch HMG 762B** (Japan)[2]	*295*	36 x 54 x 37	28	—	L	700	860	4
3 **Matsui 170S** (UK)[3]	160	35 x 54 x 42	27	—	L	700	740	5
4 **Miele M720** (W Germany)	*450*	37 x 56 x 42	27	√[4]	L	780	780	4
5 **Neff 6160.14** (Japan)[7]	*375*	31 x 56 x 43	31	√	L	700	790	4
6 **Osaki 1060** (Taiwan)[8]	120	35 x 54 x 40	26	—	L	600	600	10
▶ 7 **Panasonic Genius NN6808** (Japan)[9]	270	31 x 56 x 42	30	√	L	700	750	6
8 **Philips Space Cube 50 AVM 742** (Sweden)[11]	300	40 x 54 x 42	32	√	D	750	740	8
9 **Samsung RE606ST** (Korea)[12]	200	35 x 54 x 42	25	—	L	700	680	5
10 **Sharp R5A50W** (UK)	200	35 x 55 x 42	32	√	L	700	700	5
11 **Siemens HF1670/2** (Japan)[13]	*390*	36 x 54 x 37	28	—	L	700	810	4
12 **Toshiba Deltaware ER7820E** (UK)[14]	200	38 x 56 x 41	26	—	L	650	710	9
13 **Toshiba ER8730E** (UK)[15]	150	36 x 46 x 51	26	—	L	650	740	9
1 COMBINATION OVENS								
1 **Bosch HMG 8420** (W Germany)[16]	*730*	39 x 56 x 51	28	√	D	600	600	4
2 **Brother MF2200** (UK)	380	38 x 55 x 50	22	√[4]	L	650	650	5
3 **Siemens HF74020** (W Germany)[17]	*800*	38 x 56 x 50	28	√	D	600	580	4
▶ 4 **Toshiba ER9630EW** (Japan)[18]	300	36 x 53 x 49	23	√[4]	L	650	660	5

▶ Recommended in the Buying Guide ◀

KEY TO RATINGS best ◩ > ◪ > □ > ◩ > ■ worst

1 Type
We've divided this Table into microwave-only ovens and combination ovens, which combine conventional cooking methods with microwave energy. The separate 'combination ovens' Table gives information and test results for the various combination options.

2 Target price
For ovens we didn't find widely available in our price survey, we give manufacturers' prices in *italics*.

3 External dimensions
Height × width × depth rounded up to the nearest whole centimetre. Depth includes protrusions at the back. Check ventilation requirements for each oven: up to 10cm at the back or the sides may be needed.

4 Oven space
We tell you the usable oven volume to the nearest litre. All would take a 27cm diameter plate. We show you which would take a 31 × 29cm rectangular dish. With some ovens (those with a [4]) you would

7 Features			8 Microwave performance											
			Cooking		Defrosting		Reheating							
Accessories	Programmes	Timers	Sponge	Meat loaf	Mince	Strawberries	MAFF tests	Our tests	Recipe book 9	Convenience drawbacks 10	Building in 11	Radio/TV interference 12		
m	BT	C	□	■	□	□	—	×	■	F	[1]	√	1	
a(g)	CDM	C	◪/■	□	□	□	—	√	■	—	eg	√	2	◀
a(g)	ABCDM	C	◪/■	■	◪/□	◪/□	—	××	■	—	—	√	3	
a(g)nz	DKMT	C	■	■	□[5]	■	—	×	■[6]	LM	e	√	4	
a(g)	CDKM	C	□	□	■	□	—	√	■	—	e	√	5	
a(g)	ABDM	C	□	◪/■	□	■	√	(√)	■	P	—	A	6	
a(g)	ACDM	C	□	□	■[10]	□	—	√	■	E	e	√	7	◀
mp	BDMT	C	◪/□	■	■	■	—	×	■	K	e	√	8	
a(g)	ABCD	C	□	□	◪/◪[5]	□	—	××	■	EP	—	√	9	
a(g)	ACDM	C	□	■	□	□	—	×	■	—	e	√	10	
a(g)	CDKM	C	◪/■	□	□	□	—	√	■	—	e	√	11	
a(g)	ADM	C	■	□	◪/◪	□[5]	√	√	■	EL	ef	√	12	
a(g)	DM	C	□	□	◪/□[10]	■[10]	√	(√)	■	EL	e	√	13	
bex	M	H	◪/□	■	◪/◪	□	—	××	■	AE	e	C	1	
a(m)dhjxz	CDKM	C	□	□	□[10]	□	—	×	■	A	e	√	2	
bex	M	H	◪/□	■	◪/◪	□	—	××	■	AE	e	√	3	
a(m)dghxz	ADM	G	□	□	□[5]	■[5]	×[19]	(√)	□	E	e	√	4	◀

have to deactivate the turntable to fit the dish in.

5 Door hinge

D = drop-down door

L = door hinged on left-hand side

[1] Built-in only, price includes kit. Similar EMWS732 *£450*, dial timer and manual controls

[2] Similar HMG 760B *£295*, colour difference; HMG 732B/730B £245, dial timer and manual controls

[3] Exclusive to Currys

[4] Turntable has to be deactivated

[5] Auto-defrost and manual defrosting gave same results

[6] Supplied book written for oven with 600 to 700W output

[7] Similar 6165.14 *£374* and 6166.14 *£380*, colour differences

[8] Exclusive to Rumbelows. Similar NEI 620 *£140*, cosmetic differences; NEI 630 *£129*, and the Morphy Richards 400 £140 (exclusive to Asda), similar but dial timers and manual controls

[9] Similar NN6858 *£270*, colour difference

[10] Best result from auto-defrost

[11] Similar AVM 764 *£270*, no probe, no sensor reheat or autoweight defrost

[12] Similar RE606TC, *£170*, no sensor cooking

[13] Similar HF1672 *£391*, colour difference; HF1610/HF1612 *£305*, manual controls, no auto-cook or auto-defrost

[14] Similar ER7820EW *£200*, colour difference; ER7620 *£170*, mechanical timer and manual controls; Hotpoint 6655 *£320*, cosmetic differences

[15] Similar ER8730EW *£150*, colour difference; ER888 *£160*, stainless steel oven cavity; ER761 *£180*, has auto-recall

[16] Similar HMG 8460 *£730*, colour difference

[17] Similar HF74040 *£799*, colour difference; HF7200/HF72020 *£666*, manual controls, no fan, no 4-hour timer

[18] Similar ER9630E *£330*, colour difference; ER9530 *£260*, mechanical timer and manual controls

[19] MAFF tests carried out without plastic rack supplied

6 Microwave power

We give, in watts, the manufacturer's *stated* maximum power output. This is the figure you'll see in sales literature and instructions, and it's also the one you need to know if you have to make adjustments to microwave cooking instructions which are based on a lower- or higher-rated oven – see 'Cooking time calculator'. We also give the maximum power output we recorded during our tests, rounded to the nearest 10 watts.

Differences between the 'stated' power output and the one we recorded can be explained by different methods used for measuring power output. But microwave oven manufacturers have been moving towards a standard international method, which we used as the basis for our power output tests. By now the majority of new models in the shops will have a power output figure which is based on this standardised method.

Cooking time calculator

If your microwave oven has a lower – or higher – stated output than that given in a recipe or cooking instructions, here's how to adjust cooking and reheating times.

Power output in recipe/on packet

×

Cooking/reheating time on food packet (minutes)

÷

Your oven's stated power output

=

Number of minutes to heat for

So, if you have a 500-watt oven, but the food packet recommends reheating for 4 minutes at 650 watts, you'll need to reheat for 5 minutes 12 seconds. (650 times 4, divided by 500 equals 5.2.)

We also give the number of pre-set microwave power levels you can choose from: typically, they range from 'warm/gentle' at the low-power end, to 'full/high' at high power.

7 Features

Accessories

a(g) = glass turntable
a(m) = metal turntable
b = removable wire/metal shelf(ves)
d = anti-splash trivet/tray
e = glass tray/shelf
g = plastic defrosting rack
h = one or more trivets
j = insulating mat
m = ceramic cooking tray on oven base
n = stirring rod
p = plate cover
x = one or more catalytic oven linings
z = turntable can be deactivated for large dishes

Programmes

A = autostart: oven can be set to start and stop at specified times of the day
B = memory: stores cooking programmes
C = auto-cook: you generally programme in the type and weight of food, and the cooking time is worked out automatically. On some ovens, auto-cook works by detecting vapour from food
D = auto-defrost: on some ovens you programme in the type and weight of food, and the defrost time is worked out automatically; with others, the oven automatically divides the defrosting time you set into separate defrost and standing periods
K = 'keep warm' setting
M = multiple sequence cooking: you pre-set a sequence of power levels and/or cooking times, so don't need to set individual stages separately

T = temperature probe cooking: you insert the probe into the food before cooking, and programme a final temperature. The oven should stop automatically when the pre-set temperature is reached (see 'Probing the probes').

Timers All the ovens have electronic touch-type timers which you can set for a maximum time:

C = up to 99 minutes

G = microwave, convection and combi up to 99 minutes, grill up to 30 minutes

H = microwave and combination up to 90 minutes, convection and grill up to 4 hours

8 Microwave performance

Where we got an unsatisfactory result the first time, we repeated the test if we could change any of the factors involved – by raising the food on a rack, for instance. We show a repeat test by a split rating: the second rating shows the best result we could achieve.

Cooking and defrosting We followed the oven manufacturers' instructions for all our cooking and defrosting tests. The Genoese sponge test is designed to check how well the oven can cook a cake-type mixture in a round container. The sponge should rise evenly and have a consistent colour and texture. We also cook a 1kg meat loaf to assess evenness of heating in a thick brick-shaped food. A standard recipe is used and the temperature recorded in different positions using five special thermometers. A visual assessment is also carried out to look for raw or over-cooked areas. We assess how evenly ovens can defrost a 400g block of mince and 250g of strawberries.

With both tests, we're looking for areas which start to heat up or cook before others are properly defrosted. Where both methods were available, and where recommended, we tried both manual and automatic defrost settings; ratings in the Table are based on the method which gave the best results in the end. Manual defrosting generally gave better results than automatic programmes, but where auto-defrost was more successful we've shown this with footnote [10].

◪ = food was evenly cooked or thawed

□ = food was at least satisfactorily cooked or thawed

◩ = food was under- or over-cooked in parts; or it was unevenly thawed, so that some of the food was still frozen while other parts were beginning to cook

Reheating The Ministry of Agriculture, Fisheries and Food (MAFF) commissioned research into the ability of domestic microwave ovens to reheat food to a satisfactory temperature. Results from those tests showed up considerable differences between ovens, some of which were able to heat food far less effectively than others. We show which of the ovens we've tested were also tested by MAFF, and whether on the basis of these tests, they were described by AMDEA (the Association of Manufacturers of Domestic Electrical Appliances) in their subsequent press release as satisfactory or not.

MAFF used mashed potato in its tests. We wanted a more life-like test, so we decided to use a range of shop-bought cook-chill foods, chosen because of their different textures. We reheated spare ribs lasagne and curry in each oven three times, following instructions on the food packets and any reheating recommendations in the ovens' instructions. At the end of the cooking time, we measured the temperature in four different positions in each dish, giving a total of 36 temperature measurements per oven. Results for reheating in the Table are based on each oven's ability to heat these foods consistently and evenly to at least 70°C.

MAFF tests

√ = described as 'satisfactory' in the AMDEA press release on the MAFF tests

x = not described as 'satisfactory' in the AMDEA press release on the MAFF tests

— = not in MAFF tests

Our tests

√ = satisfactory for all our foods

(√) = up to 4 out of 36 temperature measurements below 70°C

x = between 5 and 12 temperature measurements below 70°C

xx = 14 or more temperature measurements below 70°C, and at least one temperature in the 40s recorded in at least one food

9 Recipe book

We assessed the contents, and how easy they were to use. We also assessed the most up-to-date version of each oven's instructions. We were concerned to find little advice on how to adjust cooking times in recipes and cook-chill instructions for ovens with different power outputs. (See 'Cooking time calculator'.)

10 Convenience drawbacks

A = at least some controls and/or timer difficult or fiddly to set

E = viewing poor due to dim light and/or dark mesh in viewing panel

F = oven door has to be opened to stop or cancel a programme

K = ceramic tray awkward to remove

L = door release control stiff/awkward to operate

M = turntable awkward to remove

P = difficult to see some displays on control panel without stooping

11 Building in

e = building-in kit available from manufacturer

f = if built-in with another appliance, microwave oven should go underneath

g = if building in with a Bosch built-in oven, microwave oven should go on top

12 Radio and TV interference

A = likely to cause interference in medium wave band

C = likely to cause interference in short wave band

None is likely to interfere with your TV

Electrical safety

All models were satisfactory in our tests or had British Electrotechnical Approvals Board (BEAB) approval.

Fire containment test

We do this test because in the past fires have started in some microwave ovens when foods have been set to cook for too long. In some cases, the fire has then spread to the surrounding kitchen, or has damaged the oven so that it's no longer safe to use. To do the test we put a potato in the oven, set the timer and power to maximum and leave the oven on. If the potato catches fire, we give a 'satisfactory' rating to ovens which contain the fire and are safe to use afterwards. All the ovens tested for this report were satisfactory.

COMBINATION OVENS

Combination ovens cook by convection heat (like an ordinary oven), or by microwave energy, or by a combination of

COMBINATION OVENS: CONVENTIONAL COOKING

	1 Combination settings		2 Cooking levels	3 Performance	Fan		Combination			4 Surface temperatures
	Oven	Grill		Convection	Batch bake	Grill	Fruit cake	Pork	Combination grilling	
1 Bosch HMG 8420	B	B	6	□	□	□	◪/□	□	□	CD
2 Brother MF2200	C	—	2	□	□	—	◩	◩	—	√
3 Siemens HF 74020	B	B	6	□	□	□	◪/□	□	□	CD
4 Toshiba ER 9630EW	B	—	5	□	□	[1]	◪/◩	□	—	D

[1] Not tested since manufacturers do not recommend for toast

KEY TO RATINGS best ▣ > ◩ > □ > ◪ > ■ worst

the two. Some of them also have grills. Here we show which cooking options are available for the combis we've tested, and how well they did in our tests. See the main Table for how they performed on normal microwave power.

All the ovens can be used on microwave power only, convection heat, fan-assisted convection heat, combined convection and microwave power; all but the Brother have a grill as well. The Bosch and Siemens also offer fan-assisted grilling and combined grill and microwave power.

1 Combination settings

We tell you whether the combination settings are pre-set, or whether you can select any microwave power level or convection temperature.

B = manual: you set the convection/grill temperature and microwave power level you want

C = microwave power is pre-set: you set the convection temperature

2 Cooking levels

The maximum number of levels you can position food on for cooking, using accessories such as shelves or trivets where supplied, and deactivating the turntable where possible. On most combis you generally can't use more than a couple of levels at once.

3 Performance

Convection This rating is based on baking single trays of small cakes.

Fan On fan-assisted convection heat, we did a batch bake, cooking two trays of cakes at the same time.

Grill We made toast following manufacturers' recommendations. Both the Bosch and Siemens ovens took six slices from a large sliced loaf, and toasting took less than four minutes, excluding pre-heat time. We assessed how much of the toasting area was effectively heated:

□ – 76 to 85 per cent of the area was evenly toasted. With both grills there was an untoasted area in the centre

We didn't do this test in the Toshiba because there are no exposed grill elements, and the manufacturer doesn't recommend toasting bread. We also used the fan-assisted grill setting in the Bosch and Siemens to cook pork kebabs, with satisfactory results.

Combination cooking We cooked a rich fruit cake and a joint of roast pork. A split rating shows results for the first (unsatisfactory) run, and for a second attempt to get a better result.

Combination grilling We cooked chicken portions in the Bosch and Siemens using a grill-plus-microwave setting.

4 Surface temperatures

Ordinary microwave ovens don't get hot on the outside, but some combis do. We used the same test method that we use for cookers. Parts of some oven doors and some oven casings got hot enough to cause pain or discomfort if you were to touch them.

C = side of oven casing

D = oven door

PREVIOUSLY RECOMMENDED MODELS

Because we've expanded our test programme and because some of the microwave ovens we recommended previously were not described as 'satisfactory' in AMDEA's press release on the MAFF tests, we decided to retest previously recommended ovens which are still available.

We repeated the meat loaf test, increasing the number of temperature measurements to five, and also carried out reheating tests with three cook-chill foods. Where manufacturers of these ovens have changed their cooking instructions, or introduced trivets to raise food during cooking in the light of the MAFF tests, we incorporated all these factors in our new tests. Other results – for cooking the sponge and for defrosting meat and strawberries – are brought forward from our previous tests.

1 Type

We've divided this Table into microwave-only ovens and combination ovens which combine conventional cooking methods with microwave energy.

[1] Our latest tests used the 25mm rack now included with this model

[2] Similar Matsui 200 £99, exclusive to Currys, cosmetic differences

[3] Exclusive to Currys. Model in tests made in Korea; now made in UK. Manufacturer tells us performance should be the same. Similar Saisho MW2000 £140, exclusive to Dixons, and Samsung RE-630TC £160, exclusive to Electricity Boards (prices vary from Board to Board), cosmetic differences

[4] Exclusive to Currys. Our latest tests used the trivet now included with this model

[5] Our latest tests used the trivet now included with this model

PREVIOUSLY RECOMMENDED MODELS: RETEST RESULTS

	2 Target price	3 Microwave power: Stated maximum power output	Recorded maximum power output	4 Performance: Microwave cooking: Sponge	Meat loaf	Microwave defrosting: Meat	Strawberries	Microwave reheating: MAFF tests	Our tests
	£	W	W						
1 MICROWAVE ONLY									
1 Boots Hedge Rose [1]	79	550	490	◤	□	◪/◪	□	x	x[1]
2 Goodmans Cuisine 2000 [2]	140	500	520	▰	□	◪/□	□	√	(√)
3 Matsui 170TC [3]	140	650	680	◤	◤	◪/◪	□	√	x
1 COMBINATION									
1 Matsui 260 [4]	200	650	600	□	◪/□	◪/□	◤	x	x[4]
2 Samsung RE-990CT [5]	200	650	610	□	□	◪/□	◤	x	(√)[5]

KEY TO RATINGS best ▰ > ◤ > □ > ◪ > ■ worst

2 Target price
For ovens we didn't find widely available in our price survey, we give manufacturers' prices in *italics*.

3 Microwave power
We give, in watts, the manufacturer's *stated* maximum power output (what you'd see in sales literature and instructions) and the maximum power output we recorded during our tests. See 'Microwave power' for why these two figures may be different.

4 Performance
Where we got an unsatisfactory result the first time, we repeated the test if we could change any of the factors involved – by raising the food on a rack, for instance. The second rating shows the best result we could achieve.

---

*A **Which?** Best Buy is the product or products which offered the best combination of price and performance in our tests. A **Which?** Best Buy is not necessarily the model with the best test results, nor the one with the most features; nor is it necessarily the cheapest. Other models mentioned in the Buying Guides have particular strengths which may be best suited to your needs.*

FRIDGES

Worktop-height and Taller

From *Which?* November 1989

To minimise the risk of food poisoning, you must keep your fridge cold: 5°C or colder. All the fridges tested for this report can manage this, but you won't know what temperature your fridge is at by looking at the thermostat control. We think it's about time all manufacturers built thermometers into their fridges. But until they do, it's essential to buy a fridge thermometer.

Most fridges with frozen food compartments have a particular problem at cool room temperatures: if you get the fresh food compartment at the right temperature, the frozen food section is likely to be several degrees too warm. This isn't a health risk, but it does mean you can't rely on your two-star compartment to store food at −12°C for a month, which is what it should do. When tested at a room temperature of 16°C, the fridges only managed between −3°C and −8°C. In other words, we got only one-star performance (one week's storage at −6°C) from those two-star compartments.

FACTS, FIGURES AND TEST RESULTS

1 Types

We've grouped the fridges according to their size (worktop-height or taller), and whether they're the simple larder type or have a frozen food compartment.

The Bauknecht KDC1533 has a three-star compartment, which can store frozen food for three months. All the other frozen food compartments are two-stars: they should keep frozen food for one month. None is suitable for freezing fresh food.

The Indesit R1402WG larder fridge has a no-star compartment which can be used for making ice cubes, but not for storing food.

The Asko Polar KS3501 tall fridge is different from all the other fridges: it has two doors and two compartments.

2 Target price

This is what you should expect to pay if you shop around. Several brands aren't widely available in high-street electrical chain stores. For these, we give the manufacturer's guide prices, in *italics*. Use the manufacturer's phone numbers, below, to find stockists in your area.

AEG ☎ 0753 872118; Asko Polar ☎ 081-568 4666; Bauknecht ☎ 061-905 1600; Bosch ☎ 0895 838383; Liebherr ☎ 0532 459493; Snowcap ☎ 081-800 8088.

3 Dimensions

Height × width × depth All the worktop-height fridges will fit under a standard height (87cm) kitchen work surface. Bear depth in mind if you have any deep skirtings, pipes or sockets that might get in the way. The Table tells you the width and depth (including space to let air circulate, if needed) of each worktop-height fridge, and the full dimensions of the tall fridges.

BUYING GUIDE

WORKTOP-HEIGHT LARDERS
If you already own a separate freezer, go for a larder fridge – one without a frozen food section. They're generally easier to keep at the correct temperature, need no defrosting, and are cheaper to run.

BEST BUY The **Frigidaire R1590** £140 has good temperature control, and is cheap to buy and run. But it has several convenience drawbacks.

The **Liebherr KT1910-5** *£180*, **Philips ARG193/PH** £180 (now superseded by **Philips Whirlpool ARG716**), and **Zanussi DR56/L** £185 (**Electrolux RF593** is similar) cost a bit more, but have useful features.

WORKTOP-HEIGHT WITH FROZEN FOOD SECTION
If you need a frozen food compartment:

BEST BUY the **Zanussi DR50/2** £140 has good performance at a middle-range price, with no serious convenience drawbacks.

TALL LARDERS
All the ones we tested performed well.

GOOD VALUE The **Electrolux RP1016** £240, **Hotpoint Iced Diamond 8149W** £250 and **Philips ARG711/PH** (£240) (now superseded by **Philips Whirlpool ARG729**) are a similar price, and have few convenience drawbacks. The **Proline R111** £220 (**Scandinova KS315-47** is similar) is cheap for its size, but has several convenience drawbacks.

How close to side wall With some fridges, you have to open the door beyond 90° to remove the shelves. The Table tells you how much extra space you'll need, if any.

4 Storage volumes

For comparing the sizes of fridges, we've used the storage (or 'net') volume. This gives a better guide than the 'gross' volume (usually quoted by manufacturers) which includes space taken up by shelves, thermostat housing, and so on.

Worktop-height/fresh food
I = 80 to 99 litres
II = 100 to 119 litres
III = 120 to 139 litres
IIII = 140 to 159 litres
IIIII = 160 to 179 litres

Worktop-height/frozen food
I = 5 to 9 litres **II** = 10 to 14 litres
III – 15 to 19 litres

Tall larder (fresh food)
▶ = 200 to 224 litres
▶▶ = 225 to 249 litres
▶▶▶ = 250 to 274 litres
▶▶▶▶ = 275 to 299 litres
▶▶▶▶▶ = over 300 litres

5 Convenience drawbacks

A panel of testers assessed all the fridges to see how easy they were both to use and to clean.

FRIDGES

	Target price [2]	Height [3 Dimensions]	Width	Depth	How close to side wall	Fresh food [4 Storage volumes]	Frozen food	Convenience drawbacks [5]	Recommended thermostat setting [6]	Temperature control [7]	Electrical efficiency [8]	
	£	cm	cm	cm	cm							
[1] WORKTOP-HEIGHT LARDER FRIDGES												
1 **Ariston MC140S** (Italy)	160		50	60	[7]	III	—	DNRSTVWY	◩	▩	□	
2 **Bosch KTR1541** (W Germany)	*220*		50	60	0	IIII	—	DQVWY	◩	▩	◩	
3 **Electra EO5T-8** (UK) [1]	150		53	56	15	III	—	ADNRVW	◪	▩	◪	
4 **Eurotech LR1001** (Italy) [2]	130		51	58	0	III	—	DQRSTW	□	□	◩	
▶ 5 **Frigidaire R1590** (Hungary)	140		55	60	35	IIII	—	ADEQTVW	▩	▩	◩	◀
6 **Hotpoint Iced Diamond 8129W** (UK)	180		55	60	0	IIII	—	ADTVW	◩	◩	◪	
7 **Indesit R1402WG** (Italy)	110		51	56	38	II	—	DNQRSTVWXY	◩	▩	◪	
8 **Indesit R1458** (Italy)	130		51	56	0	IIII	—	DNQRSTVWXY	◪	□	■	
9 **Lec L5025** (UK)	140		50	61	0	IIII	—	ADQRV	□	▩	■	
▶ 10 **Liebherr KT1910-5** (W Germany)	*180*		60	60	[7]	IIIII	—	DERVY	◪	▩	□	◀
11 **NEI 142** (Romania)	100		55	61	42	IIII	—	ABCDQTVWY	◩	▩	□	
▶ 12 **Philips ARG193/PH** (Italy) [3]	180		55	60	45	IIIII	—	JRTWY	◩	▩	◩	◀
13 **Tricity L5009** (UK)	150		50	61	33	III	—	DKRT	▩	□	◪	
▶ 14 **Zanussi DR56/L** (Italy)	185		55	60	29	IIII	—	D	◩	▩	□	◀
15 **Zanussi ZR60/L** (Italy)	240		60	60	[7]	IIIII	—	DR	◪	▩	◩	
[1] WORKTOP-HEIGHT FRIDGES WITH FROZEN FOOD COMPARTMENT												
1 **Ariston MP140S** (Italy)	160		50	59	0	II	II	DNRSTVWY	□	◪	◪	
2 **Bauknecht KDC 1533** (Italy)	*230*		55	60	0	III	III	DQRVWY	▩	▩	□	
3 **Electrolux RF573** (Italy)	160		55	59	43	III	II	DFGKMRSTW	□	◪	■	
4 **Frigidaire R1516** (Hungary)	100		55	60	[7]	II	III	DNQTVW	□	◩	□	
5 **Hotpoint Iced Diamond 8221W** (UK)	190		55	60	0	II	II	ADTVW	▩	◪	◪	
6 **Lec R4025** (UK)	130		50	54	[7]	I	I	ADQRV	□	◩	■	
7 **Lec R5025** (UK)	135		50	61	17	II	I	ADQRV	▩	◩	■	
8 **Philips ARG185/PH** (Italy) [4]	140		46	60	34	II	II	DNQRSV	□	□	■	
9 **Snowcap 150DL** (USSR)	*90*		57	60	0	II	II	DHPQRVWXY	◪	◩	◪	
10 **Tricity R4008** (UK)	125		46	52	41	I	I	DFLQSTVWY	▩	▩	■	
11 **Tricity R5009** (UK)	140		50	61	0	II	I	DKRT	▩	▩	■	
▶ 12 **Zanussi DR50/2** (Italy)	140		50	60	[7]	II	I	DTVW	◩	▩	◪	◀
[1] TALL LARDER FRIDGES												
1 **AEG Santo 2500KA** (W Germany)	*280*	127	54	58	0	▶▶	—	DTY	◪	◩	◩	
2 **Asko Polar KS3501** (Sweden)	*370*	185	60	60	0	▶▶▶▶▶	—	AMRQTW	◩	▩	▩	
3 **Bosch KSR2512** (W Germany)	*325*	146	60	60	0	▶▶	—	DNQVY	▩	▩	▩	
▶ 4 **Electrolux RP1016** (UK)	240	136	55	60	0	▶▶▶	—	DJRS	▩	▩	▩	◀
▶ 5 **Hotpoint Iced Diamond 8149W** (UK)	250	136	55	61	0	▶▶▶	—	DVW	▩	▩	▩	◀
6 **Lec L7625** (UK)	160	120	50	62	0	▶	—	DRQV	▩	▩	□	
7 **Liebherr KS3220** (W Germany)	*398*	146	60	60	0	▶▶▶▶▶	—	DKVY	▩	▩	▩	
▶ 8 **Philips ARG711/PH** (Italy) [5]	240	140	59	60	0	▶▶▶▶	—	DWY	□	▩	▩	◀
▶ 9 **Proline R111** (Denmark) [6]	220	155	60	60	19	▶▶▶▶▶	—	CKMVWY	▩	▩	▩	◀
10 **Zanussi DR85/L** (Italy)	240	130	52	60	0	▶	—	DV	□	◩	◩	

▶ Recommended in the Buying Guide ◀

KEY TO RATINGS best ▩ > ◩ > □ > ◪ > ■ worst

Some features make a fridge very convenient to use: a bottle grip in the door rack is useful to help prevent bottles and cartons from toppling over; a hinged flap in a fridge shelf lets you stand tall bottles in the main compartment; adjustable shelves and racks let you choose a layout that's best suited to the sorts of things you want to store.

The AEG Santo 2500KA and Bauknecht KDC1533 have solid shelves. You may find these more convenient than the grid type for storing small items. They also help stop liquids dripping from one shelf to another, and may thus cut down the risk of cross-contamination – a major cause of food poisoning.

Overall, four fridges were rated by our convenience assessors as unsatisfactory for ease of use: the **NEI 142** has many sharp edges and dirt traps; the **Snowcap 150DL** has too little shelf storage area, and the drip trays are difficult to remove and replace; the **Tricity R4008** hasn't got an interior light, its thermostat marker isn't clear, and only one tall bottle can be stored at a time in the door rack; the **Asko Polar KS3501** has an ineffective light in the top compartment, no light in the bottom compartment, and a door handle that's uncomfortable to use.

We've listed each fridge's drawbacks; decide how important they are to you.

A = door handle uncomfortable or difficult to grasp
B = many sharp edges
C = dirt traps
D = no rollers/castors
E = no adjustable feet
F = thermostat marker not clear
G = defrost control difficult to press
H = drip trays difficult to remove/replace
J = shelves difficult to adjust
K = door racks difficult to adjust
L = no interior light
M = dim interior light
N = shelves in main compartment not adjustable
P = inefficient use of storage space in main compartment
Q = door racks not adjustable
R = inefficient use of door storage space
S = no enclosed dairy compartment
T = no means of standing tall bottles in main compartment
V = no fittings to stabilise items in door rack
W = no meat dish/thaw tray
X = door hinges not reversible
Y = no plug fitted

[1] Exclusive to Electricity Board showrooms
[2] Exclusive to Iceland/Bejam stores
[3] Superseded by Philips Whirlpool ARG716
[4] Superseded by Philips Whirlpool ARG715
[5] Superseded by Philips Whirlpool ARG729
[6] Exclusive to Comet
[7] Tested previously. Test method changed, results not comparable

Defrosting All the larder fridges defrost automatically, so there's nothing for you to do. Fridges with frozen food compartments need to be defrosted, manually, every few months. All except one have a satisfactory method of collecting and removing the defrost water: with the Bauknecht KDC1533, the water collects in the bottom of the fridge, and you have to mop it up.

6 Recommended thermostat setting

In many cases, you can't rely on the manufacturer's recommended setting to keep the fridge at the best storage temperature. We've down-rated fridges that were too warm or cold. You'll need to buy a fridge thermometer to help you get the right temperature: 2°C to 5°C in the fresh food compartment; −12°C in a two-star compartment, −18°C in a three-star.

7 Temperature control

We measured how well the fridges coped with room temperatures between 10°C and

32°C. To work out the rating, we deducted marks if the fresh food compartment got too warm or fell below 0°C, and if the frozen food compartment got too warm.

The main problem with fridges with frozen food compartments is that the two compartments are often out of balance at cool room temperatures.

8 Electrical efficiency

This tells you how economical the fridges are to run, taking into account the storage volumes of the fresh food and frozen compartments. A fridge rated ■ uses more than twice as much electricity as one with a ◪ rating. The likely quarterly running cost of the worktop-height and tall larder fridges ranged from £2 to £4; the fridges with frozen food sections cost between £2.50 and £5. Clearly, having an efficient fridge won't save you much money, but conserving energy is good news for the environment as well as for your pocket.

Noise

We measured the noise made by the fridges when running, and assessed their vibration at switch-on and switch-off. None made enough noise to be a nuisance.

Electrical safety

All fridges were either satisfactory in our tests or have British Electrotechnical Approvals Board (BEAB) approval.

SIMILAR MODELS

Bold numbers correspond with those in the Table:

Worktop-height larder fridges
- **3** Candy C45 (£150) and Kelvinator KO5 (£150)
- **6** 8129P and 8129A (both £180)
- **9** L5029 (£155)
- **14** Electrolux RF593 (£185)

Worktop-height fridges with frozen food compartment
- **3** Zanussi DR56/2 (£160)
- **5** 8221P and 8221A (both £190)
- **6** R4029 (£135)
- **7** R5029 (£145)

Tall larder fridges
- **5** 8149P and 8149A (both £250)
- **6** L7629 (£170)
- **9** Scandinova KS315-47 (£230)

Consumers' Association produces a wide variety of books and Action Packs on different subjects. For a full list, write to CA at the **Which?** *Bookshop, 359/361 Euston Road, London NW1 3AL, or call in on Monday to Friday between 9.30 and 5.*

'Similar models' are products which we would expect to perform similarly to ones we have tested. They may look different (cosmetic differences) or have slightly more or fewer features. They may be better suited to your needs than the tested models.

FREEZERS

Worktop-height, Tall Upright and Chest Freezers

From *Which?* September 1990

To help your choose the freezer your peas will be happiest in, we look at how to decide which type to go for. We give our full test results on 38 freezers with our Buying Guide on the best performers.

Which freezer?

Both chest (which have lids) and upright freezers (with doors which open outwards) are equally good at freezing fresh food and keeping food frozen – but see 'Freezer problems'. You get more storage space for your money with a chest freezer, but price isn't the only thing to consider.

Where will the freezer fit?

Uprights outscore chests, because they usually take up less floor space, and having to lift the lid of a chest means it may use more vertical space when open than a

BUYING GUIDE

WORKTOP-HEIGHT UPRIGHT FREEZERS

If you're looking for a freezer to fit under a work surface:

BEST BUYS

the **Philips Whirlpool AFB726** (£200) has good freezing capacity and doesn't use much electricity – but it can't store large items. The **Eurotech UF3002** (£150) also did well and is fairly cheap, but it has several convenience drawbacks.

The **Indesit F4218WG** (£190) is a good performer, and is fairly cheap to buy, but it's pricey to run. The **Philips Whirlpool AFB740** (£280) also did well, and is reasonably efficient. But it costs more to buy.

TALL UPRIGHT FREEZERS

We haven't picked any tall uprights as Best Buys, because none has the ideal combination of having good performance, and being cheap to run and reasonably priced.

CHEST FREEZERS

BEST BUY

If you need only a small chest freezer, go for the **Zanussi CF64** (£205).

There wasn't much to choose between the larger chest freezers, and none stood out as a Best Buy. We recommend the **Electrolux TC1160** (£260), **Iceline CF306** (£200), **Philips Whirlpool AFB570** (£250), and **Zanussi CF132** (£260) tall upright freezer. And if you need to get at your food frequently, you'll have to keep the chest freezer lid clear – though this may not be a problem if you don't plan to keep your freezer in the kitchen.

Small uprights are easier to incorporate into a fitted kitchen, because they have usable worktop space, or can be placed under a kitchen work surface.

Getting at your food

Chest freezers can store large or awkwardly-shaped items more easily than uprights, but getting at food can be difficult – especially if you're short or have a problem bending. Upright freezers are more convenient, because their storage shelves and pull-out baskets make it easier to find a particular item.

Reliability

Freezers are among the most reliable domestic appliances. Chest freezers, however, tend to be more reliable than uprights.

Freezer problems

The Indesit F4113WG, Frigidaire FV2115 and Proline F90 (now discontinued) upright freezers couldn't keep food at −18°C or colder, which reduces the food storage time – but isn't a health risk.

If you own one of these freezers, turn the thermostat to the maximum (coldest) setting. Put a freezer thermometer between two packs of food on the top shelf on the side opposite the door hinge, and leave it overnight. Read the thermometer while it is still in the freezer, then repeat the test. If it's warmer than −18°C, contact Frigidaire, ☎ 051-355 0571, or your local Comet or Indesit service centre – numbers in the phone book. If the freezer is faulty, they'll repair it for no charge.

FACTS, FIGURES AND TEST RESULTS

1 Types of freezer

We've divided the freezers into three groups: upright freezers which can fit under a work surface, tall upright, and chest. They can all fast-freeze fresh food (but see 'Freezing capacity'), and all the uprights have reversible doors.

2 Target price

This is the price you should expect to pay if you shop around. For freezers which weren't widely available in our price survey, we've given the manufacturers' guide prices, in *italics*. Use the following phone numbers to find stockists in your area: **AEG** (0753) 872324; **Bauknecht** 061-905 1600; **Bosch** 081-573 1199; **Candy** 051-334 2781; **Liebherr** (0532) 459493.

3 Dimensions

Height x width x depth This is the overall space you'll need to fit in the freezer, including space needed to let air circulate around it. There are two height measurements for chest freezers: the first is with the lid closed, and the one in brackets is with the lid fully open.

How close to side wall With some upright freezers, you have to open the doors beyond 90° to remove baskets. These can't be placed with the door hinge against a wall. The Table tells you how much extra space you'll need to add to the width measurement above, if any.

Storage volume For comparing the sizes of freezers, we've used the storage (or 'net') volume. This gives a better guide than the 'gross' volume (which includes space taken up by shelves and baskets) often quoted by shops and manufacturers.

4 Convenience

In use/cleaning Our panel of testers assessed the freezers for such things as positioning and use of controls and indicators, whether there were any sharp edges or dirt traps, and access to contents. The Table gives each model's overall rating. The NEI had many sharp edges.

Drawbacks We've listed here general convenience drawbacks. Drawbacks which are specific to keeping the freezer temperature correct, and to freezing food, are given in the relevant sections of the Table. Decide how important they are to you.

A = door handle uncomfortable/difficult to grasp
B = no rollers/castors for easy moving
C = no adjustable feet for levelling
D = no plug fitted
E = no grille to prevent items falling down back of freezer. This isn't a drawback if you're putting the freezer under a worktop
F = lack of storage flexibility – large items (a big turkey, say) won't fit
G = chest freezer basket fits in main compartment, but not in small compartment
H = no interior light in chest freezer
I = no lid lock on chest freezer
J = chest freezer basket doesn't slide easily

5 Defrosting

Two of the tall upright freezers are 'frost-free' and so never need defrosting. For all the others, which need defrosting manually, we give a rating for how convenient they were to defrost.

√ = frost-free
□ = effective method of collecting and removing defrost water
◪ = water collects at bottom of freezer, and you have to bale it out
■ = water spills on to floor

6 Freezing

Capacity This is the number of kg of fresh food we could freeze down to −18°C in 24 hours, by following manufacturers' instructions. The Electrolux TF776W couldn't freeze the minimum required by the International Standard without the already-frozen food becoming too warm. The Mondia C1600 also failed the Standard: it couldn't freeze fresh food within 24 hours.

Efficiency Bigger freezers tend to freeze more at a time than smaller ones. So to make a fair comparison between freezers, our rating takes their size into account.

◩ = 12 to 14.9kg per 100 litre storage volume
□ = 9 to 11.9kg per 100 litre storage volume
◪ = 6 to 8.9kg per 100 litre storage volume
■ = 1 to 5.9kg per 100 litre storage volume

Drawbacks

K = no fast-freeze light (to remind you to switch the fast-freeze off)
L = no separate fast-freeze control – you have to re-set the thermostat
M = freezing tray tips when partly pulled out

7 Warm-up time

This is the maximum number of hours the freezer could be off (in the event of a power cut, or if you turn it off by accident, say) before the micro-organisms that spoil food start to grow.

8 Temperature

Stability A ◩ means the freezer doesn't tend to be affected by large changes in room temperature.

FREEZERS

	② Target price	③ Dimensions: h × w × d	How close to side wall	Storage volume	④ Convenience: In use/cleaning	Drawbacks	⑤ Defrosting	Capacity
	£	cm	cm	litres				kg/24hrs
① WORKTOP-HEIGHT UPRIGHT FREEZERS								
1 **Bosch GSD1340** (W Germany)	*240*	85 × 50 × 60	0	84	□	BF	◪	10
2 **DKK GS110** (E Germany)	110	85 × 55 × 60	0	86	◪	BDE	□	7
3 **Electra E40-0** (UK)[1]	170	85 × 53 × 56	13	103	◪	ABE	■	8
► 4 **Eurotech UF3002** (Italy)[2]	150	85 × 50 × 57	1	98	◪	ABE	□	14
5 **Frigidaire FV1260** (Hungary)	150	85 × 55 × 60	1	103	◪	ABCF	■	12
6 **Hotpoint Iced Diamond 8729W/A/P** (UK)	240	85 × 55 × 60	1	104	◪	AB	■	10
7 **Indesit F4113WG** (Italy)	140	85 × 51 × 56	5	103	◪	BD	◪	[10]
8 **Lec U3825** (UK)[3]	165	84 × 50 × 61	10	87	◪	ABEF	□	7
9 **Liebherr GS1502** (W Germany)	295	85 × 60 × 60	0	110	□	BF	□	15.5
10 **NEI 144** (Romania)	120	87 × 56 × 61	1	98	◪	BDEF	□	8
► 11 **Philips Whirlpool AFB726** (Italy)	200	85 × 55 × 60	0	114	□	BF	□	14
12 **Tricity Bendix UF400A/W** (UK)	180	85 × 51 × 60	5	80	□	B	□	8.5
13 **Zanussi DV45** (Italy)[4]	200	85 × 55 × 60	0	106	□	B	□	6
① TALL UPRIGHT FREEZERS								
1 **AEG Arctis 310GS** (W Germany)	*389*	173 × 60 × 60	0	262	□	BEF	□	19
2 **Bauknecht GKC2413WS** (Italy)	*350*	139 × 60 × 60	3	198	□	F	□	28
3 **Bosch GSD2612** (W Germany)	*445*	146 × 60 × 60	0	208	□	BF	□	22
4 **Candy C17FF** (UK)	*270*	118 × 53 × 56	11	121	◪	ABE	√	5.5
5 **Electrolux TF776W** (UK)	260	136 × 55 × 65	0	190	□	BE	□	[11]
6 **Frigidaire FV2115** (Yugoslavia)[5]	220	144 × 60 × 63	0	188	◪	BCDE	□	[10]
7 **Hotpoint Iced Diamond 8759W/A/P** (UK)	290	135 × 55 × 61	0	174	◪	ABE	■	14
► 8 **Indesit F4218WG** (Italy)	190	132 × 55 × 61	0	178	□	BDE	□	25.5
9 **Lec U6325** (UK)[6]	200	119 × 53 × 66	14	146	◪	ABE	□	13.5
10 **Liebherr GS2601** (W Germany)[7]	*452*	146 × 60 × 60	0	198	◪	BF	□	27
11 **Mondia FF1500** (Italy)[8]	300	157 × 60 × 60	0	222	◪	BDE	√	12
► 12 **Philips Whirlpool AFB740** (Italy)	280	140 × 60 × 60	1	197	□	F	□	25
13 **Zanussi DV85** (Italy)	320	140 × 60 × 60	0	200	◤	—	□	19
① CHEST FREEZERS								
1 **Electrolux TC810** (Denmark)	220	85(151) × 89 × 67	—	213	■	BDEHI	□	10
► 2 **Electrolux TC1160** (Denmark)	260	86(151) × 115 × 67	—	305	◪	BDE	□	18.5
3 **Iceline CF206** (Denmark)[2]	180	85(147) × 78 × 65	—	181	◪	EG	□	11.5
► 4 **Iceline CF306** (Denmark)[2]	200	85(149) × 108 × 65	—	281	◪	EG	□	14
5 **Lec F6529** (UK)	200	93(150) × 82 × 65	—	178	◪	E	◪	13
6 **Lec F9129** (UK)	220	93(150) × 103 × 65	—	257	◪	E	□	10
7 **Mondia C1600** (Rep of Ireland)[8]	190	86(142) × 106 × 65	—	267	◪	ABHIJ	◪	[11]
8 **Norfrost C105** (Rep of Ireland)[9]	96	84(133) × 60 × 60	—	102	■	AHI	◪	6
9 **Philips Whirlpool AFB567** (Italy)	200	89(150) × 87 × 66	—	199	◪	DEJ	□	12
► 10 **Philips Whirlpool AFB570** (Italy)	250	89(151) × 118 × 66	—	306	□	DEJ	□	19.5
► 11 **Zanussi CF64** (Spain)	205	85(154) × 66 × 70	—	169	◪	EIJ	□	10
► 12 **Zanussi CF132** (Spain)	260	85(154) × 119 × 70	—	352	◪	EJ	□	22

► Recommended in the Buying Guide ◄

KEY TO RATINGS best ◩ > ◤ > □ > ◪ > ■ worst

6 Freezing: Efficiency	Drawbacks	7 Warm-up time	8 Temperature: Stability	Recommended thermostat setting	Drawbacks	9 Electrical efficiency	
		hours					
□	—	16.5	▧	□	—	□	1
◪	—	13	▧	□	NPQ	□	2
◪	—	13	◩	◩	OQ	■	3
◩	—	14	▧	□	OQ	□	4 ◀
□	—	19	▧	□	NOQ	■	5
□	—	14	▧	▧	Q	■	6
[10]	—	[10]	[10]	[10]	NOQ	[10]	7
◪	KL	11	◩	▧	Q	■	8
◩	—	22.5	▧	□	—	▧	9
◪	—	11	◩	◪	OQ	■	10
◩	—	12.5	▧	▧	Q	◩	11 ◀
□	—	11	▧	□	Q	■	12
◪	—	14.5	▧	▧	Q	□	13
◪	—	28.5	▧	■	—	□	1
◩	—	27.5	◩	◩	—	□	2
□	—	20	◩	▧	—	◩	3
■	—	6.5	◩	□	OQ	■	4
[11]	—	19	◩	◩	Q	■	5
[10]	—	[10]	[10]	[10]	NQ	[10]	6
◪	—	11	▧	▧	Q	■	7
◩	—	17.5	▧	□	Q	■	8 ◀
□	KL	10.5	▧	▧	Q	■	9
◩	—	20	▧	◪	—	□	10
■	L	11	▧	□	Q	■	11
◩	—	26.5	◩	□	—	□	12 ◀
□	M	12	▧	◩	Q	■	13
■	L	24.5	▧	◪	Q	◪	1
◪	K	20	▧	◪	Q	◩	2 ◀
◪	—	22.5	▧	▧	—	◪	3
■	—	20	▧	▧	—	◩	4 ◀
◪	—	29	▧	□	Q	■	5
■	—	28	◩	▧	Q	◪	6
[11]	—	32	▧	▧	Q	■	7
◪	—	19	◩	□	Q	■	8
■	—	25.5	▧	◩	Q	◪	9
◪	—	30	▧	□	Q	◩	10 ◀
■	—	24	▧	▧	Q	□	11 ◀
◪	—	34	▧	◩	Q	▧	12 ◀

Recommended thermostat setting In many cases the settings given in the instruction books didn't keep the freezers at −18°C. We've deducted marks if the freezer was too warm or cold. The AEG and Liebherr models don't have a recommended setting.

Most of the freezers don't have a thermometer. We think they should all be fitted with accurate built-in thermometers. The Liebherr GS1502 and the Bauknecht GKC2413WS have built-in thermometers that can be read from the outside. This makes it easy to check the freezer's temperature without having to open the freezer door. Since we tested, Iceland tell us that they have also introduced externally mounted built-in thermometers to the two Iceline chest freezers we tested.

Drawbacks

N = no marked settings on thermostat control
O = thermostat control awkwardly placed
P = thermostat control at floor level on the front of the freezer
Q = no built-in thermometer

9 Electrical efficiency

Some freezers need more than twice as much electricity to keep the same amount of food frozen. Our electrical efficiency rating tells you how economical the freezers are to run. Generally, the larger the freezer, the less electricity it uses per litre of storage

[1] Exclusive to Electricity Companies. Candy 40 and Kelvinator 40 are similar, and similar price; cosmetic differences only
[2] Exclusive to Iceland/Bejam shops
[3] U3829 (£180) is similar; cosmetic differences only
[4] Electrolux TF422 (£210) is similar; cosmetic differences only
[5] Replaced by FV2125; cosmetic differences only
[6] U6329 (£210) is similar; cosmetic differences only
[7] GS2603 (£512) is similar, but has high temperature alarm
[8] Exclusive to Currys
[9] Tricity Bendix CF400 (£120) is similar; cosmetic differences
[10] Both the samples we tested had performance problems – see 'Freezer problems'
[11] We couldn't calculate freezing capacity – see 'Freezing'

volume, irrespective of its efficiency. So we've rated the worktop-height freezers using a different scale, but these ratings can't be directly compared with tall upright and chest freezers.

Some freezers that you may see in the shops have extra thick cabinet insulation which helps save electricity. However, they cost more to buy and so it would take several years before the initial expense was compensated for by the electricity saving you could make.

Electrical safety

All fully tested models were satisfactory in our tests or were British Electrotechnical Approvals Board (BEAB) approved.

Noise

We measured the noise made by the freezers when running, and assessed their vibration at switch-on and switch-off. None made enough noise to be a nuisance. The Candy C17FF and Zanussi CF132 were the noisiest.

Consumers' Association takes no advertising in any of its publications. It pays for all the goods and services it reviews. It receives no money from Government, trade or industry. All its income is derived from sales of its magazines, books and research. It is independent of all interests other than those of the consumer. It allows no exploitation of its recommendations in advertising or promotion. If readers of this guide see any ad making use of CA material in the press, in catalogues or in shops, please send details to Consumers' Association, Dept AWM, 2 Marylebone Road, London NW1 4DX.

FRIDGE-FREEZERS

Plus Advice on Safe Food Storage

From *Which?* May 1990

Recent food poisoning scares have brought the humble fridge into the limelight. It's no longer just a white box, but a vital element in limiting the growth of food-poisoning bacteria. Here we tell you how to keep your fridge-freezer as cold as possible, and show you why this isn't as easy as it should be.

A chilling solution?

Food-poisoning bacteria are inactive or grow only slowly at low temperatures. So it's important to keep your fridge cold: 5°C or lower. To help you do this, you could buy a fridge-freezer which has an enclosed chill compartment. These are specifically designed to keep the temperature at about 0°C, and so help to limit bacterial growth and keep food fresh for longer. This sounds like a good idea, but how well do they work?

We've tested three fridge-freezers with a chill compartment. The Hotpoint 8590P and Philips Whirlpool ARG664 have small compartments in the fridge; the Zanussi DF102/3T has a completely separate chill compartment between the fridge and freezer.

In our tests, all the chill compartments were colder than the rest of the fridge, but since none of them has the benefit of a built-in thermometer, *you* won't know what temperature they're set at. And because they don't have their own thermostat control you can't set the temperature accurately anyway: they're dependent on the control in the main fridge section.

You don't need a special chill compartment to keep food fresh, since you can create the same effect in an ordinary fridge – by keeping the top of the fridge at 5°C, the bottom should be at 0°C. You can make sure it is by checking it regularly with a fridge thermometer. This is essential if you're storing products such as raw and cooked meats, fish, and cook-chill food. Keep this sort of food at the bottom, just above the salad drawers, because our tests show that this is usually the coldest part of your fridge.

Beating back the bugs

If you're storing a mixture of raw and cooked food, take care not to let the raw foods come in contact with, or drip on to, the cooked foods. Use the warmer (top) part to store things such as juice, yoghurt, and margarine, which don't need to be kept so cold. And never leave the door open for longer than is absolutely necessary: the fridge can warm up quickly.

Keeping in control

Keeping your fridge at the right temperature is an important part of keeping food safe. But most fridge manufacturers don't make setting or measuring the temperature particularly easy.

Very few thermostat controls tell you anything about the temperature; generally you just set the control to a number (some don't even have any numbers to help you). There's no industry standard for what the numbers mean – different manufacturers use different numbered scales. The only thing they have in common is that the higher the number, the colder the fridge will be. But because fridges are affected by the temperature outside the cabinet, the same thermostat setting can give different cabinet temperatures at different room temperatures (in winter and summer, say).

Some fridge-freezers (usually ones with separate controls for fridge and freezer) have a built-in freezer thermometer to help you keep the freezer at −18°C. But none has a built-in fridge thermometer. The Philips Whirlpool ARG731 (and the similar Bauknecht KGC2883) and the Bosch two-control models have integral thermostat/thermometers. They allow you to set the thermostats to a temperature, rather than to a meaningless number. They all worked well in our tests.

A question of standards

We'd like to see *all* fridges (and fridge-freezers) fitted with integral thermostat/thermometers on the outside of the fridge so that it's easy to set the right temperature and you don't have to let warm air into the fridge when reading the temperature. But to be absolutely sure that you can measure (and set) the temperature in your fridge accurately, we think that the current standards should have a requirement for this. Many manufacturers already fit freezer thermometers, but our tests show that not all of them are accurate. We think the Standards should require all makers to fit accurate thermometers in both fridge *and* freezer.

We've written to fridge manufacturers to persuade them to fit thermometers as a matter of course. And we've argued that they should support us in trying to change the current Standards.

BUYING GUIDE

ONE-CONTROL TYPE

If you don't want a big freezer, or you store mainly pre-frozen food, a one-control fridge-freezer might be your best choice.

BEST BUY **Electrolux TR916W** (£260). Good all-round performance, and average price for its size

The **Candy Compact 10R** (*£290*) did well, and you get a lot of freezer storage space. For a smaller freezer we recommend the **Zanussi DF65/14** (£220). Cheap to buy, but fairly pricey to run

TWO-CONTROL TYPE

These generally cost more than the one-control type, but they have several advantages: they're better at freezing fresh food, the freezer temperature can be controlled more accurately, and they usually have warning lights.

BEST BUY The **Frigidaire FR2865/A** (£270) has pretty good performance, especially freezing capacity, and is very cheap

The **Philips Whirlpool ARG731** (£350) and **Scandinova RF7054** £350, exclusive to Comet, are both good all round

If you want a frost-free fridge-freezer, the **Electrolux TR1177** (£500) did the best.

Controlling freezer temperatures

It's hard enough to get your fridge at the right temperature, but there's an extra difficulty with fridge-freezers: making sure the freezer compartment is at the correct temperature as well. This is fairly easy if you've got a model which has separate controls for both fridge and freezer. But fridge-freezers which share one control for both compartments can be out of balance, because the freezer is dependent on the fridge thermostat. So even if you manage to get the fridge temperature right, the freezer can be several degrees warmer than it should be, and frozen food may not stay in good condition for as long.

Fridge-freezers with separate controls usually have them on the outside of the appliance, at the top. But some will have them inside the fridge and freezer compartments. With models which have a shared control for both fridge and freezer, the control is almost always inside the fridge.

Testing the temperature

To check that your fridge and freezer are at the right temperatures, you need to buy a fridge and freezer thermometer, and follow our advice.

To check the fridge temperature, put the thermometer in the warmest part of the fridge, which is usually the middle of the top shelf. After a couple of hours, read the temperature, ideally without taking the thermometer out of the fridge. If the temperature is higher than 5°C, turn the thermostat control to a colder setting (a higher number), and check the temperature again the following day. Our tests have shown that setting the temperature to 5°C in the warmest part of the fridge should mean that that the bottom of the fridge is about 0°C. But to check that it is, put the thermometer on the shelf above the salad drawer.

It's worth checking your freezer even if it's got a built-in thermometer since it may not be measuring the warmest part. Put the thermometer on the edge of the top shelf (or at the front of the top basket) on the side the door opens. Leave the thermometer for a couple of hours before reading it. Try to get the temperature at −18°C. If it's any warmer the quality of the frozen food will deteriorate more quickly. If it's colder than −18°C, you're wasting energy. If you need to adjust the thermostat control, wait at least a day before checking the temperature again.

It can be tricky to get the right temperatures in a fridge-freezer with a shared control for both fridge and freezer. It's more important to store your fresh food at the correct temperature, so use the thermometer to get your fridge cold enough.

Which fridge-freezer?

There's a massive choice of fridge-freezers in the shops. Our Buying Guide highlights the models which we think offer a good blend of price and performance, but there are other things you need to take into account before you go shopping.

Fridge or freezer on top?

You can buy fridge-freezers with either the fridge above the freezer, or the freezer above the fridge. If you want a big freezer, look at the fridge-on-top type; with these the fridge and freezer are often the same size. With the freezer-on-top type, the freezer is always smaller than the fridge. Generally, our panel of assessors found it more convenient to have the fridge on top.

One control or two?

Most fridge-freezers have one thermostat control to set the temperature in both fridge and freezer. The other type has a separate control for each compartment. One-control models are usually cheaper, but they don't necessarily offer the best value.

Two-control models are generally better at keeping the correct storage temperatures, because you can set the temperatures in the fridge and freezer independently. With a one-control type, the freezer temperature is dependent on the fridge thermostat. So at low room temperatures the cooling system in the fridge stops working, even though the freezer still needs cooling.

And, from the convenience point of view, most of the two-control models we tested have warning lights which tell you that the mains is on, if the fast-freeze is on, and if the freezer is too warm.

The freezer factor

If you don't need a big freezer, or you store mainly pre-frozen food, a one-control model will probably suit you well.

GREEN GUIDE

Ozone-friendly fridges?

ICI has developed a new coolant which doesn't damage the ozone layer. It should be commercially available in 1991 – though fridge manufacturers still need to iron out some problems before they can use it instead of the harmful CFCs. The major manufacturers told us that they won't be able to use the new coolant for some time.

If your old fridge is broken and not worth repairing, the CFCs used as a refrigerant in the cooling system can be recycled. ICI has set up a nationwide scheme to encourage local councils and businesses to collect refrigerant from old appliances and send it to ICI. Look out for notices in your area, telling you who is recycling, or ask your council.

But the CFCs used in the cabinet insulation can't be recycled. At the moment, it isn't possible to stop them from being released into the atmosphere when the insulation is broken up. As a partial solution, most fridge manufacturers have reduced the amount of CFCs they use in the insulation. Bosch have started to use CFC-free insulation in some models.

Until *all* fridge manufacturers use CFC-free insulation, the best thing to do, if you care about the environment, is to put off buying a new fridge. If you have to get a new one, try to sell your old one secondhand, rather than scrapping it.

Energy efficiency

Fridge-freezers vary in how efficiently they use electricity. Some need more than twice as much electricity to keep the same amount of food cool. So if you're looking for a new fridge-freezer, it's worth taking the 'Electrical efficiency' rating in the Table into account.

However, if you want to freeze a lot of fresh food, you'd be better off with a two-control type. In our tests, fridge-freezers with a shared control for fridge and freezer weren't good at freezing. Many could freeze food, but only at the expense of allowing the fridge to drop below freezing point. With others, we couldn't measure freezing capacity, because either food already in the freezer became too warm, or the fresh food wasn't frozen in 24 hours.

No more defrosting?

Defrosting a freezer can be a messy and time-consuming chore. For convenience, fridge-freezers with two controls have the edge. Defrosting is more convenient because most let you switch the freezer off while leaving the whole appliance switched on at the mains, so you can leave the fridge on. With one-control fridge-freezers, you have to switch off the whole appliance if you want to defrost the freezer.

If you don't like defrosting, you might think it's worth paying extra for a frost-free model which never needs it.

FACTS, FIGURES AND TEST RESULTS

1 Types

The fridge-freezers fall into four groups:

- models with one thermostat control to set the temperature in both compartments, and the fridge on top of the freezer
- models with one control, and the freezer on the top
- models with two controls (one each for fridge and freezer), and the fridge on top
- one model with two controls, freezer on top.

2 Target price

This is what you should expect to pay if you shop around. Some brands weren't widely available in our price survey. For these, we give the manufacturers' guide prices, in *italics*. Use the phone numbers to find stockists for those models in your area. **AEG** ☎ 0753 872324; **Ariston** ☎ 0322 526933; **Asko Polar** ☎ 081-568 4666; **Bosch** ☎ 0895 838383; **Candy** ☎ 051-334 2781; **Fagor** ☎ 081-801 7212; **Frigidaire** ☎ 0977 603111; **Liebherr** ☎ 0532 459493.

3 Dimensions

Height x width x depth This includes space needed at the back to let air circulate.
How close to side wall With some fridge-freezers, you have to open the doors beyond 90° to remove shelves or baskets. These can't be placed with the door hinge against a wall. The Table tells you how much extra space you'll need, if any.

4 Convenience

In use/cleaning Our testers evaluated the fridge-freezers for ease of use and ease of cleaning. Most were satisfactory.

Drawbacks

We assessed each model for overall convenience drawbacks; decide how important they are to you. Drawbacks which are specific to the fridge and freezer are given in the relevant sections of the Table.

A = door handle uncomfortable/difficult to grasp
B = sharp edges
C = dirt traps
D = no rollers/castors
E = no adjustable feet
F = no marked settings on thermostat(s)
G = no indicator lights for: mains on; fast-freeze on; freezer temperature warning light

FRIDGE-FREEZERS

	Model	2 Target price	3 Dimensions h × w × d	How close to side wall	4 Convenience In use/cleaning	Drawbacks	5 Fridges Storage volume	Chill compartment	Convenience drawbacks	6 Freezers Storage volume	Convenience drawbacks	Freezing capacity
		£	cm	cm			litres			litres		kg/24 hours
	1 ONE CONTROL/FRIDGE ON TOP											
	1 **Ariston RF225S** (Italy)	*279*	147 × 51 × 59	0	□	BCDGJ	104	—	NO	108	Z	7.5
▶	2 **Candy Compact 10R** (UK)[1]	*290*	183 × 53 × 57	37.5	□	DG	107	—	NOQ	152	TVZ	11
	3 **Electra E44** (UK)[2]	260	155 × 53 × 57	39	□	DG	108	—	NOQ	106	TVZ	7.5
▶	4 **Electrolux TR916W** (UK)[3]	260	135 × 55 × 59	0	□	DG	100	—	L	108	TVZ	12
	5 **Electrolux TR871** (Italy)[4]	260	148 × 55 × 60	0	□	DG	168	—	O	59	TZ	3
	6 **Hotpoint Iced Diamond 8633W/A/P** (UK)	280	135 × 55 × 60	0	□	ADGI	93	—	LNO	109	TZ	7
	7 **Kelvinator K33** (UK)[5]	200	120 × 53 × 57	39	□	DG	78	—	LNOQ	78	TVZ	0
	8 **Lec T4325** (UK)[6]	240	146 × 54 × 64	34	□	CDG	100	—	O	100	TVZ	10
	9 **Lec T5625** (UK)[7]	240	146 × 53 × 64	29	□	CDG	142	—	LO	79	TVZ	3.5
	10 **Liebherr KSD 2714-5** (W Germany)	*556*	146 × 60 × 60	0	□	DGJ	180	—	N	57	TZ	5
	11 **Philips Whirlpool ARG648** (Italy)	280	138 × 56 × 61	0	□	D	108	—	KO	101	VZ	6
	12 **Philips Whirlpool ARG649** (Italy)	320	160 × 55 × 61	41	□	DJ	155	—	O	99	VZ	6
	13 **Zanussi DF62/21FF** (Italy)	330	148 × 55 × 60	0	□	DG	166	—	O	57	YZ	2.5
	1 ONE CONTROL/FREEZER ON TOP											
	1 **AEG Santo 2200DT** (W Germany)	*289*	127 × 54 × 58	0	□	DG	167	—	NQ	46	TZ	3.5
	2 **Bosch KSV2621** (W Germany)	*359*	145 × 60 × 60	0	□	DGJ	189	—	N	68	TZ	5
	3 **Bosch KSV3121** (W Germany)	*409*	166 × 60 × 61	0	□	DGJ	239	—	N	67	TZ	5
	4 **Bosch KSV4312** (Greece)	*520*	178 × 71 × 66	0	□	GJ	315	—	N	97	TZ	5
	5 **Fagor U2290CB** (Spain)	*291*	147 × 60 × 59	0	□	GJ	169	—	NO	72	TZ	0
	6 **Frigidaire RF2615** (Yugoslavia)	*200*	139 × 60 × 61	0	□	DGJ	187	—	LNO	67	TZ	0
	7 **Hotpoint Iced Diamond 8326W/A/P** (UK)	250	135 × 55 × 60	0	□	ADGI	164	—	NO	63	TZ	4
	8 **Lec T2125** (UK)[8]	200	121 × 50 × 61	3	◪	ADG	109	—	LR	58	TVZ	2.5
	9 **Liebherr KSD2314-5** (W Germany)	*415*	124 × 60 × 60	25	□	DGJ	173	—	NO	47	TZ	4.5
	10 **Zanussi DF50/14** (Italy)	195	126 × 50 × 59	0	□	DG	130	—	NQ	44	TZ	0
▶	11 **Zanussi DF65/14** (Italy)	220	142 × 53 × 59	0	□	DG	174	—	NO	40	TZ	5
	1 TWO CONTROL/FRIDGE ON TOP											
	1 **AEG Santo 3110KG** (W Germany)	*429*	157 × 60 × 60	0	◤	—	189	—	—	81	V	11.5
	2 **AEG Santo 3510KG** (W Germany)	*469*	177 × 59 × 60	0	◤	—	188	—	—	126	V	10
	3 **Asko Polar KNF3056** (Sweden)	*529*	184 × 60 × 61	0	□	—	154	—	NOP	107	—	13
	4 **Bosch KGE7002** (W Germany)	*444*	166 × 59 × 60	0	◤	J	178	—	LN	95	—	17
	5 **Bosch KGE3434** (W Germany)	*484*	186 × 59 × 60	0	◤	J	182	—	LN	134	—	17
	6 **Derby KG1814** (Denmark)	*536*	183 × 60 × 61	0	□	DF	174	—	KOP	92	—	10
	7 **Electrolux TR1056W** (UK)	330	166 × 55 × 65	2	◪	D	127	—	LM	139	Z	9
▶	8 **Electrolux TR1177** (Sweden)[9]	500	175 × 60 × 60	0	□	CD	182	—	N	109	—	13
	9 **Fagor Supermatic UC2380L** (Spain)	*388*	170 × 60 × 58	1	□	J	199	—	LN	69	—	10
	10 **Frigidaire FR2715** (Yugoslavia)	*290*	172 × 60 × 60	0	◪	AEHJ	198	—	LNOQ	107	WZ	8
▶	11 **Frigidaire FR2865/A** (Hungary)	270	168 × 55 × 60	33	□	ADE	141	—	LNOQ	105	V	16.5
	12 **Hotpoint Iced Diamond 8553W/A/P** (UK)	350	167 × 55 × 64	0	□	—	164	—	NO	108	Z	12
	13 **Hotpoint 8590P** (Italy)	460	180 × 59 × 60	0	◪	AG	190	√	OS	79	TWZ	3.5
	14 **Liebherr KGD3923** (W Germany)	*645*	196 × 60 × 60	0	□	DJ	217	—	KNO	116	—	16
	15 **Ocean CB18/20** (Italy)	310	178 × 60 × 62	0	□	D	182	—	NO	137	TZ	11
▶	16 **Philips Whirlpool ARG731** (Italy)[10]	350	158 × 55 × 61	0	□	J	155	—	O	95	—	14
	17 **Philips Whirlpool ARG657** (Italy)	400	180 × 59 × 61	2	□	AJ	184	—	O	129	Z	12
	18 **Proline NF6148** (Italy)[11]	330	177 × 60 × 60	0	□	CDJ	171	—	N	110	Z	0
	19 **Scandinova RF4872** (Denmark)[12]	380	185 × 60 × 60	0	□	IJ	126	—	KNO	177	—	12
▶	20 **Scandinova RF7054** (Denmark)[13]	350	185 × 60 × 60	20	□	IJ	191	—	KNO	133	—	13
	21 **Zanussi DF56/45** (Italy)	340	166 × 55 × 60	0	□	—	156	—	O	110	XZ	10
	22 **Zanussi DF102/3T Superchill** (Italy)	490	170 × 60 × 60	0	□	—	199[14]	√	MO	53	—	9.5
	1 TWO CONTROL/FREEZER ON TOP											
	1 **Philips Whirlpool ARG664** (Italy)	340	159 × 56 × 59	0	◪	FGJ	172	√	O	52	TZ	4

	Warm-up time	Defrosting	7 Temperature: Stability – Fridge	Stability – Freezer	Recommended thermostat settings – Fridge	Recommended thermostat settings – Freezer	8 Electrical efficiency		
[15]	9	■	●	●	□	●	□	1	
◪	13	■	●	●	□	●	◐	2	◄
◪	10	■	●	□	●	●	□	3	
□	20	□	●	●	●	●	□	4	◄
[15]	17	□	◪	●	◪	●	□	5	
◪	14	■	●	●	●	●	◪	6	
[16]	10	■	●	■	●	●	■	7	
[15]	11	□	□	□	●	■	◪	8	
■	14	□	□	□	●	◐	◪	9	
◪	19	□	●	●	●	●	◐	10	
◪	14	□	□	◪	◪	◪	□	11	
[15]	13	□	●	□	●	●	◐	12	
■	14	√	●	◪	●	●	■	13	
[15]	18	◪	◪	●	●	◪	□	1	
◪	23	□	●	◐	□	□	●	2	
[15]	25	◪	●	●	□	●	●	3	
■	28	□	□	◐	●	□	●	4	
[17]	15	◪	□	□	●	●	◐	5	
[17]	21	◪	●	●	●	□	◪	6	
[15]	15	□	●	●	●	●	◪	7	
■	13	□	●	●	●	●	■	8	
[15]	18	◪	◪	□	◪	■	◪	9	
[17]	15	◪	●	●	□	●	□	10	
◐	10	■	●	●	◪	□	◪	11	◄
◐	20	□	●	●	◐	◪	□	1	
◪	21	□	●	●	◪	◪	□	2	
◐	18	√	●	●	◪	□	■	3	
●	19	□	●	●	●	●	◐	4	
◐	25	□	●	●	●	●	●	5	
□	14	◪	●	◐	●	●	◐	6	
[15]	12	□	●	●	●	□	□	7	
□	12	√	●	●	●	◪	□	8	◄
◐	15	◪	●	●	□	◐	□	9	
◪	15	□	●	◪	●	◪	□	10	
●	19	■	●	●	●	□	□	11	◄
□	16	■	●	●	●	●	□	12	
■	8	√	□	◐	□	□	■	13	
◐	16	□	●	●	◪	◪	●	14	
□	14	□	●	●	□	◪	◐	15	
◐	18	□	●	●	●	●	◐	16	◄
□	22	□	●	●	●	◐	◐	17	
[17]	12	√	●	●	●	◐	■	18	
◐	14	□	●	◐	●	◪	◐	19	
□	15	□	●	●	●	◐	●	20	◄
□	18	□	●	●	●	◐	◐	21	
●	7	√	●	□	◐	◐	■	21	
◪	6	√	●	●	●	◐	■	1	

H = controls at floor level
I = thermostat settings difficult to see
J = no plug fitted

5 Fridges

Storage volume For comparing the sizes of fridge-freezers, we've used the storage (or 'net') volume. This gives a better guide than the 'gross' volume (which includes space taken up by shelves, thermostat, and so on), often quoted by shops and manufacturers.

Chill compartment Those with a √ in this column have an enclosed chill compartment (see 'A chilling solution?').

Convenience drawbacks

K = door racks awkward to adjust
L = door racks not adjustable
M = shelves not adjustable for height
N = no fittings to stabilise items in door rack
O = no meat dish/thaw tray to retain liquids
P = light ineffective
Q = no means of storing bottles upright in main compartment
R = fridge is small and awkward to use
S = thermostat difficult to grasp

[1] Kelvinator K100-8 (£290) is similar
[2] Kelvinator K84 (£250) is similar
[3] Tricity ED790W (£200) and Zanussi DF35/45 (£300) are similar
[4] Zanussi DF62/26 (£300) is similar
[5] Candy C6RT (£220), Electra E33 (£230; exclusive to Electricity Boards), and Kelvinator KR34 (£210; exclusive to Rumbelows) are all similar
[6] T4329 (£270) is similar
[7] T5629 (£270) is similar
[8] T2129 (£220) is similar
[9] Zanussi DF67/41FF (£470) is similar
[10] Bauknecht KGC2833 (£300) is similar
[11] Exclusive to Comet, Mondia FFR9002 (£400, exclusive to Currys) is similar
[12] Exclusive to Comet
[13] Exclusive to Comet. Scandinova KF350-47 is similar, and a similar price
[14] Including 41 litres in chill compartment
[15] Froze food satisfactorily, but fridge temperature fell below zero during freezing
[16] Froze food satisfactorily, but fridge temperature too high
[17] We couldn't measure freezing capacity because either food already in the freezer became too warm, or the fresh food wasn't frozen in 24 hours

► Recommended in the Buying Guide ◄

KEY TO RATINGS best ● > ◐ > □ > ◪ > ■ worst

6 Freezers

Convenience drawbacks

T = no separate fast-freeze control
V = no cards supplied for recording food in freezer baskets
W = thermostat difficult to grasp
X = fast-freeze light appears on when it isn't
Y = fast-freeze switch awkwardly placed
Z = no built-in freezer thermometer

Freezing capacity

This is the number of kg of fresh food we could freeze down to −18°C in 24 hours, by following manufacturers' instructions. Bigger freezers tend to freeze more at a time than smaller ones. So to make a fair comparison between freezers, our rating takes their size into account.

◩ = 15kg or more per 100 litres
◸ = 12 to 14kg per 100 litres
□ = 9 to 11kg per 100 litres
◪ = 6 to 8kg per 100 litres
■ = 1 to 5kg per 100 litres

Warm-up time

This is the maximum number of hours the freezer could be off (in the event of a power cut, for instance) before the micro-organisms that spoil food start to grow.

Defrosting

The seven frost-free models never need defrosting, so get a √ in this column. All the others have an auto-defrost fridge, but the freezer will still need defrosting manually.

√ = frost-free so never needs defrosting
□ = satisfactory method of collecting and removing defrost water
◪ = water collects at bottom of freezer
■ = water spills on to floor or into fridge

7 Temperature

Stability

◩ means the fridge-freezer doesn't tend to be affected by large changes in room temperature.

Recommended thermostat settings

In many cases the settings recommended in the instruction books didn't keep the fridge-freezers at the best temperatures. We've deducted marks if the fridge and freezer were too warm.

8 Electrical efficiency

This tells you how economical the fridge-freezers are to run, taking into account the storage volumes of both compartments.

Frost-frees defrost automatically two or three times in every 24 hours. During these defrost periods, the freezer temperature rises by 2°C to 3°C. We set their thermostats to make sure they were −18°C (the current Standard for conventional freezers) when defrosting. This means the freezers were colder than −18°C most of the time, wasting electricity and increasing running costs.

Electrical safety

All models were satisfactory in our tests or had British Electrotechnical Approvals Board (BEAB) approval.

Noise

We measured the noise made by the fridge-freezers when running, and assessed their vibration at switch-on and switch-off. None of the fridge-freezers we tested made enough noise to be a nuisance. The Asko Polar KNF3056, Liebherr KGD3923, and Proline NF6148 were the noisiest.

*See page 8 for how to use **Which? Buying Guide**.*

FOOD PROCESSORS

22 Models from £30 to £140

From *Which?* July 1990

Food processors are fast and very versatile. You'll probably find one useful if your cooking involves lots of slicing, shredding or chopping. Spending a lot on a food processor will generally give you a machine with a larger capacity than a cheaper model and it may come with more attachments included in the price, but it won't necessarily work better.

We look at what processors do well and at where their limitations lie, and give our rundown on the features to look out for – and avoid.

BUYING GUIDE

BEST BUY

The **Braun MC200 Type 4177** is good value at £40. It gave good all-round performance but had a few convenience drawbacks

The **Kenwood FP600** £74 gave good all-round performance and was fairly convenient to use. But it's almost twice the price of the Braun. The **Kenwood FP300** £50 is convenient and did well in most of our tests.

Processor plus points

All food processors are good for:

Slicing and grating Processors really come into their own with tedious slicing and grating jobs. Typically, processors we've tested can slice just over a pound of carrots in under 30 seconds, or a cucumber in less than ten seconds. Grating a pound of cheese generally takes no more than a minute.

Chopping For our tests we chop a selection of vegetables with different textures – as if for soup. Even processors with fairly small capacities can chop over half a pound of vegetables in around 20 seconds. Processors can also chop nuts quickly, but not always very evenly, so if the appearance of the nuts is very important, you may prefer to chop them by hand. And it's a matter of seconds to make breadcrumbs.

Blending We assess how well processors blend food by making mayonnaise, which most do well. Processors are also generally good at quickly reducing food to a purée for soups, pâtés, puddings and baby food.

Processor limitations

Some food preparation tasks aren't quite as successful in a food processor, either because the amount you can prepare at a time is limited by the processor's capacity, or because the right attachment isn't available:

Mixing cakes If you only make cakes from time to time, all processors give satisfactory results. But if cake-making is your top priority, and you like to bake in bulk, you may do better with a traditional table mixer.

Kneading dough Processors can take a lot of the hard work out of breadmaking, but most can cope with only a fairly small amount of dough at a time. If you're a keen breadmaker and want to make several loaves per session, you may find it irritating to have to weigh up for and mix just one loaf at a time.

Whisking egg whites Most processors we've tested can't whisk egg whites satisfactorily. Processors which have produced good results have had special whisk attachments which look like traditional egg beaters. But you may find it cheaper to buy a fairly basic processor, plus a cheap electric hand-held mixer (from around £13), than a more expensive processor that can whisk egg whites well too.

What to look for

Although processors work quickly, setting them up and cleaning them afterwards can be time-consuming. If attachments are fiddly to fit, or the controls awkward to use, it may all seem like too much trouble – especially for small quantities of food.

We pick out some of the features that affect how easy a processor is to use, and show the drawbacks and plus points to look for when you're choosing one.

Fast to process but slow to clean

Food processors can save you a lot of time when you're cooking, but some are much easier to clean than others. If a processor has lots of nooks and crannies, you may need to be extra diligent about washing it up to make sure that you get at any trapped bits of food. The inside of the blade column can be particularly awkward to wash and dry. A dishwasher may solve the washing-up problem provided your processor has dishwasher-proof accessories – see the Table.

When big isn't always beautiful

You can't always process small amounts of food effectively in a large processor, or you may feel that you lose so much around the bowl or on the blade, that it's not worth assembling your processor to purée some baby food, or chop a few herbs. The Magimix models we tested had an extra mini-bowl and mini-blade designed for small amounts of food.

Storing up trouble?

Processors generally come with lots of different attachments which you'll need to keep somewhere. It's important from a safety point of view that sharp metal blades and discs are kept out of the hands of children, but it's also infuriating if the one attachment you need in a hurry disappears to the back of a kitchen drawer. Models which have a storage box provide a neat solution – see Table for those which have one.

Good processing needs fine control

Because a processor works so quickly, it's critical that you keep your eye on food while the machine is working. If you don't, the food you intended to chop could end up as an unintentional purée. It's easier to avoid over-processing food if controls are well positioned and easy to identify rather than low down and less easy to tell apart or awkward to operate – see 'Convenience' in the Table for any problems we found.

FACTS, FIGURES AND TEST RESULTS

1 Target Price

The price you can expect to pay if you shop

around is in ordinary type. Prices in *italics* are manufacturers' guide prices for machines not so widely available in the shops.

2 Capacity

A food processor's capacity is limited by its bowl size and by how much heavy mixture it can cope with at any one time.

Cake/dough We give the largest amount of fruit cake mixture, in one-egg multiples, and the amount of bread dough, in multiples of one small-size loaf (340g flour) each machine could cope with.

Liquid We also give you the manufacturers' recommendations for the maximum volume of liquid (in litres) you can put in each processor. One litre is about four half-pint servings of soup.

3 Accessories

All the processors came with a bowl (with handle), lid and food guide (to push food down the hopper), and attachments for basic mixing, kneading, whisking, blending, slicing, shredding and chopping tasks.

Included If the accessories or attachments for the following additional tasks are included in the price we give them in capital letters.

Optional Small letters indicate accessories you can buy separately.

A = dust cover
B = storage rack or box for accessories
C = separate blender goblet (additional to food processor bowl)
D = mini-processing bowl and blade for small quantities
E = attachment for fine slicing/shredding
G = chipping
H = juice extracting (eg for citrus fruit)
J = juice separating (eg for carrots)
K = sieving/straining
L = ice-cream making
M = peeling
N = milling (spices)
P = you'll be able to buy a replacement bowl (costs between £5 and £30, depending on the food processor)

A — in the Table means that none of these accessories is included in the price.

4 Features

Speeds We tell you the number of marked speed settings. (v) means that you can set speeds in between marked settings to give more variable control. All except the Kenwood FP600 have a pulse option which gives more control if you want to process food in short bursts. With the Kenwood you have to use the on/off control to achieve the same effect.

Other

Q = flex storage
R = speed/function guide on machine – shows which speed to use for which task/accessory
S = double/expanded feed tube – one large tube for items such as cucumbers and one for smaller items like carrots
T = drip-feed facility in lid/feed tube – useful for making mayonnaise
U = dishwasher-proof bowl, blade and other accessories

5 Performance

We carried out the following tests using the basic food processor attachments. We also tell you if the result was improved by using an alternative accessory.

Mixing – all-in-one cake and fruit cake
Kneading – bread dough
Whisking – our ratings are based on whisking four egg whites
Slicing/Shredding – grating cheese, slicing carrot and cucumber
Chopping – vegetables (without liquid) and nuts

Blending – mayonnaise. Owing to concern about possible contamination of eggs with salmonella, the Department of Health recommends that you don't eat foods made with raw eggs. It's also important that you ensure good hygiene when preparing food and cleaning equipment afterwards.

6 Convenience

We note any convenience drawbacks we found:

q = control(s) awkward to operate
r = some attachments/parts awkward to clean
s = speeds poorly marked
t = tends to move/vibrate
u = some attachments fiddly or awkward to assemble or dismantle
v = no storage for loose sharp inserts
w = lack of adequate finger grips on some attachments; risk of cuts
x = liquid added through the feed tube tended to leak through a hole in the blade shaft onto the base of the processor

A — in the Table means that we didn't find any drawbacks relating to convenience in our tests.

FOOD PROCESSORS

	1 Target price	2 Capacity: Cake/dough	Liquid	3 Accessories: Included	Optional	4 Features: Speeds	Other	5 Performance: Mixing	Kneading
	£		l						
1 **Braun MC100 Type 4176** (Spain)	35	2/1	0.7	—	p	1	Q	□	□
► 2 **Braun MC200 Type 4177** (Spain)	40	2/1	0.7	—	p	5(v)	QR	□	◩
3 **Braun UK12** (W Germany)[2]	50	4/1	0.7	EG	ahjp	2	Q	□	◩
4 **Braun UK22** (W Germany)	69	4/1	1.0	EG	ahjp	6	Q	□	◩
5 **Braun UK40** (W Germany)[4]	85	5/1	1.0	BEG	ahjp	6(v)	QRS	□	□
► 6 **Kenwood FP300** (UK)	50	3/1	0.8	—	abeghjkp	2	QU	◩	◩
7 **Kenwood FP400** (UK)[6]	60	3/1	0.8	—	abeghjklp	3	U	□	◩
► 8 **Kenwood FP600** (UK)[7]	74	3/1	0.8	AEGH	jklnp	8	RU	□	◩
9 **Kenwood FP700** (UK)[8]	100	6/3	0.8	ACEG	hjmnp	2	QSU	□	□
10 **Magimix 3000** (France)	89	3/1	1.1	BD	aeghj	(v)[9]	QU[10]	□	□
11 **Magimix 4000** (France)	110	3/2	1.4	BD	aeghj	(v)[9]	QU[10]	□	◩
12 **Magimix 5000** (France)	140	3/3	2.1	BD	aeghj	(v)[9]	QU[10]	□	□
13 **Moulinex 20** (France)	30	2/1	0.8	E	p	1	Q	□	□
14 **Moulinex 30** (France)	40	3/1	0.8	—	p	1	QRST	◩	◩
15 **Moulinex 35** (France)	50	3/1	0.8	BGH	p	4(v)	QRST	□	◩
16 **Moulinex 50** (France)	49	4/1	0.8	EG	hjp	3	Q	□	□
17 **Moulinex 55** (France)	63	4/1	0.8	EG	hjp	11(v)	QR	□	□
18 **Moulinex 65** (France)	73	4/1	0.8	BEG	hjp	11(v)	QR	□	□
19 **Moulinex 75** (France)	100	4/1	0.8	BEGHJ	p	11(v)	QR	□	□
20 **Philips HR2880** (Netherlands)	60	3/1	1.0	BE	ghjp	2	QRTU	□	□[11]
21 **Philips HR2881** (Netherlands)	70	3/1	1.0	BEG	hjp	(v)[9]	QRTU	□	□[11]
22 **Tefal 8612** (France)	47	2/1	0.8	HJ	p	1	RSTU[12]	□	□

► Recommended in the Buying Guide ◄

KEY TO RATINGS best ◼ > ◩ > □ > ◪ > ■ worst

7 Mechanical safety

Misfitted lid The rotating blades and discs on a food processor are potentially very dangerous, so it's important that there are adequate safety precautions to stop you from touching them. Most processors have a safety interlock to prevent the blade or disc from operating if the lid isn't fitted properly.

We carried out a test to see if it was possible to misfit the lid and override the safety interlock. √ means that the processor can't be operated unless the lid is properly secured.

Whisking	Slicing/shredding	Chopping vegetables	Chopping nuts	Blending	6 Convenience	7 Mechanical safety: Misfitted lid	7 Mechanical safety: Hopper access	
■[1]	□	□	□	□	uvx	√	A	1
□	□	◤	□	□	uvx	√	A	2 ◀
■[3]	◤	◤	□	◤	v	√	X	3
◤	◤	◤	□	◤	v	√	X	4
◤	□	◤	□	□	—	√	X	5
■[5]	◤	□	□	◤	v	√	A	6 ◀
◪[5]	◤	□	◪	□	v	√	A	7
◤	◤	◤	□	□	qv	√	A	8 ◀
◤	◤	◤	□	◤	rv	√	A	9
■	◤	◤	□	◤	qt	√	X	10
■	◤	◤	□	◤	qt	√	X	11
■	◤	◤	□	◤	qt	√	X	12
◪	□	◤	□	◤	ruvw	√	X	13
■	□	□	□	◤	v	√	X	14
■	◤	□	□	□	q	√	X	15
■	◤	◤	◪	◤	v	√	A	16
■	◤	◤	◪	◤	v	√	A	17
■	◤	◤	◪	◤	—	√	A	18
■	◤	◤	◪	◤	—	√	A	19
■	◤	◤	□	◤	rs	√	√	20
■	◤	◤	□	◤	rs	√	√	21
■	□	□	□	◤	v	[13]	X	22

Hopper access Another area we've been concerned about is the possibility of touching the moving cutting discs of a food processor through the hopper or feed tube.

A draft International Standard limits the width and height of the hopper. All the processors we tested are within the proposed limits. But with ten models (marked A in the Table) our tester could still touch the discs with her fingertips through the feed tube. And with another ten machines (marked X in the Table) our tester could reach moving parts with her whole hand. We think machines in this second group present an unnecessary risk and don't consider any of them for recommendation in the Buying Guide. We have campaigned for stricter limits on hopper dimensions for some time, to make access to moving parts through the hopper less easy, and will be keeping up the pressure.

When using a food processor, don't take risks – always use the food guide provided to push food down the hopper.

Electrical Safety

All models were satisfactory in our tests or had British Electrotechnical Approvals Board (BEAB) approval.

[1] Result with metal blade. With optional whisking disc (£1.65), rating was □
[2] Similar model UK9 (£44), without chipping/fine-slicing attachment and UK120 (*£50*) with larger bowl and without chipping attachment
[3] Result with whisking disc. With optional bowl and whisk (£12.95) rating was ◪
[4] Similar model UK240 *£70*, without whisking bowl and dough hook
[5] Result with whisking disc. With optional geared whisk (£11), rating was □
[6] Superseded by FP404 *£70*, with variable speed control. Similar model FP410 (£60), with lower-rated motor
[7] Superseded by FP505 *£80*, with variable speed control and separate blending attachment. Similar models FP610 (£80), with lower rated motor; FP550 (£70), without attachments for fine shredding or juice extracting and no cover
[8] Similar model FP800 (£120), with electronically variable speed control
[9] Manufacturer tells us speed alters automatically according to task
[10] Temperature of dishwasher programme should not exceed 60°C
[11] □ rating was achieved using metal blade; ◪ with kneading attachment
[12] Juice extractor is the only accessory which is not dishwasher-proof
[13] Processor can be operated with lid misfitted, but no access to dangerous moving parts

TOASTERS

Two-slice and Four-slice Models

From *Which?* November 1989

Browned off with your old toaster? The 34 models we've tested vary in more ways than just the number of slots in the top. Some make toast more evenly than others, some are less fiddly to use than others, and some did better than others in our durability test.

Only half came unscathed through the test that simulates five years' use, and one toaster caught fire during our electrical safety testing.

FACTS, FIGURES AND TEST RESULTS

1 Types

All the toasters we tested can toast one slice at a time. Two-slice toasters either have a slot for each slice of bread or a single long slot which takes two slices. The four-slice toasters had two long slots. The Dualit had 1950s styling in chrome, and was very wide-bodied indeed. The Tefal Toast'n'Grill was also large, and had an integral grill section.

2 Price

We give target prices – you should be able to match these if you shop around. Prices in *italics* are guide prices supplied by manufacturers.

3 Slot width

With all the two-slice long slot toasters and the four-slice Tefal 8446, the slot width changed automatically for bread of different thicknesses.

III = will take thick sliced bread, crumpets and half baps
II = will take thick sliced bread and crumpets
I = will take thick sliced bread

4 Speed

We made four batches of toast and averaged out the time taken. The first batch usually takes about half a minute longer than the other three. How quickly the bread toasts can also vary with the freshness of the bread. To make sure our tests were fair, we used sliced bread that had been kept in controlled conditions.

- ◩ = less than 1min 50sec
- ◩ = 1min 50sec to 2min 10sec
- □ = 2min 10 sec to 2min 30sec
- ◪ = 2min 30sec to 2min 50sec
- ■ = more than 2min 50sec

5 Toasting quality

After 'running in' each toaster until we found the setting at which it made toast a golden shade of brown, we toasted several batches of our sliced bread to compare how evenly the toasters cooked, and how consistent they were from batch to batch. Results were assessed by a panel of people who use toasters regularly. Our panel found unevenly toasted bread less acceptable than toast which was merely stripy – and the ratings in the Table overleaf reflect this.

BUYING GUIDE

TWO-SLICE TOASTERS

Toasters with one long slot usually cope with a range of toastables, though the slots are often so deep that it's hard to fish out small items.

One-slot type

BEST BUYS **Boots Long Slot** £20; **Swan Elegance 20436** £18 or similar **Swan 20437** £18

The **Tefal 8437** £20 or similar **Tefal 8438** £18 also did well.

Two-slot type

BEST BUY **Boots 21** £20

The **Braun HT50** £30 did very well, but was expensive. The **Hinari T2B Lifestyle** *£14*, and similar **Hinari T2G** *£15*, and the **Rowenta TA03** £17 also performed well and could take crumpets, but they were a bit slow; and the Hinaris were hard to find in the shops.

FOUR-SLICE TOASTERS

Large families and busy households may find the idea of a four-slice toaster attractive. The four-slice toasters were generally less convenient than the two-slice ones, and most had surface temperatures we considered a little too high.

The **Hinari T4B** *£16*, similar **Hinari T4G** *£13*, and **Oster 3241** *£19* did best in our tests, but were hard to find in the shops. The **Rowenta TA04** £23 was a bit slow and more expensive, but also did well.

6 Convenience

The 'Advantages' and 'Drawbacks' are based on a laboratory assessment of how easy it was to use and clean the toasters, and on how useful the instructions were. None was particularly awkward, but some were liked better than others.

Advantages

a = plug fitted
b = can switch off element for one-slot operation
c = cord storage
d = wall-mountable
e = easy to eject toast manually
f = frozen bread setting
g = grill
h = hinged or removable crumb tray

Drawbacks

p = our thick sliced bread protrudes from top of slot while toasting
s = small or thin slices can shoot out when they pop up
t – frozen bread setting gave dark or black toast (other settings could be used)
u = browning controls awkward to use
v = awkward to eject toast manually
w = fingers get hot removing small slices
x = awkward to clear crumbs/dirt traps

7 Durability

We put two samples of each of the models tested through 4,000 toasting cycles – about the same as using them twice a day

TOASTERS

	Model	Price (2) £	Slot width (3)	Speed (4)	Toasting quality (5)	Convenience (6): Advantages	Convenience (6): Drawbacks	Durability (7)	Surface temperature (8)	
	(1) TWO-SLICE LONG SLOT WITH GRILL									
	1 **Tefal 8720 Toast'n'Grill** (France)	38	III	□	□	g	sw	◩	◩	
	(1) TWO-SLICE/LONG SLOT									
►	1 **Boots Long Slot** (Hong Kong)	20	III	◩	◩	f[1]	uvw	◩	◩c	◄
	2 **Haden HT2L** (Hong Kong)	17	III	■	◩	f	ux	□	◩	
	3 **Kenwood TT400** (Hong Kong)	16	III	◩	◩[2]	cef[1]	u[2]w	□	◩c	
	4 **Krups 196** (Switzerland)	23	III	◩	□	ce	—	◩	◩c	
	5 **Morphy Richards 44120** (UK)	19	III	◩	◩	—	suvw	◪	◩c	
	6 **Philips HD4571** (Austria)	20	III	□	◩	cde	—	□	◩c	
	7 **Rowenta TO68** (W Germany)	20	III	▩	□	c	x	□	◩c	
	8 **Russell Hobbs Microchip 5600** (UK)	24	III	□	◩	cef[1]	xw	□	◩c	
	9 **Swan 00434** (UK)	25	III	▩	◪[3]	cfh	t	□[3]	◩c	
►	10 **Swan Elegance 20436** (Hong Kong)	18	III	□	◩	f[1]	uw	◩	◩c	◄
►	11 **Tefal 8437** (France)	20	III	◩	□	—	uv	◩	◩	◄
	12 **Tefal 844215 Innovation** (France)	22	III	◩	□	—	w	◩	◩c	
	(1) TWO-SLICE/TWO-SLOT									
►	1 **Boots 21** (W Germany)	20	I	□	◩	ac	p	◩	◩c	◄
►	2 **Braun HT50** (W Germany)	30	I	◩	◩	cf[4]h	p	◩	◩c	◄
	3 **Carlton 200 Duo** (China)[5]	15	III	◩	□	h	p	◪	□	
	4 **Dualit Auto 2** (UK)	50	II	□	□	abh	u	□	□	
►	5 **Hinari T2B Lifestyle** (Hong Kong)	14	II	◪	◩	f	p	◩	◩	◄
	6 **Morphy Richards 44210** (UK)	18	II	▩	□	—	puvw	◪	◩c	
	7 **Oster 3240** (Hong Kong)	14	II	◩	□	—	swx	◩	◩	
	8 **Philips HD4580** (Hong Kong)	15	II	◪	□	h	s	◩	□	
►	9 **Rowenta TA03** (Hong Kong)	17	II	◪	◩	fh	w	◩	◩	◄
	10 **Russell Hobbs 5468** (UK)	18	II	◩	◩	f	tw	◩	□	
	11 **Salton 3816** (Hong Kong)	14	II	□	□	h	sw	□	□	
	12 **Swan 20425** (Hong Kong)	17	II	▩	□	h	wx	□	◩	
	(1) FOUR-SLICE									
	1 **Frigidaire FCL444** (Hong Kong)	18	III	□	□	h	pv	□	□	
►	2 **Hinari T4B Lifestyle** (Hong Kong)	16	II	□	◩	f	psw	◩	□	◄
►	3 **Oster 3241** (Hong Kong)	19	II	□	◩	—	swx	◩	□	◄
	4 **Philips HD4585** (Hong Kong)	22	II	□	◩	h	ps	◩	◪	
►	5 **Rowenta TA04** (Hong Kong)	23	II	◪	□	fh	ptw	◩	□	◄
	6 **Russell Hobbs 5484** (UK)	24	II	◪	◩	ef	w	□	◪	
	7 **Salton 3818** (Hong Kong)	20	II	■	□	h	psw	◪	□	
	8 **Swan 20428** (Hong Kong)	24	II	□	□	h	pvwx	◩	◩	
	9 **Tefal 8446** (France)	30	III	◩	□	—	ux	□[6]	□	

► Recommended in the Buying Guide ◄

KEY TO RATINGS best ▩ > ◩ > □ > ◪ > ■ worst

for five years. If minor faults were found, we repaired them or tested another sample. Only about half of the toasters came through our tests in good condition. Most common faults were with the pop-up mechanism or element failure.

- ◩ = both samples passed, only minor faults
- ☐ = one sample failed or both passed after minor repairs
- ◪ = two samples failed

Tefal 8720 Toast'n'Grill

The Tefal Toast'n'Grill has a small grill section alongside its single toasting slot. Turn it on its side to operate it as a grill.

We tested the grill using three items suggested in its instruction book: a frozen individual lasagne, a small frozen pizza and a small chilled flan.

The Tefal cooked them evenly, though we found the base of our flan and pizza rather soggy. The toaster section also performed satisfactorily – see Table. Our 5in diameter pizza was the largest thing we could fit on the grill pan. But if you want a grill the size of a toaster, and are happy to pay £20 over the odds for your toaster, the Tefal Toast'n'Grill had no major problems.

[1] Performance of frozen bread setting not tested
[2] Manufacturer tells us models now have a modified browning control which could affect toasting quality and convenience
[3] Manufacturer tells us that modifications should improve toasting quality and durability
[4] Has infra-red sensor to control toasting time
[5] Exclusive to Currys
[6] Manufacturer tells us durability has been improved
[7] Exclusive to Electricity Boards
[8] Exclusive to Electricity Boards and has fitted plug
[9] Exclusive to Comet
[10] Exclusive to Marks and Spencer and has fitted plug
[11] Has a different electronic browning control which may affect performance
[12] Exclusive to Woolworth

TOASTERS SIMILAR TO THOSE IN TABLE

Unless footnoted otherwise, the difference between the listed model and the one in the Table is cosmetic only. The **bold** figure matches the one in the appropriate section of the Table.

	Target price	Similar to toaster number in Table
	£	
1 TWO-SLICE/LONG-SLOT		
Boots Hedge Rose	26	**9**
Boots Camargue	26	**9**
Electra[7]	24	**9**
Electra Saffron[8]	25	**9**
Morphy Richards 44121	19	**5**
Proline Coolwall[9]	17	**2**
Rowenta T070	17	**7**
Russell Hobbs 5604	22	**8**
St Michael[10]	29	**9**
Swan 00435	24	**9**
Swan 00436	24	**9**
Swan 20437	18	**10**
Tefal 8438	18	**11**
Tefal 844216	22	**12**
1 TWO-SLICE/TWO-SLOT		
Braun HT40[11]	20	**2**
Empire HC0601	15	**3**
Empire HW8283	15	**3**
Frigidaire FCL222	16	**3**
Hinari TL2 Lifestyle	14	**3**
Hinari T2G	15	**5**
Kenwood TT100	17	**12**
Morphy Richards 44211	18	**6**
Russell Hobbs 5469	20	**10**
Salton 3817	14	**11**
Swan 20447[12]	16	**12**
Swan 20419	16	**12**
1 FOUR-SLICE		
Empire HB0602	20	**1**
Empire HW8272	20	**1**
Hinari TL4	16	**1**
Hinari T4G	13	**2**
Kenwood TT550	22	**8**
Russell Hobbs 5489	27	**6**
Tefal 8448	28	**9**

Safety warning

We tested eight Morphy Richards 44210 toasters. Six had switch faults of varying seriousness; another caught fire during safety tests. Morphy Richards told us that, since we bought our samples, they had modified this toaster (and the similar 44211). If you have one of these toasters and the batch number marked on the gold 'tested' label is between 0189 and 2089, you can get a modified replacement by returning it to: Customer Services Dept., Morphy Richards Ltd, Mexborough, South Yorkshire S64 8AJ.

For further enquiries phone Morphy Richards on 0709 582402, extension 237. You can ask for a prepaid label for the postage, or you can ask for a refund for postage by letter sent with the toaster.

8 Surface temperatures

Thirteen of the toasters in our Table are 'cool wall' type (c under surface temperatures in the Table). As you can see from the ratings, they do stay cool, and should cause no problems if you touch the walls or handles (though the area round the slot still gets hot). For the other toasters, check our ratings.

Electrical safety

Apart from the Morphy Richards 44210 (see left), all the toasters were satisfactory in our tests or had British Electrotechnical Approvals Board (BEAB) approval.

COFFEE MAKERS

For Filter, Espresso or Cappuccino Coffee

From *Which?* December 1989

How do you like your coffee? Whether you want a mid-morning mugful or frothy post-prandial cappuccino, there are a few essentials for all tastes.

The coffee There are many types of beans, blends and roasts to choose from, so it's worth experimenting to find one you like. Try to make sure the type of grind is suited to the method of coffee making you're using, although this can be varied as well. Filter coffee is usually a medium roast, medium to fine grind. Espresso coffee is often a much darker roast, ground very finely.

Most important of all, the coffee should be as fresh as possible. In the *Good Food Guide* taste test (see Box), the clear favourite was coffee from a freshly opened vacuum pack; the worst cups came from a pack which had been open four days.

Strength Aim to get a full flavour without any bitterness. Again, it's worth experimenting with different amounts of coffee to find a taste you like. In the *Good Food Guide* taste test, a cup of espresso coffee made with half measures was preferred to one made with the full amount.

Hot and fresh Good coffee doesn't like to be kept waiting: drink it while it's hot, and try pre-warming the cups. Our tasters were least impressed by coffee which was made and kept hot for 20 minutes before being drunk: 'unidentifiable as coffee'; 'not even a decent warm drink'.

Good coffee guide

What makes a good cup of coffee? Three *Good Food Guide* tasters tried to find out. They compared two methods of coffee making: a widely available plunger-type filter jug, La Cafetière, using a well-known vacuum-packed ground coffee (Lyons Original medium-ground, medium roast), and an espresso machine (the Krups Espresso Mini 963) using the most popular espresso coffee, Lavazza.

Various permutations were tried with a freshly opened pack of coffee, four-day-old coffee, full strength and half-strength coffee, freshly made coffee, and coffee which had been kept warm for 20 minutes. One conclusion was that people will always disagree over what tastes good.

But other recommendations were clear:

- coffee should be freshly made from a newly opened pack
- if made too strong, the flavour of espresso coffee can become too bitter tasting
- it is harder to make a good cup with a plunger-type coffee maker: the best of the cups from La Cafetière was put in fourth place, after three variations of the espresso, although that may have more to do with the type of coffee than the method of making it.

BUYING GUIDE

FILTER COFFEE MAKERS
Useful if you often need large amounts of coffee, or as a change from instant:

- can make half a dozen cupfuls in about ten minutes
- can keep it warm for up to an hour, if you're not too fussy about the taste
- easy to use
- comparatively cheap to buy.

For good coffee making and no convenience drawbacks:

BEST BUYS **Philips Café Comfort HD7200** £18 (and the similar **Philips HD7201** *£19*, **HD7203** £20), the **Russell Hobbs 3313 Country Style** £19, **Russell Hobbs 3320 Reflections** £19

ESPRESSO COFFEE MAKERS
For those who want that continental flavour, an espresso machine gives you strong rich coffee in a matter of minutes. But make sure you really do want espresso or cappuccino coffee, and are prepared to put up with the drawbacks:

- only small amounts made at one time
- can be messy and fiddly to use/clean
- more expensive to buy than filter machines.

For good performance and better ease of use than other machines:

BEST BUY machines: **Russell Hobbs Café Espresso 3335** £40

Filter, espresso or cappuccino An electric filter coffee maker consists of a tank of cold water which is heated and allowed to drain through a filter containing the ground coffee. The hot coffee usually collects in a jug under the filter, and a hotplate keeps it warm in case you don't drink it all at once.

With the most popular type of espresso machine, the water is heated up and then forced through a small round metal filter which holds tightly packed ground coffee. This produces a small amount of strong coffee with a lot of flavour. We tested this type; more expensive machines have a pump which forces the water through under even greater pressure, to extract the maximum flavour. Cappuccino is espresso with heated frothy milk. It doesn't taste as strong as undiluted espresso, and is usually served in bigger cups. The milk is frothed by a steam pipe on the espresso machine. Skimmed milk makes more froth than full-fat milk, but it won't be as creamy.

FACTS, FIGURES AND TEST RESULTS

1 Type
We've separated filter coffee makers and espresso machines in the Table.

2 Price
What you should expect to pay in the shops. Where a model wasn't widely available in our price survey, we give the manufacturer's guide price in *italics*.

3 Features

Useful features to look for:

a = mains ON/OFF indicator

b = machine READY indicator tells you when it's ready to froth milk or make coffee

c = jug removable while coffee still filtering. Anti-drip device stops coffee splashing on to the hotplate.

d = manual shut-off to stop flow if cups fill up

e = water capacity marks on tank, inside or out

f = separate water level indicator, such as a ball float in a tube

g = clip to keep filter in holder when knocking out coffee grounds

h = removable drip tray

j = steam pipe can be used to froth milk while coffee is being made

k = capacity scale on jug/cup

Other features include:

l = permanent filter: saves cost of paper filters, but needs to be cleaned after each use

m = swivel filter holder: gives easy access to filter

n = mains flex storage

p = separate jug which heats up milk and keeps it warm

q = filter attachment for filling two cups instead of jug

4 Quantity

The maximum number of cups which we measured could be filled in one go. For filter machines, we calculated the number of typical (0.2 litre) coffee cups. Espresso coffee is usually served in much smaller demi-tasse cups, about a quarter the size of normal coffee cups; for espresso machines we calculated the number of these which could be filled.

5 Time

How long it took for the maximum amount to be made. The espresso machines were usually quicker the second time, if used continuously.

6 Coffee temperature problems

We made the maximum amount of coffee for all the machines, and measured the initial temperature. Ideally, if you're adding cold milk, the black coffee should be at least 80°C. A few machines didn't make the coffee hot enough. With the espresso machines, this matters less because espresso coffee is more likely to be drunk black or with hot frothed milk. Coffee which is made at about 90°C or hotter is more likely to lose its flavour; five machines made coffee which was too hot.

If you don't always drink all the coffee when it's freshly made, you'll need a filter machine which will keep it warm. To test this, we poured away half the maximum amount of filter coffee and measured the temperature again an hour later to see how well it had been maintained. Most filter machines have a hotplate and/or insulated jug to keep coffee warm, but several failed to keep it warm enough. A few actually heated it up too much.

The **Melitta Aroma Comfort** had a detachable hotplate, and the **Philips Café Gourmet HD5560** and **Salton Filter Perc 3625** claimed to keep coffee warm when unplugged. All three let the coffee get far too cold when left unplugged for half an hour.

To see how they would cope with making just a single cup of coffee, we tested every machine with the minimum amount of coffee they could make, and measured the initial temperature. Most of the filter machines made coffee which was not hot enough.

COFFEE MAKERS

	Price	Features	Quantity	Time	Coffee temperature problems	Convenience drawbacks
	2	3	4	5	6	7
	£		cups	min		
1 FILTER MACHINES						
1 **Black & Decker DCM200** (Hong Kong)	22	aceklm	5	11	— [1]	—
2 **Black & Decker DCM321** (Hong Kong)	15	acfkmn	6	12	CE	—
3 **Boots 65-78-039** (Switzerland)	20	acfln	5	10	E	—
4 **Braun Aromaster Compact 10 KF32** (W Germany)	20	acekmn	6	10.5	CE	—
5 **Braun Aromaster 10 KF42** (W Germany)	26	aceklmn	6	10.5	E	—
6 **Braun Aromaster 10 Special KF72** (W Germany)	30	acekmn	6	10	CE	—
7 **Cordon Bleu 5550** (W Germany)	13	f	5	13	—	M
8 **Krups Compact Aroma 10 Gold 133** (W Germany)	37	acfklmn	6	11	E	—
9 **Krups Compact Thermaroma 138** (W Germany)	*39*	afn	4.5	8	CE	M
10 **Melitta Aroma Comfort** (W Germany)	40	acfkmn	6	8.5	E	—
11 **Melitta Aromaline SCM12** (Hong Kong)	*24*	acfkn	7	12	E	G
12 **Morphy Richards 47400** (UK)	*22*	acflmn	6	13	E	—
13 **Moulinex Aroma Extra 07601** (France)	20	acfkn	7	15.5	CE	L
14 **Moulinex 854** (Spain)	13		5	10.5	AE	JL
15 **Philips Café Cino HD5365** (Taiwan)	20	afl	2	8.5	—	—
16 **Philips Café Comfort HD7200** (Netherlands)	18	af	4.5	9	—	—
17 **Philips Café Duo HD5190** (Netherlands)	19	aehln	1.5 [2]	6	AE	—
18 **Philips Café Gourmet HD5560** (Switzerland)	40	acem	2	9	—	—
19 **Philips Café Lait HD5746** (Netherlands)	50	acenp	4.5	10	D	—
20 **Philips Café Royal 1200 HD5752** (Netherlands)	22	acfmn	6	11.5	E	—
21 **Philips Café Therm HD5750** (Netherlands)	50	aen	4.5	8	B	—
22 **Rowenta FK25** (W Germany)	22	acflmn	6	12	E	—
► 23 **Russell Hobbs 3313 Country Style** (Switzerland) ◄	19	cen	5	10	—	—
24 **Russell Hobbs 3317 Reflections** (Switzerland)	24	acfln	5.5	13	ACE	—
25 **Russell Hobbs 3319 Sovereign** (Switzerland)	35	acfln	5.5	11.5	E	—
► 26 **Russell Hobbs 3320 Reflections** (Switzerland) ◄	19	aekn	5	11	—	—
27 **Russell Hobbs 3325 High Style** (Switzerland)	30	acfln	5.5	10	E	—
28 **Salton Filter Continental 3619** (Hong Kong)	20	acfln	6.5	12	DE	—
29 **Salton Filter Perc 3625** (Hong Kong)	*20*	af	3.5	8	BDF	G
30 **Tefal Coffee Maker Elite** (France)	25	acflmn	6.5	12	AE	H
1 ESPRESSO MACHINES						
1 **Bialletti Cappuccino Super** (Italy)	60	abdglnq	7 [3]	6.5	AE	GK
2 **Cordon Bleu Espresso/Cappuccino 7102** (Spain)	35	ahjkl	4	3.5	E	—
3 **Cordon Bleu Deluxe 7116** (Spain)	40	adgjkln	4	5	—	—
4 **Gaggia Fantastico** (Italy)	50	ajklnq	4	8.5	—	—
5 **Gran Gala Cappuccino 4TZ** (Italy)	55	adgl	5	6	B	—
6 **Krups Espresso Mini 963** (Switzerland)	53	ahjklnq	4	5.5	B	—
7 **Morphy Richards 47500 Espresso/Cappuccino** (Switzerland)	33	agjklnq	4	5	E	—
8 **Moulinex Espresso Cappuccino** (Italy)	38	adhklnq	4	4.5	BE	—
9 **Rowenta ES01** (Spain)	40	adghklnq	3	3.5	A	G
► 10 **Russell Hobbs Café Espresso 3335** (Switzerland) ◄	40	ajkln	4	5	—	—
11 **Salton Cappuccino 3408** (Italy)	38	adhkln	4	4	—	—
12 **Tefal Espresso 2315.10** (Italy)	*45*	abdhkln	4	4	—	—

► Recommended in the Buying Guide ◄

[1] Recommended minimum amount may be too weak
[2] Two small cups (each 0.1 litres) provided. No hotplate
[3] Filter must be refilled after four cups

Only six filter machines and five espresso machines passed all our coffee-making tests; the rest had one or more of these drawbacks:

A = maximum amount of coffee – initial temperature less than 80°C
B = maximum amount of coffee – initial temperature over 89°C
C = temperature after one hour less than 80°C
D = temperature after one hour over 89°C
E = minimum amount of coffee – initial temperature less than 80°C
F = minimum amount of coffee – initial temperature over 89°C

7 Convenience drawbacks

Our user panel assessed how easy it was to set up the machine, make a jugful of coffee and clean up afterwards. Generally, the users were very satisfied with the filter machines.

Espresso machines do generate a lot of steam pressure which, although not dangerous, can be alarming. Be prepared for gusts of steam, spluttering and hissing – and perhaps a bit more cleaning up later.

Particular drawbacks which were noted include:

G = some difficulty setting the machine up, such as fitting the filter or judging the water level
H = jug pours badly when full
J = uncomfortable jug handle
K = some parts awkward to wash
L = poor instructions
M = controls or displays, such as ON/OFF switch, may be difficult to understand or read

Milk frothing

We tested each espresso machine to see how well it would froth skimmed milk for making cappuccino. The fastest frothers were the **Cordon Bleu Deluxe 7116**, the **Gaggia**, **Krups**, **Morphy Richards** and **Salton**, which could all froth a demi-tasse cupful of milk to twice its volume in under 30 seconds. Some of the other steam-pipes were quite short, which made it harder to froth small amounts in a jug: the more milk needed, the longer it takes. The **Tefal** was the slowest frother; it took two and a half minutes because the water tank had to be refilled after the coffee was made.

We also tested a separate electric frothing machine called **Mister Cappuccino** (£30) to see how it compared. It took longer to heat up than most espresso machines. Once ready, it frothed the milk as fast as the others, and made much more froth – twice as much as the best espresso. It would be worth considering if you often make lots of cappuccino coffee.

Electrical safety

All the machines passed our electrical safety tests or were BEAB approved (have British Electrotechnical Approvals Boards approval) or BEAB approved via CCA (have BEAB approval via another European approval authority).

Descaling

If you have hard water, your coffee maker will collect scale and take longer to make coffee. How quickly this happens depends on how often you use the machine and how hard the water is. Manufacturers' recommendations for descaling range from every six weeks to every six months; some suggest after 40 operations or simply when brewing takes longer than usual.

A common descaling solution is a mixture of distilled malt vinegar and water. Citric acid solutions can also be used. There are also several brands of descaler recommended for coffee makers.

GREEN GUIDE

All coffee filter papers which have been bleached with chlorine may contain dioxins. Sounds serious, but don't let such news put you off that after-dinner cup.

Dioxins are a group of 210 chemicals, 17 of which may be dangerous. If you drink filter coffee, it's possible that some of the minute quantities of dioxins in some filter papers could end up inside you. The quantities involved are very small and the effect is uncertain. At the moment, the government does not regard the presence of dioxins in paper products such as filter papers as a risk to health.

If you want to avoid filter papers which have been chlorine bleached, there are now several brands on the market.

Similar models to those in the Table

Model numbers match those in the appropriate section of the Table. Unless we say otherwise, similar models listed here are only cosmetically different.

FILTER MACHINES

1 **Black & Decker DCM200:** Black & Decker DCM250, *£33*, with timer

2 **Black & Decker DCM321:** Black & Decker DCM323G, *£40*, with permanent filter and timer

3 **Boots 65-78-039:** Russell Hobbs 3314, *£23*

4 **Braun Aromaster Compact 10 KF32:** Braun KF32PF, *£24*, with permanent filter

5 **Braun Aromaster 10 KF42:** Braun KF46, *£23*, no permanent filter

7 **Cordon Bleu 5550:** Cordon Bleu 5553, *£14*

8 **Krups Compact Aroma 10 Gold 133:** Krups Compact Aroma 130, *£30*, smaller capacity and no permanent filter; Krups Compact Aroma 131, *£33*, no permanent filter

11 **Melitta Aromaline SCM12:** Melitta SCM5, *£17*, smaller capacity

16 **Philips Café Comfort HD7200:** Philips HD7201, *£19* with anti-drip device; Philips HD7203, £20, with anti-drip device and larger capacity

20 **Philips Café Royal 1200 HD5752:** Philips HD5753, £25, has larger capacity and permanent filter; Philips HD5751, £20, smaller capacity; Philips HD5757, *£35*, larger capacity and timer

22 **Rowenta FK25:** Rowenta FK27, £30, with permanent filter

28 **Salton Filter Continental 3619:** Salton Filter Gold 3620, *£28*, with permanent filter

ESPRESSO MACHINES

6 **Krups Espresso Mini 963:** Krups 967, *£56*, different steam pipe

WATER FILTERS

Under-sink and On-tap Filters

From *Which?* August 1990

Thinking of buying a water filter? Our test results and buying advice will help you choose one, but if you're concerned about any aspect of your tap-water, the first step is to contact your supplier, who must tell you what's in your water (see 'The water in your taps').

You may find out that your water meets the Water Supply (Water Quality) Regulations – in which case you don't need to buy a filter at all. But if you're not happy about the taste, you could try a filter. Buy a jug filter (costing around £10) to find out if it improves the taste. The Waymaster Crystal was our Best Buy when we tested jug filters, but all reduced the amount of chlorine – one of the substances which gives water an unpleasant taste. An activated carbon on-line filter will also remove chlorine, and our taste test shows it may improve the taste. It will also be more convenient to use, and will work out cheaper in the long run. All the filters in this report contain activated carbon.

If you're fed up with scale in your kettle and scum in your drinks, you need a filter that reduces water hardness. A jug filter is a cheap and effective way of doing this. Or you could get an on-line filter with a scale inhibitor, or buy a reverse osmosis or distillation unit – none of which we've tested.

If your supplier tells you that some substances in your water exceed the limits in the Regulations, you need to know whether they are linked with possible health risks, or just affect the look of the water. Taking into account how much they exceed the limits, it's up to you to decide whether you think it would be worth buying a filter.

None of the filters tested for this report could reduce nitrates. If you're worried about nitrates, you could buy a jug filter that reduces nitrates, such as the Waymaster Crystal. Alternatively, you could get a nitrate-reducing cartridge for an online filter, or you could go for a reverse osmosis unit or distillation unit.

The water in your taps

How do you find out what's in your water? You could find out about some substances yourself, using a water testing kit. But we don't think there's any point doing your own testing, because the results won't be as full or as accurate as the information you can get from your supplier. Because what's in your water may change over time, you'd have to test frequently, and so spend more on kits.

Your water supplier (listed under 'Water' in the phone directory) is legally obliged to tell you what's in your water. Ask for a free detailed list of what's in the water supplied to your area, and for information about how your water compares with the Water Supply (Water Quality) Regulations. And ask if any improvements are being made to the water quality.

When you ask your water supplier for a breakdown of what's in your water, you'll be sent a page or two of information. It may look complicated, but there are only two columns you need to look at.

The first column tells you the name of each substance (or 'determinand') your supplier has analysed the water for. And the column headed 'Max' tells you the maximum amount of each substance measured in the water. The '<' symbol alongside a figure means that the amount of a particular substance is less than the figure shown. The data is based on several measurements taken throughout the year, to get an accurate picture of the water quality. The information you get may cover a year's worth of measurements, though this could vary between suppliers.

We've outlined some of the most common substances which may exceed the levels set by the Regulations and (where appropriate) stated the maximum amounts permitted in the Regulations. The amounts are expressed in milligrams (mg) per litre, and micrograms (μg) per litre, a thousand times smaller than a milligram.

At the moment, Regulations cover water quality in England, Wales and Scotland; Regulations for Northern Ireland are in the pipeline.

Nitrates

(maximum permitted: 50mg per litre)
Over the last few years, the levels of nitrates in water in some parts of the country have risen. This is probably because of the increased use of nitrogen fertilisers in farming. High levels of nitrates can increase the risk of *methaemoglobinaemia* ('blue baby syndrome'), a very rare blood condition which can affect bottle-fed babies. In *all* age groups, the body converts nitrates to nitrites, which have been shown to cause cancer in animals. However, studies haven't confirmed a link between nitrates and cancer in humans.

BUYING GUIDE

For a filter that reduces metals and organic chemicals:

BEST BUY **Fileder Ametek HM** (£180) had the best all-round performance. It reduced aluminium, lead, iron, manganese, organic chemicals – and chlorine

The **Citmart Everpure BW100** (£148) did almost as well, and is cheaper.

Metals

Aluminium

(maximum permitted: 0.2mg per litre)
Aluminium occurs naturally, but is also added during the purification process of some tap-water. Too much aluminium can discolour the water. It may also be one of the factors that causes Alzheimer's disease – a type of dementia – but as yet there's no solid proof.

Iron and manganese

(maximum permitted: 200μg per litre and 50μg per litre respectively)
Both these substances occur naturally in water, but corroding pipes can also add iron to water. They both discolour tap-water, but at the levels found in the UK, they aren't a health risk.

Lead

(maximum permitted: 50μg per litre)

Lead can damage the brain and nervous system, cause anaemia, and affect muscles. Children are especially vulnerable to the effects of lead. Most lead in drinking water comes from lead pipes in the home, and this is more of a problem in soft water areas.

If you think your house may have lead pipes (many pre-1976 houses do), ask your water supplier for advice. If you choose to replace lead pipes, you may be able to get a grant from your local council to help towards the cost.

Organic chemicals

Polycyclic aromatic hydrocarbons (PAHs)

(maximum permitted: 0.2μg per litre)
Some water mains pipes are lined with coal tar pitch. Parts of this lining can break off through wear and tear, and release PAHs into the water. Tests have shown that large doses of some polycyclic aromatic hydrocarbons cause cancer in animals.

Trihalomethanes (THMs)

(maximum permitted: 100μg per litre)
Water suppliers add chlorine to water to kill harmful bacteria. But the chlorine can react with substances in the water to form trihalomethanes, the most common being chloroform. Studies suggest that these chemicals might increase the risk of cancer.

Trichloroethene

(maximum permitted: 30μg per litre)
Also called trichloroethylene. This is used for degreasing metal in industry. Waste trichloroethene probably gets into the tap-water because of careless dumping. Trichloroethene can cause cancer in animals.

Hardness

Hardness is a measure of how much calcium is dissolved in the water; the higher the figure, the harder the water. Some of the hardness comes out as scale when you boil a kettle, and it also causes scum in hot drinks.

As a rule of thumb, water containing 100 to 200mg per litre of calcium carbonate per litre is moderately hard; over 200mg per litre is hard. Although we've highlighted hardness, the specific amount in your water isn't important; what's more important is whether you're bothered by the scale and scum.

Who cares about your water?

The UK has been taken to the European Court of Justice for failing to implement the EC water quality Directive, for high nitrate levels in parts of England, and for high lead levels in parts of Scotland. The Court isn't likely to make a decision for a year or so.

If you're not happy with any aspect of your water, complain to your supplier. Ask for a copy of their 'Customer Code of Practice' for the correct procedure. If the supplier can't resolve your problem, try your local Customer Service Committee – part of the Office of Water Services. (The Code of Practice gives their address.) OFWAT is a Government Department which acts as the watchdog over the water suppliers. Or you can contact your local Environmental Health Officer.

Which filter suits you best?

Concern about the quality of our tap-water has led to many new water filters coming on to the market. But before you start looking through manufacturers' glossy brochures, find out from your water supplier what problems there are, if

Filter-using tips

- When using a jug filter, give it and its water reservoir a weekly clean, and always keep the filtered water in the fridge – to slow down bacterial growth in the water.
- You will still need to boil water for making a baby's feed, to kill the bacteria. But, of course, the only substance you can remove by boiling is hardness (left in the kettle as scale).
- With both jug and under-sink activated carbon filters, there's no way you can tell when the filter cartridge has reached the end of its life. Manufacturers suggest you watch out for a slower flow rate or a worse taste. If they also advise you to change the cartridge after a certain period of time, you should follow these instructions.

any, with your water. There's no point in buying a filter if you don't need one; nor is there any point buying a filter that can't solve your particular problem.

A water filter could cost you anything from £10 to £500. To help you decide which kind is best for you, we've listed the pros and cons of the main types you're likely to find in the shops. For this report, we tested the most popular on-line types – activated carbon and ceramic under-sink filters, and on-tap filters. Under-sink filters are connected to the mains water supply in the kitchen, and the water comes out through a separate tap fitted on the sink.

Jug filter (£10 to £20)

This consists of a plastic or glass jug, with a plastic container on top. You pour tap-water into this container, and the water passes through a filter cartridge and collects in the jug, which you can then keep in the fridge.

All the jug filter cartridges we've tested contained activated carbon and ion-exchange resins (see 'Activated carbon under-sink filter'). Most jug filters also contain silver, which is meant to reduce bacterial growth in the filtered water.

√ No installation necessary

√ Reduces level of most metals, organic substances, chlorine, and water hardness

× Although some jugs take some aluminium out of the water, others don't remove any

× Most jugs don't reduce nitrates

× Hard to know when the cartridge has reached the end of its useful life

× You can filter only a small amount of water at a time (one to two litres)

× Because of their short life (typically 60 to 100 litres) you have to buy new filter cartridges regularly

× Although the jug is cheap, the cost and life of each cartridge means that jug filters are expensive to use compared with other types of filter.

Distiller (About £400)

A distillation unit can be fitted under a sink, or put on a worktop. It boils the water. Then either air or water is used to cool the steam until it condenses back to water which is collected in a storage tank. Substances with a boiling point that's higher than water – which is almost everything else – are left behind in the boiling chamber. A distiller may also have an activated carbon filter to take out some organic substances that condense with the steam and so stay in the water.

We haven't tested distillers. The following is based on tests by our sister organisations in the United States and Canada.

√ Removes virtually everything from the water
√ No need to replace a cartridge
× Expensive
× Water-cooled distillers waste water; air-cooled ones can be noisy
× Very low flow rate
× Produces warm water, which you may need to refrigerate before drinking
× Needs regular cleaning
× Bulky.

Reverse osmosis under-sink filter (About £250 to £500)
At the heart of these filters is a plastic sheet, known as a semi-permeable membrane. This has such small holes that it can stop almost all substances. Typically, a complete reverse osmosis system consists of a sediment filter (which removes undissolved particles), the plastic membrane, an activated carbon filter, and a 10-litre storage tank. The tank is necessary because reverse osmosis filters are very slow at producing filtered water. Without a tank, you may not be able to draw enough water as it's being filtered.

We haven't tested this filter type. The following pros and cons are based on recent tests carried out by our sister organisations in the United States and Canada.
√ Reduces metals, nitrates, organic substances, chlorine, bacteria, and water hardness
√ Semi-permeable membrane has a high capacity (typically 4,000 litres), so doesn't need replacing very often
× Expensive
× Complicated installation
× Wastes a lot of water: only about 10 to 25 per cent of the water which goes through the unit ends up in the storage tank; the rest goes down the drain
× Very low flow rate
× Needs high water pressure to work well
× Filtered water is at room temperature
× The whole system is bulky.

Activated carbon under-sink filter (£40 to £200)
An activated carbon filter is riddled with tiny channels. As water passes through these channels, substances such as chlorine and organic chemicals stick to the walls of the channels. The cartridge is much larger than that of a jug filter, so lasts a lot longer, and needs changing less often. Many under-sink carbon filters also contain ion-exchange resins. These attract particles such as metals from the water, and replace them with harmless substances like hydrogen.

Many carbon filters also have silver in them (meant to reduce bacterial growth).
√ Reduces metals (aluminium, lead, iron), organic chemicals, and chlorine
√ High-capacity cartridges (at least 2,000 litres) so don't need replacing very often
√ Although the main unit can be fairly expensive, the cost of filtered water is cheap
√ Good flow rate
√ Filtered water always available on tap – no storage tank needed
× They don't reduce water hardness, and most don't reduce nitrates
× Hard to know when the cartridge has reached the end of its useful life.

Ceramic under-sink filter (£100 to £250)
These have a texture similar to a clay pot. The ceramic barrier has very small holes which let the water through but trap several different substances. Ceramic filters usually also contain activated carbon, ion-exchange resins, and silver.

√ Reduces metals, organic chemicals, and chlorine
√ Ceramic cartridge has a high capacity (typically 1,500 to 4,000 litres) so doesn't need replacing very often
√ Filtered water always available on tap – no storage tank needed
× Doesn't remove nitrates or hardness
× Clogs easily, so needs frequent cleaning
× Slower flow rate than carbon filters.

On-tap filters (£10 to £100)
These filters are either so small that the whole filter fixes on to a tap, or else the filter stands on the worktop, and a tube connects it to the tap.

The advantages and disadvantages of activated carbon on-tap filters are the same as for activated carbon under-sink filters. Apart from being less bulky and easier to install, the on-tap reverse osmosis models have the same pros and cons as the under-sink type.

FACTS, FIGURES AND TEST RESULTS

1 Types
For this report we've looked at the most popular types of filters: activated carbon and ceramic under-sink filters, and activated carbon on-tap filters.

Except for the Berglen Tapmate Springclear AC200, the under-sink filters come with a self-piercing valve, which screws into the mains water supply pipe so the filter branches off the pipe. This means your existing cold tap still gives unfiltered water, and a new tap (supplied with the filter) gives filtered water. The Berglen Tapmate Springclear is designed to fit directly on to the mains pipe, so all the cold water that reaches the kitchen sink is filtered.

The Leisure Care Major on-tap filter sits on the worktop; a tube connects it to the tap.

2 Price
We checked the price and availability of each filter around the country. Only the Berglen Tapmate Springclear was readily available. Some filters are available only direct from the manufacturer, through sales representatives. The Table gives the manufacturers' guide prices for the main unit and for replacement cartridges. Use the phone numbers, below, to find stockists in your area.

Aldous & Stamp ☎ 081-0659 1833; **Berglen** ☎ 081-204 3434; **Citmart** ☎ (0303) 262211; **Fileder** ☎ (0622) 691886; **Friskan** ☎ (0474) 325771; **Leisure Care** ☎ (0983) 299119; **NSA** ☎ (0628) 776044; **Opella** ☎ (0432) 357331; **Vertac** ☎ (0480) 495757.

The Fileder Ametek HM needs two cartridges at a time; one for metals, and one for organic substances and chlorine. With the NSA 100S, you replace the whole unit rather than the cartridge.

3 Cartridge
Type All the cartridges contain activated carbon, which reduces the amount of chlorine and organic substances. One also has a ceramic filter. Most filters contain a small amount of silver which is meant to prevent the growth of bacteria (see 'Bacterial growth').

A = activated carbon
C = ceramic
I = ion-exchange resin
S = silver

Life according to manufacturer
Manufacturers usually give a figure in litres for how long the cartridge will last. But

WATER FILTERS

	2 Price: Main unit	Replacement cartridge	3 Cartridge: Type	Life according to manufacturer	4 Instructions	5 Drawbacks: Installation	In use	6 WFBS listing	7 Filtering performance: Aluminium	Lead	Other metals	Organic chemicals	Chlorine	8 Flow rate	
	£	£		litres/months											
1 UNDER-SINK FILTERS															
Aldous & Stamp Aqua Clear (UK)[1]	75	14	A,S	2,500/6	0	—	—	x	-	-	-	-	0	0	
Berglen Tapmate Springclear AC200 (UK)	40	10	A	7,500/3	+	ABC	—	x	+	+	++	0	+	+	
► **Citmart Everpure BW100** (USA)[2]	148	42	A	6,800/12	+	E[6]	—	√	++	+	++	0	++	-	◄
► **Fileder Ametek HM** (USA)	180	30[5]	A,I	6,000/12	0	B	—	√	++	++	++	+	++	-	◄
Friskan Bon Del (USA)	184	114	A,S	19,000	0	AB	F	√	-	-	0	--	0	0	
NSA 100S (USA)	178	—	A,S	45,000/36	0	AB	—	√	+	+	++	+	++	-	
Opelia Castalia Filterclear (UK)[3]	70	12.50	A,S	1,900/3	++	—	G[7]	x	--	--	--	--	--	+	
Vertac Purely Water PW 1003/H (UK)[4]	234	20	A,C,I,S	4,000/6	+	—	H	x	++	+	++	0	++	--	
1 ON-TAP FILTER															
Leisure Care Major (UK)	80	17	A,S	25,000/12	0	D[6]	—	x	0	+	+	0	+	+	

► Recommended in the Buying Guide ◄

KEY TO RATINGS best ++ > + > 0 > - > -- worst

— = not applicable

[1] Tested with standard cartridge. A different cartridge is available which the manufacturer claims reduces nitrates

[2] BW400 (£135) is similar, but doesn't have a scale inhibitor

[3] We tested the 'Taste and Odour' cartridge. A 'sediment' cartridge is also available

[4] Tested with standard cartridge. Different cartridges are available which the manufacturer claims reduces nitrates and scale. EP1003/H (£99) is similar, but has a plastic housing

[5] Price for both cartridges

[6] Manufacturers claim that new fittings don't have this problem

because there's no way of knowing how much you've filtered, they also advise you to change it after a certain time (six months, say), or when the flow rate drops appreciably, or when the taste of the water gets worse.

In our tests, all the cartridges lived up to the manufacturer's claimed life, except the NSA, which managed only 30,000 litres before the flow rate dropped to less than half the initial flow rate. But the life of any cartridge will probably vary, depending on the water pressure and the amount of contaminants in the water.

The Fileder Ametek HM is now fitted with an automatic shut-off device. This stops water going through the cartridges once it has reached the end of its useful life.

4 Instructions

We assessed the instructions for clarity and usefulness of both the text and diagrams.

5 Drawbacks

Installation All the filters were fairly easy to install, and shouldn't be a problem for a competent do-it-yourselfer. Otherwise, a plumber shouldn't charge much for fitting one.

If you buy an under-sink filter, it must conform to the Water Byelaws. The simplest way to be sure it does is to look for one that has been tested according to the UK Water Fittings Byelaws Scheme – see 'WFBS listing'.

The Water Byelaws insist that you fit a device called a non-return valve upstream of the filter to prevent water going back into the mains supply. Manufacturers don't have to include one with their filter, so make sure you get one, £1 or so, from a plumber's merchant, for example.

The Byelaws recommend that you fit an isolating valve upstream of the filter. This lets you release the pressure on the filter, which can make it easier to change the cartridge or repair the filter. If the filter doesn't come with one, expect to pay a couple of pounds.

A = non-return valve not supplied
B = isolating valve not supplied
C = compression joints (to fit filter to mains supply) are needed but not supplied
D = some seals leaked under pressure
E = self-piercing valve leak difficult to stop

In use The activated carbon filters don't need any maintenance, and the cartridges are very easy to change. Ceramic cartridges clog quite quickly, and have to be cleaned with a brush. How often this chore needs to be done depends on the quality of the water and how much you filter. But it could be as often as every two to four weeks.

F = needs spanner (not supplied) to change cartridge
G = filter casting difficult to unscrew and screw tight when changing cartridge
H = ceramic cartridge clogs easily, and needs to be cleaned regularly with a brush

6 WFBS listing

The WFBS tests filters to BS6920 to ensure that materials used in the filter's construction don't contaminate the water. Filters which have passed the Standard have a √ in the Table, and are listed in the *Water Fittings and Materials Directory*, which should be in your local library. The WFBS doesn't test the life or performance of the filter.

You can fit an unlisted filter if it's equal to or better than approved ones, and you don't need to prove this; it's up to your water supplier to show that your filter *doesn't* conform to the Byelaws. But whatever filter you buy, you're obliged to tell your water supplier at least five days before you fit it.

7 Filtering performance

We tested the filters using both fresh water and water we had 'spiked' with several substances at the limits laid down in the Water Supply (Water Quality) Regulations. We filtered to the manufacturer's claimed capacity or to the point where the flow rate became unsatisfactory (we took this as 50 per cent of the initial flow) if that was sooner. Then we analysed how well each cartridge reduced the level of the various substances over its whole life. Generally, the cartridges removed the same amount throughout their lives.

The rating for 'organic chemicals' takes into account trichloroethene, fluoranthene (a polycyclic aromatic hydrocarbon), and chloroform. The rating for 'other metals' includes iron and manganese. None of the filters could reduce the amount of nitrates, though you can buy a separate nitrate cartridge for the Aldous & Stamp Aqua Clear and the Vertac Purely Water. We haven't tested these special nitrate filters.

We also tested the filters for removing chlorine, which can make water taste unpleasant, and hardness. None of the filters reduced the water hardness. The manufacturer of the Citmart Everpure claims that it has a scale inhibitor which prevents the hardness substances from forming in the water when it's boiled. We weren't able to do a long-term practical trial to test this.

- ◪ = 80 per cent or more removed
- ◩ = 60 to 79 per cent removed
- □ = 40 to 59 per cent removed
- ◪ = 20 to 39 per cent removed
- ■ = less than 20 per cent removed

While testing the Opella Castalia Filterclear with the 'spiked' water, we found that it dumped some of the previously collected lead, iron, and aluminium back into the filtered water during the cartridge's lifetime.

After we'd filtered the amount of 'spiked' water which was equal to the manufacturer's claimed cartridge life, we stopped all the filters, waited 30 minutes, then turned them all back on. Many filters dumped previously-collected substances back into the filtered water. But it's important to remember that the 'spiked' water was a stiff test for the filters, and not representative of typical tap-water, or usage. But even in this test, the following filters didn't dump anything: Citmart Everpure, Fileder Ametek HM, and Vertac Purely Water.

8 Flow rate

We found large differences between the filters. Ceramic filters are especially slow, and need cleaning regularly to keep them flowing at all. We don't think they're suitable if you have low water pressure (around 50lb per square inch or lower). Ask your water supplier for advice if you think your water pressure is low.

Other tests

Bacterial growth Harmful bacteria in drinking water are killed by the chlorine which water suppliers put in the water. But a few harmless ones may still remain. At high levels, they could cause stomach upsets in vulnerable people, such as the very young and the elderly.

We tested whether the filters let bacteria grow in the cartridge, and whether any bacteria then flushed through into the filtered water. Over a three-month period, we filtered ten litres a day through each filter, and analysed the filtered water for bacteria. All the cartridges added some bacteria to the water, but even the highest levels we found shouldn't do you any harm. Interestingly, the cartridges with silver in them to reduce bacterial growth didn't always have the lowest levels of bacteria.

Silver Because silver can be a health risk in high concentrations, we measured how much silver the cartridges which contained it released into the filtered water. Although they all added some, they were within the Regulations, and shouldn't present a health risk.

Taste An expert taste panel compared hard unfiltered tap-water, water filtered through each under-sink and on-tap filter, and water filtered through the Waymaster Crystal jug filter (which did well in February 1989).

Each taster found at least one sample of filtered water that tasted better than the unfiltered sample. But the tasters didn't agree on which ones tasted best, so the overall scores for the filters were similar – and, overall, no better than the unfiltered water. You may find that one filter makes the taste of your tap-water more palatable to you than others.

The ratings given in the Tables are based on **Which?***'s latest tests of each product. The date of the original report is noted just below the main heading.*

A **Which?** *Best Buy is the product or products which offered the best combination of price and performance in our tests. A* **Which?** *Best Buy is not necessarily the model with the best test results, nor the one with the most features; nor is it necessarily the cheapest. Other models mentioned in the Buying Guides have particular strengths which may be best suited to your needs.*

'Similar models' are products which we would expect to perform similarly to ones we have tested. They may look different (cosmetic differences) or have slightly more or fewer features. They may be better suited to your needs than the tested models.

Consumers' Association takes no advertising in any of its publications. It pays for all the goods and services it reviews. It receives no money from Government, trade or industry. All its income is derived from sales of its magazines, books and research. It is independent of all interests other than those of the consumer. It allows no exploitation of its recommendations in advertising or promotion. If readers of this guide see any ad making use of CA material in the press, in catalogues or in shops, please send details to Consumers' Association, Dept AWM, 2 Marylebone Road, London NW1 4DX.

If you're new to **Which?***, we hope you'll find enough in* **Which? Buying Guide** *to consider subscribing to the magazine itself – see the advertisement on page 287 for how to get three trial issues completely free.*

CLEANING AND LAUNDRY

Dishwashers • Washing Machines • Tumble Driers
Vacuum Cleaners

DISHWASHERS

Full-size, Slim and Table-top

From *Which?* November 1989

New to dishwasher ownership? There are a few pros and cons you need to bear in mind.

Pros

- Most dishwashers cope well with washing and drying crockery, cutlery and glassware.
- They save you time as well as effort; perhaps three hours a week for a family of four. A dishwasher is ideal for doing lots of washing up when you feel least like it – especially after a party.

Cons

- They're not good at everything. Delicate china, glassware and some cutlery can be spoiled by the hot water and the detergent, which is more aggressive than washing-up liquid. Pans may need to be soaked or re-washed by hand.
- Using a dishwasher is more expensive than washing up by hand – about £1.15 a week for a family of four, compared with around 50p a week.
- You may need to buy more crockery and cutlery: it's more economical not to use the machine until it is full.

What to watch out for in a dishwasher

We've picked out design features that affect how easy a dishwasher is to use. Look out for these when you're buying a dishwasher. The Table of test results shows which machines have which convenience drawbacks.

- Filters should be easy to remove and replace. Rinse-aid and salt dispensers should be easily reached for refilling.
- Hinged flaps and racks on the baskets and a handle on the cutlery basket can make loading and unloading easier.
- Make sure baskets slide in and out smoothly. The height of the top basket may be adjustable to let you fit in larger dinner plates below.
- Indicators that let you know when rinse aid and salt dispensers are empty are useful.
- Regulators let you set the water softener to suit the water hardness in your area, and also let you adjust the amount of rinse aid used in each wash – so you can use the smallest amount necessary.

Sizing up the options

A full-size dishwasher, which takes up about as much space as a front-loading washing machine, holds 12 or 14 place-settings, and is the obvious choice if you've got a family or entertain a lot. If you've got slightly less room, you might be able to fit in a slim dishwasher. The ones we've tested are only 41 or 45cm wide (instead of the normal 60cm), and take four or seven place settings.

Table-top machines take four or six place-settings. You can put one on a work surface or draining board, and either plumb it in or run it from the taps. Table-top models may have fewer programmes and features than larger machines. In particular they don't have built-in water softeners, so if you've got hard water, some of your washing up may be left with whitish spots.

NE550 table-top dishwasher, £150

Both our four-place-setting NE550s flooded and/or cut out during testing. Network Electronic Industries (NEI), the NE550's UK distributors, modified our machines. But the problems continued, and we stopped testing.

Our experience was matched by that of a *Which?* reader who had had two NE550s, both of which flooded. She sent us a letter from NEI to its service engineers which acknowledges the problem, and advises owners to 'rinse excess food and heavy grease from dishes before placing in the washer' and to 'avoid washing pots and pans'.

NEI tell us that all NE550s should have been modified, and that this should make flooding impossible. We're not convinced that the modification has solved all the problems, and this, together with the advice not to wash pots and pans, makes the NE550 a poor choice.

BUYING GUIDE

FULL SIZE

For a cheap 12-place-setting

BEST BUYS

dishwasher which will wash and dry satisfactorily: **Indesit D320BG**, £220

SLIM

We recommend the: **Servis**

GOOD VALUE

Secret Compact 4400 £220 (four place-settings, and built-in or built-under/ slide out design)

The **Bosch SPS5121** £330 is more expensive, but might be worth considering for its seven-place setting capacity.

TABLE-TOP

If space makes a table-top machine your only option, the **ASKO ASEA Cylinda 700** had good performance and takes six place-settings, but is expensive at £345.

In our original report we also recommended the **Bendix Table Top Compact 78868** (now discontinued – see page 285).

FACTS, FIGURES AND TEST RESULTS

1 Target price

What you should expect to pay if you shop around: where a model wasn't widely available in our price survey, we give the manufacturer's guide price in *italics*.

2 Dimensions

Dimensions are rounded up to the nearest centimetre where necessary. All of the full-size dishwashers are 85cm high (including the worktop) by 60cm wide by 60cm deep. (You may be able to remove the worktop if you want to put it *under* a work surface.)

Depth includes space needed at the back of the machine, eg for hoses, but doesn't include any controls at the front. Allow between 55cm and 65cm extra at the front for opening the door (up to 40cm for table-top dishwashers).

3 Water supply

Most dishwashers are intended to be plumbed into the cold water supply, but you can often use hot water instead. (Check first that your hot water doesn't exceed the manufacturer's recommended temperature: some recommend cold fill only.) If you do use the hot supply, this will be used for all the rinse cycles (some of which are usually cold), as well as for washing. So it's unlikely to save much money, even if your hot water is heated cheaply, although it may save some time.

One machine is hot-and-cold fill, and is connected to both pipes.

c = cold fill
C = cold fill recommended
h = hot fill (maximum recommended temperature in °C)
h/c = hot-and-cold fill

4 Place-settings

The maximum number of place-settings the machine will hold (dinner, soup and side plates, a saucer, cup, glass, knife and fork, and three spoons) with room for a few extra items.

5 Programmes

We tell you how many programmes the

DISHWASHERS

	Target price (1)	Dimensions h × w × d (2)	Water supply (3)	Place-settings (4)	Programmes (5)	Indicators (6 Features)	Regulators	Baskets	Other features
	£	cm							
FULL SIZE									
1 **AEG Favorit 420** (W Germany)[1]	300		h(70)c	12	4	irs	RS	bhl	FP
2 **AEG Favorit 667** (W Germany)	400		h(70)c	12	6	iors	SW	chu	FP
3 **Ariston Aristella LS1054** (Italy)[1]	280		h(60)/c,c	14	9	ors	RW	bhlu	F
4 **Hotpoint Super Plus 7821** (UK)	300		h(70)[3]c	12	3	iors	RS	c	FP
► 5 **Indesit D320BG** (Italy)	220		h(55)C	12	7	or	R	clu	—
6 **Miele G572** (W Germany)	550		h(60)c	12	7	irs	RS	ch	FP
7 **Philips ADG662** (W Germany)	330		h(70)C[5]	12	3	irs	RSW	chu	FP
8 **Philips ADG664** (W Germany)[1]	380		h(65)C	12	4	iors	RSW	chu	FP
9 **Servis Starlet 4153** (Spain)	300		c	12	6	ors	R	hu	F
10 **Zanussi DW41** (Italy)	350		h(60)C	12	4	iors	RS[6]	u	FP
SLIM									
► 1 **Bosch SPS5121** (W Germany)	330	85 × 45 × 60	c	7	5	iors	RS	ch	FP
► 2 **Servis Secret Compact 4400** (Italy)[1,8]	220	54 × 41 × 52	c	4	3	os	—	c	—
TABLE-TOP									
► 1 **ASKO ASEA Cylinda 700** (Sweden)[1]	345	50 × 54 × 63	h(80)C	6	3	—	R	—	FP

– = does not have this feature or not applicable
[1] Machine tested with old type of detergent, but not re-tested – see 'Performance'
[2] Hot-and-cold fill; includes cost of heating the hot water outside the machine with a gas boiler
[3] Hot-fill hose costs £11.50 direct from manufacturer
[4] No economy programme, or economy programme tested offers no significant saving in electricity and/or water; other programmes (if available) for lightly soiled loads, say, may give greater savings
[5] Hot-water-only conversion pipe for this model costs £16.68 direct from manufacturer
[6] Water softener regulator can be altered only by a service engineer

machine has. All have a *normal* programme, and most have a *rinse and hold* option to help stop food drying on items waiting to be washed; an *intensive* wash for pots and pans and heavily soiled items; a *slightly soiled* wash for things not needing much cleaning, and an *economy* programme – although this may save time rather than money – see 'Performance'.

Less common are a *delicate wash* for china and glassware; and *plate warm or dry*, which uses hot air to warm plates. In addition, there may be options for pre-washes, extra rinses, half-loads and drying without heat.

6 Features

Indicators

i = programme progress indicator
o = machine 'on' light
r = rinse aid refill indicator
s = salt refill indicator

Regulators

Let you control the amount of rinse aid used, alter the setting of the water softener to suit the hardness of your water, or regulate the water pressure for different types of loads.

R = rinse aid
S = water softener
W = water pressure

7 Performance – normal programme: Time	Electricity cost	Water consumption	Washing	Drying	Setting	7 Performance – economy programme: Time	Electricity cost	Water consumption	Washing	Drying	8 Convenience drawbacks	9 Stability (kg)	
■	□	□	(◩)	(◩)	economy 50°C	□	◩	◩	(■)	(□)	—	16	1
◪	□	◩	⧄	⧄	A 50°C	□	⧄	◩	◩	□	—	17	2
◪	◪[2]	◪	(◪)	(⧄)	2	□	□[2]	◪	(◪)	(⧄)	dh	18	3
◪	□	◩	(□)	(⧄)	[4]	[4]	[4]	[4]	[4]	[4]	h	23	4
◪	□	□	◩	□	[4]	[4]	[4]	[4]	[4]	[4]	cl	14	5 ◀
◪	□	◩	⧄	⧄	univ 55°C	□	◩	◩	◩	⧄	—	19	6
◪	◪	□	⧄	□	[4]	[4]	[4]	[4]	[4]	[4]	h	19	7
◪	□	◩	(◩)	(⧄)	[4]	[4]	[4]	[4]	[4]	[4]	h	13	8
■	◪	□	◩	◩	[4]	[4]	[4]	[4]	[4]	[4]	eg	16	9
◪	□	◩	⧄	⧄	[4]	[4]	[4]	[4]	[4]	[4]	a[7]h	18	10
□	◩	⧄	⧄	⧄	economy	□	⧄	⧄	□	■	—	13	1 ◀
□	◩	⧄	(◩)	(□)	light	◩	⧄	⧄	(◪)	(□)	—	—	2 ◀
□	◩	◩	(◩)	(⧄)	[4]	[4]	[4]	[4]	[4]	[4]	bc[9]h	18	1 ◀

[7] Manufacturer tells us this can be adjusted by a service engineer
[8] Top loading with hinged removable lid; must be either built-in so lid forms part of the work surface, or built-under so it pulls out like a drawer. Kit with runners for building under/sliding out £22
[9] Manufacturer tells us door catch has been changed

▶ Recommended in the Buying Guide ◀

KEY TO RATINGS **best** ⧄ > ◩ > □ > ◪ > ■ **worst**

Baskets

Adjustable baskets give extra flexibility for fitting in large or awkward items.

b = removable rack(s) or flap on upper basket
c = hinged top rack
h = handle on cutlery container
l = removable rack(s) on lower basket
u = upper basket height adjustable for different sized plates

Other features

F = adjustable feet for altering the height and/or levelling the machine
P = plug fitted

7 Performance

For each machine, we tested the highest temperature 'normal' programme with a full load of dirty dishes.

We then ran all its economy options *unloaded*, to find out which, if any, saved a significant amount of electricity and/or water; the economy programme results in the Table (based on an identical, full, dirty load) are for those programmes which saved most electricity and/or water (as opposed to those which just saved time).

Our crockery, cutlery and glassware was soiled with food which is especially difficult to remove: egg yolk, porridge and spinach on the plates, tea in the cups, and dried-on milk in the glasses. The dirty load was left in the machine overnight. After washing it the next day, we assessed a range of items to see how clean and dry they were. Apart from one hot-and-cold fill machine, we used cold water only.

On the whole, economy programmes we've tested don't wash as well as normal programmes. This is due to the lower wash temperature and/or shorter wash time which are responsible for the saving in electricity and/or water. Some manufacturers say that their economy programme is suitable only for lightly-soiled dishes, which may be the explanation for some of our disappointing results.

We've changed the type of detergent we use, from a specially-formulated detergent used in dishwasher testing all over the world to a leading brand of detergent which is widely available in the shops. We changed detergents because we were concerned about a decline in washing performance over the last two years; tests suggested our original detergent was at fault.

Machines tested with the old detergent, but *before* washing performance started to fall off, are still included in the Table, but are indicated by footnote [1], and performance ratings are shown in brackets. Because of the change in detergent these aren't strictly comparable with new results.

Time

◪ = Up to 60 minutes
□ = 61 to 75 minutes
◪ = 76 to 90 minutes
■ = 91 to 105 minutes

Electricity cost

Based on the average cost of full-price electricity (6.2p per KWh).

■ = 4 to 6.9p
◪ = 7 to 9.9p
□ = 10 to 12.9p
◪ = more than 13p

Water consumption

(see 'Green Guide')

■ = up to 20 litres
◪ = 21 to 30 litres
□ = 31 to 40 litres
◪ = 41 to 50 litres

8 Convenience drawbacks

We assessed how convenient each machine was to use – particularly opening and closing the door, using the baskets, dispensers, and controls, and cleaning the filter. We highlight any major drawbacks in the Table.

a = door tended to spring back up when opened
b = awkward rinse aid dispenser
c = awkward/uncomfortable door handle/catch
d = cramped basket design
e = confusing or awkward controls
g = basket 'stops' are easily overridden so loaded baskets can be inadvertently pulled out
h = filter awkward to remove and/or clean
l = awkward salt dispenser

9 Stability

We applied weights to the door to see how easily the machine would tip if, say, a child climbed on to it. (The average weight of a four-year-old child is 16kg.)

Other tests

Noise In comparison with other appliances, such as washing machines, none of the dishwashers was particularly noisy, but the Servis Starlet 4153 was slightly noisier than the others.

Electrical safety All the dishwashers were satisfactory in our tests, or have BEAB (British Electrotechnical Approvals Board) approval or are BEAB via CCA approved (another European approvals authority has tested the machine).

Water protection Back-siphonage (when dirty water is drawn back into the mains water supply) is a potential health hazard. All the dishwashers either have the UK Water Fittings Byelaws Scheme approval, or were satisfactory in our back-siphonage tests.

We also tested to see if any of the dishwashers would flood your kitchen if there were problems such as a power cut, a jammed programmer or an inlet valve sticking open. Early models of the Servis Secret Compact 4400 had no flood protection but the manufacturer says current production should be satisfactory.

Models similar to those in the Table

Model numbers match those in the appropriate section of the Table. Unless we say otherwise, similar models listed here are only cosmetically different. *Integrated* models are built-in, and can be fitted with a door panel to match kitchen units.

FULL SIZE

1 AEG 435, *£290*; AEG 435U, *£446*, built-in and 435i, *£500*, integrated.
2 AEG 665i, *£640*, integrated.
3 Ariston LS1044, £260, cold-fill only; Ariston ILS12 *£455*, built-in; Ariston KLS12, *£555*, integrated; Ariston LS1064, *£320*, cold-fill only, delay timer; Ariston LS1094, *£350*, delay timer, extra insulation.
4 Hotpoint 7870, £290 from Currys, adjustable upper basket.
5 Indesit D325BG, £240 from Currys; Indesit D321BG, £220, from Comet.
6 Miele G572i, *£650*, integrated.
7 Philips ADG660, *£300*, polypropylene interior; Bauknecht GSF 2130, *£320*, delay timer.
8 Philips ADG666, *£400*, more programmes; Philips ADG668, *£440*, more programmes and features.
9 Servis 4155, *£280*; Servis 4163/65, *£300*, more programmes.
10 Zanussi DW401, £300, fewer programmes, no hot air drying; Zanussi EDW407, £300, fewer programmes, no hot air drying, delay timer (exclusive to Electricity Board); Bendix 78488, *£340*; Bendix 78688, *£280*, fewer programmes, no hot air drying.

Dishwater safety
On some Candy, Kelvinator and Electra dishwashers made between 1986 and 1988, water can leak on to the electrics at the base of the machine. If you own one, look for a serial number ending D86, D87 or D88 on the top left-hand corner of the door frame. If yours has one, contact Candy on 051-334 2781 (ask for 'dishwasher recall') or write to Department A, PO Box 88, Wirral, Merseyside L62 3QW. They'll arrange for an engineer's visit and modification (free). Don't use your machine unattended until it's been fixed.

SLIM

1 Bosch SPS5122, *£390*; Bosch SPS6122, *£440*, extra programme; Bosch SPS2102, *£320*, fewer programmes; Bosch SP15320/2, *£560*, integrated; Hotpoint 7800, £300, fewer programmes; Hotpoint 6820, £500, fewer programmes, integrated; Siemens SR 1303, *£270*, fewer programmes; Siemens SR 1520, *£340*; Siemens SR 7523, *£570*, integrated; Neff 5523.25i, *£570*, integrated, push-button controls; Neff 5421.11S, *£523*, fewer programmes, built-in.

GREEN GUIDE

Energy
A dishwasher uses quite a lot of electricity – particularly on its hotter, more intensive programmes. Different models do vary in how much electricity they use, but only a few machines we've tested have economy programmes which combine good wash performance with real savings in electricity. The most energy-efficient way to use your dishwasher is to run it only when it's full.

Water
Dishwashers do vary greatly in the amount of water they use – by up to 20 litres on a normal wash programme. See the ratings under 'Water consumption' in the Table on page 90 for which machines use least water.

2 Bauknecht GSC4, *£250*, and Philips ADG 901, *£305*; Philips ADG 945, *£200* – none of these suitable for building in.

TABLE-TOP

1 ASEA 750, *£350*, more programmes.

'Similar models' are products which we would expect to perform similarly to ones we have tested. They may look different (cosmetic differences) or have slightly more or fewer features. They may be better suited to your needs than the tested models.

Consumers' Association produces a wide variety of books and Action Packs on different subjects. For a full list, write to CA at the ***Which?*** *Bookshop, 359/361 Euston Road, London NW1 3AL, or call in on Monday to Friday between 9.30 and 5.*

WASHING MACHINES

Front Loaders, Top Loaders and Washer-driers

From *Which?* January 1990

If space isn't a problem, you'll probably want a full-size front-loading machine. They'll take 4kg to 5kg of mixed cottons in the maximum load, and are designed to fit in with standard 60cm-width kitchen units. Most are around 85cm high, to fit neatly under worktops. If you want the front to fit flush with your unit doors, check the space any existing pipework takes up at the back: you could find your choice of machine will be limited.

Front loaders start at around £200. Typically, at the lowest end of the price range, you'll get a spin speed of 800 rev/min, few features, and little choice of programme. For around £250 to £350, you'll get more choice in features and more flexible programming options – as well as a selection of machines with good spinning performance, so your clothes should feel drier at the end.

If you can spend more than £350 – up to £450, say – you can buy a machine with very good performance all round. But paying this much doesn't necessarily guarantee you'll get good performance. With some models, you could well be paying for little more than high-tech appearance, flashing lights and programmes that you're not often going to use. You will certainly have to pay £400 or more if you want a model with suitable panels and fixings to co-ordinate with the colour scheme of your fitted kitchen.

Most of the machines described as being 'environmentally-aware' will also cost you over £400, but see 'Green Guide' on page 100.

Top loaders

A top-loading washing machine might be worth considering if you find it awkward to bend down far enough to use a front loader.

If space is tight, you may want to consider a drum-type top loader. These take the same maximum load as front loaders, and work in a similar way, except the opening to the drum is on the top: you load and unload by opening the top flap to put the washing in and reaching in to get it out. They're fairly awkward to use, but they're usually 15cm to 20cm narrower than full-size front loaders. You can't use one under the work surface; indeed, with heights of 88cm to nearly 90cm, you may not be able to fit one under it. But assuming the hoses are long enough, you could roll it out to use. Or you could fit one in a corner: they don't need space to open the door (though remember you'll have to be able to get to the filter to clean it).

If someone in your family is sensitive to the low-foaming automatic-type detergents, it would be worth investigating one of the few tub-type top loaders on the market. They've got an agitator in the middle of the stationary tub, and can use any washing powder or liquid detergent. They're over 100cm high, and take up no less floor space than a front loader; but they are less awkward to use than drum-type top loaders.

Top loaders start at around £370, but you can expect to pay over £400 for a maximum spin speed of 1,000 rev/min or more.

Compacts

If you're really tight for space, there are a few very small machines. They're about three-quarters the size of a full-size machine, and they take about half the usual maximum load. They wash satisfactorily, but they have low maximum spin speeds, so they'll leave your washing feeling quite wet. The top-loading AEG 280 Digitronic is smaller than most top-loaders, but it will still take 4.5kg in its maximum load.

Washer-driers

If you have the space for a full-size washing machine, but none to spare for a tumble drier as well, you could consider buying a washer-drier. They wash and tumble dry in one drum, but most will

BUYING GUIDE

FULL-SIZE FRONT-LOADING
£250 TO £350

BEST BUY **Hotpoint Electronic 800 De Luxe 9524** £300

The **Candy D4-104X** £280 didn't perform quite as well on the synthetic washing programme, but is £20 cheaper. The **Electrolux WH828 Electronic** *£340* performs well, but is more expensive.

The **Indesit 823** was originally recommended as a Best Buy but has been discontinued (see page 285).

£350 TO £450

GOOD VALUE If you want a computerised machine, the **Hotpoint Microtronic 1000 De Luxe 9554** £390 performs well

The **Hotpoint Electronic 9544** £370, with a spin speed of 1000 rev/min, is similar to the recommended 9524, but has more programmes, so may be worth considering.

GOOD BUT PRICEY The **AEG Lavamat 981 Sensortronic** £450 also performs very well all round

FULL-SIZE TOP-LOADING
The **Philips Slimster 850 T12 AWG090** £370 is worth considering if you want a top-loader

COMPACT
The **Candy Aquamatic 3** £280 is worth considering you want a compact front-loader

WASHER-DRIERS
In our original report we recommended the **Hoover A8548/50** as worth considering but this model has been discontinued (see page 285).

Remember that for many of our recommended machines, there are similar models with cosmetic differences which might suit you.

dry only about half of their maximum wash load at one time. This usually means you have to take some of the washing out between washing and drying, though some will take 3kg or so right through both cycles without stopping.

Most of them are condenser driers: they use cold water from your house supply to cool the warm, moist air so that it condenses and can be drained away. If you're worried about the amount of water they use for this process, you could consider an air-venting one. They blow the warm moist air out of the machine. To avoid condensation indoors, you should use a vent hose to direct this air outside through a window or a permanently installed vent in the wall.

WHAT TO LOOK FOR IN A WASHING MACHINE

Most of the washing machines and washer-driers we've tested will wash, rinse and spin at least satisfactorily. So you need to decide which programmes and features will be useful to you. Good spinning performance, low running costs, and convenience may also affect your choice.

Programmes and features: what do you need?

Standard wash programmes Most clothes that are machine-washable have care labels showing which programme is most suitable, in the form of wash-tub symbols. The new wash-tub symbols indicate both the wash temperature and the wash action recommended. All our tested machines claim to have programmes which will wash at the correct temperatures for most things.

Whichever labels are used, life's easier if the symbols are clearly displayed on the controls or a programme guide on the machine, where you can easily refer to them – not just in the instruction book, which can easily get lost.

Flexibility Some washing machines have their main programmes and temperature preset, so you have to set only one control (though there may be a separate economy button). With others, you set the programme and temperature you want separately; these may be slightly more complicated, but you gain greater flexibility.

Similarly, some machines have a pre-wash which is built in only to certain programmes, while others have pre-wash as a separate option which you can select. A separate option is more flexible, but could be inconvenient if it means having to go back to the machine to set the main programme; some machines have both types.

Built-in delay timers A built-in timer lets you use the machine at night without having to add a time-switch – useful if you have an Economy 7 meter for your electricity. But see 'Safety warnings'.

Remember that if a computerised machine doesn't have a built-in delay timer, it is unlikely that it can be used with an independent time-switch. This is because the machine can't be programmed until the electricity supply is connected: in other words, after the time-switch has operated.

Economy programmes These are available on most machines. The most common is half-load (or reduced load) which cuts down on the amount of water and detergent needed when you want to wash only a few things. But most 'half-loads' don't really halve the amounts of water, detergent or electricity used, compared with the machine's full load, so doing two half-loads is not as economical as waiting until you can do a full load.

Reduced-temperature washes are useful for lightly soiled clothes, or easy-care fabrics, and with biological detergents. Generally, they still use about the same amount of water as the main programme; you make your saving because they use less electricity.

A quick-wash programme may be useful for freshening up a lightly soiled load in about half an hour.

Wool programme All machines we've tested have a wool programme which has been approved by the International Wool Secretariat for washing woollens with 'Machine Washable' on the label.

Other wash programmes You may come across a 'multifabric' programme which allows you to mix different fabric types in the wash. It sounds useful, but it's a long, low-temperature soak, generally taking four to five hours. 'Drain' just means you can drain the water out without spinning if you want to drip-dry the washing. 'Cold wash' means just that: the machine only takes in cold water. 'No heater', on the other hand, means washing at the temperature of the incoming water.

Spin speeds: numbers aren't everything

As you can see from the Tables, the all-but-identical machine with the higher spin speed is the one that typically commands a higher price. Is the difference likely to be worth the extra?

For the same diameter drum, the faster a machine spins, the drier your washing is likely to be at the end. That, in turn, will cut the drying time – and, if you have a tumble drier, your running costs. For instance, a 4kg load of mixed cottons spun in a 1,000 rev/min machine takes about an hour to tumble dry, at a cost of about 13p. The time and cost would double if the same load were spun in a 500 rev/min washing machine.

But, as you can see from the ratings in the Tables, that's not the whole story. The difference between 850 and 1,100 rev/min, say, is not so critical. Some machines which claim upwards of 1,000 rev/min maximum spin speed never actually spin that quickly when loaded, or don't spin at that speed for very long; and some machines with lower claimed spin speeds spin for a longer time, so achieving good spinning efficiency. So don't be mesmerised by a fast spin speed for its own sake.

With delicate and easy-care fabrics, you don't want a roaring spin, which will scrunch them up, anyway. With most fast-spin machines, either there is a lower spin-speed option button, or a suitable speed will be selected automatically at the end of each programme. Some machines have a variable spin-speed control, so you can select a higher or lower spin speed if you want.

All our tested machines have 'spin delay' (sometimes called 'rinse hold'), which is useful if you aren't going to be around at the end of a programme. The washing sits in the last rinse water rather than settling into creases after having been spun.

Running costs: a balanced economy?

Detergent Some machines use detergent more efficiently than others, either by the way they circulate the wash water or by special valves on the drainage system. Others pre-fill the machine with some water before the detergent is washed from the dispenser, so not so much gets away. Not all of these efficient machines are self-consciously 'green machines' (see 'Green Guide'), though if you can use less detergent, there will be that much less of it for the waste system to deal with.

We've given a rating for detergent loss in our Tables; it reflects how much of the detergent you put in to the machine actually gets used. Some washing machines allow 25 per cent and more of the detergent to drop unused straight through the drum.

Electricity The electricity cost ratings in our Tables are based on the cost of washing full wash loads, using full-price electricity. For hot-and-cold-fill models, we have included the cost of heating the water outside the machine. These electricity costs will apply to you if your house hot water is heated by full-price electricity, whether you have a hot-and-cold or cold-fill machine. Assuming you wash one hot cotton load and four 'synthetic' washes a week, the cost would be between £4 and £7 a quarter.

In practice, many people don't pay this much, and others could reduce their costs. If you have an Economy 7 meter, and you run your machine only during the cheap-rate period, your running cost would be about a third of those figures.

Gas or oil, for example, also cost less to heat water than full-price electricity, reducing the washing costs a bit for hot-and-cold-fill. But, unless you're using Economy 7, the machine still needs some full-price electricity for its pump and motor, and to get the wash water hotter than that in your hot water taps for some programmes. And some machines fill only with cold water on some programmes; that water must be heated up.

Water Water metering is already being introduced in some places. It is planned that the traditional form of charging by rateable value will be banned from the year 2000, and metering is one of the alternative methods being looked at. This, combined with the rising cost of complying with European Community standards for the quality of our water, means that you should be thinking about the likelihood that you will be paying directly for the water you use.

All washing machines use a lot of water, but there are big differences between models. The best machines, which use less than 70 litres of water per wash, would, on current average water charges, cost no more than around £3.50 per quarter (assuming five washes per week). Machines which use over 100 litres per wash will cost upwards of £6.

Reliability and servicing: the breakdown story

When you're paying around £200 or more for a washing machine, you want to know how reliable it's likely to be. We monitor washing machines in use through our panel of members; they keep diaries on how often their machines break down and how quickly they can get things put right.

By analysing these records for machines which are at least three years old, but have been bought in the last five years, we can tell you how reliable machines of fairly recent production have been for 11 makers. We don't have enough recent machines of the other makes to allow us to comment. Compared with all machines in this age bracket (including other brands), **Zanussi** have been more reliable than average; **Ariston**, **Candy**, **Hotpoint**, **Indesit**,

Philips and **Servis** have been below average, while **AEG**, **Bendix**, **Electra** and **Hoover** machines have not been significantly different from the average.

According to our members, most repairers arrived within three days of being called. The **Hotpoint** repairers were rather quicker to respond than average, arriving within two days.

When they came, most **Indesit** repairers finished the job on the spot. Most of the other manufacturers' repairers needed another day or two, presumably to fetch parts or equipment they hadn't brought with them. But **Bendix** took four days, on average, and the **AEG** repairers seven.

We asked these 11 manufacturers about their call-out charges: how much their own repairers will charge just to come and look at your machine if something goes wrong. Many have arrangements with local repairers, so they emphasised that they could only offer an average charge. Some of the call-out charges cover labour for minor repairs, but it's often up to the engineer on the spot to decide how much labour is involved.

11 MAKERS COMPARED

	Breakdowns	Call-out	Completion	Charge
				£
AEG	—	—	x	23
Ariston	x	—	—	17
Bendix	—	—	x	17a
Candy	x	—	—	22al
Electra	—	—	—	21ael
Hoover	—	—	—	34hl
Hotpoint	x	√	—	21
Indesit	x	—	√	17
Philips	x	—	—	24al
Servis	x	—	—	11.50
Zanussi	√	—	—	18hl

√ = more reliable/quicker than average
x = less reliable/slower than average
— = average reliability/number of days
a = average charge, varies around the country
e = varies from Board to Board
hl = includes about an hour's labour
l = includes some labour

GREEN GUIDE

Washing machines generally have had a poor 'eco-image' for using a lot of water, and wasting a lot of detergent and energy because of poor design. But amidst the furore over specially designated 'green machines', we should point out that some manufacturers have for many years been making washing machines with energy-saving and water-saving features: it's up to you to make the best use of them.

The best way to save energy is to use the lower-temperature programmes, especially when your washing isn't all that grubby. Choosing a half-load option if you're not washing much is better than nothing, but waiting to wash a full load is better, for saving both energy and water.

Using pre-wash and lots of rinses may be reassuring, but is often not necessary. Think about using the shorter programmes if you can.

If you find a liquid detergent which suits you, you can virtually eliminate wasteful detergent loss by using a 'wash-ball'. You fill this with a detergent – usually liquid, though there is one specially concentrated powder – and put it directly into the drum.

Convenience: those little things

Convenience is a very subjective thing; one person's awkward door catch is, for another, one that will keep the children out. But it is possible to draw up a checklist of common convenience irritations, so we try to save you unpleasant surprises, like doors which can be opened when the machine is on rinse-hold.

Special needs We also give further guidance to people with disabilities. Most of the convenience drawbacks we look out for can be a problem for anyone: a small, smooth flat knob is annoyingly fiddly for anyone with a wet hand, and can be impossible to turn with an arthritic hand. A door which doesn't open very wide, and seems actively to obstruct attempts to use the machine, is a nuisance for anyone; a door which doesn't open right out can mean time-consuming manoeuvring when trying to load and unload for someone in a wheelchair.

SAFETY WARNINGS

Washing machine fires

The fire statistics for 1987 show that nearly 2,000 fires were started by washing machines and dishwashers. Given that there are more than 20 million of these appliances in our homes, 2,000 fires may not seem many. The trouble is, the number has doubled since 1981.

More use of plastics in these machines seems a likely cause, but a lot of detailed work needs to be done investigating how and when the fires happened before we know for sure. We've urged manufacturers and the Government to do this analysis.

If you want to use a machine at night, make sure you have strategically placed smoke detectors which will wake you up if there's a problem. And don't leave it on when you leave the house unless it's absolutely essential.

We'd like to hear of any experiences you've had with a washing machine or dishwasher fire in the last three years. Write to Dept PSS at Consumers' Association, 2 Marylebone Road, London NW1 4DX.

Creda washing machine recall

Creda have recalled some of their washing machines: water and detergent could leak on to wiring. If you own one of the following machines, don't use it unattended; contact Creda; ☎ (0800) 886688, or Creda-Care, PO Box 421, Stoke-on-Trent, ST11 9SH, to arrange a free check and modification.

The machines affected are **Creda** models **17011**, **17021**, **17022**, **17024** and **17221**; **Jackson** models **27401** and **27402**; and **Electra 17015**, **17016** and **17207**. Only those with a serial number ending **C188** to **C1288** or **C189** to **C389** are affected.

We didn't find this fault in our tests, and neither did BEAB; we've supported a call for a test for it to be included in the British Standard.

Hot washer-drier doors

During the drying cycle, glass doors on washer-driers tend to get hot; many manufacturers' instructions do warn you about this. But there have been alarming reports of children burning themselves on these doors.

During our tests on the **Candy Turbomatic 48WD** for this report, we found a temperature in excess of 112°C on the glass door. So we went back to look for high surface temperatures on our previously tested washer-driers. The **Candy Turbomatic 38WD**, which we have recommended previously (though it has now been modified so much that our performance results are no longer representative) had a similarly hot door, as do the other Turbomatic washer-driers.

Neither the British Standard for washing machines nor that for tumble driers sets a limit for the temperature of the doors. We use available medical evidence on the reaction of skin to hot surfaces to assess temperatures; our recommended maximum temperature for accidental contact with glass is 87°C.

Candy told us they are working on a protective guard that can be fitted over the door to stop children touching the glass. They are also looking into modifications to the machines themselves, to reduce surface temperatures.

In the meantime, if your washer-drier has an unprotected glass door, don't let small children play unattended near it during the drying cycle.

Servis/Electra washer-driers

A safety warning has been issued by Servis and Electra concerning certain models of washer-driers produced before August 1989. There is a risk that, in use, a wire may fracture and touch a rubber hose which could smoulder.

The model numbers with the serial numbers of the affected machines are listed in the Table below.

MODEL NUMBERS	SERIAL NUMBERS
SERVIS SAPPHIRE 9543	000004 TO 002332
SERVIS SAPPHIRE 9545	000004 TO 002039
SERVIS SAPPHIRE 9633	000005 TO 003096
SERVIS SAPPHIRE 9635	000003 TO 003004
SERVIS 1100 9700	000001 TO 005906
ELECTRA 9900E	000001 TO 002077

The risk of fire is small, but Servis warn that these machines should not be used unattended until a modification has been made. This can be arranged, free of charge, by phoning Freephone 0800 833 198, Mon to Fri and Sat morning; call if in any doubt. Or write, quoting daytime telephone number, to Servis Group Ltd, Washer Dryer Announcement, Darlaston Road, Kings Hill, Wednesbury, West Midlands WS10 7TE.

FACTS, FIGURES AND TEST RESULTS

All the tested machines will wash between 4kg and 5kg of mixed cottons in their maximum load, except for the Zerowatt Tropic (6kg) and the Candy Aquamatic 3 (3kg).

Maximum synthetic and delicate loads are usually smaller.

1 Types

We've divided our Tables into compact, front-loading and top-loading machines. Several manufacturers have changed their model ranges since we tested them, so we aren't able to include them in the Tables.

2 Target price

You should be able to match these target prices if you shop around. Prices in *italics* are manufacturers' guide prices for machines which were difficult to find in the shops.

3 Depth

Full-size front-loading machines will all fit in the space you'd need for a standard 60cm wide kitchen unit, and are about 85cm high, so will fit under the work surface. We give depth, including space for hoses at the back, but not for controls or knobs at the front.

The compact machines, front-loading and top-loading, are 65cm to 69.5cm high, and 45cm to 51cm wide. The non-compact drum-type top loaders are 88cm to 89.5cm high and 40cm to 45cm wide. The tub-type top loader in the Table is 104cm high and 56cm wide.

4 Controls/indicator lights

Controls

A = automatic; main programme is pre-set
M = manual; you set temperature, wash action, etc
b = has built-in delay timer
i = programme stage reached is indicated on the machine; either by symbols on the programme dial or by lights

Indicator lights

d = door locked
h = heater on
m = mains on
o = machine on
p = programme set
q = programme finished alarm
r = machine rinsing
s = spin delay
u = door unlocked
v = machine spinning
w = machine washing

5 Programmes

Pre-wash

A = automatic pre-wash before the main programme for the hot cotton wash (95°C), and possibly other programmes
M = manual; you can set pre-wash before any programme, then you have to go back to the machine to set the main programme

Other wash programmes

C = cold wash
H = half load programme or button; or machine automatically suits wash to load size
M = multifabric (long soak)
N = no heater
Q = quick wash
T = reduced temperature option(s)
V = variable thermostat (so you can reduce the temperature of a programme)
X = drain (for washing to be drip-dried)

6 Spin

Programmes

All have 'spin delay'. All but the Proline T1000 have 'rinse and spin', which, along with 'spin alone', is useful for clothes you've hand-washed.

S = spin alone
V = variable spin-speed button or selector

Maximum spin speed

The figures given are manufacturers' maximum stated spin speeds.

7 Washing test results

How clean Our performance tests are based on the maximum load for the programme indicated by the 'wash-tub' at the top of the column (on the 95°C programme for cotton, this will be the maximum load the machine can wash).

How long The time taken to complete a

wash will vary mainly with the temperature of the incoming water. The times are based on hot-fill at 60°C and cold at 15°C.

Water consumption The ratings are based on how much water, both hot and cold, is used in the washing programme. Assuming five washes a week, at current average metered water charges, those rated ▩ would cost about £3.50 per quarter, those rated ◪ or lower £6 or more per quarter.

C = cold-fill only
▩ = 0 to 70 litres
◩ = 71 to 85 litres
□ = 86 to 100 litres

WASHING MACHINES

		Target price [2]	Depth [3]	Controls/indicator lights [4]	[5] Programmes: Pre-wash	Other	[6] Spin: Programmes	Maximum speed	[7] Washing test results (95): How clean	How long	Water consumption	Electricity costs
		£	cm							hours		
	[1] COMPACT/top-loading											
	1 **AEG Lavamat 280 Digitronic** (W Germany)[D]	460	64.0	Mio	AM	CHQTVX	SV	1000	◩	1½	■C	◩
	[1] COMPACT/front-loading											
►	1 **Candy Aquamatic 3** (Italy)	280	43.5	A	A	TX	S	600	□	2	▩	◩
	[1] FRONT-LOADING											
	1 **AEG 561-W Electronic** (W Germany)	350	60.0	Mio	AM	CHQTVX	SV	850	◩	□	2	□
►	2 **AEG Lavamat 981 Sensortronic** (W Germany)	450	60.0	Mio	AM	CHQTVX	SV	1200	◩	1½	◩	□
	3 **Blomberg WA1210/88** (W Germany)	*640*	60.0	Mio	A	HTV	S	1200	◩	1½	□	□
	4 **Bosch V454** (W Germany)	350	58.0	Mio	A	CHQVX	S	800	◩	1½	□	□
	5 **Bosch WFK 6010** (W Germany)	500	58.0	Mdio	A	CHQTVX	SV	1100	◩	2	◩	□
►	6 **Candy D4-104X** (Italy)	280	51.5	Aio	AM	CHV	S	1000	◩	□	2	□
►	7 **Electrolux WH828 Electronic** (Italy)	*340*	58.5	Mio	AM	HVX	S	850	◩	1½	□	◩
	8 **Hitachi Autoset 1000** (UK)	400	57.0	Abhioq	AM	HMQTX	S	1000	◩	1½	□	□
	9 **Hoover Logic 800 A3780/78** (UK)	290	56.5	Aio	M	T	S	800	◩	1¾	◪	□
	10 **Hoover Logic 1200 A3786/88** (UK)	350	55.5	Ahiorsw	AM	HQT	S	1200	◩	1½	□	□
	11 **Hoover Computer Logic 1300 A3794/96** (UK)	420	56.5	Abdips	A	HMQTV	SV	1300	◩	1½	□	□
	12 **Hoover Logic 1300 A3790/92** (UK)	370	56.0	Abhioqrsvw	AM	HQT	S	1300	◩	1½	◪	□
►	13 **Hotpoint Electronic 800 De Luxe 9524** (UK)	300	54.5	Ais	M	HNQ	S	800	◩	1¾	□	□
►	14 **Hotpoint Electronic 1000 De Luxe 9544** (UK)	370	54.5	Aims	AM	HNQT	SV	1000	◩	1½	□	□
►	15 **Hotpoint Microtronic 1000 De Luxe 9554** (UK)	390	55.0	Abioprsvw	A	HMQT	S	1000	◩	1½	□	□
	16 **Hotpoint Micro Profile 1400 De Luxe 9565** (UK)	450	58.0	Abiopqrsvw	AM	HMQT	SV	1400	◩	2	◩	□
	17 **Indesit Omega W1130** (Italy)	285	53.0	Adho	A	CHQTX	—	1100	◩	2	□	□
	18 **Proline T1000** (Italy)[1]	220	56.0	Mo	A	HT	S	1000	◩	2	■C	□
	19 **Servis Quartz Plus 6032** (UK)	*350*	55.0	Abdhioprsu	AM	HMNQTX	S	1000	◩	1½	□	□
	20 **Zerowatt Spazio 081** (Italy)	*400*	45.0	Mo	A	CHVX	—	800	◩	2	◩	□
	21 **Zerowatt Mille** (Italy)	*460*	54.5	Mo	A	CHVX	V	1000	◩	2	◩	◪
	[1] TOP-LOADING											
	1 **Hotpoint Electronic 1050 De Luxe 9605** (UK)[T][2]	400	60.0	Aims	—	HNQT	S	1050	◩	2	■	■
►	2 **Philips Slimstar 850 T12 AWG090** (France)[D]	370	60.0	Ai	A	HQ	V	850	◩	1¾	□	□
	3 **Philips 1100 AWG013** (France)[D]	440	63.0	Mio	A	QTV	SV	1050	◩	1½	□	◩

[1] Exclusive to Comet
[2] No pre-wash option, but instructions suggest using HLCC5 or HLCC6 main washes
[D] Drum-type top load
[T] Tub-type top loader

◪ = 101 to 115 litres
■ = more than 115 litres

Electricity costs For the HLCC programmes, these ratings are based on washing full loads using full-price electricity at 6.2p per kWh.

Economy costs This rating is for electricity costs on an Economy programme. Many machines have more than one economy option; our rating is, where possible, based on a reduced-temperature full load; otherwise on a half-load programme.

The quarterly running costs assume you wash five loads a week on that programme.

Economy costs	How clean	How long (hours)	Water consumption	Electricity costs	Rinsing	Spinning	Detergent loss	8 Convenience: General drawbacks	Special needs drawbacks	Special needs good features	9 Unbalanced load	10 Noise	
◩	◩	1	□C	▩	□	◩	▩	cd	bgiko	EU	◩	□	1
◩	□	1	▩	▩	□	■	◪	adfr	knosx	—	◪	□	1 ◀
◩	◩	1	◩	▩	□	□	▩	j	—	—	◪	□	1
◩	◩	1	▩	▩	◩	▩	▩	j	●	ESUYZ	◩	□	2 ◀
◩	◩	1	◩	◩	□	▩	▩	hj	—	—	◩	◪	3
◩	◩	1¼	▩	▩	□	◩	□	j	—	—	◩	◪	4
◩	◩	1	▩	▩	◪	□	▩	fj	iksy●	OUX	◪	◪	5
◩	□	1	◩	◩	◩	◩	□	ajp	—	—	◩	◪	6 ◀
◩	◩	1¼	▩	▩	◩	□	□	prw	—	—	◪	□	7 ◀
□	□	¾	◩	▩	◩	◩	□	—	gkx	IJOSZ	◪	□	8
◩	◩	1	□	◩	□	□	□	—	—	—	◪	◪	9
◩	◩	¾	□	▩	□	◩	□	epv	—	—	■	■	10
◩	◩	1	□	▩	□	◩	□	o	kn	GIOSXZ	■	◪	11
◩	◩	¾	□	▩	□	◩	□	ep	gikny	U	◪	■	12
◩	◩	¾	◩	▩	◩	◩	▩	r	—	—	◩	◪	13 ◀
□	◩	¾	◩	▩	◩	◩	▩	r	—	—	■	◪	14 ◀
◩	◩	1	◩	▩	□	◩	▩	r	—	—	■	◪	15 ◀
◩	◩	1¼	◩	◩	□	▩	▩	—	—	—	▩	■	16
◩	◩	1	◩	◩	□	◩	◪	fhjp	—	—	◪	■	17
◩	□	1¼	■C	▩	◩	□	□	acjpv	giklnsyz	X	◪	□	18
□	◩	¾	□	◩	□	□	▩	—	—	GNOSUXZ	◪	◪	19
◩	□	1¼	▩	◩	◪	□	□	acehjp	iklnsyz	—	◩	□	20
◩	◩	1¼	▩	◩	□	□	□	acefhjp	giknosxyz	—	◩	◪	21
◪	◩	¾	■	□	□	◩	▩	—	—	—	■	□	1
◩	◩	1	▩	▩	□	◩	▩	cdfr	bgikoy*	—	◩	◪	2 ◀
◩	◩	1¼	□	▩	□	▩	▩	cdr	biksyz	U	□	◪	3

▶ Recommended in the Buying Guide ◀

KEY TO RATINGS best ▩ > ◩ > □ > ◪ > ■ worst

In practice, you'd probably use different programmes from time to time, which would slightly increase or reduce these figures.

- ◩ = less than 6.2p per wash (less than £4 per quarter)
- ◸ = 6.2p to 12.5p per wash (£4 to £8 per quarter)
- □ = 12.5p to 19p per wash (£8 to £12 per quarter)
- ◪ = 19p to 25p per wash (£12 to £16 per quarter)
- ■ = 25p to 31p per wash (£16 to £20 per quarter)

Rinsing If someone in your family is particularly sensitive to detergents, you may want to go for a rating of ◸ or ◩

Spinning This is especially important if you plan to hang your clothes inside to dry. Alternatively, the better the rating, the lower your tumble-drying costs will be.

- ◩ = cottons feel dry
- ◸ = cottons feel damp, but water can't be wrung out
- ■ = cottons feel wet

Detergent loss If you measure out the detergent you put into the machine by eye, or even if you carefully put in the amount recommended on the packet, many machines don't make use of all you put in. If 25 per cent of the detergent drops unused straight through the drum, you would be wasting a quarter of every packet of detergent you buy. The best machines lose less than five per cent, and some of these lose none.

- ◩ = loses less than 10 per cent
- □ = loses 11 to 20 per cent
- ◪ = loses more than 20 per cent

8 Convenience

General drawbacks Our testers use a checklist, drawn up over many years of testing washing machines, to pick out these drawbacks; check which ones matter to you. Think about actually using the machines when you go to look at them; play with the controls, and open the doors and detergent dispensers before you buy. A dash means we found no particular drawbacks.

- a = narrow door opening angle and loading/unloading awkward
- c = door catch awkward
- d = detergent dispenser not removable, difficult to clean
- e = detergent dispenser awkward to remove and/or replace for cleaning
- f = filter fiddly to remove/clean/replace
- h = no HLCC symbols, no programme guide on machine
- j = no wheels or castors to make it easier to move for cleaning; may be optional extra, but will raise the height of the machine
- m = minor controls stiff/have poor grip
- p = main programme control awkward
- r = no laminated worktop; may be optional extra
- v = poor visibility of programme settings
- w = dark window in door; difficult to see if stopped on 'rinse hold' with water in drum; these machines let you open the door during rinse-hold

Special needs For our assessment of features which are particularly useful, or problematic, for people with disabilities, we consider the needs of partially-sighted and blind people, wheelchair users, those with mobility problems, people with stiff or weak hands, and frail elderly people. However, most of the poor features we single out could be a problem for anyone. A dash in both columns means the machine has not been assessed.

Special needs drawbacks

- b = two hands needed to open door
- g = some force needed to open or close door

i = door catch hard to grip
k = sharp edges on door/dispenser/control
l = poor stop on dispenser, could be pulled out easily by mistake
n = door opens less than 90°
o = hard to get at dispenser
s = fine control needed to set programme accurately
u = dispenser compartment(s) small
x = some force needed to open dispenser
y = main programme control hard to grip
z = some force needed to operate main programme control

Special needs good features

E = programme stages identifiable by people who are blind
G = no force needed to open or close door
I = door catch easy to grip/use
J = easy to see labelling
K = large opening for loading and unloading
N = door opens fully
O = easy to get at dispenser
S = easy to set programme accurately
U = dispenser compartment(s) large
X = no force needed to open dispenser
Y = main programme control easy to grip
Z = no force needed to operate main programme control

Good for some people, a problem for others

★ = controls at rear top of machine
● = loading door opens to right

9 Unbalanced load

Putting a heavy towelling robe, for example, into a washing machine on its own may cause the machine to move across the floor. The best had no problems; those rated ■ 'jumped' on the initial spin or started moving.

10 Noise

Our ratings for noise are based on the noisiest part of the cycle (usually spinning)

□ = sound level similar to being inside a cruising motor coach
◪ = similar to nearby traffic in town
■ = similar to a vacuum cleaner 1m away (may interfere with telephone conversations in the same room)

Electrical safety

All the tested machines are either approved by the British Electrotechnical Approvals Board (BEAB), approved by BEAB via another European approvals authority or were satisfactory in our electrical safety tests.

WASHER-DRIERS: DRYING

See Key to washing machines Table for explanations and background on columns 2 to 10 in the 'Washing' part of the 'Washer-driers' Table.

Type

All tested machines were front-loading and had condenser driers.

4 Indicator lights

t = tumble drier on

8 Convenience

t = tumble drier control small with poor grip

12 Timer

The maximum time you can set in one go. At the end of the run, a cooling or airing cycle usually operates with the drum continuing to turn for a few minutes.

13 Heat settings

Machines have a low heat setting for drying more delicate fabrics or synthetics. All the tested machines have reverse tumbling,

WASHER-DRIERS: WASHING

	Target price (2)	Depth (3)	Controls/indicator lights (4)	5 Programmes: Pre-wash	5 Programmes: Other	6 Spin: Programmes	6 Spin: Maximum speed	7 Washing test results (95°): How clean	How long	Water consumption	Electricity costs	Economy costs
	£	cm							hours			
1 **AEG Lavamat 2060 Turbo** (W Germany)	750	60.0	Mio	A	CHQTVX	SV	1100	◤	2	◪C	□	◤
2 **Bosch V697** (W Germany)	650	60.0	Mhiot	A	CHQTVX	S	900	◤	1¾	◪	□	◤
3 **Candy Turbomatic 22WD** (Italy)	*400*	51.5	Mhiot	AM	CHV	S	800	◤	2	□	□	◤
4 **Candy Turbomatic 48WD** (Italy)[1]	430	51.0	Mbot	AM	CHVX	SV	1200	◤	2	□	□	◤
5 **Creda Supaspeed 17316** (UK)[2]	380	58.5	Aim	AM	HQ	SV	1150	◤	1½	◤	□	◤
6 **Electrolux WD1036** (Italy)	410	55.0	Aot	A	QX	S	1000	◤	1½	□	□	—
7 **Electrolux WD1038** (Italy)	400	60.0	Ao	AM	HTX	S	1000	◤	1¾	□	□	◤
8 **Hoover A8552/54** (UK)	440	57.0	Aost	M	HMT	S	1300	◤	1½	◪	□	◤
9 **Hotpoint 1000 De Luxe 9934** (UK)	440	56.5	Aimos	M	HQT	S	1000	◤	2	◤	◪	□
10 **Philips AWG 997** (Italy)	420	51.0	Mo	A	CHVX	SV	1000	◤	2	◪	□	◤
11 **Servis Sapphire 9633/5** (UK)	460	61.0	Abdhiost	A	HMQTX	—	1300	◤	1½	◪	□	□
12 **Zanussi Jetsystem WDJ1013** (Italy)	480	55.0	Miot	M	CHQVX	SV	1000	◤	2¼	◤C	□	◤
13 **Zanussi WDT1061** (Italy)	430	55.0	Adit	A	HQTX	S	1000	◤	1½	□	□	◤
14 **Zerowatt Tropic** (Italy)[3]	595	61.5	Mhot	A	HVX	S	1000	◤	1½	■	□	□

WASHER-DRIERS: DRYING

	Timer (12)	Heat settings (13)	14 Maximum drying load: Cotton	Towelling	Polycotton	Wash/dry maximum (15)	16 Drying test results – Drying time: Cotton	Towelling	Polycotton	Drying cost: Cotton	Towelling	Polycotton
	minutes		kg	kg	kg	kg						
1 **AEG Lavamat 2060 Turbo**	80	2	2.25	2.25	2.00	—	◤	◤	◤	□	◪	□
2 **Bosch V697**	120	3	2.75	2.75	2.00	2.75	◤	□	◤	□	■	□
3 **Candy Turbomatic 22WD**	[4]	2	2.50	3.00 (2.50)	1.50	2.25	◤	◪(□)	□	□	■(■)	◪
4 **Candy Turbomatic 48WD**[1]	120	2	3.00	3.00	1.50	3.00	◤	◪	◪	□	■	□
5 **Creda Supaspeed 17316**[2]	90	2	2.30	1.80	1.80	2.30	◤	□	□	□	◪	□
6 **Electrolux WD1036**	120	2	2.25	2.25	1.50	2.25	◤	□	◪	□	■	□
7 **Electrolux WD1038**	180	2	2.25	2.25	1.00	2.25	■	■	■	◪	■	■
8 **Hoover A8552/54**	120	2	3.00	1.50	1.00	3.00	□	□	□	□	◪	◤
9 **Hotpoint 1000 De Luxe 9934**	100	2	2.30	2.30	1.80	2.30	◤	□	□	□	◪	□
10 **Philips AWG997**	120	2	2.50	2.50	1.50	2.50	□	◪	□	□	◪	□
11 **Servis Sapphire 9633/5**	[5]	2	2.05	1.70	1.00	2.05	□	◪	◪	□	◪	□
12 **Zanussi Jetsystem WDJ1013**	120	2	2.25	2.25	1.50	2.25	□	◪	◪	◪	■	□
13 **Zanussi WDT1061**	120	2	2.25	2.25	1.50	2.25	□	□	□	◪	■	◪
14 **Zerowatt Tropic**[3]	120	2	4.00	3.00	2.50	4.00	◤	□	□	□	◪	□

[1] Very hot door: see 'Safety warning'
[2] Since our tests, manufacturers tell us they have increased the size of their recommended drying loads; this could affect performance ratings
[3] When we tested this machine, the recommended load of 7kg caused the door to bow and leak, and on one sample the catch broke. The manufacturers tell us the maximum load size they now recommend is 6kg, and that they are modifying the door. If you have had this problem with this machine, please send us the details, and if necessary, we will take it up with the manufacturers. Write to Dept PSS at our London address.
[4] Timer marked in ten programme divisions; ironing damp to bone dry
[5] 99min timer plus 10min cooling; can set for delicates and airing-only

	How clean	How long 50 (hours)	Water consumption	Electricity costs	Rinsing	Spinning	Detergent loss	General drawbacks	8 Convenience: Special needs drawbacks	8 Convenience: Special needs good features	9 Unbalanced load	10 Noise	
	□	1	◤C	▨	◪	◤	◪	cj	gi●	SYZ	▨	◪	1
	◤	1¼	□	◤	◤	◤	□	jp	—	—	◪	◪	2
	◤	1	▨	▨	◤	◪	□	ajp	—	—	◤	□	3
	□	1	▨	▨	▨	□	□	efjmptv	gklosuxyz	—	◤	□	4
	◤	1¼	◤	▨	◤	◤	▨	r	k	GIJNX	■	◪	5
	◤	1	▨	▨	□	◤	▨	rw	gknsz	OUX	◪	◪	6
	◤	1	▨	▨	◤	◤	▨	prw	—	—	◤	◤	7
	◤	¾	□	▨	▨	◤	□	eptv	gikny	U	◪	■	8
	◤	1	◤	◤	◪	◤	□	r	—	—	◪	■	9
	□	1¾	▨	▨	◤	□	□	ejpt	gksyz	K	◪	□	10
	□	¾	□	▨	▨	◤	□	—	gkx	IJNOSZ	■	◪	11
	◤	1	▨C	▨	◤	□	▨	apt	—	—	◤	□	12
	□	1	▨	▨	◤	□	▨	aejpt	gknsz	OUX	◤	□	13
	□	¾	□	▨	◤	◤	◪	aej	iklsyz	K	◪	◪	14

	Evenness: Cotton	Evenness: Polycotton	Tangling cotton	Creasing polycotton	17 Water consumption (condenser drying): Cotton	Towelling	Polycotton	
	□	□	◤	□	◤	◤	□	1
	□	□	◤	□	■	■	■	2
	□	□	◤	◪	□	◪	◤	3
	◪	◪	□	□	◤	■	◤	4
	◪	◪	□	□	▨	◤	◤	5
	□	□	◤	◪	◤	◤	◤	6
	□	◪	□	◤	◪	■	◤	7
	■	◪	□	◤	▨	▨	▨	8
	◪	◪	◤	◤	▨	◤	▨	9
	◪	◪	◪	□	◤	□	▨	10
	◪	◪	□	□	◤	◤	▨	11
	◪	◪	◤	◤	◤	□	◤	12
	◪	◪	□	◤	◤	□	◤	13
	◪	□	◤	◪	◪	◪	◪	14

KEY TO RATINGS best ▨ > ◤ > □ > ◪ > ■ worst

which changes the direction of the drum during drying and cooling cycles; this is supposed to reduce tangling and creasing.

14 Maximum drying load

We give manufacturers' recommended loads. The figure in brackets in this column, and the rating in brackets under 'Drying time', are for the smaller load the manufacturer recommends to reduce creasing.

15 Wash/dry maximum

The maximum amount of washing you could set the machine to wash and dry in one go. Remember, if you use a detergent 'wash-ball', you have to take it out between wash and dry cycles.

16 Drying test results

Our drying performance figures are based on maximum loads. The ratings for drying costs are for each kg of a full drying load. The overall drying time and cost for a full load varies according to the capacity of the drier, as well as the type and dampness of the load.

Drying time

◤ = between 15 and 30min per kg
□ = between 30 and 45min per kg
◢ = between 45 and 60min per kg
■ = over 60min per kg

Drying cost This is based on full-price electricity at 6.2p per kWh.

◤ = 2p to 3p per kg
□ = 3p to 4.5p per kg
◢ = 4.5p to 6.2p per kg
■ = over 6.2p per kg

Evenness

□ = fairly even
◢ = uneven with wet patches
■ = very uneven

Tangling cotton

◤ = slight tangling
□ = some tangling
◢ = moderate tangling

Creasing polycotton

◤ = little creasing
□ = moderate creasing
◢ = severe creasing

17 Water consumption

Condensing washer-driers take in water during the drying cycle, using it to cool the warm moist air so the water vapour condenses out and can be drained away. This adds to the total water consumption of the machine; our rating here is based only on the amount of water used during the drying cycle.

Assuming you wash five full loads a week, you'll probably use the drier part only seven times a week (not ten, because you probably won't dry every full wash load), machines rated ▨ would cost around £1.80 per quarter, and those rated ■ about £5 at current average metered water charges, for drying alone.

▨ = 0 to 25 litres
◤ = 26 to 40 litres
□ = 41 to 55 litres
◢ = 56 to 70 litres
■ = more than 70 litres

SIMILAR MODELS TO TESTED MACHINES

The machines in these Tables are similar in performance to our tested machines. Some are more up-market or down-market versions; some have more or fewer features, programmes and/or cosmetic differences. Some washing machines are sold exclusively by one retailer.

Also listed are similar models with a different spin speed from the tested model; their spinning performance could well be different, but otherwise they should perform much the same.

1 Types

This Table is split by type: front-loading and top-loading washing machines, washer-driers.

2 Target price

You should be able to match the target prices if you shop around. Prices in *italics* are manufacturers' guide prices for machines which were difficult to find in the shops.

3 Tested model

The number in this column matches the one next to the tested model in the appropriate part of the Tables.

For example, you can expect the AEG Lavamat 539 Electronic to perform in a similar manner to the AEG 561-W Electronic which is number **1** in the Table, under the front-loading washing machines heading, apart from having an 800rev/min spin speed, rather than an 850rev/min spin speed.

4 Differences

Spin speed = the number is the spin speed of the machine in this Table

C = cosmetic differences (eg in styling or colour) which have no effect on performance

P = programme differences (eg more or fewer programme options)

▶ Similar to models recommended in the Buying Guide ◀

[1] Exclusive to Electricity Boards; prices vary from Board to Board
[2] Exclusive to Currys
[3] Exclusive to Rumbelows
[4] Exclusive to Comet

Models for building-in

[A] Can be built-in or free-standing
[B] Version for building-in available

SIMILAR MODELS

	2 Target price	3 Tested model	4 Differences	
1 WASHING MACHINES/FRONT-LOADING				
AEG Lavamat 539 Electronic	340	**1**	800 spin speed	
▶ **AEG Lavamat 720**	*600*	**2**	CP	◀
▶ **AEG Lavamat 971 Sensortronic**	400	**2**	1000 spin speed	◀
▶ **AEG Sensortronic 693**	*530*	**2**	1400 spin speed CP	◀
▶ **AEG Sensortronic 770**	*800*	**2**	CP	◀
Aristocrat Logic 1300 A3640	*340*	**12**	C	
Blomberg WA1260	*725*	**3**	1250 spin speed P	
Bosch WFK 6410	*530*	**5**	C	
Bosch WFM 3010	400	**5**	900 spin speed CP	
Bosch WFM 3410	*430*	**5**	900 spin speed CP	
▶ **Candy D81X**	*280*	**6**	800 spin speed C	◀
Electra 695OE[1]	300	**19**	C	
▶ **Electrolux WH818**	280	**7**	C	◀
Hitachi FW131B/W	*430*	**8**	1300 spin speed CP	
Hitachi FW133B/W	*450*	**8**	1300 spin speed CP	
Hoover A3616[1]	285	**9**	C	
Hoover A3618/20[1]	370	**12**	C	
Hoover A3628[3]	350	**10**	C	
Hoover A3668[2]	300	**9**	C	
Hoover A3770[4]	280	**9**	C	
Hoover A3798	*350*	**10**	1000 spin speed C	
Hoover A3802	*280*	**9**	C	
Hoover A3804	340	**10**	1100 spin speed C	
▶ **Hotpoint 9513W[2]**	280	**13**	CP	◀
▶ **Hotpoint 9519W[3]**	280	**13**	CP	◀
▶ **Hotpoint 9533W/P[2]**	350	**14**	CP	◀
▶ **Hotpoint Electronic 1000 Plus 9534**	350	**14**	CP	◀
▶ **Hotpoint Electronic 800 Plus 9514**	280	**13**	CP	◀
Indesit Exc 1100	*290*	**17**	C	
Indesit Omega W1032[3]	280	**17**	1000 spin speed C	
Indesit Omega W1035[2]	300	**17**	1000 spin speed C	
Indesit Omega W1232[3]	300	**17**	1200 spin speed C	
Servis Electronic 3301/5	310	**19**	CP	
Servis Quartz 6033/4/5/6	350	**19**	C	
Servis Sapphire 6043/4/5/6	380	**19**	CP	
Servis Sapphire 6063/4/5/6	*420*	**19**	1300 spin speed CP	
Siemens WV2760	*350*	**4**	C	
Zerowatt ZW258	*440*	**21**	800 spin speed C	

	2 Target price	3 Tested model	4 Differences
1 WASHING MACHINES/TOP-LOADING			
AEG Lavamat 480 Digitronic	*470*		65cm version of the AEG Lavamat 280 Digitronic – a compact top loader

	2 Target price	3 Tested model	4 Differences
1 WASHER-DRIERS			
AEG Lavamat 2040 Digitronic	600	**1**	CP
AEG Lavamat 2045 Digitronic [A]	675	**1**	CP
Bosch V695	600	**2**	C
Bosch V698	*1,020*	**2**	C
Bosch V6982[B]	*650*	**2**	C
Candy Turbomatic 26WD	*400*	**3**	C
Creda 17308 Supaspeed XL[1]	420	**5**	CP
Creda 17317 Supaspeed SDL	420	**5**	CP
Electrolux WD1039	*430*	**7**	CP
Electrolux WD3000	460	**12**	C
Hoover A8500[1]	*430*	**8**	C
Hoover A8544[2]	370	**8**	C
Hoover A8568	*420*	**8**	C
Hotpoint 9924WD	400	**9**	800 spin speed P
Neff 5061.13S	*1,030*	**2**	C
Servis Sapphire 9543/4/5/6	430	**11**	1000 spin speed CP
Siemens WV9600[B]	*650*	**2**	C
Zanussi Jetsystem WDJ1015	500	**12**	C
Zanussi WDJ1055 B/W	*480*	**13**	C

WHAT THE WASH-TUB SYMBOLS MEAN

A new system for care labelling for clothes was introduced in 1987. You may see the new wash-tubs referred to as either HLCC (Home Laundry Consultative Council), ITLC or ITCLC (International Textile Care Labelling Code) symbols. Both new and old symbols will be in use.

The new symbols show wash temperture and wash action recommended. The bar under the new symbol indicates the action: no bar means normal ('maximum') action; a single bar means reduced (medium) machine action; a broken bar means much reduced ('minimum') action. You can mix loads if you use the lowest temperature and/or the most reduced wash action shown on the label.

Old	New	Examples of application
1 / 95	95	White cotton and linen articles without special finishes
2 / 60	60	Cotton, linen or viscose articles without special finishes, where colours are fast at 60°C
3 / 60	60 (bar)	(Not used in UK) White nylon and white polyester/cotton mixtures are included in 50 (bar)
4 / 50	50 (bar)	Nylon; polyester/cotton mixtures; polyester cotton and viscose with special finishes; cotton/acrylic mixtures
5 / 40	40	Cotton, linen or viscose articles, where colours are fast at 40°C but not at 60°C
6 / 40	40 (bar)	Acrylics, acetate and triacetate, including mixtures with wool; polyester/wool blends
7 / 40	40 (broken bar)	Wool, wool mixed with other fibres; silk
8 / 30	30 (bar)	(Not used in UK) See items included in 40 (broken bar) and 40 (bar)
9 / 95	95 (bar)	(Not applicable in UK)
		Hand wash (Do not machine wash)
		Do not wash

*The ratings given in the Tables are based on **Which?**'s latest tests of each product. The date of the original report is noted just below the main heading.*

TUMBLE DRIERS

Air-vented and Condenser Driers

From *Which?* October 1990

There's something cheerful about a line of freshly-laundered washing snapping in the sunshine – until the rain comes, and you have to rush out to pull everything indoors. To help you beat the British weather, and if you haven't got anywhere outside to dry your washing, we've looked at 33 tumble driers, including the first gas-heated model to be generally available in the UK. And we show you what you get for your money, and what features are worth paying for.

Drying with gas

Gas-heated tumble driers are common in laundrettes in this country, and Americans have been using them in their homes for years. We've tested the **White Knight BG411**. It's about the same size and capacity as an ordinary tumble drier, and it still needs electricity to turn the drum and operate some of the controls. But instead of heating the circulating air with electric heating elements, the White Knight uses gas: it's connected to the supply by a flexible pipe at the back. You must have a window or vent open in the room when you use it, though you don't need a flue.

It costs £225 from British Gas showrooms (including installation in a room which already has a gas supply), which makes it around £90 more expensive than our Best Buys for basic all-electric full-sized models. But the White Knight will cost around £4 to run per quarter, compared with around £12.50 for an ordinary drier using full-price electricity. The **Cannon RA10**, £272, with reverse tumble, and **Parkinson Cowan 45GT**, £300, with reverse and intermittent tumble, are similar models and should have similar performance.

Tumble types

Air-vented: full-size

These will generally dry a 4 to 5kg mixed cotton washload in around an hour and a half. Air-vented ones blow the damp air out of their exhaust vents. To avoid condensation, you should direct this damp air outside, through a window or hole in the wall, by means of a vent hose (usually £10 to £20 extra from the machine manufacturer). All we've tested vent from the rear, but some can have hoses fitted to the side, or front, instead. They usually have a timer, often with a maximum of 120 minutes, two heat settings (the lower setting for delicate or synthetic fabrics), and a cool tumble at the end of the cycle. Reverse tumble changes the direction in which the drum revolves during drying and cooling, in an effort to reduce tangling and achieve more even drying. Intermittent tumble means that the drier tumbles the clothes occasionally, after the drying cycle has finished, to minimise creasing.

To protect clothes from overheating, and to save electricity, some basic machines have temperature sensors which lower the heat as the load gets drier.

But you still have to set the timer, and the machine will continue for the set time.

Air-vented: compacts

If you are pushed for space, or rarely have much to dry, think about a compact drier. Most take about the same time to dry their smaller maximum loads, but perform about as well, as the full-size ones do with theirs. They have most of the basic features, but some vent from the front only.

Air-vented with programmed drying

These have programmes which you select depending on the type of fabric you want to dry, and the level of dryness you want: ironing damp or bone dry, for example. The drier will stop itself when its sensors detect that the load is dry enough. Separating loads into fabric types will get the best out of autosense programmes.

Condenser

If you can't position your drier so that it can vent the moist air away through a window or wall, choose a condenser model. These cool the air so that the water condenses out of it and collects in a storage tray in the drier or, in some cases, it can be piped away. But you'll have to pay a lot more for a condenser drier.

GREEN GUIDE

The drier washing is before tumble drying, the more energy, as well as time and money, you'll save: use a washing machine with good spinning efficiency.

BUYING GUIDE

AIR-VENTED: FULL SIZE

BEST BUYS **Philips Whirlpool AWB650**, £130 (and similar **White Knight Sensordry Dual Heat**, *£135*)

The **Creda Reversair Sensadry 37543/44**, *£155* (and similar **DL37545/46**, *£165*, and **Electra 37465**, £150) and **Electra 37463**, £160, also rated highly and are good value.

The gas-powered **White Knight BG411**, £225, is pricey, but performs well and has very low running costs.

AIR-VENTED: COMPACTS

BEST BUY **Creda Compact Reversair 37324**, £120, is the best performer of the smaller machines.

AIR-VENTED WITH PROGRAMMED DRYING

BEST BUY **Creda Sensair 37549**, £220, performs well at a price below the competition.

The **AEG Lavatherm 630**, £320, is very good, but pricey.

CONDENSER

If you need a condenser drier the **AEG Lavatherm 740**, £470, has programmed drying and performs well.

A word of warning
Children climbing into driers can suffer horrific accidents if the machine begins to operate. The doors of the full-size Hotpoint machines in our Table can be locked shut. The **AEG Lavatherm 630** and **740, ASKO Asea 7002, Bosch WTL4610** and **Miele Novotronic T454** have an 'on' switch which has to be reset every time the door is opened. This provides an additional level of safety. We are pressing for safeguards like this to be a requirement of the British Standard.

FACTS, FIGURES AND TEST RESULTS

1 Type
We've divided our Table into four sections; each type will suit different needs (see text). Numbers or letters following an oblique (/) in the model name indicate different colours.

2 Typical price
This is the price you can expect to pay; if you shop around, you may get £10 to £20 off some machines. Prices in *italics* are manufacturers' guide prices for machines we didn't find so widely available.

3 Stacking kit
We give the manufacturer's price for a kit which allows you to stack your tumble drier on a washing machine of the same make.

4 Dimensions
Rounded up to the nearest centimetre.
Check dimensions carefully on a model you want to fit in with your existing kitchen units. You may need extra space: up to 20cm for driers which vent from the side or rear.

5 Indicators/Controls
B = finish buzzer
D = door release button
F = filter-needs-attention light
M = machine-on light
O = on/off control
T = built-in delay timer
A built-in delay timer means you can pre-set the drier to use cheaper Economy 7 electricity, if you have the right meter. You could use a separate time-switch with most other driers. If you plan to use a machine at night, make sure you have smoke detectors which will wake you if there's a problem.

6 Other features
C = castors, wheels or rollers
G = drying guide on drier
H = vent or drain hose included in price
I = intermittent tumble (see text)
L = loading door can be locked shut
P = plug fitted
R = reverse tumble (see text)
W = laminated worktop

7 Capacity
We give the manufacturer's recommended maximum loads (brackets indicate where towelling load differs from mixed cotton).

8 Performance
To compare driers which have different maximum capacities, we base our performance ratings on the time taken and cost per kilogram for each type of load. We rinsed and spun our towelling and cotton loads using a washing machine with a maximum spin speed of 1,000rpm. Polycotton loads were spun at 500rpm.

TUMBLE DRIERS

	2 Typical price	3 Stacking kit	4 Dimensions h x w x d	5 Indicators/Controls	6 Other features	7 Capacity: Cotton/towelling	Polycotton
	£	£	cm			kg	kg
1 AIR-VENTED: FULL SIZE							
1 **Bosch WTA 2310** (W Germany)	290	37	84 x 60 x 58	M	GPRW	4.5 (5.0)	2.0
2 **Candy Turbo Dry D7R** (Italy)	*200*	10	85 x 60 x 55	MO	GRW	4.5	2.0
▶ 3 **Creda Reversair Sensadry 37543/44** (UK)	*155*	16	85 x 59 x 58	—	CGR	5.0[1]	3.0
▶ 4 **Electra 37463** (UK)[2]	160	12	85 x 59 x 58	T	CP	4.5[3]	3.0
5 **Electrolux WT252** (Italy)	190	7	85 x 60 x 57	DM	GPR	4.5	2.0
6 **Hoover Logic D6530/32** (UK)	190	9	85 x 59 x 56	DMO	CGRW	4.5	2.0
7 **Hoover Autosense D6526/28** (UK)	150	—	85 x 59 x 50	—	GW	4.0	2.0
8 **Hotpoint Reversomatic Dryer Plus 9325W/A/P** (UK)	180	7	85 x 60 x 50	T	CGHLPR	4.1 (3.0)	2.0
9 **Hotpoint Plus 9315W/A** (UK)	150	7	85 x 60 x 57	—	GLP	4.1	2.0
10 **Hotpoint Reversomatic Deluxe 9335W/A/P** (UK)	210	7	85 x 60 x 58	BDMT	CGHILPR	4.1	2.0
11 **Indesit TD1000** (UK)	160	13	85 x 59 x 58	T	CGW	4.0	3.0
▶ 12 **Philips Whirlpool AWB650** (UK)[4]	130	25	85 x 60 x 53	—	—	4.5	2.0
13 **Philips Whirlpool AWB672 Deluxe** (UK)[5]	180	25	85 x 60 x 53	—	CGHPR	4.5	2.0
14 **Servis Gem 260W/B/A/C** (UK)	*180*	19	85 x 56 x 55	D	CGRW	4.0	1.8
15 **Servis Quartz Plus 2703/4/5/6** (UK)	190	19	85 x 56 x 55	DMOT	CGIRW	4.0	1.8
16 **White Knight Sensordry Deluxe CL511** (UK)	*160*	16	85 x 60 x 53	MO	CGHIPR	4.5	2.0
▶ 17 **White Knight BG411** (UK)[6]	225	16	85 x 60 x 57	—	CGWP	4.5	2.25
1 AIR-VENTED: COMPACTS							
1 **Bendix 74688** (UK)[7]	120	—	68 x 50 x 46	—	PR	3.0 (1.7)	1.3
2 **Bendix 74488E** (UK)[7]	140	—	68 x 50 x 59	T	PR	4.0 (2.25)	1.75
▶ 3 **Creda Reversair 37324** (UK)	120	—	67 x 49 x 48	F	CR	3.0	2.0
4 **Hotpoint Deluxe 9304W/A** (UK)	115	—	68 x 50 x 54	—	GHP	2.7	1.2
5 **Servis 2154** (UK)	100	—	67 x 49 x 43	—	—	3.0 (1.3)	1.3
6 **White Knight Sensordry CL311** (UK)	105	—	67 x 51 x 53	—	CGH	3.0	1.5
1 AIR-VENTED WITH PROGRAMMED DRYING							
▶ 1 **AEG Lavatherm 630** (W Germany)	320	40	85 x 60 x 60	BDMOT	IPRW	5.0	2.0
2 **ASKO Asea 7002** (Sweden)[8]	*400*	√	82 x 60 x 60	BMO	HP	5.0[1]	2.2
3 **Bauknecht TRA 965WS** (W Germany)	*340*	23	85 x 60 x 60	BFMO	GIPRW	5.0[1]	2.5
▶ 4 **Creda Sensair 37549** (UK)	220	16	85 x 59 x 58	BFMT	CGHIRW	5.0[3]	3.0
5 **Hoover Computer Logic D6538/40** (UK)	*270*	9	85 x 59 x 57	BDFMO	CIRW	4.5	1.8
6 **Hotpoint Sensor Deluxe 9345W/A/P** (UK)	290	7	85 x 60 x 58	BDFMOT	CHILPRW	4.1 (3.0)	2.0
7 **Miele Novotronic T454** (W Germany)	500	40	84 x 60 x 60	BDMO	GIPRW	5.0	2.0
1 CONDENSER							
▶ 1 **AEG Lavatherm 740** (W Germany)	470	40	85 x 60 x 60	BDFMO	GIPRW	5.0	1.5
2 **Bosch WTL 4610** (W Germany)	*500*	37	84 x 60 x 58	BMO	IPRW	4.5 (5.0)	2.0
3 **Creda Condensair 37550** (UK)[9]	300	16	85 x 59 x 58	FM	CGRW	4.5	3.0

▶ Recommended in the Buying Guide ◀

KEY TO RATINGS best ◩ > ◪ > □ > ◪ > ■ **worst**

[1] We tested with 4.5kg; manufacturers have increased stated maximum capacity, which could affect the results
[2] Electra models available from Electricity Companies. Prices vary from region to region.
[3] We tested with 4kg; manufacturers have increased stated maximum capacity, which could affect the results
[4] Being superseded by similar Philips Whirlpool AWG210
[5] Being superseded by similar Philips Whirlpool AWG220/1

8 Performance: Drying Time – Cotton	Drying Time – Towelling	Drying Time – Polycotton	Drying Cost – Cotton	Drying Cost – Towelling	Drying Cost – Polycotton	Evenness	Tangling	Creasing polycotton	9 Convenience drawbacks	10 Electrical safety	11 Stability	
▨	◩	▨	□	□	□	□	□	□	A	√	13	1
◩	□	◪	□	◪	□	□	□	□	—	√	5	2
◩	□	▨	□	◪	◩	□	□	□	—	B	11	3 ◀
◩	□	▨	□	◪	◩	□	◩	□	—	B	15	4 ◀
▨	◩	□	□	◪	□	□	◩	◩	ACN	B	16	5
◩	□	◩	□	◪	□	□	□	□	E	B	15	6
◩	□	□	□	◪	□	□	◩	□	E	B	12	7
◩	◪	□	□	■	□	□	◩	□	E	B	10	8
□	◪	□	□	◪	□	□	□	□	EN	B	14	9
◩	◩	◩	□	◪	□	□	◩	□	BEN	B	12	10
◩	□	□	□	◪	◩	◪	□	□	—	B	10	11
◩	□	◩	□	◪	◩	□	◩	□	—	B	10	12 ◀
◩	□	◩	□	◪	□	□	◩	◩	—	B	22	13
□	◪	■	□	◪	◩	◪	□	□	—	√	9	14
□	■	■	□	◪	◩	□	▨	□	—	B	14	15
◩	□	■	□	◪	◩	□	□	◩	—	B	9	16
◩	◩	◩	▨	▨	▨	◪	□	□	—	√	9	17 ◀
◪	■	■	□	◪	□	□	□	◩	DE	B	7	1
◩	■	■	□	◪	□	□	□	◩	DE	B	10	2
□	◪	◩	□	◪	◩	□	▨	◪	—	B	8	3 ◀
□	■	□	□	■	□	◪	◩	◪	D	B	14	4
■	■	■	◪	◪	□	□	◩	◩	CE	B	5	5
□	■	■	□	◪	□	□	□	◩	—	B	9	6
▨	◩	□	□	□	◩	□	◩	◩	A	√	12	1 ◀
◩	◩	◩	□	◪	□	□	◩	◩	f	√	14	2
□	◪	◩	□	◪	◩	□	◩	◩	—	√	18	3
◩	□	▨	□	◪	◩	□	◩	□	—	D	18	4 ◀
◩	□	◩	□	◪	◩	□	□	◩	E	B	11	5
◩	◪	◩	□	◪	□	◪	□	◩	EN	B	13	6
▨	◩	▨	□	□	◩	□	◩	◩	—	√	11	7
▨	◩	◪	□	◪	□	□	□	□	—	√	15	1 ◀
◩	□	◩	□	◪	□	□	◩	□	—	√	11	2
◪	■	□	□	◪	□	□	□	□	—	B	9	3

[6] Price from British Gas (see text)
[7] Current, re-designed, door may be more convenient
[8] Manufacturer tells us current production has higher power fan: could affect performance
[9] Being superseded by similar Creda Condensair 37551

Drying time
◩ = less than 15 minutes per kg
◤ = 15 to 20 minutes per kg
□ = 21 to 25 minutes per kg
◪ = 26 to 30 minutes per kg
■ = more than 30 minutes per kg

Drying cost
Based on full-price electricity at 6.7p per kWh (and gas at 42.8p per therm):
◩ = less than 2p per kg
◤ = 2p to 3.5p per kg
□ = 3.5p to 5p per kg
◪ = 5p to 6.5p per kg
■ = more than 6.5p per kg

The overall drying time and cost for a full load varies according to the capacity of the drier as well as the type and dampness of the load. But, on average, drying two cotton loads, two towelling and two polycotton a week, will add around £12.50 to your quarterly electricity bill. On Economy 7 cheap-rate electricity, it would cost around £4.50 per quarter, about the same as a gas-heated drier.

Evenness
The combined rating shown is for full cotton and polycotton loads
□ = fairly even
◪ = uneven with wet patches

Tangling
◩ = no tangling
◤ = slight tangling
□ = moderate tangling

Creasing
Manufacturers sometimes suggest that you dry half the recommended polycotton load to reduce creasing; when we tested this, the smaller loads were less creased, but typically took about five minutes longer per kg.
◤ = slight creasing
□ = moderate creasing
◪ = severe creasing

9 Convenience drawbacks
A = fitting/using vent hose awkward
B = vent hose not removable for storage
C = loading/unloading awkward
D = door awkward to use: narrow grip or force needed to open or close it
E = filter awkward to remove and clean (manufacturers recommend that fluff filters be cleaned after each cycle)
F = can't be pre-set to use Economy 7
N = comparatively noisy (when tested with a full cotton load): could be annoying, especially if used at night

10 Electrical safety
All the driers passed our electrical safety tests (√) or are approved by the British Electrotechnical Approvals Board (B).

11 Stability
We put weights on the open doors of the driers to simulate a small child climbing on them. We give the weight at which either the drier tipped forward, or the hinge or door distorted or broke. As a guide, the average weight of a four-year-old child is 16kg.

Reliability
Tumble driers are, on the whole, fairly reliable. Our domestic appliance reliability survey shows no outstandingly reliable brands.

Key to Table
√ = satisfactory in our tests/included in price
— = does not have this feature/not supplied by manufacturer

SIMILAR MODELS
These machines are similar in performance to our tested machines. They may have more or fewer featurers and/or cosmetic differences. Numbers in **bold** show the driers in the Table to which the models are similar.

Full-size

3 Creda 37542, *£145*; DL37545/46, *£165*; SDL37547, *£190*; Electra 37465, £150

6 Hoover D6534/36, £220

8 Hotpoint 9371, £190 from Currys

9 Hotpoint 9370, £160 from Currys

11 Indesit TD105, *£140*

12 White Knight Sensordry Dual Heat, *£135*

15 Servis Sapphire Autodry 2753/4/5/6, £200

17 Cannon RA10, £272; Parkinson Cowan 45GT, £300: both prices include installation (see text)

Compact

3 Creda 37325, £110; Electra 37288, £105

4 Hotpoint 9303W/A, £110

5 Servis 2164, *£120*

6 Carlton 3101, £100 from Currys; Philips Whirlpool AWG200, *£120*; Zanussi TD61, £110

Consumers' Association takes no advertising in any of its publications. It pays for all the goods and services it reviews. It receives no money from Government, trade or industry. All its income is derived from sales of its magazines, books and research. It is independent of all interests other than those of the consumer. It allows no exploitation of its recommendations in advertising or promotion. If readers of this guide see any ad making use of CA material in the press, in catalogues or in shops, please send details to Consumers' Association, Dept AWM, 2 Marylebone Road, London NW1 4DX.

VACUUM CLEANERS

Upright and Cylinder Models

From *Which?* May 1990

We help you to choose the type of vacuum cleaner that will suit you best, and give verdicts on two more expensive cleaners which claim to have special advantages. We don't think they're worth the extra.

Upright or cylinder?

Uprights pick up more dust than cylinders – that's what our practical tests have shown. With their revolving brushes and beater bars they pick up much more dust than cylinder cleaners which rely solely on suction. An upright's brushes also help remove fluff and cat or dog hairs, and can improve the surface appearance of cut-pile carpets (as opposed to looped pile).

One advantage of a cylinder cleaner is its better manoeuvrability for cleaning around and under furniture – cleaning under a bed or sofa, for example, is no problem with almost any cylinder cleaner, but uprights need a clearance of about 15cm to 20cm, unless you use their hose attachments.

But a lot depends on the type of carpets you have and the type of dirt that gets trodden into them – sand and heavy grit (which can damage carpet fibres) tend to penetrate deep down in the pile where they are difficult to remove with suction alone.

Upstairs, downstairs

Cleaning stairs with an upright cleaner or a cylinder which will not stand on a stair can be a problem, particularly if the reach from the machine is limited and it is too heavy for you to hold with one hand. Most cylinder cleaners are now designed so that they can stand on one end and be lifted from stair to stair by the handle at the other end. (It helps if the air does not comes out at the end it stands on – it may get blocked by a thick stair-carpet.) Telescopically adjustable tubes are good because you can shorten them for convenient cleaning of stairs above where you are standing.

Suction power

Advertisements for vacuum cleaners often stress how powerful they are, basing this on the wattage of their motors. But this can be misleading. Some cleaners are much more efficient than others at creating suction. In one of our tests we measure suction power, and we've found that this often bears little relationship to the rated wattage of the cleaner. You'll need strong suction for cleaners with a turbo nozzle – these depend on the air flow to make a brush revolve.

Recirculating dust

Nearly all vacuum cleaners let some fine dust through their filter systems and back into the room. If you suffer from asthma or sensitivity to dust, choose a cleaner rated ◩ in our 'Dust in exhaust' column in the Table, and do your vacuum cleaning with the windows open.

BUYING GUIDE

UPRIGHT CLEANERS

These are good for cleaning large areas of carpet, getting out deeply-embedded dirt and animal hairs.

If you want one cleaner to deal with both carpets and other jobs, try an upright with its hose permanently attached. More of this type are becoming available, but none is ideal.

BEST BUY

If you want a separate hose, the **Electrolux Twin Turbo de Luxe 1065**, £100, is a good choice. In our original report we also recommended the **Electrolux Electronic 616** as the Best Buy upright cleaner with hose attached.

CYLINDER CLEANERS

Cylinder or canister cleaners are good for getting around and under furniture, for cleaning stairs, rugs, walls and curtains, cleaning out your car and clearing up after d-i-y jobs.

BEST BUYS

The cylinder cleaners which did best in our tests without being excessively expensive were the **AEG de Luxe Electronic 607**, £120, and **Miele S228i**, £110.

The AEG had an electronic suction control and telescopic tubes, but was heavier.

BEST BUYS

For a lighter and less expensive cleaner we choose the **AEG Compact Electronic 406**, £90, or **Philips HR6520 T520**, £80, or similar **HR6521**, *£90*.

A bagful of dust

When buying a vacuum cleaner it is a good idea to buy a supply of spare dust bags. We have had many complaints about the unavailability of bags, particularly for new models. If the shop has not got them in stock, insist that they order them for you.

Two 'special' cleaners

The Medivac Microfilter MO2 *£344*, Dust Monitor £55 extra, is a canister-shaped cleaner and is promoted for those with asthma or other breathing problems. Our tests show that it is extremely good for preventing dust particles coming back into the room, has powerful suction and is good at carpet-cleaning. But it's heavy to move around and difficult to store. The Dust Monitor tells you when there is no more dust being sucked up, but it is very time-consuming to use. Before paying out so much for the Medivac we suggest you see how you get on with a vacuum cleaner rated ■ for 'Dust in exhaust'.

The Vorwerk VK120/ET340 4-in-one *£340* can be used as a normal upright or, by removing the head and rearranging the handle, as a cylinder cleaner, or – with the strap contained in the handle – it can be slung from the shoulder for carrying. It was convenient to use and it had few serious disadvantages. But other vacuum cleaners can offer similar performance at a much lower price – in fact you could have one each of our Best Buy uprights and cylinders for less than the Vorwerk.

FACTS, FIGURES AND TEST RESULTS

What we tested

Most manufacturers make several versions of the same cleaner, with or without such features as an automatic flex-reel and 'electronic' speed control. In most cases we tested a mid-price to top-of-the-range model to see how such features work.

To simplify the Table and make it easier to see the differences that matter between models, we have assumed a 'standard' vacuum cleaner has these features:

- a hard plastic case around its disposable paper dust bag
- a fully-variable 'electronic' suction control affecting the motor speed
- an automatic spring-loaded flex reel
- a bag-full indicator
- built-in storage for a crevice tool, upholstery nozzle and dusting brush.

And that the vacuum cleaner comes with:

- a flexible hose
- one or more extension tubes
- a carpet/floor nozzle (except for uprights)
- a crevice tool, upholstery nozzle and dusting brush.

1 Types

We've split our Table into upright and cylinder cleaners and uprights which convert into cylinder types.

2 Target price

The prices shown are the lowest that you should find without too much difficulty. Prices in *italics* were given to us by manufacturers for cleaners we didn't find in our survey. When shopping for an upright check a tool-kit is included. All prices for uprights in our Table include the price of tools, bought as an extra if necessary. Our survey showed that Electrolux and Hoover dominate the market and are more widely available than other brands.

3 Similar models

Key letters to a similar model's name or number indicate advantages, disadvantages or features it has which our tested model doesn't; in brackets are features on the tested model which the similar model lacks. We also show similar models exclusive to certain retailers.

4 Extra features

Extra features the cleaner has, not on our 'standard' model.

a = automatic suction adjustment depending on fabric
b = has boost setting for difficult jobs
c = cleaner is canister-shaped (round)
d = adaptor plate for blowing is available for £3.75 extra
f = fabric bag rather than hard plastic around dust container
j = extension hose supplied
m = carpet nozzle with motorised brush available as an extra
n = can be used with a permanent filter, cloth bag, or dust container, and no paper dust bag
p = shoulder strap provided for carrying
r = dust bags can be re-used
s = flexible hose is stretchable
t = has talking signals for bag full, etc
x = wall rack supplied for storing tools
y = has 'economy' setting for normal cleaning
z = turbo brush nozzle available as an extra

5 Advantages and disadvantages

Our key shows how the different models differ from our 'standard' vacuum cleaner.

Advantages

B = can be used for blowing
F = floor/carpet or hard floor nozzle supplied with tools for upright
G = storage for tubes or hose on cleaner
L = headlamp
M = additional carpet nozzle with motorised brush supplied
P = comes with a 13-amp plug attached
Q = remote control on grip for suction
R = radiator brush supplied
S = electric socket for a motorised nozzle
T = telescopic tubes, adjustable for length
U = revolving brush can be stopped for cleaning hard floors
V = swivel connection for hose
W = wall or ceiling brush supplied
Z = additional turbo-brush nozzle (airflow powered) supplied

Disadvantages

a = no flex reel
b = no bag-full indicator
c = no crevice tool supplied
d = no dusting brush supplied
e = flex reel is manually operated
f = high pushing force needed over carpets
g = motor has only two speed settings
h = storage position of hose obstructs handle
i = difficult to disconnect hose or nozzle
j = carpet height control difficult to adjust
k = awkward to lift and carry
l = nozzle storage space difficult to open
m = awkward to manoeuvre around furniture
n = no storage for small nozzles
o = attachments may come apart or fall off
p = doesn't use disposable bags – can be messy to empty
q = awkward to convert for use with hose
r = carpet nozzle awkward to use on stairs
s = no suction control by user
t = telescopic tubes do not lock well in position
u = no upholstery nozzle supplied
v = vent on tube rather than electronic suction control
w = will not reach under low furniture
y = handle may be awkward to release from vertical position
z = tends to fall over when hose being used

Performance

6 Dust pick-up This depends both on the strength of suction and on the design of the carpet nozzle. For uprights, it may also depend on having exactly the right height setting for the carpet being cleaned.

Our ratings are based on using a standard wool Wilton carpet of medium pile height. Most cleaners picked up less dust from a nylon cord-type test carpet. Nearly all cleaners will pick up dust from hard floors easily.

7 Fibre pick-up Our ratings for this show how well a cleaner should cope with hairs which cling to a carpet.

8 Cleaning skirtings and corners It is useful to have a vacuum cleaner that will clean close to edges with its normal carpet nozzle. Most of the cleaners reached to within 1cm side-on to the skirting board but few would clean to within 2cm front-on to achieve a ◩ or ■ in our combined rating.

9 Bag clogging Fine dust can block the pores of a dust bag or filter and reduce suction before the container is full. Our ratings show that cylinder cleaners are generally better than uprights for picking up fine dust.

10 Working of bag-full indicator This should show when suction has been reduced and dust pick-up is significantly affected.

11 Blocking of airways and tubes With some designs of upright cleaner, dirt picked up when using the tube attachments has to go through the fan blades before entering the bag. Debris can get stuck in the fan blades and be very difficult to clear. Blockages are seldom a serious problem with cylinder cleaners, so for this report we give ratings for upright cleaners only.

12 Suction power Our ratings are based on using all cleaners with their hose attachments but without a nozzle.

Convenience

Ratings in this section are based both on measurements and on our user trials.

13 Weight Although some of the cylinder cleaners were rather heavy, they nearly all had convenient handles and so were easy to carry – though their hoses, tubes and nozzles could be cumbersome. A heavy upright cleaner may be very awkward for taking up and down stairs.

▣ = less than 4.5kg □ = 6 to 8kg

■ = over 10kg

14 Reach from the plug This shows how far you can get without changing to another socket outlet or using an extension flex.

▣ = 10m or more □ = 6m to 8m

◩ = 8m to 10m ◪ = less than 6m

For cleaning stairs you may want to leave the cleaner at the bottom and reach up with

VACUUM CLEANERS

	Target price (2)	Similar models – letters after each price show different advantages, disadvantages or features, which it doesn't have eg (A, a), or has in addition eg A, a (3)	Extra features (4)	Advantages
	£			
1 UPRIGHT VACUUM CLEANERS WITH HOSES ATTACHED				
1 Hoover Turbomaster Total System U5096 (UK)	140	Total System U5094 £130 **as**	rs	GLU
2 Panasonic MC-E43N (Spain)	120	MC-E41N £100 (L) **s**; MC-42N £110 (L)	jrs	GL
3 Philips HL3687/B (Italy)	90		r	G
1 UPRIGHT VACUUM CLEANERS WITH SEPARATE HOSES				
4 Electrolux Lite Special 1030A (UK)	60	Lite Deluxe 1040A £70 (f)	fr	
▶ **5 Electrolux Twin Turbo de Luxe 1065** (UK)	100	1055 £90 **v**; 1045 £100 **v**[3]; 520 £70 **v**[14]	r	
6 Goblin Commander XPC 19152 (UK)	70	S18104 *£70* f; S18103 *£60* f[15]; 19104 £70[14]	r	L
7 Hitachi Powerhouse CV560DP (Japan)	100	CV560D £80 **as**; CV560DC *£90* **s**	rs	
8 Hoover U1284 Sprite (UK)	65		frs	
9 Hoover Turbomaster Hard Bag U5078 (UK)	120	U4362 £100 **bf**; U5080 Electronic £140 (**as**)	rs	LU
10 Moulinex Major 830 (France)	*85*	801 *£60* **ab** f[15]; 841 *£70* **ab** f		
11 Philips HL3686/T (Italy)	80		r	
1 UPRIGHTS WHICH CONVERT TO CYLINDER-TYPE				
12 Kirby Heritage Legend II (USA)[4]	700		fpxz	BFLPRUW
13 Vorwerk VK120/ET340 4-in-one (W Germany)[10]	*340*		fp	FPRTW

▶ Recommended in the Buying Guide ◀

KEY TO RATINGS best ▣ > ◩ > □ > ◪ > ■ **worst**

the hose. Most cleaners gave about 3m reach from the machine, but uprights with hoses attached were mostly nearer 2m.

15 Dust bag capacity The dust bags of most upright and cylinder cleaners held from 2 to 7 litres.

16 Cleaning fitted carpets This includes back and forth cleaning as well as manoeuvring around furniture, getting close to edges and, for cylinder cleaners, the ease of pulling them along by the hose.

17 Cleaning stairs Our ratings take all aspects of stair cleaning into account.

18 Cleaning upholstery and curtains These ratings include, for upright cleaners, the use of the tool kit in general – connecting and taking apart hose, tubes and nozzles.

19 Changing dust bags Bag changing was easy on many cleaners. If you want to re-use dust bags, the job is obviously messier. And bear in mind that re-used dust bags mean less efficient suction.

Other tests

20 Dust in exhaust This may or may not be important to you – see 'Recirculating dust'.

21 Noise Our ratings are based on the machines set up for cleaning carpets, at maximum suction setting.

5 Compared with our 'standard' vacuum cleaner

	Performance							Convenience							Other tests			
Disadvantages	Dust pick-up 6	Fibre pick-up 7	Cleaning skirtings and corners 8	Bag clogging 9	Working of bag-full indicator 10	Blocking of tubes 11	Suction power with hose 12	Weight 13	Reach from plug 14	Dust bag capacity 15	Cleaning fitted carpets 16	Cleaning stairs 17	Cleaning upholstery and curtains 18	Changing or emptying dust bag 19	Dust in exhaust 20	Noise 21	Durability 22	
	▩	▩	◪	□	□	◪	◪	◪	□	□	◩	◪	□	◩	◪	■	▩	1
ay	▩	▩	□	□	■	□[6]	□	□	□	□	▩	◪	□	◩	◩	◪	◩	2
adhms	▩	▩	□[22]	□	■	□	□	□	□	◪	□	■	□	◩	◩	◪	▩	3
abnoqsw	▩	▩	□	◪		■	■	▩	□	◪	◩	◪	◪	◩	◪	■	◩	4
anw	▩	▩	□	◩	N/T	□	◪	□	□	□	◩	◪	□	◩	◩	◪	▩	5 ◀
abgjnq	◩	▩	■	◪		◪	◪	◩	□	□	□	◪	◪	◩	◩	■	◩	6
dn	□	▩	◩[22]	◪	N/T	▩	□	□	□	◪	◩	◪	□	◪	◩	□	◩	7
abknqv	▩	▩	◪[22]	◪		◪	◪	◩	◪	□	◩	◪	□	◪	◪	■[2]	◩	8
answ	▩	▩	◪	◩	▩	◪	□	□	□	□	◩	◪	□	◩	□	■	▩	9
knvz	▩	▩	◪	◩	N/T	◪	■	□	□	◩	□	■	◪	□	◪	◪	◩	10
ans	◩	▩	□[22]	◪	■	◪	◪	□	□	◪	◩	◪	□	◩	◩	■	▩	11
abkmns	▩	▩	▩	◩		□	□	◪	▩	▩	◪	◪	◪	□	□	◪	◩	12
ans	▩	▩	◪	□	◩	◪	◪	◩	□	◪	▩	□	□	◩	▩	◪	▩	13

See overleaf for explanation of footnotes

VACUUM CLEANERS

	Target price (2)	Similar models – letters after each price show different advantages, disadvantages or features, which it doesn't have eg (A, a), or has in addition eg A, a (3)	Extra features (4)	Advantages
	£			
(1) CYLINDER AND CANISTER VACUUM CLEANERS				
► 1 **AEG Compact Electronic 406** (W Germany)	90	400 £75 (y) **v**[17]; 408 £100[3]	yz	PV
2 **AEG Compact Electronic 415** (W Germany)	100		myz	GPSV
► 3 **AEG de Luxe Electronic 607** (W Germany)	120	604 £120; 608 £130[3]	myz	GPRSTV
4 **Band 402** (Czechoslovakia)	35		n	
5 **Bosch Alpha 31** (W Germany)[16]	130	Alpha 30 £100 (Ty) **v**; Alpha 32 £150 Q	nyz	GRTV
6 **Electrolux 154B** (UK)[5]	*50*			
7 **Electrolux 1820 Lite Electronic** (UK)	75	1800 Super £60 **av**; 1810 Deluxe £70 **v**	r	V
8 **Electrolux Dolphin 2230** (UK)	110	2210 £100 **v**[13]; 2220 £100 y[13]; 2225 £110[3]; 2260 £125 Q[12]	br	BG
9 **Goblin Rio XPC** (Rep of Ireland)	40	Rio 800 £40 (**g**)**v**[13]	n	
10 **Goblin Solo De Luxe 1000** (Rep of Ireland)[8,9]	60	Solo £50 **ab**; Solo Electronic 30411 £*76* (**v**)		
11 **Hitachi Powerhouse CV590** (Singapore)	65		n	
12 **Hoover S4412 Jet 1000 Twin Speed** (UK)	60	S4410 Jet £45 (**g**)**v**[13]	n	
13 **Hoover Compact Electronic S3710** (France)	90	S3076 £70 **av**[13]; S3708 £70 **v**[13]; S3712 £120 M	r	G
14 **Hoover S3724 Sensotronic System 200** (France)	110	S3722 System 100 £90[13]; S3726 System 300 £130 QSab; S3732 Audio 300 £150 Qabt	r	GV
15 **Medivac Microfilter MO2** (UK)[21]	*344*[1]	Medivac 1000 £*263* (Z) **v**[17,25]	cm	BPSZ
► 16 **Miele S228i** (W Germany)	110	S240i £150 (**v**) STma	yz	BPRV
17 **Miele S248i Compact** (W Germany)[8]	150	Black Diamond S256i £180 (**v**) Sm[12]	z	GPTV
18 **Miele S275i** (W Germany)	170	S280i £180 a; Silverstar £200 a	mz	BGPSTV
19 **Nilfisk GS90** (Denmark)	200	GS80 £220[19]	cdmnxz	RS
20 **Numatic HRV-200 Henry** (UK)	85	EVR-370 Edward £100[20]	cmnz	PS
21 **Panasonic MC-E61** (Spain)	50		n	
22 **Panasonic MC-E89N** (Spain)	90	MC-E83 £70 **v**		
23 **Panasonic MC-E97** (Spain)	130	MC-E96 £115 **v**	r	GTV
24 **Philips HR6300 T300** (Netherlands)	50	HRT320 £50[3]; HR6350 £*70* (**bcd**) V		
► 25 **Philips HR6520 T520** (Netherlands)	80	HR 6521 £*90*		V
26 **Philips HR6720 T720** (Netherlands)	*110*	HR6760 £110 a	mz	GSTV
27 **Rotel U65.0** (Poland)[8,11]	40			
28 **Rowenta Powermaster RS350** (France)	90	RS320 £90		GRSTV
29 **Samsung VC-1400** (Korea)	65	VC1500 £*95* MS[17]		T

► Recommended in the Buying Guide ◄

KEY TO RATINGS best ▨ > ◩ > □ > ◪ > ■ **worst**

[1] Price is £300 if you can show that you have a medical requirement (no VAT payable)
[2] Extremely noisy
[3] Available from Currys
[4] Available through Kirby (UK) Ltd; ☎ 0527 61034
[5] Sold mainly through mail order catalogues
[6] Several members reported clogging during normal carpet cleaning – very difficult to clear; manufacturer tells us that the problem should be less on latest production.
[7] Extremely low dust emission
[8] Current production has slightly more powerful motor
[9] Current model has a different floor/carpet nozzle which may affect performance
[10] Available from Vorwerk (UK) Ltd; ☎ 0734 794753

5 Compared with our 'standard' vacuum cleaner

Performance (6–12) · **Convenience** (13–19) · **Other tests** (20–22)

Disadvantages	6 Dust pick-up	7 Fibre pick-up	8 Cleaning skirtings and corners	9 Bag clogging	10 Working of bag-full indicator	11 Blocking of tubes	12 Suction power with hose	13 Weight	14 Reach from plug	15 Dust bag capacity	16 Cleaning fitted carpets	17 Cleaning stairs	18 Cleaning upholstery and curtains	19 Changing or emptying dust bag	20 Dust in exhaust	21 Noise	22 Durability	
dn																		1 ◄
																		2
																		3 ◄
adnv					N/T													4
mr																		5
abmns																		6
f																		7
f																		8
abdgmnp																		9
dnv																		10
dfnpuv													[23]					11
abdgnp																		12
																		13
k																		14
abn										[18]					[7]			15
v															[24]			16 ◄
dv																		17
																		18
abfnv															[26]			19
benv																		20
adnv																		21
f																		22
i			[22]															23
abcdfnv																		24
i																		25 ◄
ilt																		26
afmnv																		27
																		28
																		29

[11] Available from Index, or through Littlewoods, Brian Mills or John Moores catalogues
[12] Slightly more powerful motor [13] Sightly less powerful motor
[14] Available from Co-op stores [15] No tools included in price
[16] Manufacturer tells us UK model has more powerful suction than the German version tested.
[17] Different floor/carpet nozzle; may affect performance
[18] Larger dust bag now available
[19] Has metal rather than plastic body
[20] Has larger capacity dust container
[21] Available from Taylormaid Products Ltd; ☎ 0625 539401
[22] Cleans close to skirtings on one side only
[23] Not tested because no upholstery nozzle is supplied
[24] Manufacturers tell us an improved filter is now provided
[25] Has normal rather than 'absolute' filtration
[26] Special filters available to reduce emissions further

22 **Durability** The durability rating takes into account all faults and failures of our test samples, but are, unfortunately, no more than an indication as to what might happen to your sample in many years of use.

Reliability data from members indicates that Electrolux and Miele S228i cylinder cleaners have been more reliable than average; Goblin 1000 and Hoover Sensotronic less so. We did not find significant differences among uprights.

Electrical safety
All were satisfactory in our tests or had BEAB approval. Members' letters suggest that there could be a problem with the Panasonic MC-E43N; if the flex is caught under the revolving brushes, the insulation can be worn through to expose bare wires. Be careful to keep the flex clear and, as with any electrical device, inspect the flex regularly.

HAND-HELD VACUUM CLEANERS

From *Which?* August 1990

Knock over an ashtray, spill the sugar, or drop a cup of coffee – a hand-held vacuum cleaner should suck up the mess in seconds. And as well as coping with accidents, a hand-held vacuum cleaner could be just what you want for jobs like cleaning the stairs, the inside of the car or upholstered furniture – saving you the time and trouble of setting up and lugging around your main cleaner.

That's what the ads suggest. But we found: they don't hold much dust; they have relatively weak suction; cordless models don't run for long; and most let fine dust back into the room. None we tested would be an acceptable substitute for your main vacuum cleaner. So, before you buy one, consider whether you'd do just as well by making fuller use of the tools that come with your present cleaner, or by taking a less technical route – like a sponge.

BUYING GUIDE

MAINS-POWERED

BEST BUY

The **Hoover Dustette S1122** £45 with tool kit, was the best lightweight portable cleaner to do all your above-the-floor jobs including cleaning your stairs.

CORDLESS – DRY

Short running time and limited suction mean rechargeable cleaners are mainly suitable for jobs like picking up spills and cleaning the car. The **Black & Decker HC150** £30, or, for larger areas, the **Black & Decker H350** £35 with wider clip-on nozzle, and longer running time, are our choices.

CORDLESS – WET OR DRY

For a small cleaner to cope with wet spills as well, we pick the **Hoover Dubl-Duty 500 S1105** £35; it was noisy but was easier to use than the others. But a cloth or sponge would be at least as good in most situations.

See page 8 for an explanation of Best Buy.

FACTS, FIGURES AND TEST RESULTS

1 Types

Mains powered Sizes and shapes varied greatly. The Bissell and Moulinex could be used like uprights, whereas the Goblin, Hoover Brush Vac and Dustvac were all-in-one machines for carrying only. The Hoover Dustette could be used with or without its hose and tubes.

Cordless battery-powered These all came with a charger built into a 13-amp plug and a flex from that to a rack which you could screw to a wall. When you're not using the cleaner, you put it in the rack and the batteries are charged automatically.

2 Price

In our price survey we found fewer variations than usual between shops. Most of the Black & Decker and Hoover models were widely available; some of the others were harder to find – prices in *italics* are those recommended by the makers.

3 Measurements

Weight This includes attachments necessary for cleaning upholstery or a car interior.

Reach from plug Mains cleaners only.

Running time Some of the battery-powered cleaners would run at full speed for less than five minutes even when fully charged; if you like to do a thorough job on your car, or have a long flight of stairs, you will need one of the longer-running models. After an initial charge of about 16 hours, batteries can be recharged overnight – or in a few hours if they're not completely run down. The cost of electricity for charging would be only a few pence per week even if left on continuous charge.

Dust capacity Most of the cleaners could hold only a very small quantity. We used standard rubber pellets for this test; the cleaners might hold more light dust or fluff. But when we tried to pick up sand and gravel – as you might have in your car – we discovered that nearly all spilt some of the sand when held nozzle-down.

The Hoover Dustette lost just about all its contents if you held its body vertically – so it's best used with its hose attachment. The Brush Vac would not pick up much sand – its revolving brush just scattered it about. You might have a similar problem with household spills of, say, sugar or salt.

Wet capacity None would suck up much more than half a pint of liquid.

Width of track The Hoover Dustvac and most of the battery cleaners had nozzles less than 10cm wide so wouldn't be much use for cleaning an area of carpet.

4 Features and attachments

B = clip-on nozzle with revolving brush driven by a separate motor
C = reusable cloth filter
D = disposable paper dust bag (can be reused)
E = torch head can be used instead of vacuum cleaner head
F = flex can be wound around the handle or clip-on crevice tool
H = long handle or tube allows upright use
J = reusable foam filter
L = light shows when battery is being charged
M = incorporates belt-driven revolving brush
S = storage for accessories in wall charging unit
T = two year guarantee supplied
b = battery charger/mains plug
c = crevice tool
d = dusting brush

f = floor/carpet nozzle
q = squeegee nozzle for wet pick-up
r = replacement filter supplied
s = stretchable hose
t = extension tube or tubes
u = upholstery nozzle or all-purpose nozzle (may be integral with body)
v = upholstery nozzle with brush attached
w = wall or floor brush
x = wall rack/charging point
y = wall rack for battery unit, cleaner and torch

Only the Hoover Dustette used paper bags. All the others had cloth or foam filters; to empty, you take off the nozzle end of the cleaner and tip out the filter bag, or the container under it. The Pifco's alternative torch head would stay bright for about two hours on a full charge.

5 Performance

Suction power There was a wide variation in the suction produced by these cleaners but even the best did not compare with a

HAND-HELD VACUUM CLEANERS

		2 Price	3 Measurements: Weight	Reach from plug	Running time	Dust capacity	Wet capacity	Width of track	4 Features and attachments	5 Performance: Suction power	Resistance to filter clogging	Dust pick-up	Cleaning skirtings and corners
		£	kg	m	min	litres	litres	cm					
	1 MAINS POWERED												
	1 Bissell Magic Broom 3100E (China)	*37*	1.4	5.0		0.9		20	CFHcfu	◩	■	□	◩[1]
	2 Goblin Handy 11511 (Hong Kong)	20	1.1	4.6		0.5		10	CFTctuv	◩	■	□	□
▶	**3 Hoover Dustette S1122** (UK)	45[2]	2.4	4.6		0.9		13	Dcdstu	◩	■	◩	◆
	4 Hoover Brush Vac S1083 (Taiwan)	40	1.7	4.8		0.3		13	CMdu	□	■	◩	□
	5 Hoover Dustvac S1262 (UK)	*33*	1.2	4.7		0.3		9	Cu	◩	■	—	◆
	6 Moulinex Petivac 237 (France)	20	1.0	4.6		0.8		14	CHcdtuw	□	■	◪	◩
	1 CORDLESS – DRY ONLY												
	7 Black & Decker HC110 (UK)	20	0.6		4	0.4		8	Cbux	■	□[4]	—	◩
▶	**8 Black & Decker HC150** (UK)	30	0.7		5	0.4		8	CSbcruvx	◪	◩[4]	—	◆
▶	**9 Black & Decker H350** (USA)	35	0.8		11	0.3		14	BCSbcfrux	◪	◪	□	□[1]
	10 Pifco Power House 1485 (Hong Kong)	*27*	0.8		9	0.5		11	CELbcvy	◪	■	□	◆
	11 Steinel Vacu-Fix 3000 1401 (Switzerland)	*28*	0.5		4	0.3		8	Cbux	■	■[5]	—	◩
	12 Steinel Vacu-Fix Super 0135 (Switzerland)	*30*	0.5		2	0.3		8	Cbux	◪	■[5]	—	◆
	1 CORDLESS – WET OR DRY												
	13 Black & Decker Spillbuster HC220 (UK)	25	0.7		7	0.3	0.25	8	Cbqux	■	◆	—	◆
	14 Hoover Dubl-Duty 300 S1103 (Taiwan)[6]	25	0.8		7	0.3	0.25	8	Cbux	■	■	—	◆
▶	**15 Hoover Dubl-Duty 500 S1105** (Taiwan)[6]	35	0.9		10	0.4	0.25	8	CSbcqux	◪	■	—	◆
	16 Moulinex Handivac 168 (Hong Kong)	*20*	0.8		6	0.3	0.22	7	JLburx	■	□[4]	—	◆

▶ Recommended in the Buying Guide ◀

KEY TO RATINGS best ◆ > ◩ > □ > ◪ > ■ **worst**

normal mains-powered vacuum cleaner. (All would have been rated ■ on the scale used in our main vacuum cleaner report.) Efficiency for many jobs will relate to suction power, although the design of the nozzle used is also important for carpet cleaning and wet pick-up.

Resistance to filter clogging We tested the effect of sucking up an amount of talcum powder related to the capacity of each cleaner. As you can see from the ratings, in nearly all cases the filters became blocked and the cleaner almost stopped sucking. On a few cleaners, however, the filter mesh was so coarse that most of the talc went right through and back into the room. We don't recommend any of these cleaners for picking up plaster or other fine dust.

Dust pick-up These ratings for the amount of dust picked up are comparative with those given for the full-sized cylinder cleaners. They should not be used to indicate the *speed* of cleaning an area. We do not give ratings for the cleaners with narrow nozzles only.

Cleaning skirtings and corners Most of the cleaners would be quite good for going round the edges of your carpet. You could get even closer with the Bissell and Black & Decker H350 if you took off their carpet nozzles.

Threads and fibres Most cleaners would pick up threads, but fibres – equivalent to animal hairs which can cling to the pile – were more of a problem.

Cleaning under low furniture You might think that these small cleaners would be good for reaching under things, but many of them had to be tilted up in order to get the nozzle flat to the floor, and so would not clean under a bed or easy chair.

Threads and fibres	Cleaning under low furniture	6 Dust in exhaust	7 Noise	8 Convenience: House	Car	Wet spills	Emptying	
◪	□	◪	■	□	□		□	1
◪	□	□	■	□	□		■	2
□	□	◪	◪	◤[3]	◤[3]		■	3 ◀
□	□	■	■	◪	◪		◪	4
□	◪	□	◪	□	□		◤	5
◪	◪	◪	◪	□	◪		□	6
□	◪	■	◤	□	□		□	7
◪	◪	■	◪	□	◤		◤	8 ◀
□	□	◪	□	□	◤		□	9 ◀
◪	■	◪	□	◪	◪		◪	10
■	◪	■[5]	◤	◪	◪		◤	11
□	◪	■[5]	◤	◪	◪		◤	12
■	□	◪	□	■	◪	■	□	13
◪	◪	◪	◪	◪	◤	◤	◤	14
◪	◪	◪	■	□	◤	◤	◤	15 ◀
■	◪	■	□	■	◪	◪	◪	16

6 Dust in exhaust

None of the cleaners was effective at preventing fine dust from coming back into the room. Those rated ■ could throw out enough dust to get into your eyes and throat if you did not watch what you were doing, and the cloth outer bag of the Dustette let

[1] Rating would be better with carpet nozzle detached
[2] £35 plus £10 for the tool kit
[3] Less good without the optional tool kit
[4] Most of the fine dust went right through the filter
[5] Material of filter has been changed since our tests
[6] Models now made in France, Hoover say these have longer running time.

through additional dust if you knocked it on anything.

7 Noise
For their size most of these cleaners made an excessive amount of noise. Our rating scale is the same as we used for our main vacuum cleaners report.

8 Convenience
We arranged for a panel of users to try the cleaners for various tasks in the **house**, to clean up sand from the interior of a **car**, and – with the wet/dry cleaners – to suck up **spilled milk**. We then asked them to **empty** the cleaner or change its bag, whichever was appropriate.

Ratings in the Table do not necessary apply to convenience for any particular task. If, for example, you drop an ash tray on to the carpet, it will be more convenient to grab a cordless vacuum cleaner off its rack than go to the cupboard, get out a cylinder cleaner, unwind its flex, and plug it in. But if you knock over a large flower pot, none of the cleaners would hold enough dirt to be useful.

Electrical safety
The Hoover Dustette and Dubl-Duty models were BEAB approved. Our tests on all the others, including the charging units of the battery models, showed them to be satisfactory.

SOUND AND VISION

CD Players • Personal Stereos • Car Stereos
Stereo Systems • Video Recorders • Satellite TV
Binoculars • Compact Cameras • Slide Projectors

CD PLAYERS

Separate and Portable Players

From *Which?* April 1990

Compact discs can give superb sound quality, but what sells CD to most people is probably convenience. What's more, some record companies no longer issue new releases on vinyl LP; a CD player has become essential if you're not to limit your choice of classical music. But many people will still want a record player as well, for their existing record collection, or for music that's not available on CD.

If you're considering buying CD equipment, you'll have to choose from three broad categories:

- complete stereo systems which include CD as well as radio, tape and (usually) record player: cost, anything from £200 to £1,000
- 'separate' CD players like those we've tested for this report. This kind of player isn't much use by itself, but it's what you'll want if you're putting together a stereo system from separate units, or adding to an existing one. We've tested models in the £150 to £400 range
- portable players. We've tested two small battery-operated models which you can listen to on headphones or play through a hi-fi system. You can also buy larger portable radio cassette recorders which include a CD player.

Generally speaking, complete package systems are easy to buy, set up and use but sound quality can be disappointing. This is where systems put together from separates can score – though they're not cheap.

Assuming that – like most people – you've already got a record-playing system of some kind, the first decision may well be whether to add a CD player to it, or scrap it and buy new. This is partly a practical matter of whether there's a means of connecting the CD player to your system. But, more importantly, if the system is old or wasn't up to much in the first place, you're unlikely to get the full benefit of CD sound quality.

For this report we've tested 20 separate CD players – for use with an amplifier and loudspeakers. Four of these are 'multi-disc' types which take five or six discs at once.

FACTS, FIGURES AND TEST RESULTS

Sound quality

Our listening panel assessed the sound quality of each CD player through very high quality hi-fi equipment. This was backed up with a series of lab tests.

Our CD players sometimes sounded slightly different from each other, but in most cases it wasn't possible to rate one as consistently better or worse than another. These differences are very small compared with the other things which can affect how your hi-fi system will sound in your home, which is why we don't include a 'sound quality' rating in our Table.

BUYING GUIDE

BEST BUYS Choose between the **Philips CD 610** (£160, but see Table footnote [4] and 'Reliability worries'), **Rotel RCD855** (£250) or **Technics SLPJ46A** (£200). Others did well, but cost more. The **Technics SLPC20** (£270) multi-disc player is easy to use and good value

BEST BUY Of the portable CD players that we tested, the **Technics SLXP2** (£150) was good all round

In past tests we've found that the best small portable models can sound as good as larger ones when played through a hi-fi system. As a hi-fi player, the Technics SLXP2 was the better of the two we tested this time. Both portables gave good results with the earphones supplied, though using better earphones did improve sound quality.

1 Types

Standard players The normal type of separate which accepts just one disc at a time. Many of these have remote control.

Multi-disc players Four models have a disc holder which can take several discs: you can select or programme tracks from any of the discs in any order.

The Technics has a rotating 'turntable' on top – a bit like a record player – which holds five discs; the Sony has a similar arrangement in a drawer at the front; the Philips and Pioneer have removable magazines which take six discs. We found the Sony/Technics system more convenient, though you may well find the whole idea an unnecessary complication and prefer a standard player.

Portables The two portables come with lightweight earphones, carrying strap and adaptor to run them from the mains. They can also run off standard disposable or rechargeable batteries; the Technics played for 4½ hours on a set of two alkaline batteries, and the Sony for nearly eight hours on a set of four.

The Sony earphones have a headband; the Technics phones are the small in-ear type without a headband.

All the players could play 8cm CD singles without needing a special adaptor, though the Philips and Pioneer multi-disc players need a special magazine for them.

2 Target price

This is the price you can expect to pay by shopping around. The CD market changes very rapidly, so you may find that models have been discontinued since this report was first published and are difficult to find. On the other hand, you may be able to find such models for less than our target price.

3 Width

Full-size players are all much the same shape and style: they come in one of two widths – around 35cm or 43cm – to match other midi-sized or full-width hi-fi components.

For the portables we've given all the dimensions as footnotes to the Table: as well as being smaller, the Technics is lighter (360g with batteries) than the Sony (530g). For comparison, a typical personal cassette player weighs about 300g.

FEATURES

4 Track access

On most players, if you want to jump forwards or backwards to a particular track, you press the 'next' or 'previous' button the appropriate number of times (or hold it in while it counts up or down).

A = direct access keypad (on the player and/or on the remote control) – this is more convenient, especially on CDs with lots of tracks: you just press '+10' then '5' for track 15, for example.

Searching through the disc at high speed is another way to find the part of a disc you want, especially one with very long tracks. There are often several search speeds: for example, one speed with sound audible, and another faster one without sound (when you'd use the player's displays to tell roughly where you're up to on the disc)

E = these are the most convenient models for searching: you get two search speeds *with* sound, and the search speeds up automatically if you hold the button down (on other CD players you may have to select the 'pause' mode if you want to search using the faster speed)

CD PLAYERS

1	Target price 2	Width 3	Features: Track access 4	Displays 5	Programming 6	Repeat 7	Other 8	Test results: Error correction 9	Ease of use and snags 10	Shock resistance 11	Noise of operation 12	
	£	cm										
1 STANDARD PLAYERS												
Akai CD25 (Taiwan)	180	42	AC	IKLN	32 PQRST	Y	acde	□	◩	◩	▩	
Arcam Alpha (UK)	380	43	AECD	IJ	20 QR	Y	ae	▩	◩	◩	▩	
Denon DCD620 (W Germany)	200	43	A	IJLMN	20 PQRS	YZ	acdg	□	◩	◩	▩	
JVC XLZ411 (Singapore)[1]	200	43	AECD	IJKLMN	32 PQRSU	XYZ	abcdefg	◩	◩ m	▩	▩	
Kenwood DP730 (Singapore)	180	36	AE	IJLMN	20 PQRST	XY	fg	◩	□	◩	▩	
Marantz CD50 (Belgium)[2]	270	42	ACD	IJKLMN	20 PQRTUVW	XYZ	abcdefg	▩	□h	◩	▩	
Memorex CD2400 (Japan)[3]	170	35	F	I	15 P	XY	—	▩	□l	◩	▩	
NAD 5325 (Japan)	220	42	AE	IKL	20 PR	XY	a	◩	□j	◩	▩	
Onkyo DX1700 (Japan)	220	43	AE	IJLMN	20 PQRT	XY	acfg	◩	◩	▩	◩	
► **Philips CD 610** (Belgium)[4]	160	42	AECD	IJN	20 QRT	YZ	acf	▩	▩	◩	▩	◀
Philips CD 630 (Belgium)	250	42	AED	IJKLMN	30 PQRSTUV	YZ	abcefg	▩	◩	◩	▩	
Pioneer PD4350 (Malaysia)[5]	200	42	—	IJLM	20 PT	Y	af	◩	◩	◩	◩	
► **Rotel RCD855** (Taiwan)	250	44	AE	IJ	20 QRTU	Y	ae	▩	◩	◩	▩	◀
Sony CDP228ES (Japan)	400	43	AD	IJKLMN	20 PQRSTV	XYZ	abcdeg	▩	◩ m	◩	▩	
Sony CDP470 (Japan)	160	43	A	IJKLMN	20 PQRST	XYZ	acdg	◩	◩ m	▩	▩	
► **Technics SLPJ46A** (W Germany)[6]	200	36	AE	IJLMN	20 PQRSU	Y	acefg	▩	◩	◩	▩	◀
1 MULTI-DISC PLAYERS												
Philips CDC586 (Belgium)	230	42	A	KLM	30 PQRTV	XY	acf	▩	□hjln	▩	▩	
Pioneer PDM610 (Japan)	280	42	A	IJLM	32 PRSTW	XY	abcd	◩	□hlm	◩	▩	
Sony CDPC500 (Japan)	200	43	—	IJLM	32 PRT	Y	acd	□	□	◩	▩	
► **Technics SLPC20** (Japan)	270	43	AE	IJM	20 PQRST	Y	a	▩	◩ l	◩	▩	◀
1 PORTABLES												
Sony D22 (Japan)	150	[7]	—	I	T	X	cd	◪	□jl	◩	▩	
► **Technics SLXP2** (Japan)	150	[8]	E	IJ	18 PQT	Y	abcd	▩	◩ l	◩	▩	◀

► Recommended in the Buying Guide ◀

KEY TO RATINGS best ▩ > ◩ > □ > ◪ > ■ **worst**

F = only one search speed (with sound)

As well as (or instead of) being divided into tracks, a few discs are coded with 'index' points at specific places in the music (details on the CD box)

C = you can search out an index point from the stop mode

D = you can jump to the next or previous index point in the play mode – more convenient.

5 Displays

All models tell you the number of the track being played and how long the track has been playing, but you may have to press a button to select one or the other:

I = total playing time on disc

J = track number *and* time displayed together – useful

K = index number

L = total playing time left

M = time left on track being played

N = a 'calendar' display showing which tracks on the disc have been programmed – this is particularly convenient.

6 Programming

Each player (except the Sony portable) lets you programme a number of tracks into its memory before you start listening; it will then play just those tracks in the order you selected them. The Table shows how many tracks will fit into each player's memory; for some types of music, 15 (the least) may be barely enough.

P = you can include a track in a programme more than once

Q = you can check ('review') programme contents during play

R = you can check the programme in stop mode

S = you can add to the programme during play

T = you can play tracks in random order

U = you can sample the beginning of each track automatically before deciding whether to include it in your programme

V = an extra memory feature which recognises a disc on subsequent playings and, without further programming, plays only the tracks you chose when you previously played it. Philips call this Favourite Track Selection; the Sony version – called Custom File – also lets you assign up to ten index points to a disc for future access

W = when programming you can *omit* two or three tracks you don't like – quicker than actually selecting all the others.

7 Repeat

All players give you repeat play of the whole disc by pressing a button.

X = repeat of individual tracks

Y = repeat of programmed tracks

Z = 'A-B' repeat – between any two chosen points on a disc. Of limited use except perhaps for studying a particular passage.

8 Other

a = infra-red remote control handset. This gives you control of most features once the disc has been inserted. The

[1] Similar models XLB311 (£170) without digital output, XLB211 (£150) without digital output or remote control
[2] CD50SE (£330) is 'special edition' version with improved sound quality claimed
[3] From Tandy shops only
[4] The first three samples of the Philips CD 610 we tested had a slight distortion problem noticeable on some types of music. We suggest you check the serial number which is of the form AHOOxxxx . . .; where xxxx is higher than 8948, distortion shouldn't be a problem. If you've got a CD 610 and are worried about sound quality, contact Philips Customer Services on 081-689 2166
[5] Similar model PD4300 (£190) without remote control
[6] Similar model SLPJ26A (£150) without remote control, keypad or digital output
[7] 3.8 × 13.8 × 15cm
[8] 3.5 × 12.6 × 14.4cm

Technics portable has a remote control on the headphone lead

b = remote control of volume – saves you getting up to adjust the volume on your amplifier

c = a socket for stereo headphones. But check that there's also:

d = a means of adjusting headphone volume

e = 'digital' output – could give slightly higher sound quality when used with special amplification equipment or future digital recorders

f = link to connect to other hi-fi units of the same make so that, for example starting to play a CD automatically switches the amplifier over to CD

g = 'edit' feature: this helps you compile a sequence of tracks from a disc which will fit on to a blank cassette of a specified length with a minimum amount of tape left unused. Generally this was quite tricky to understand, though the Technics SLPJ46A worked well and was easy to operate, if you think you'd use it.

TEST RESULTS

9 Error correction

Manufacturing imperfections or superficial damage to a disc can cause 'errors' in the stream of numbers which the player reads off it. Most of the time, the player can compensate without audible effect, but if a more serious error occurs, it may produce ticking sounds over the music, or even skip across or stick (though this doesn't harm the disc or player).

All the players' error correction was satisfactory, but for best possible sound and the least likelihood that you'll have to take a disc back to the shop, it's sensible to choose a player with a ◪ rating in the Table.

10 Ease of use and snags

The rating includes our testers' assessment of each player's displays, controls (including labelling and the feel of the buttons), remote control (if provided) and programming. Particular snags:

h = inconvenient to insert disc

j = displays hard to read

k = controls stiff/poorly labelled

l = slower than average to reach a particular track after pressing play. Fast access time is probably a bigger plus on models with remote control

m = poor instructions – this shouldn't be a problem once you're used to the player

n = you can't programme using the remote control.

11 Shock resistance

Some players are more prone than others to jumping or stopping momentarily if jarred while playing, though this isn't generally a problem.

CD portables don't stand up to being carried around while playing as well as personal cassette players do; there wasn't much to choose between the two we tested.

12 Noise of operation

This is the noise produced by the player mechanism itself (not through the loudspeakers). Most players were very quiet, though some produced a slight whirring sound which might be annoying, particularly on classical music.

Electrical safety

All the players passed our electrical safety tests.

This test was carried out jointly with consumer organisations in Belgium, France and the Netherlands.

Reliability worries

There's a worrying trend of CD player unreliability; 14 per cent of players (of all types) in our survey had gone wrong at least once. Most frequent faults were failure to load the disc properly, and skipping or sticking during play (on all or most discs). Of the brands where we had enough replies to be significant, Philips players were a bit worse than average (18 per cent had gone wrong).

As in our previous survey, we found that a disturbingly high number of people had had problems with faulty discs: about one owner in three. Skipping or sticking were the most common faults. Though most people had no difficulty in getting the retailer to exchange a faulty CD, it's clear that quality control isn't good enough. After all, the absence of pops and crackles is supposed to be CD's big selling point.

Survey details

In November 1989 we carried out a postal survey among a random sample of 2,000 *Which?* subscribers of whom 1,163 responded. We also compared the data with the 3,600 members who took part in our 1988 survey.

PERSONAL STEREOS

Cassette only and Cassette/Radios

From *Which?* June 1990

In Britain, one in four people now owns a personal stereo. If you're thinking of joining them, we tell you what to look for. All the personal stereos we tested have a cassette player, and (except the Saisho PS 450) come with fast forward and rewind. Here we look at the other cassette features and at what you get with a radio. In the Verdicts we say which features the players did and didn't have.

Toning up

Most players have tone controls which can help to compensate for poor sound. Treble and bass controls are good enough, but you can also get a graphic equaliser (basically a treble and bass control plus one in between), or, less usefully, a bass boost control which emphasises the bass.

To reduce the background hiss on tapes, most players have Dolby B. This is worth having, though only better players make the most of it.

Changing sides

Most players have reverse play which plays the second side after the first has finished, without you having to turn the tape over. Loop play does this continuously. All of the players with these functions also have a switch which lets you play the other side of the tape at any point. Most players have 'autostop' at the end of a tape, which saves on batteries.

Limiting the volume

If you're worried about hearing damage, the Sony WM 3000 – designed for children – has a switch which limits the maximum volume at which you can play tapes.

Radio daze

You won't have to pay much more if you want a radio as well as a cassette player. But personal stereo radios are very sensitive to fluctuations in the radio signal, which can make the station you're listening to fade in and out. None of the radios could pick up long wave, and even if FM stereo is available, you'll get clearer listening with the mono signal – only the Saisho didn't have a switch to let you choose this.

Tuning in

Radios with digital tuning – where you tune to a number – have pre-set buttons. These make it easier to switch stations by letting you pre-tune your favourite ones. Radios with analogue tuning have dials which can be difficult to use accurately. None of these has pre-set buttons.

Our ratings

Sound quality Using the headphones supplied, our panel listened to cassettes of a wide variety of music, and to MW and FM radio. These results were backed up by our technical measurements. And we also give a rating for the quality of radio reception. We tested the players with our

BUYING GUIDE

Personal stereos don't stay on the market very long so you may have difficulty finding the models tested for this report. Of the ones looked at this time, we recommended:

BEST BUY For a player with cassette only, the **Aiwa HS G58** £45 had good sound and useful features. In our original report we also recommended the now discontinued **Aiwa HS T170** as a Best Buy – see page 285

BEST BUY For a player with a radio, the **Aiwa HS T11** £40 was the best

Best Buy small headphones, the Sennheiser HD50 (£25), and say which players sounded significantly better with them.

Running costs For the same cost of batteries, players with an above-average rating will last about one and a half times longer than those with a below-average rating

Ease of use We examined the convenience of the controls, how comfortable the headphones were, and how easy the radio was to tune.

CASSETTE PLAYERS

AIWA HS G58 (£45)
Sound quality: ◩
Running costs: □
Ease of use: ◩
Verdict: Good sound for the money. Has treble and bass controls, bass boost and reverse play. Slow rewind speed and no autostop. Best Buy.

AIWA HS P202 (£60)
Sound quality: ◩
Running costs: ◩
Ease of use: ◩
Verdict: Good sound. Has reverse and loop play. Slow rewind speed.

BOOTS PS 88 (£22)
Sound quality: □
Running costs: ◩
Ease of use: □
Verdict: Has graphic equaliser and loop play. No autostop.

PANASONIC RQ P300 (£70)
Sound quality: ◩
Running costs: ◪
Ease of use: □
Verdict: Good sound quality, improved further with our Best Buy headphones. Has loop play and bass boost. Also supplied with rechargeable battery and charger. Slow rewind speed. Discontinued – replaced by RQ P303 £60, with cosmetic differences only.

PHILIPS AQ 6498 (£35)
Sound quality: □
Running costs: □
Ease of use: □
Verdict: Has loop play and bass boost.
The Philips AQ 6598 £50 (with radio) is similar, but has graphic equaliser and no bass boost.

REALISTIC SCP 350 (£40)
Sound quality: □
Running costs: ◪
Ease of use: ◩
Verdict: Not supplied with headphones – we used Realistic headphones Nova 37 (£12) in our tests. Sound improved with our Best Buy headphones. Has loop play but no autostop. From Tandy shops.

SONY WM 3000 (£25)
Sound quality: □
Running costs: ◸
Ease of use: ◸
Verdict: Designed for young children. Sound improved with our Best Buy headphones. Has sound limiter switch to limit maximum usable volume (which is not difficult to turn off). No autostop or Dolby B.

CASSETTE/RADIO PLAYERS

AIWA HS T11 (£40)

Sound quality:		**Radio reception:**	□
cassette	◸	**Running costs:**	□
FM radio:	◸	**Ease of use:**	□
MW radio:	□		

Verdict: Good sound and performance. Has treble and bass controls, and bass boost. Analogue tuning. Best Buy.

FERGUSON PS 67 (£50)

Sound quality:		**Radio reception:**	□
cassette	□	**Running costs:**	□
FM radio:	◪	**Ease of use:**	□
MW radio:	◪		

Verdict: Sound improved with our Best Buy headphones. Has graphic equaliser but no Dolby B. Digital tuning with ten presets.

SAISHO PS 450 (£20)

Sound quality:		**Radio reception:**	◪
cassette	◪	**Running costs:**	□
FM radio:	■	**Ease of use:**	◪
MW radio:	□		

Verdict: Poor sound quality. Has graphic equaliser but not Dolby B. No rewind; fast forward speed slow. Analogue tuning difficult to use. No mono switch. Available from Dixons.

SANYO MGR 78 (£28)

Sound quality:		**Radio reception:**	◪
cassette	□	**Running costs:**	◪
FM radio:	◪	**Ease of use:**	□
MW radio:	□		

Verdict: MW reception slightly better than FM. Has graphic equaliser but no Dolby B. Analogue tuning.

The Sanyo MGP 28 £18 has no radio.

SHARP JC 534 (£60)

Sound quality:		**Radio reception:**	◪
cassette	■	**Running costs:**	◪
FM radio:	◸	**Ease of use:**	□
MW radio:	◸		

Verdict: Poor cassette sound for the money. Has graphic equaliser, reverse and loop play and bass boost. Slow rewind speed. Analogue tuning slightly difficult to use.

TOSHIBA KT 4049 (£50)

Sound quality:		**Radio reception:**	◪
cassette	□	**Running costs:**	□
FM radio:	□	**Ease of use:**	□
MW radio:	□		

Verdict: MW reception better than FM. Has graphic equaliser and loop play. No autostop. Analogue tuning.

KEY TO RATINGS best ◩ > ◸ > □ > ◪ > ■ **worst**

CAR STEREOS

Mid-priced Car Radio Cassette Players

From *Which?* July 1990

If you're thinking about changing your car radio cassette player, our tests on 13 mid-priced sets will help you choose. And we give our verdicts on sets with Radio Data System (RDS) and car radio compact disc players.

RDS: convenience on the move?

Car radios which can pick up RDS should be a great benefit if you listen to the radio when driving. RDS is an inaudible signal transmitted along with FM broadcasts. This improves car radio convenience by giving you features such as a display showing the station name and automatic re-tuning as you drive out of one transmitter's range and into another. And if you prefer listening to cassettes, players with an RDS radio have the ability to switch automatically from the cassette player to the radio when traffic news is being broadcast.

Most manufacturers sell car radio cassette players which can pick up RDS, but they're not being widely bought. To see what the current sets can do, we've looked at the Philips DC682 (£370) and Pioneer KEH9000RDS (£450). The main features are:

The name in the number

When you tune to a station, its name appears on the display panel on the front of the set. This makes it much easier to find the station you want without having to remember the number.

High-powered pick-up

While you're tuned to a station, the radio checks that it's receiving the strongest signal in the area you're travelling in. And if the reception gets weak, the radio automatically switches to a stronger transmitter broadcasting the same station.

Tuning into traffic

With RDS sets you can listen to a tape or have the radio silent but switched on (called 'muted') and be interrupted when a local station transmits traffic news. After the bulletin has finished, the set switches back to whatever you were listening to.

To make the sets do this, you first need to tune the radio to a station which is broadcasting RDS traffic signals – at the time of our test, only five BBC stations in the South East and Midlands and three commercial ones (in Essex, London and Manchester) did this. An indicator light appears on the display panel to tell you when you've found one. Or you can press a button which makes the set automatically find the station with the strongest signal. Then you 'mute' the radio or play a tape, and let the set do the rest.

This traffic news feature has an important limitation: you can't listen to one station and hear traffic news on another, and you're limited to the number of bulletins on one station. But what the sets *can* do is re-tune from one RDS traffic station to another as you travel out of the first one's range. And soon there should be sets capable of using the BBC's national and local station network. These will re-tune to any BBC station in a given area as they give travel information. We don't know to what extent the commercial stations will provide such a network, though many already transmit a few of the RDS features.

Our verdict

There's no doubt that RDS greatly improves car radio convenience, but we're not convinced that the time's yet right to get one. We think it's worth waiting until RDS transmissions are more widely available, and until the sets have more features to exploit RDS to the full. And although prices are dropping quite quickly – some sets now cost around £250 – they should be better value in the future.

Until then, the first choice for most people will be a radio cassette player. We've tested sets in the popular £150 to £250 bracket. They all have stereo FM, and AM (medium and long wave) radio wavebands, and they play tapes. We've also looked at a typical compact disc radio unit to see if it's worth splashing out on digital sound.

In-car CD: better sound for your car?

Another alternative to buying a standard radio cassette player is a car radio with a CD player rather than cassette. If you already have a collection of CDs, there's the obvious advantage that you don't need to record them on to tape in order to play them in the car. But even fairly cheap sets are twice the price of the radio cassette players in this report – and you could spend a lot more on separate units, which have the player in the car boot.

CD may not sound significantly better than a tape while driving because of the general noise in the car, and CDs can be more fiddly to load and eject than a tape.

CD on test

We looked at the Pioneer DEH-55 CD radio which costs £400. To play a CD, you push it halfway into a slot, then it's loaded automatically. Most home CD players have a programmable memory which lets you choose in advance which tracks you hear and in what order. This could be a useful feature on a car player, but the Pioneer doesn't have it. It does have 'random play' which plays the tracks in a different order each time the button is pressed. And to save you jumping from one track to another to find one you want, the player has 'intro scan', which plays the first few seconds of each track.

Sounding out CD

In our car listening tests, the CD player sounded better than the cassette players on test when the car was parked. But when driving, there wasn't a significant difference between CD and tape, because of the general noise in the car. However, this difference will probably depend on the quality of your speakers (poor ones will limit the CD's potential) and the particular car.

Discs can have manufacturing defects or superficial damage. How well a player copes with these problems depends on its 'error correction'. In our tests, the Pioneer wasn't as good as the home CD players in our tests.

A car CD player should be able to work properly under normal driving conditions. We put the Pioneer through a rigorous road test, which included driving over bumpy roads, speed ramps, and doing emergency stops. It was satisfactory in all our tests.

What to look for

Security Car stereos are a popular target for thieves, so it makes sense to buy a set which is harder to steal. All the sets in this report have at least one security feature.

> ## BUYING GUIDE
>
> **BEST BUYS**
>
> The **Hitachi CSK492E** (£200), did well in our tests. It's easy to use with useful features. The **Panasonic CQH07** (£180) also did well. It's cheaper than the Hitachi, but has fewer radio pre-sets

The most common way of making sure that your radio cassette player is safe from thieves is removing the whole unit from the dashboard. This lets you lock the set in the boot, or take it with you when you leave the car – a sure way of protecting it, but also the least convenient.

The Grundig has a detachable front panel. When you take it off, it leaves the rest of the set unusable, so not worth stealing. This is more convenient than carrying around the whole set.

With two of the sets, you have to key in a four-digit number before they'll work. Car stickers warn people that the set is useless unless you know this code number. This method of security is convenient, but relies on the would-be thief reading the stickers, and you remembering the number.

The Pye comes with a key which locks it into the dashboard. This should make the set harder to remove, but a determined thief might cause more damage to the car fascia trying to steal it.

The simplest method of deterring a thief is by disguising the set. The Aiwa has a hinged front cover to hide the controls.

Pre-set tuning This is a very useful feature on any radio, but especially on a car radio. It's a quick and easy way of finding the station you want. You select a station, then press a button to store it in the radio's memory. You can then recall the station whenever you want simply by pressing a button, instead of searching the waveband. All the sets we tested have pre-set tuning (some cheaper ones don't).

Typically, the radios can store six stations on stereo FM, and six each on medium and long wave (AM). To increase the number of pre-sets on FM, many radios have two or more FM bands (each one covering the whole frequency range) which can all store stations. The radios we tested with this feature could store between 12 and 24 stations. The others are generally limited to six.

The Sharp's pre-set tuning is less convenient than the others, because all the memorised stations are recalled using only one button. To select a station, you have to keep pressing the button until you reach the right one. The other radios have either five or six buttons, so each station can have its own pre-set button.

Automatic store At the touch of a button, most radios can automatically store the strongest stations in that particular area. These can then be selected using the pre-set buttons.

This is a useful feature for a car radio, because some of the strongest stations will be the local ones, which give traffic information. But the sets with only one FM band have the drawback that when you use this feature, the strongest stations will override any existing pre-set stations.

Variable station strength search To make it easier to tune to strong stations, pressing this button makes the radio skip over all the weaker stations. This is useful if you're interested in searching through only the strongest ones.

Dolby noise reduction This helps to reduce the background hiss on a tape. But in our listening tests in a moving car, the sets with noise reduction didn't sound significantly better than those without.

Reverse play and auto reverse All except the Blaupunkt have these features. Reverse play lets you play the other side of a tape at any time – saving you the bother of taking it out and turning it over. Auto reverse automatically starts playing the other side of a tape, when the first side finishes. Some of the sets we tested have the drawback that when the tape reverses, the 'fast forward' and 'fast rewind' controls swap their function. Although the sets have an indicator to tell you which way the tape is going, this could be confusing.

Music search A few of the cassette players can search a tape quickly, to find the beginning of the next or previous track. This is a useful feature because it should reduce the time spent fiddling with the cassette player's controls. Though if you listen mostly to classical music, this feature may be of limited use.

Cassette mechanism Most of the cassette mechanisms don't disengage from the tape when the power is turned off with a tape still in the player. This could cause damage to the player, and lead to tape stability problems. So if you buy a player with this drawback, you must remember to eject the tape before leaving the car.

Tone controls Most sets have separate bass and treble tone controls to let you boost and reduce the high and low notes. Four sets have graphic equalisers which are more versatile. This can be useful to compensate for speaker deficiencies. The Blaupunkt has a single tone control. This allows only limited changes to the sound.

Loudness control When listening at low volumes, the ear isn't very sensitive to low and high frequencies, so you can use a loudness control to boost the bass and treble.

CD input socket Four sets have a socket on the front panel for connecting a portable CD player, so you can play a CD through your car speakers.

Remote control If you can't reach your set easily, you may be tempted by one which comes with a remote control device. The Audioline has a remote control which you stick on the dashboard near the steering wheel. But it only changes the radio station; it doesn't operate the cassette player.

Choosing and using speakers

Although most new cars come fitted with speakers, there are several reasons why you might want to change them: they'll probably be of limited quality; they might not be in the best position for sound quality; or you may want more speakers.

Take your pick

You need to buy speakers to suit your radio cassette player (they should match the power range recommended by the set's manufacturer). But there's no reason why they should be the same make as your player.

You need to listen to a selection of speakers before you buy. But it can be difficult to get an accurate idea of how they'll sound in your car, because shops usually have the speakers mounted on boards. A few dealers have a demonstration car which will give you a much better idea.

Some speakers come mounted in small boxes, which are designed for fixing on a surface such as the rear parcel shelf. Others are designed for mounting flush in doors, dashboards, footwells, or rear parcel shelf. The same speakers can sound different in different parts of the car, so we asked several car audio installers to tell us the places they thought gave the best sound in different cars. We also did listening tests using combinations of flush-mounted and surface-mounted speakers in different places.

Sounding out the experts

From what dealers told us about a variety of cars, and our tests with a hatchback, if you want only a single pair of speakers they'll sound best in the front doors. This position gives the best stereo effect, and a good amount of bass. The rear parcel shelf can give very good bass, but poor stereo effect. And some people don't like the sound coming from behind them. If you want a second pair for rear seat passengers to listen to, they'll sound better in the rear doors than on the parcel shelf. But if the driver wants the effect of four speakers, it's best to put the second pair on the parcel shelf.

We also compared the sound of similar-priced surface-mounted and flush-mounted speakers on the parcel shelf. Our listening panel preferred the surface-mounted type because they had a better quality bass sound and the music was directed towards the listener rather than the roof.

Installing the system

After you've chosen your set and speakers, the final task is fitting the system. As long as you know about car electrics, you can do it yourself. But you may want an experienced installer to do it – you can expect to pay from £25 to £50 for a simple installation. Many cars come fitted with the aerial on the front wing. To save hassle and money you'll probably want to leave it there, though putting it on the roof should give better reception, and reduce the likelihood of electrical interference from the engine. If your installation does suffer from interference, such as crackling, whining, or clicks when the indicator is used, you'll need to buy, and fit, suppression components to do away with the problem.

Dealing with a dealer

If you look out for a dealer who belongs to the Car Radio Industry Specialist Association (CRISP), you can be reasonably sure that your system will be installed properly. CRISP runs training courses for its members, and does spot checks to make sure the dealers' work reaches a certain standard. You also get a nationwide guarantee: if you buy a system from a CRISP member, and it breaks in a different part of the country in the first year, you can get it mended free by the nearest CRISP dealer.

For a list of CRISP dealers write to Mr W Lawrie, 1 Grosmont Drive, Toothill, Swindon, Wiltshire, SN5 8LR.

FACTS, FIGURES AND TEST RESULTS

1 Target price

This is what you should expect to pay if you shop around. For sets which weren't widely available, we give the manufacturers' guide prices, in *italics*. Use their phone numbers, below, to find stockists in your area. The prices don't include speakers because you generally buy these separately; see 'Choosing and using speakers' on page 146. Car radio cassette players can be bought from high street electrical shops, as well as specialist car audio shops, listed under 'car radio dealers' in the Yellow Pages. These dealers can usually install the set too. Aiwa ☎ 081-897 7000; Grundig ☎ 0788 577155; Pye ☎ 081-689 4444; Roadstar ☎ 0734 321032.

2 Features

Security

A = can be removed from dashboard
B = front panel can be removed
C = four-digit security number
D = can be locked into dashboard
E = hinged front cover to hide controls

General All the sets can drive either two or four speakers.

F = single tone control
G = separate bass/treble tone controls
H = graphic equaliser
I = loudness button
J = CD input socket
K = remote control for radio
L = clock

3 Ease of use

A panel of assessors used each set in road trials, to evaluate such things as the display, labelling, position and size of controls, ease

CAR RADIO CASSETTES

	Target price 1	2 Features: Security	General	Ease of use 3	Radio features 4	5 Number of pre-sets: FM	MW	LW	6 Reception: FM	AM	Cassette features 7	Tape motion 8	
Aiwa CT-Z3601 (Korea)	*199*	AE	GIJ	□	N	12	6	6	□	◸	OQ[5]	□	
Alpine 7179LS (Japan)	180	A	GI	□	N	12	6	6	▣	□	Q[5]S	◸	
Audioline 550 (Korea)	180	A	HKL	◪	MN	6	6	6	▣	□	OQ	◪	
Blaupunkt Cambridge SQM39 (W Germany)	170	C	F	◪	MN	24	6	6	◸	◸	S	◸	
Grundig WKC3841 (Portugal)	*230*	BC	G	◸	M	6	6	6	◸	□	Q[5]	□	
▶ **Hitachi CSK492E** (Singapore)	200	A	GI	◸	M	18	6	6	▣	◸	OQ[5]RS	◸	◀
Memorex 12-9386 (Korea)[1]	180	A	H	◪	MN	6	6	6	◸	◪	Q[5]	□	
▶ **Panasonic CQH07** (Japan)	180	A	GI	◸	M	12		6[4]	▣	◸	OQ	◸	◀
Philips DC699 (France)	250	A	HIJ	□	MN	15	10	5	◸	□	OQ[5]RS	□	
Pioneer KE3500 (Japan)[2]	180	A	GI	[3]	MN	18		6[4]	▣	□	OQ[5]RS	□	
Pye CC82 (Korea)	*170*	AD	GI	□	MN	6	6	6	◸	□	PQ	□	
Roadstar RC921LB (Korea)	*160*	A	GIJ	□	MN	6	6	6	◸	□	OQ	□	
Sharp RGF834E (Malaysia)	170	A	HJ	◪	MN	8	5	3	▣	□	OQ[5]R	◸	

▶ Recommended in the Buying Guide ◀

KEY TO RATINGS **best** ▣ > ◸ > □ > ◪ > ■ **worst**

of using pre-sets, searching the wavebands, ease of playing a tape.

4 Radio features

All the radios have stereo FM, and medium and long wave AM. They all have digital tuning: to find a station you press 'up' and 'down' buttons, and the radio jumps from one station to the next. To tell you which station you're tuned to, the frequency is displayed on the front panel. All the radios can be connected to an electric aerial, so that the aerial goes up and down when the radio is turned on and off.

M = automatic store

N = variable station strength search

5 Number of pre-sets

We've given the maximum number of stations which each set can store on FM and medium and long wave.

6 FM and AM reception

Our ratings are based on a series of laboratory measurements, to find out such things as how well the sets pick up weak stations (when you're a long way from the transmitter, say) and their ability to reject interference from unwanted stations. Our in-car listening tests backed up these findings. In particular, several sets had problems receiving weak stations: the Aiwa, Blaupunkt and Memorex weren't as good as the rest on FM, and the Memorex and Sharp were poor on AM.

Sound quality

We also measured, and listened for, how accurately the radios reproduced the whole musical range from bass to treble. They were all satisfactory except the Alpine, which didn't have enough treble on FM, even with the treble tone control at maximum.

The Audioline had a high-pitched whine for the whole time the radio or cassette player was on.

In our car listening tests, we found that all the radios sounded similar on FM. But when we tried them on medium wave, the Aiwa and Memorex sounded muffled and the Audioline sounded slightly harsh. In our long wave tests the Aiwa sounded rather muffled.

[1] Exclusive to Tandy shops

[2] Tested as KEH3090B. Manufacturers claim new model has improved Dolby noise reduction

[3] Front panel has been changed since our tests, so we can't give an ease of use rating

[4] This is the maximum number of pre-sets shared between medium wave (MW) and long wave (LW)

[5] 'Fast forward' and 'fast rewind' controls swap function when tape is reversed

7 Cassette features

All the cassette players have fast forward and fast rewind controls for searching a tape. The Philips has 'play' and 'stop' buttons, which means you don't need to eject a tape if you want to switch from the cassette player to the radio. This is more convenient because most eject controls are fairly stiff.

O = Dolby noise reduction

P = tape noise limiter (not Dolby)

Q = reverse play and auto reverse

R = music search

S = cassette mechanism disengages when player off

8 Tape motion

We measured the cassette players for tape speed stability. Slow and fast variations in speed (called 'wow' and 'flutter') are particularly noticeable on music with sustained notes. Our tape motion rating takes these into account. We also found that most players were running fast, which raises the pitch of the music, though this type of error wasn't as noticeable as variations in tape speed.

Sound quality
We measured whether the sets accurately reproduced the whole musical range from bass to treble and listened to the sets in a stationary car. There wasn't much between them.

Amplifier power
We measured the power output of the sets. The Alpine, Blaupunkt, Grundig, Hitachi and Pioneer gave 4 to 5 watts per channel (continuous power into 4 ohms). This should be adequate as long as you choose fairly sensitive speakers – ones which don't need much power to sound loud. The other sets had more power (10 to 14 watts per channel) and would be suitable for a wider range of speakers.

Consumers' Association takes no advertising in any of its publications. It pays for all the goods and services it reviews. It receives no money from Government, trade or industry. All its income is derived from sales of its magazines, books and research. It is independent of all interests other than those of the consumer. It allows no exploitation of its recommendations in advertising or promotion. If readers of this guide see any ad making use of CA material in the press, in catalogues or in shops, please send details to Consumers' Association, Dept AWM, 2 Marylebone Road, London NW1 4DX.

STEREO SYSTEMS

Packages from £530 to £800

From *Which?* October 1990

Package systems are most people's first choice when looking for a new stereo. And systems which don't include a record player – smaller and neater than a typical 'midi' system – are becoming more popular as CDs become more common. For this report, we've tested packages (some with and some without record players) costing between £530 and £800, and one similarly-priced separates system.

We've criticised package stereos previously for having poor sound quality. But this time round, our listening panel was more impressed by the sound.

BUYING GUIDE

BEST BUYS The **Proton A1 3000** (£650 without speakers) and the **Rotel separates** (£780) had the best all-round sound

You can add a record player to either system, or go for the **Aiwa XD-91CD** (£700) which did reasonably well in all our tests.

Benefits of packages

The main advantages of a package compared with a system put together from separate components (amplifier, CD player, etc) should be:

- you get a lot for your money. Systems with CD, record player, cassette deck, and radio are common, and they often have stacks of features. Remote control is particularly useful
- generally they're easy to set up
- all the components match visually
- they take up less space.

However, not all package systems have these advantages. Many features are next to useless, unless you enjoy pressing buttons (see 'Gimmicks'). Also, the more expensive packages (like many of those in this report) are in fact made up of a number of separate components, which take up a lot of space, and can be very complicated to set up.

The Proton in this report doesn't come with speakers or a record player. This may be a good idea, because you can listen to different speakers (and record players too, if you want one) in a hi-fi shop, and choose the ones which give the best sound.

The separates alternative

There are two benefits of putting together a system which is made up from separate components: because you can buy each component separately, you can mix brands to get the best quality and value, and it's easy to improve the system by switching components in the future. A separates system will generally sound better than a package, though you would need to spend at least £800 for a complete set-up.

Package features

Don't be tempted into buying a package system just because it's loaded with features. Although some features are definitely worth having, others are less useful.

Useful features

Remote control handset Lets you operate the system from your armchair. A very handy gadget, though many we tested were fiddly to use.

Auto source selection This saves you having to select the music source on the amplifier. When you start playing a CD, for example, the amplifier automatically switches to CD.

Synchronised recording Helps you record from CD or record player. The cassette deck senses when play starts, and begins recording automatically.

Preset tuning This lets you programme radio stations into a memory. Once the stations have been programmed in, you simply press a button to select.

CD 'calendar' display All the CD players let you programme a number of tracks into a memory. They then play just these tracks in the order you selected them. Some also have a 'calendar' display to show you which tracks are in the memory.

Gimmicks

Graphic equaliser This is a row of controls which lets you tailor the tone quality of the music more precisely than one or two ordinary tone controls. But a model with 14 separate controls seems more trouble than it's worth for home hi-fi.

Spectrum analyser This is a row of indicator lights which displays the frequencies in the music from bass to treble. It looks quite pretty, but doesn't do anything useful.

Listening style selector A complicated programming feature, which lets you preset the volume level, graphic equaliser, and sound source, so that a particular combination can be listened to at the touch of a button.

STEREO SYSTEMS

	Target price (1)	Dimensions: Main unit h × w × d	Dimensions: Height with record player lid up	Dimensions: Speakers h × w × d	General features (2)	Radio: FM reception (3)	Radio: FM sound quality (4)	Radio: AM reception (3)	Radio: AM sound quality (4)	Cassette features (5)
	£	cm	cm	cm						
▶ 1 **Aiwa XD-91CD**[1]	700	62 × 36 × 35	89	52 × 30 × 23	ABCDFG[4]H	□	□	◪	□	IJLMP
2 **JVC W71CDX**[1]	700	60 × 36 × 38	87	44 × 27 × 19	BCDFG[4]H	◪	□	◪	◩	IJKLMP
3 **Pioneer S555D** (Japan)	800	68 × 36 × 38	95	31 × 25 × 22	BCDFG[4]H	◪	□	□	□	IJKLMNP
▶ 4 **Proton A1 3000** (Taiwan)	*650*[3]	17 × 42 × 37	—	—	ABD	◪	◪	□	□	IKLMNO
▶ 5 **Rotel separates** (Taiwan/UK)[2]	780	36 × 45 × 32	—	44 × 25 × 27	BE	◪	◪	◪	□	KNP
6 **Technics CDX50**[1]	750	50 × 36 × 32	77	46 × 27 × 24	BDFGH	□	◪	◪	◩	IJKLMNP
7 **Yamaha Astarte C10** (Japan)	*530*	26 × 30 × 30	—	22 × 15 × 25	CDF	□	◪	□	□	IJKMO

▶ Recommended in the Buying Guide ◀

KEY TO RATINGS best ▣ > ◪ > □ > ◩ > ■ **worst**

FACTS, FIGURES AND TEST RESULTS

The Yamaha comes with speakers and stands but no record player – it doesn't even have connections for you to add one yourself. The Proton doesn't have speakers or a record player. We listened to the Proton through Celestion 3 speakers, Best Buys in our last speaker report.

1 Target price

This is what you should expect to pay if you shop around. Two brands weren't widely available in our price survey. For these, we give the manufacturers' guide prices, in *italics*. Phone them to find stockists: Proton ☎ 0494 890277; Yamaha ☎ 0923 33166.

2 General features

All the systems have a spare input socket for things like TV sound.

A = socket for external microphone
B = tone controls
C = graphic equaliser
D = remote control operates amplifier, and all sound sources
E = remote control operates CD player only
F = timer
G = auto source selection
H = spare record/play sockets for tape

Radio features

All the radio tuners have the same features:

three wave bands FM stereo, and medium and long wave (AM), which are mono

digital tuning Stations are located using 'up' and 'down' controls, and the frequency is displayed digitally

preset tuning This lets you programme radio stations into a memory. Once set, you simply press a button to select a station

autoscan The radio jumps automatically from one station to the next, making it easy to search up and down the bands

stereo/mono switch In some places, or with a poor aerial, reception of FM stereo broadcasts might be poor. To get better results, all sets permit mono reception.

3 FM and AM reception

How well the sets pick up weak stations, and reject interference from unwanted stations.

4 FM and AM sound quality

Ratings are based on lab and listening tests using our own high quality 'broadcasts'.

5 Cassette features

All but the Proton and Hotel have twin cassette decks. Both decks play tapes, but only one can record. All twin decks except the Yamaha can copy (or 'dub') a tape from

Play/record sound quality	Record player features	Record player sound quality	CD player features	CD player sound quality	Overall ease of use	
□	QS[5]	□	ab(30)cdegh	◩	□	1 ◀
◩	Q	◪	b(32)h	□	□	2
□	RS	◪	ab(24)cdegh	◩	◪	3
□	—	—	b(20)ch	■	◩	4 ◀
◩	—	—	ab(20)cfg	■	◩	5 ◀
◪	QST	◪	ab(20)cdeh	◩	□	6
◪	—	—	b(20)cdf	◩	◪	7

— = not applicable
[1] System components from three or more countries
[2] We tested the RT850AL radio tuner (£180), RA810A amplifier (£120), RD845 cassette deck (£130), RCD855 CD player (£250), and RL810/II speakers (£100)
[3] Expect to pay an extra £100 for speakers
[4] Except record player
[5] Except switch for selecting record size

one deck to the other in about half the normal playing time.

All decks can record on ferric (type I) and chrome (type II) tapes, and all except the Yamaha can record on metal (type IV) tapes. Which type you choose will depend on how much you want to pay, and how fussy you are about the sound. Decks which let you set the recording level manually should give better results if used properly.

I = auto reverse – automatically switches to the other side of the cassette when one side has finished

J = relay play – you first load both compartments with tapes. When the first tape finishes, the second tape starts playing automatically

K = counter to help find part of a tape

L = automatically detects tape type

M = music search – the deck searches a tape quickly, and starts playing when it finds the beginning of the next or previous track

N = manual recording level control

O = Dolby B noise reduction

P = Dolby B and C noise reduction

6 Play/record sound quality

Our panel assessed the sound quality using commercial tapes, and recordings (from CD) made on the decks.

7 Record player features

Q = fully automatic play – after putting a record on the turntable, you simply press a button, and play begins

R = arm lift and return only

S = all controls on front panel

T = synchronised recording – recording starts just before the music starts

8 CD player features

The Pioneer can take two discs at a time; the rest are standard one-disc players.

On all the players, you can move backwards or forwards from one track to another, by pressing the 'next' or 'previous' button. Searching through the disc at high speed (with sound audible) is another way of finding the part you want. All but the Proton can do this.

a = direct-access keypad – lets you select a track by pressing the number key which corresponds to the track number

b = programmable memory (number of tracks) – lets you choose in advance which tracks you hear and in what order

c = programme review

d = 'calendar' display of tracks in programme – shows the contents

e = programme additions during play

f = auto track sampling – as a reminder of the tracks on a disc, it plays the first few seconds of each automatically

g = random play – plays the tracks in a different order each time

h = synchronised start when recording – the cassette starts recording just before the music starts

CD error correction

Discs can have slight manufacturing defects or superficial damage. How well a player copes with these problems depends on its 'error correction'. In our tests, all the players were good, though the Aiwa wasn't as good as the rest.

9 Overall ease of use

We assessed each set for such things as the 'feel' of the controls, how well they were labelled and spaced, clarity of displays, and ease of using the remote control.

Electrical safety

All were satisfactory in our tests.

VIDEO RECORDERS

Including Hi-fi Stereo and S-VHS Recorders

From *Which?* June 1990

Any video will record TV programmes so you can watch them when *you* want, or play back pre-recorded tapes. Some give rather better picture quality than others; some seem to go out of their way to confuse you, while others are a bit easier to use. But apart from this, you need to decide which features it's worth paying extra for.

The main features

Twin speed A 'long-play' model can run at half speed to fit twice the recording time on a cassette. This is useful if you're away a lot, provided the timer has enough settings (most now do).

Hi-fi stereo With the start-up of stereo sound TV transmissions in some areas, manufacturers of both videos and TVs are paying more attention to sound quality. A hi-fi video can record stereo sound in much higher quality than an ordinary mono one, and most current hi-fi models are fitted with the *Nicam* decoder needed to receive stereo broadcasts from BBC, ITV and Channel 4 when available.

If sound quality matters to you, a hi-fi model is well worth the extra £200 or so, though you need a stereo sound TV or stereo hi-fi system to make best use of it (you can also use it to record in sound-only, but with the advantage over an ordinary stereo cassette deck of a longer uninterrupted recording time). On the other hand, a mono video is perfectly adequate for use with an ordinary TV.

Super VHS S-VHS models (around £900 to £1,000) can give a significantly sharper, clearer picture than ordinary VHS. But the picture quality which your aerial picks up – or which your TV can make use of – may limit the quality you actually get. S-VHS is really a bigger plus on a camcorder than on a home video.

S-VHS models can also record in standard VHS, or play back standard VHS recordings. But special blank tapes (around £10 for three hours) are needed to make S-VHS recordings, which *can't* then be played back on a standard VHS model.

Programme indexing All videos have at least a tape counter, but many have cleverer ways of finding the part of a tape you want in a hurry – see 'Search features' in Table.

User-friendly timer These days all but the most basic models can be programmed from the remote control handset. By paying a bit more you may get more help, such as step-by-step setting instructions on your TV screen – see 'Timer setting' in the Table.

Teletext All teletext videos give you teletext if your TV doesn't have it already. On top of this:

- some can use BBC and ITV/Channel 4 teletext listings of today's or tomorrow's programmes to help you set your video's timer
- some can record the teletext subtitles along with a programme – see 'Hard of hearing?' They can't record other teletext

BUYING GUIDE

If you're not interested in the major extras like Super VHS, hi-fi Nicam stereo or twin speed recording, but want good performance choose the:

BEST BUYS **Akai VS425EK** £300, **Ferguson FV31R** £300, or **Mitsubishi HSB11** £330. The **Philips VR6293** £360 also did well and can record teletext subtitles

If you want a twin-speed recorder:

BEST BUY the **Panasonic NVJ35B** £370 has several extra features which the video enthusiast might find useful, like NTSC playback and audio dubbing

If you want hi-fi Nicam stereo:

BEST BUYS the **Mitsubishi HSB51** £570, and the **Panasonic NVF70B** £550, did best in our tests: the Panasonic has full twin speed. The **Philips VR6585** £500 – also with full twin speed – did almost as well and is quite a bit cheaper

With Super VHS and Nicam stereo the **JVC HRS5000EK** £950 is very good but also expensive.

pages, though you're unlikely to want to do this.

Digital picture These models can produce a variety of special effects like those sometimes used in TV programmes, for example, picture-in-picture (PIP) can display a second, postcard-sized picture in the corner of the screen. This would let you keep an eye on another channel, or might be useful for editing camcorder tapes. Or you can get a whole series of small pictures: either a succession of still pictures, or a visual menu of what's on each TV channel.

Editing facilities Camcorder owners may want to edit their tapes, copying the original to leave out sequences or arrange them in a different order. Some home videos have special features to make this easier.

NTSC playback

New American films are often released on video in the US before they've even reached the cinemas in the UK. However, the US TV system (NTSC) is technically quite different from the PAL system used in most of Europe, and it hasn't been possible to play an NTSC recording on an ordinary PAL video bought here. But now there are one or two reasonably priced videos which *will* play NTSC tapes through most ordinary PAL TVs (because there's a degree of technical trickery involved, some older sets may not co-operate). It's a fair bet, though, that NTSC tapes won't be easy to find over here if the film companies have their way.

Video reliability

We've analysed the returns from our monitoring panel of members owning video recorders. Altogether we've looked at data on over 1,000 VHS recorders bought between 1985 and 1987. We compared how the recorders fared in their first two years of life.

One in five of the videos in our survey had needed at least one repair. Just over one in seven had needed a repair in the *first year* after being bought new. Average cost of an out-of-guarantee repair was £32.

Ferguson, **JVC** and **Panasonic** recorders were *more reliable* than average; **Amstrad** and **Hitachi**, though they don't feature in this report, have proved *less reliable* than average in our survey.

Hard of hearing?

If you have a teletext TV and find it difficult or impossible to hear TV sound clearly, you probably value the subtitles provided for many programmes on teletext page 888. But, until recently, it hasn't been possible to record these subtitles (or indeed any other teletext pages) on video.

Videos which can record programmes with subtitles are now available: some can't record subtitled programmes unattended (using the timer); some can't record subtitles in different colours (sometimes used to make following dialogue easier).

Below we've listed all the teletext videos which the makers tell us can record subtitles under timer control (★ means an optional adaptor – £75 to £100 – is needed).

In colour Grundig VS680, ITT VR5740★, VR5760★; Philips VR6293; Salora SV9900★; *in white only:* Ferguson FV37H★; Granada GS5; ITT VR5730★; JVC HRD520, 540, 560, 610, 620, 660, 830 (all ★); Sanyo VHR5240.

FACTS, FIGURES AND TEST RESULTS

Our tests

For this report we've tested 21 video recorders. One or two major brands are missing because they were changing their ranges when we did our testing. These tests were carried out jointly with consumer organisations in Belgium and the Netherlands.

1 Types

We've grouped the videos we've tested into:

- standard VHS models with hi-fi Nicam stereo
- Super-VHS models with hi-fi Nicam stereo
- standard VHS models with normal mono sound.

All the models tested have remote controls which include all major functions.

2 Target price

The price you should be able to find by shopping around. Prices in *italics* are manufacturers' estimates. The video market changes very rapidly, so you may find that some models tested are in short supply. On the other hand, models which are about to be replaced are often reduced in price to clear stocks, so you may pick up a bargain.

3 Twin speed (long play)

A √ in this column means that record and playback at half speed (doubling the recording time) is possible. Sound and picture quality are poorer when using the half speed record/play option (except for hi-fi sound quality, which doesn't suffer noticeably) but are acceptable for when you need to fit several long programmes on one cassette. On some hi-fi recorders the half speed facility is available *only* when using it as a sound-only recorder – which rather defeats the purpose for most people.

4 Timer setting

Most timers can be set to record up to eight 'events' or chunks of programmes unattended (assuming of course that the tape is long enough). And most timers can be set for at least four weeks ahead. All have a daily repeat feature which lets you record a particular channel at a particular time every day of the week. Weekly repeat records once a week on the same channel and time slot. See 'Timer drawbacks' for the models which have more limited timers.

All the videos we tested let you set the timer using the remote control, though the exact method varies:

P = programmable remote control: you enter all the settings on the handset (which has an LCD display rather like a calculator) and then transmit them to the video by pressing a button. Handy (especially if the video itself isn't at a convenient height), provided that you find the remote control easy to understand

B = bar code reader: you set the timer for day, time and channel required by running the reader over the appropriate bar codes on the chart supplied or in listings magazines

O = on-screen display of step-by-step setting instructions on your TV screen

T = talking handset: an electronic voice says 'let's set the timer for recording,' etc

X = use of teletext programme pages as a means of setting the timer – useful for today's or tomorrow's programmes only.

All the videos also have one-touch record, giving a pre-set recording duration – usually in blocks of 15 or 30 minutes – without you having to go through the whole process.

D = start time of one-touch recording can be delayed: otherwise it starts immediately.

L = indication of time left on cassette – so you can tell if a planned recording will fit.

Some recorders retain their clock and timer settings even if the power is cut off: unless otherwise shown under 'Timer drawbacks', protection is for at least an hour.

5 Timer drawbacks

c = clock and timer protected against power failure for only a few minutes

C = clock and timer not protected against power failure at all

D = timer can be set up to only 14 days ahead

P = fewer than eight events

R = no one-touch record

W = no weekly repeat feature

6 Timer use

Our lab assessed whether the timer setting features were a help in practice, and whether the setting procedure was clear and logical. Most people find a new video a bit confusing at first; however, it's partly a matter of getting used to your particular model.

7 Picture features

All models have pause during record and still picture (freeze frame) during play – see the 'Still picture' rating in the Table for how good the still picture was. All have frame advance – which moves the freeze frame action fractionally on in time. Both frame advance and slow motion can be used for sport-type 'action replays', but otherwise aren't that useful.

Q = quick start: VHS videos take a few seconds to switch between stop and play because the tape has to thread and unthread itself from the video heads each time. The models with Q in the Table went from stop (cassette loaded) to picture in three seconds or less

VIDEO RECORDERS

	2 Target price	3 Twin speed	4 Timer setting	5 Timer drawbacks	6 Timer use	7 Picture features	8 Picture quality	9 Still picture quality	10 Search features	11 Other features	12 Sound quality	13 Remote control use	
	£												
1 VHS NICAM HI-FI													
Akai VS75EK (Japan)	550	√	DO		◐	FQSV	□	□	ITX	HL	●	◐	
Bang & Olufsen VX5000 (Denmark)	1150	√[1]	LOX[2]	R	□[3]	MPSV	□	●	GTX	HIMTU	◐	◪	
Ferguson FV37H (W Germany/Japan)	500	√[1]	DPX[2]	c	●	FSV	□	●	GITX	HLMTU	◐	●	
JVC HRD830 (W Germany/Japan)	500	√[1]	DPX[2]		●	FSV	□	●	GITX	HLMTU	●	◐	
▶ **Mitsubishi HSB51** (Japan)	570	√[1]	DLOP	c	●	FQSV	◐	●	GITX	BHLT	●	◐	◀
▶ **Panasonic NVF70B** (Japan)	550	√	BDLP	c	●	FQRSV	◐	●	GITX	HIMU	●	●	◀
▶ **Philips VR 6585** (Austria)	500	√	DLP		□	FRS	◐	●	GITX	HTU	◐	◐	◀
1 S-VHS NICAM HI-FI													
▶ **JVC HRS5000EK** (Japan)[4]	950	√	LP	c	◐	FRSV	●	●	GITX	HIMTU	●	◐	◀
1 STANDARD VHS													
▶ **Akai VS425EK** (Japan)	300		DOP		●	FQS	◐	◪	ITX	L	□	●	◀
▶ **Ferguson FV31R** (Singapore)[5]	300		LP		●	—	◐	◐	G	LT	□	◐	◀
Grundig VS600 (W Germany)	330		LP	P	□	—	□	◐	GT	LT	□	◐	
ITT VR 5730 (Japan)	380	√	PX[2]	PW	●	QSV	□	◪	GITX	LT	□	□	
▶ **Mitsubishi HSB11** (UK)	330		DLO	c	●	FQSV	◐	◐	GITX	BL	◐	◐	◀
▶ **Panasonic NVJ35B** (Japan)	370	√	BDP		●	FNRSV	◐	●	GITX	IMU	□	●	◀
▶ **Philips VR6293** (Austria)[6]	360		PX	P	□	FR	◐	●	GT	LT	□	◐	◀
Samsung SI-7220 (UK)	260		DP	CDPW	●	—	□	□	—	—	◪	□	
Sanyo VHR5200 (W Germany)	330		D	W	●	QSV	□	●	GITX	—	□	◐	
Sharp VCA615 (UK)	350	√	DOP		●	FSV	□	●	GITX	BL	□	□	
Sharp VCT310H (UK)	300		DPT		●	S	□	◐	GTX	BLT	◪	◐	
Sony SLV353 (France)	400	√	DLP		●	FQRSV	□	●	GITX	BT	◪	●	
Toshiba V309B (UK)	340		LO	C	◐	SV	□	◪	TX	—	◐	●	

▶ Recommended in the Buying Guide ◀

KEY TO RATINGS best ● > ◐ > □ > ◪ > ■ worst

[1] Half speed available only when using as a sound-only recorder
[2] Teletext adaptor optional extra
[3] Manufacturer says this model is easier to use with TV of same make
[4] Ferguson FV39S is similar
[5] FV32L is similar with twin-speed recording
[6] VR6291 is similar without teletext

S = slow motion replay
V = slow motion is variable over a range between one-fifth and 1/30 (approximately)
F = fast motion (two or three times normal speed). See also 'Search features'
R = reverse play.

These last two may have limited comedy value.

P = picture-in-picture
M = multi-picture showing you a succession of freeze frames, or a 'menu' of what's on each TV channel
N = NTSC playback

8 Picture quality

Our rating is based on both lab tests and viewing tests for:

- picture sharpness
- colour accuracy
- video noise (graininess or streaks in the picture) and dropouts (white specks in the picture).

The Super VHS model scored ● – a

whole rating better than any of the standard models – when recorded *and* played back using S-VHS. With an ordinary TV or poorer quality source material the difference was still noticeable but less marked.

9 Still picture quality

This rating is based on how steady and free of interference the still picture and fast picture search was. Videos with a ◪ or □ rating usually show some unsteadiness or interference bands across the screen in the still picture mode; more expensive videos have extra video heads to avoid this.

10 Search features

All videos have a counter counting up from zero to help you find the point on the tape you want. All except the Akai VS425EK have *zero memory* – you can reset the counter to zero at any point, and the video will stop (or start playing) automatically at that point when rewinding. Some have additional features:

T = shows elapsed tape time in hours and minutes as well as (or instead of) just numbers

G = 'go to' will wind to *any* counter reading you key in, and then stop

X = index search (or VISS) electronically marks the tape whenever a recording is started (or at any other point you choose); later the video can quickly wind to that point

I = 'introscan' will stop winding at the beginning of each programme on the tape and play a few seconds of it.

All the above systems are useful to find the programme you want on a tape, but index search and introscan are handiest because you don't have to remember to reset the counter or note down numbers. G and T is also a useful combination to have.

Once you've found the programme you want, fast picture search (which all recorders have) plays the tape forwards or backwards (without the sound) at about five to nine times normal speed.

11 Other features

All models have audio and video input and output sockets for things like:

- copying from one video to another
- copying from a video camcorder
- playing the sound through an audio system or stereo TV (if it's a stereo video)
- on hi-fi models, recording from a radio tuner or other sound source
- direct connection to a TV, giving better picture quality than the normal aerial socket.

A SCART connector – which all have – is generally the most convenient way of making TV/video connections, and most recent TVs have a matching SCART connector too.

For best results with a Super-VHS recorder a TV with an S-VHS connector is necessary: it's advisable to check carefully with the retailer if you're buying a new TV.

U = audio dubbing: lets you replace the soundtrack with a new one (though not in the hi-fi mode). You could add music or a commentary to a camcorder recording

H = headphones socket, and

M = microphone socket – both useful for making hi-fi sound recordings or audio dubbing

L = electronic lock – stops unauthorised use

T = remote control handset which can control TV functions as well as the video. You generally have to have the same make of TV for this to work

I = insert edit: lets you replace a section of a recording with new picture and sound, erasing what was there before and making a neat join with the old material at each end. All videos can do simple 'assemble' editing (copying from another recording), although the more expensive (hi-fi) models gave best results

B = 'blue mute': provides a plain blue screen and no sound if a blank channel is selected

12 Sound quality

The rating includes lab and listening tests for background hiss, clarity of treble reproduction and tape speed stability. All videos produce a small amount of *mechanical noise* while running: the Bang & Olufsen, Grundig, JVC, Panasonic, Philips and Samsung were slightly noisier than the others.

13 Remote control use

We assessed the handsets for convenient layout and clearly labelled buttons that were positive in action.

Electrical safety

All the videos we tested had British Electrotechnical Approvals Board approval or were satisfactory in our tests.

If you're new to ***Which?****, we hope you'll find enough in* ***Which? Buying Guide*** *to consider subscribing to the magazine itself – see the advertisement on page 287 for how to get three trial issues completely free.*

The ratings given in the Tables are based on ***Which?****'s latest tests of each product. The date of the original report is noted just below the main heading.*

See page 8 for an explanation of Best Buy.

SATELLITE TV

Receivers for BSB and Astra

From *Which?* September 1990

British Satellite Broadcasting (BSB) went on air in 1990. Sky and other channels available via the Astra satellite have been on the air for almost two years now.

We look at what you can get on the Astra and BSB satellites and give results on the equipment that you'll need to receive them.

A site for eyesores?

At present, you're allowed to install *one* dish per house without getting planning consent from your local authority, provided the dish is below the roof line and not larger than 90cm across. If you live in a listed building, you should check the position with your local planning authority. If you live in a rented or leased property, check with the council, landlord or freeholder. Some councils are stricter than others: Sutton, for example, has demanded that dishes fitted to their council properties be removed, claiming the fixings could damage the walls.

Since the only practicable way to receive Astra *and* BSB by satellite at the moment is to install two dishes, this could be an increasing problem. The Department of the Environment has published a consultation document which may lead to changes in the regulations about how many dishes you have and where you can put them. At the same time, various other developments are promised which might make satellite dishes less of an eyesore:

smaller dishes Developing technology means that in the South of England dishes for Astra may need to be only 45cm across rather than 60cm. But it's not yet clear whether this might cause problems with interference from other satellites

less obtrusive dishes Amstrad and Ferguson have a dish made of black metal mesh – less visible in many sites than the white or light grey dishes available up to now; and one manufacturer has a prototype dish made of glass which may blend in better with surroundings. Apart from these developments, installers could often do more to site dishes less conspicuously

combined Astra/BSB dishes At least one maker claims to have a dish which will receive Astra and BSB. You'd still need separate receiver boxes, however. This dish isn't yet generally available

Satellite on cable

If you live in an area where a new 'broadband' cable TV network has been laid, you can get Astra, BSB, other satellite channels and ordinary broadcast programmes on cable without having a dish at all. Contact the Cable Authority (☎ 071-821 6161) to check the local position. Subscription costs depend on whether you pay extra for movie or sport channels, but £19 a month is typical.

a shared dish The number of dishes that have to be installed can be greatly reduced by wiring a shared dish to many houses or flats on a housing estate. This is sometimes called SMATV (Satellite Master Antenna TV). Current cable TV regulations limit who can set up an SMATV service in a particular area: the Broadcasting Bill will relax the regulations, however, and probably make SMATV more common.

BSB and Astra compared

BSB – what's on offer

Galaxy – general entertainment mix of soaps, cop shows, and old BBC sitcoms. On air 7am to 1.30am
Now – current affairs and general interest magazine, on air 7am to midnight
Movie Channel – on air 12 noon to 2am (longer at weekends). Watching films after 6pm costs £10 a month
Sports Channel – on air 1pm to 1am
Power Station – rock music and 'youth' programming, on air 7am (10am at weekends) till 2am

What you need

BSB's satellite (Marco Polo) is in a different part of the sky from Astra, and its transmissions differ technically. This means that – at present anyway – a separate dish and receiver are required.

Two styles of dish are available: a conventional roundish type 35 to 37cm across, or a 'squarial' about 38 to 40cm square. A BSB system – dish or squarial and indoor receiver – costs from £350 to £400 plus £70 installation.

BSB is also available on cable; picture and sound quality may not be quite as good as when received via satellite.

At present there aren't any combined Astra/BSB receivers.

Astra – what's on offer

Sky One – general entertainment channel with soaps, drama, game shows and pop. On air 5.30am to 12.30am. Also Sky Radio (sound only)
Sky News – 24-hour news service
Sky Movies – on air 24 hours a day. Now scrambled (encoded), you pay a subscription to watch it
Eurosport – on air 9am to midnight
Screensport – on air 7am to 1am weekdays, round the clock at weekends
Lifestyle – mainly cookery and keep-fit programmes, talk shows, soaps and films. On air 10am to 8pm weekdays, 12 noon to 8pm weekends
Children's Channel – shares Lifestyle's channel, from 5am until Lifestyle starts. Entertainment and educational programming
MTV – 24-hour rock and pop music and videos

Other channels aimed primarily at other European countries – like *Filmnet* – are also on Astra, but need special decoders to receive them. These decoders are advertised in satellite magazines (though the channel providers don't sanction reception in the UK and may change their code, leaving pirate users with a useless decoder). There are also several German and Dutch language channels which you can receive without a special decoder.

A second Astra satellite with 16 more channels is due to be launched soon. Existing Astra dishes will be able to receive this too.

What you need

Most of the dishes you now see on houses and blocks of flats are Astra dishes. They're roughly 60cm across. You can buy a system (dish and indoor receiver box) in the high street for as little as £130. Installation is likely to cost another £70, unless you want to d-i-y (possible if you're handy with power tools and a ladder). On top of this you pay £9.92 a month to rent the Sky Movies decoder and 'smart card' to turn it on. Or you can *rent* the whole package (see 'Where to rent or buy'). Receivers are now available with the decoder built in rather than as an add-on.

More expensive dishes are available which, as well as receiving Astra, can be moved by a motor to pick up signals from satellites in other parts of the sky. Apart from other foreign language channels, there's *Cable News Network*, *Superchannel* (general entertainment), and *Discovery* (documentaries). Astra and other channels are also available on cable.

More about BSB

Transmissions on BSB are technically different from Astra's in several ways:

a better picture While Astra uses the same colour TV system (PAL) as the BBC and IBA, BSB transmits using a new system called D-MAC. With a suitable TV, D-MAC can give much better picture quality than PAL: there's less fuzziness and colour fringing. But to get the full benefit you need a TV with a SCART (or 'peritelevision') socket (most new TVs have this) which keeps separate the red, green and blue (RGB) signals that go to make up the colour picture.

A BSB receiver will also work with a video recorder or a TV without a SCART socket, but the full benefit of D-MAC is then lost.

future widescreen pictures With these, the width and height are in the ratio 16 to 9 (rather than the normal 4 to 3). This is more like the picture in a cinema, and the most obvious benefit would be on feature films. TVs with 16:9 screens aren't yet readily availabe (and at first will be very expensive). Viewers with normal screens won't miss out too much, though: they'll see films either in 'letter-box' format (with a black space top and bottom) or with the film 'panned' to concentrate the action within the 4:3 screen shape.

high-definition TV The D-MAC system can be further developed to give even better pictures as and when suitable broadcasts and TVs become available.

digital stereo This can give very high quality sound if played through a stereo system or TV with a SCART socket and stereo speakers (although Sky transmits in stereo, it uses a different system which doesn't give quite such good quality sound).

'parental control' Certain categories of programme (such as films containing bad language or those with a 15 or 18 certificate) cannot be accessed unless a four-digit code is entered on the receiver handset.

no teletext Unlike BBC and IBA programmes and Sky, BSB doesn't transmit teletext.

Every BSB receiver needs to be authorised remotely by BSB via their satellite. After installation, you need to phone BSB and answer a few questions before your system is authorised. Only if you've paid your subscription will you get access to the Movie Channel after 6pm. This authorisation is occasionally updated by BSB via the satellite, and you're supposed to leave your receiver permanently connected to the mains supply (as you would a video recorder). Power consumption even on standby is about 20 watts – so the running cost is about £14 a year.

In future, it's planned that you'd have your credit card debited to watch some programmes.

BSB satellite systems on test

We tested four systems; the Tatung with a dish, and the others with squarials. Because they're manufactured to a tight BSB specification, there's actually little difference between them in performance and features. We found installation quite straightforward and all gave very good picture and sound quality. All four systems have the following features:

- capacity for ten channels (five more than are currently in use)
- infra-red remote control of basic features (extra remote features are mentioned in the Summaries)
- on-screen messages and menus to assist setting up and channel selection and give details of the current and next programme
- standby switch on the receiver (most other controls are on the remote handset)
- sockets for SCART (or composite PAL video) and standard UHF aerial output
- built-in decoder
- 'parental control' for restricting viewing if required
- selection of widescreen or normal picture.

BUYING GUIDE

BEST BUYS All the BSB systems we tested gave very good picture and sound with a suitable TV; there was very little to choose between them. The **Philips** and the **Ferguson** are slightly easier to use than the other two. On the basis of our tests so far, it doesn't matter whether you opt for a dish or a squarial. The squarial costs more but is a bit neater.

A snag common to all four receivers: there's only one SCART output providing *either* RGB *or* PAL video, and there are no separate stereo audio sockets – the stereo output is also part of the SCART socket. This can make it awkward to feed stereo sound through a hi-fi system, or record a BSB programme in stereo on a hi-fi video. Another grumble: only a standard UHF aerial lead was supplied with each receiver. The SCART lead that you'll need to get the best picture will cost another £11 or so.

If you install your own system, you may need the advice of your TV shop to ensure that your TV has the right connections and that everything is wired up properly, especially if you're trying to link together a BSB receiver, TV, video recorder and perhaps an Astra receiver as well.

FERGUSON SRB1 (UK) £380
Includes squarial. £20 less with dish
Receiver dimensions 9×43×24cm
Extra features Remote control of colour, contrast, picture sharpness and sound volume; channel change button on receiver; panning of widescreen films when transmitted (see text); conversion for Super VHS video connection, about £50
Ease of use Remote control very fiddly, but better on-screen menus than others

ITT NOKIA SAT3300 (Sweden) £400
Includes squarial. £20 less with dish
Receiver dimensions 7×38×26cm
Similar models Salora 5903
Extra features None

Ease of use Poor instructions. Remote control a bit fiddly to use.

PHILIPS STU902 (France) £370
Includes squarial. £10 less with dish
Receiver dimensions 8×42×25cm
Similar models None
Extra features Remote control of matching TV
Ease of use Very convenient remote control but few features

TATUNG TRX2801 (UK) £400
Includes squarial. £20 less with dish
Receiver dimensions 7×42×20cm
Similar models Deccacolour DRX 2851
Extra features Remote control of colour, text display brightness, sound volume; panning of widescreen films (when transmitted)
Ease of use Remote control fairly convenient; no display of channel number on receiver

Astra satellite systems on test

We've also looked at three systems that receive signals from the Astra satellite. The dishes came with a wall mounting kit and were straightforward to install. The ITT gave the best picture, comparable to good reception from a terrestrial station. The Amstrad and ITT had stereo sound. Each receiver had remote controls, at least one SCART socket and capacity for at least 32 channels.

'Similar models' are products which we would expect to perform similarly to ones we have tested. They may look different (cosmetic differences) or have slightly more or fewer features. They may be better suited to your needs than the tested models.

BUYING GUIDE

BEST BUY

The **ITT Nokia SAT 1200** (£380) had a very good picture, stereo sound and is good for upgrading (**Salora 5902**, £380, is similar). The **Amstrad SRX200** (£180) with stereo sound was easy to install and use, and gave a pretty good picture (replaced by **SRD400**, £330, with built-in decoder and black mesh dish).

AMSTRAD SRX200 (£180) [1]
Similar models SRX100 without remote control (£130)
Ease of use Receiver very good, remote control poorer

[1] Superseded by similar SRD400 (£330) with built in decoder and black mesh dish

GRUNDIG STR20 (£350)
Similar models STR22 with stereo sound (£400)
Ease of use Most facilities on remote control only

ITT NOKIA SAT 1200 (£380)
Similar models Salora 5902 (£380)
Ease of use Most facilities on remote control only

Where to rent or buy

Astra

Comet: Amstrad SRD400 £300; NEC £400. Installation £75
DER, Focus and Multibroadcast: Ferguson with 60cm dish £300, 80cm £330; Grundig STR20 £350; ITT Nokia SAT1200 with 60cm dish £380, 85cm £430. Rental: Ferguson, Grundig, ITT

Nokia, Maspro models £12.99 a month including installation
Dixon and Currys: Amstrad SRD400 with 60cm dish £330, 80cm £370; Amstrad SRX 100 with 60cm dish £130; Amstrad SRX200 with 60cm £180
Granada and Visionhire: Salora 5902 £380, installation £80. Rental £17.29 a month including installation.
Radio Rentals: Ferguson or ITT Nokia £12.95 a month. Installation free
Rumbelows: Amstrad SRD400, 60cm £330, 80cm £360. Installation £70
Sky direct deals: rental £24.50 a month including movie channel; purchase over three years £25.50 a month or, over one year, £39.84 a month. ☎ 0506 460000 for rental, 0733 555555 for purchase

***BSB** (All models are those we tested)*
Comet: Philips with dish £360, squarial £370; Tatung (or Decca) with dish £380, squarial £400; Ferguson with dish £359, squarial £377. Installation £70
Currys: Ferguson with dish £360, squarial £380; Philips with dish £360, squarial £370
DER, Focus and Multibroadcast: Ferguson with dish £360, squarial £380; ITT Nokia with dish £380, squarial £400; Philips with dish £360, squarial £370; Tatung with dish £380, squarial £400. Rental: Ferguson, ITT Nokia or Philips £12.99 a month including installation
Dixons: Philips with dish £360, squarial £370
Granada and Visionhire: Ferguson, Philips, Salora, Tatung, dish or squarial, £380, installation £80. Rental £12.99 a month including installation
Radio Rentals: Ferguson with squarial, £12.95 a month. Installation free
Rumbelows: Ferguson or Philips with dish £360, squarial £380. Installation £70

---

*A **Which?** Best Buy is the product or products which offered the best combination of price and performance in our tests. A **Which?** Best Buy is not necessarily the model with the best test results, nor the one with the most features; nor is it necessarily the cheapest. Other models mentioned in the Buying Guides have particular strengths which may be best suited to your needs.*

BINOCULARS

From £25 to £420
From *Which?* May 1990

If you are a birdwatcher, you'll already know that a good pair of binoculars is essential for your hobby. But binoculars can also broaden your outlook when you're watching sport, at the theatre, walking, boating and even stargazing. We've sorted through the shapes, sizes and prices to help you choose the right ones for you.

Seeing by numbers

Binoculars are described by two numbers, eg 8 × 30 or 7 × 50. The first number is the *magnification* or *power* – how many times larger an object seems when looked at through the binoculars as opposed to the naked eye. The second is the diameter, in millimetres, of the *objective lens* – the lens furthest from your eye. The larger this is, the more light it gathers in – but the bigger and heavier the binoculars tend to be.

The power you need

Don't be tempted by advertisements like '20 × 50 extra high power'. Most binoculars on sale are from 7- to 10-power. Below 6-power the magnification may not be worthwhile (except for opera glasses); above 12-power the binoculars are so heavy that they become impossible to hold steady enough (unless you use a tripod) and the field of view becomes very narrow, making it difficult to locate your subject.

Eight-power is a good compromise for general use so we have concentrated on this magnification for this report. However, if you have steady hands, 10-power might be a better choice for bird-watching.

You can buy zoom binoculars on which you can vary the magnification from, say, 7- to 15-power by moving a lever. But they tend to be bulky and not so good optically as fixed-power models. They're not very popular.

In the gloom with a view

You can find out how good the binocular is likely to be for looking at things in poor light very easily. All you have to do is divide the diameter of the objective lens by the magnification. This will give you the *exit pupil* diameter. For example, an 8 × 40 binocular has an exit pupil diameter of 5mm. The larger this figure, the better.

In bright light there's no optical advantage in having a large exit pupil because the pupils of your eyes will have become smaller than the beam of light through the binocular. But even in a bright light, the larger the exit pupil diameter, the easier it should be to get the binoculars in the correct position in front of your eyes – especially useful if you're being jolted about in a boat or car, say.

Lens to lens

Most people who wear spectacles don't need to use them with binoculars because the focus adjustment can compensate for ordinary short- or long-sightedness. If you wear spectacles partly

BUYING GUIDE

GENERAL PURPOSE

Our results show that for a pair of good general-purpose binoculars you don't have to spend a fortune. One of the cheaper porro-prism models, the

BEST BUY **Zeiss Jena Jenoptem 8 × 30** £40 did well in all our tests. Its only drawback was that it would not be good if you have to wear spectacles when using binoculars.

If you wanted a smaller pair you'd have to pay much more for similar quality. The roof-prism **Minolta Mariner DCF 8 × 32** £150 was the best value of those we tested.

MINI BINOCULAR

A mini binocular that you can slip into your pocket has some advantages, but it won't be so easy to use or as good when the light is poor as our general-purpose choice.

BEST BUY Of those we tested the **Pentax DCF II 7 × 20** £70 is reasonably priced and was quite durable. Of the other minis, the **Zeiss Dialyt 8 × 20B** £205 gave an exceptionally bright image for its size; but the only model from this group to be well sealed against damp was the **Leitz Trinovid 40305 8 × 20BC** £200.

SPECTACLE WEARERS

If you have to keep your spectacles on when using binoculars our tests show your best choice would be the:

BEST BUY **Opticron High Resolution 8 × 42** £140. These binoculars had the best performance in poor light of all those tested, but you would have to take reasonable care to protect them from damp.

BEST ON TEST

If money is really no object, then the **Zeiss Dialyt BT* 8 × 30B** £420 were excellent all round.

We would expect that 10-power versions of the same type and of the same brand of binoculars in our report would have similar characteristics to the 8-power versions we've tested.

to correct astigmatism, you won't see accurately through binoculars unless you keep your spectacles on. Astigmatics have the additional problem that they can't usually wear contact lenses, a solution available to other spectacle wearers.

What we tested

We have concentrated on three types of 8-power binoculars for this report:

- porro-prism 8 × 40 – these are standard general-purpose binoculars
- roof-prism 8 × 30 – if you want equivalent performance in more compact form
- roof-prism mini 8 × 20 – for something that is small at the expense of some ease of use.

There are a lot of binoculars on the market so for this report we've tried to cover leading and widely available brands. There are many different ranges available under the same brand names: Swift, for example, make over 30 models, Tasco over 80 (though they're not all available in the UK). One other point to watch out for is the brand name Zeiss. The medium-priced East German Zeiss *Jena* brand should not be confused with the very expensive West German Zeiss *Dialyt* (although with the economic changes in Germany, this difference may not last).

Within each of our three groups there are slight variations in the specifications depending on what each manufacturer offers. And in each group we have included both cheap and expensive models. We chose standard versions, but for a number of models you can buy versions with rubber-armoured bodies; these usually cost more and may make the binoculars bulkier, but shock-resistance may be improved.

What we did

What matters with binoculars is how well you can see through them, how easy they are to use, and how durable they are.

In the laboratory we checked the specifications and measured weight, size and field of view. We also worked out how much the field of view was restricted for those who have to wear spectacles. (Spectacles keep the eyes about 2cm away from the eyepiece lenses.) We then tested for defects in the binoculars' optical systems.

We used a panel of 20 people to assess the binoculars for how easy they were to use. The same people then tested the binoculars by looking through them at a black ring against a white background. The ring had a small gap and could be rotated so that the opening appeared in different positions – 3, 6 or 9 o'clock, for example. The viewer had to identify the position of the opening. If this could be done without error, the target was moved progressively further away. In this way we obtained an average maximum distance for each model. We did this ring test both in bright and dull lighting conditions. Finally, we subjected the binoculars to dust, damp and knocks to find out how long they would be likely to last in real use.

Our tests on binoculars were carried out in conjunction with the Dutch and Belgian consumer organisations.

FACTS, FIGURES AND TEST RESULTS

1 Types

Binoculars can be made with several different arrangements of the prisms which control the path of the light going through them. The *porro-prism* type, with the prisms offset, is the traditional construction; the barrels can be made in two sections (Zeiss-type) or one piece (Bausch & Lomb type). *Roof-prism* (or Schmidt prism) binoculars have what appears to be straight-through barrels. This makes them smaller and lighter, but often more expensive than the equivalent porro-prism model. With objective lenses of around 20mm, roof-prism binoculars can be made very compact indeed, and, by using two hinges, they can fold small enough to slip into a coat pocket or handbag. We have called this type *mini* in the Table.

Ordinary porro-prism binoculars give you the greatest stereo effect, but this makes little difference in practice except when viewing close objects.

You can also buy *reverse porro* binoculars where the objective lenses are closer together than the eyepieces. This means the binoculars can be quite small. But we haven't tested that type this time.

2 Designation

Our measurements showed that actual magnification often varied from the stated figures, but not by enough to make a difference in practice. Least accurate was the Miranda, which was 9-power rather than the 8 it was designated as. Leitz and Zeiss use 'B' in their designation to distinguish models with rubber eyecaps for use with glasses from those without. Leitz also use 'C' to denote central focusing – which all our tested binoculars had (except the fixed focus Jason).

3 Price

We show target prices based on our shopping survey. It's certainly worth shopping around if you decide on expensive binoculars. You'll find binoculars in most camera shops, and many specialist dealers advertise in birdwatching magazines.

4 Size and weight

The more ▶▶s, the larger the binoculars. Our scale is based on the volume of the smallest box each binocular would fit into when folded for carrying. This varied from 200cc to 2,400cc. Within groups, weight generally went with size but the roof-prism models tended to be a bit heavier for their size than the porro.

5 Field of view

We show our measured figures in degrees for easy comparison. The figures written on binoculars are often given as the width that can be seen at a given distance – for example, 122m at 1,000m or 367ft at 1,000 yards. (Both of these mean 7° so it can be quite confusing.) Some binoculars, that take in a wider field of view than average for their magnification, describe themselves as 'wide-angle' but there seems to be no firm rule about how wide 'wide-angle' is.

A wide field of view is helpful in finding an object, but it won't necessarily help in picking out detail because, with nearly all binoculars, only the centre of the field is completely sharp. (This actually matters less than you might think because your eyes can focus on just one point at a time.)

6 Features

- B = Bausch & Lomb body type (one piece)
- C = calibration for distance between eyepieces – may make it quicker to set the binoculars, particularly if you wear glasses
- F = fixed focus – few of our panel found these binoculars satisfactory
- G = guaranteed for five years or longer – but you might have to prove that they had not been mistreated
- R = rainguard for eyepieces – this saves having to put binoculars in their case during a brief shower
- T = tripod socket – less needed with these binoculars than with those of 10-power or greater magnification
- Z = Zeiss body type – each barrel made up of two sections

7 Closest focus

Close focusing can occasionally be useful, for example, if you want to read prices in a shop window, or the programme of someone sitting two rows ahead of you at the opera. Most of the mini-binoculars could focus down to 2m but a few of the others could not focus closer than 5m or so. With the Jason Perma Focus binoculars, the only fixed focus pair in our tests, our panel could not make objects closer than 12m appear sharp. Binoculars may vary from sample to sample in this respect, so it may be worth checking several pairs in the shop before buying. Short-sightedness makes you able to focus binoculars a bit closer than normal.

BINOCULARS

		Designation [2]	Price [3]	Size [4]	Weight [4]	Field of view [5]	Features [6]	Closest focus [7]	Alignment [8]	Daylight [9]	Twilight [9]
			£		g	degrees					
	[1] PORRO-PRISM										
	1 **Adlerblick MC** (Japan)	8 × 42	170	▶▶▶▶	590	6.1	CTZ	□	□	▧	▧
	2 **Bausch & Lomb Custom** (Japan)	8 × 36	190	▶▶▶▶	670	6.4	BCGRT	◩	◩	▧	▧
	3 **Greenkat Kent** (Japan)	8 × 40	35	▶▶▶▶	560	6.4	CGZ	◩	□	◩	◩
	4 **Hilkinson Falmouth** (Japan)	8 × 40	60	▶▶▶▶	700	8.0	CGTZ	◩	◩	◩	◩
	5 **Jason Perma Focus 194** (Japan)	7 × 35	90	▶▶▶	550	6.6	FGZ	■	◩	◪	■
	6 **Minolta Standard** (Japan)	8 × 40	80	▶▶▶▶	870	9.1	CTZ	□	◩	◩	◩
	7 **Miranda** (Macau)[1]	8 × 40	25	▶▶▶▶	720	8.1	CGZ	□	▧	◩	◩
►	8 **Opticron High Resolution** (Japan)	8 × 42	140	▶▶▶▶	640	6.2	CRTZ	◩	▧	▧	▧
	9 **Pentax 65620** (Japan)	8 × 40	90	▶▶▶▶	820	7.8	TZ	◩	▧	◩	▧
	10 **Swarovski Habicht SL** (Austria)	7 × 42	320	▶▶▶▶▶	1020	6.7	BCGR	◩	◩	◩	◩
	11 **Tasco 5002RB** (Japan)	8 × 40	50	▶▶▶▶	590	5.9	GZ	◩	◩	▧	◩
►	12 **Zeiss Jena Jenoptem** (E Germany)	8 × 30	40	▶▶▶	530	8.4	GZ	◩	▧	▧	◩
	[1] ROOF-PRISM										
	1 **Bresser Linear** (Japan)	8 × 32	130	▶▶	460	7.5	G	◩	◩	□	□
►	2 **Minolta Mariner DCF** (Japan)	8 × 32	150	▶▶	550	7.1		◩	▧	◩	◩
	3 **Nikon DCF** (Japan)	9 × 30	240	▶▶	490	6.8	C	◩	▧	◩	▧
►	4 **Zeiss Dialyt BT*** (W Germany)	8 × 30B	420	▶▶	580	7.7	G	◩	▧	▧	▧
	5 **Zeiss Jena Notarem** (E Germany)	8 × 32B	130	▶▶	600	7.3	G	◩	□	◩	◩
	[1] ROOF-PRISM MINI										
	1 **Hanimex** (Korea)	8 × 21	40	▶	240	6.9		▧	▧	□	■
	2 **Jessop Flagship Supreme** (Japan)[5]	8 × 21	38	▶	230	6.7		◩	◩	◩	◪
►	3 **Leitz Trinovid 40305** (Portugal)	8 × 20BC	200	▶	220	6.5	G	◩	▧	◩	□
	4 **Minolta Pocket** (Japan)	8 × 22	75	▶	280	8.0		◩	◩	◩	□
	5 **Nikon** (Japan)	8 × 20	140	▶	210	6.6		▧	◩	◩	□
►	6 **Pentax DCF II** (Japan)	7 × 20	70	▶	210	7.4		▧	◩	◩	□
	7 **Praktica Sport** (Korea)	8 × 21	35	▶	260	6.8		▧	□	◩	□
	8 **Ranger Standard DCF** (Japan)	8 × 21	40	▶	230	6.9	G	▧	◩	◩	◪
	9 **Swift Compact DCF** (Japan)	8 × 21	70	▶	220	7.1	G	◩	▧	□	◪
	10 **Tasco Voyager II** (Japan)	8 × 21	50	▶	160	6.8	G	◩	◩	□	■
	11 **Vivitar Series 1** (Japan)	8 × 21	80	▶▶	250	6.4	G	▧	◩	◩	□
►	12 **Zeiss Dialyt** (W Germany)	8 × 20B	205	▶	190	6.4	G	◩	▧	▧	◩

► Recommended in the Buying Guide ◄

KEY TO RATINGS best ▧ > ◩ > □ > ◪ > ■ worst

8 Alignment

The two optical systems of a binocular should be exactly parallel. If they're not, your eyes may be under some strain to make the two images merge into one, and this may give you a headache. We checked two samples of each model when adjusted for someone with close-together eyes and for someone with widely-spaced eyes. If you find your binoculars particularly tiring to look through, take them back to the shop and ask to have the alignment checked (they may need to be returned to the manufacturer's agent for this). Any realignment of new binoculars should be done under your guarantee – older ones may cost around £20.

Performance		12 Durability – Resistance to:			13 Case/pouch				
Overall optical quality 10	Ease of use 11	Dust	Damp	Shock	Quality	Ease of use	Use with spectacles 14		
◩	◩	▩	□	◩[2]	H□	□	r◩	1	
▩	◩	▩	□	◩[3]	H□	□	r▩	2	
□	◩	□	■	◩	H◩	◩	r◩	3	
◩	□	▩	◪	◪	H□	◪	r◪	4	
■	◩	□	□	□	P▩	▩	r□	5	
◩	◩	▩	□	◩	P◪	□	r□	6	
◩	◩	◩	◪	□	H□	◩	r■	7	
▩	◩	▩	□	◩	P◩	◩	r▩	8	◀
◩	◩	□	□	◩	P◩	□	r□	9	
◩	◩	▩	▩	◩[2]	E–	–	◩	10	
▩	◩	◩	◪	◩	P□	□	r◩	11	
▩	◩	▩	▩	◩	H◩	□	■	12	◀
□	◩	▩	◩	◩[4]	P◪	◩	r◪	1	
◩	◩	▩	▩	◩	P◪	◩	r□	2	◀
▩	◩	▩	◩	◩	H□	◩	r◪	3	
▩	◩	▩	▩	▩	H◩	◩	r◩	4	◀
◩	□	▩	▩	◪	H□	◩	r◩	5	
□	□	▩	□	◩	P◪	□	r◪	1	
□	□	▩	□	◩	P◩	□	r◪	2	
◩	□	▩	▩	◩	E–	–	p□	3	◀
◩	□	▩	□	□	P◪	◩	r■	4	
◩	□	◩	□	▩	P◩	◩	r◪	5	
◩	□	▩	□	◩	P◪	◩	p□	6	◀
□	□	▩	■	◪[2]	P□	◩	r■	7	
□	□	▩	□	◩	P◪	□	r■	8	
□	□	▩	□	◩	P◪	□	r◪	9	
□	□	▩	◩	□	P▩	□	r□	10	
◩	◪	▩	□	◩[2]	P◪	◩	r■	11	
▩	□	▩	□	▩	P▩	□	r□	12	◀

9 Performance

This rating is based on the average distance from which our panel members could score accurately in our ring test.

The **daylight** rating takes into account scores when standing freely, and when having support for the elbows. The **twilight** rating is for standing freely, in poor light.

10 Overall optical quality

This rating includes the results of our alignment and performance tests, as well as tests for distortion and for how much of the field of view could be brought into sharp focus at one time (usually about half of the full angle of view).

11 Ease of use

This rating takes into account our panel assessments for:

- finding an object – locating it in the field of view
- focusing on the object
- following a moving object – eg a bird in flight
- holding the binoculars steady

[1] Available from Dixons
[2] Neckstrap or its attachment broke in our jerk test
[3] Manufacturer tells us resistance to shock now improved
[4] Manufacturer tells us case now strengthened
[5] Available from Jessops

- adjusting the binoculars for the distance between your eyes
- carrying the binoculars by the neck strap and in one hand
- adjusting one eyepiece to match any slight difference in vision between your left and right eye
- dealing with lens caps and any rainguard
- use in the cold: at −10°C a few binoculars became stiff to focus.

12 Durability

Dust We subjected the binoculars to a stream of fine sand for two hours, inspected them to see how much had penetrated, and checked the effect on focus and other adjustments. With a few binoculars dust got in behind the front lenses and/or the focusing became stiff. No dust got into the lens system of the Leitz 8 × 20BC mini binoculars, but after the test you could no longer push in the movable eyecaps for use when wearing glasses.

Damp None of the binoculars was affected by our artificial rain test. But in a severe test for corrosion, we dipped the binoculars in salt water, stored them in warm and humid conditions for four days, then repeated the test. We examined the binoculars immediately, and again after four weeks storage in normal dry conditions (some improved after drying out). The ratings take both inspections into account. At the end, binoculars rated ■ were unusable since they couldn't be focused, those rated ◩ were undamaged. The rest were affected by varying amounts but could still be used.

Shock We held the neckstraps against a wall covered with chipboard, extended the binoculars horizontally, and then let them drop. After two such knocks on each side we remeasured the binoculars for alignment, and checked for any other damage.

As a final test for durability we jerked 10 times on the neck straps with twice the weight of the binoculars. We have shown with footnote [2] those which failed this test; worst was the Swarovski Habicht 7 × 42; the ring on the binoculars holding the strap broke off; a difficult repair job.

13 Case or pouch

H = hard case supplied
P = soft pouch supplied
E = case or pouch available at extra cost

Cases or pouches can be leather or plastic. It's sometimes very difficult to tell which material is used – a thin layer of leather may be stuck to cardboard.

Quality We tested the cases or pouches for how well they kept out fine sand, for resistance to rain, and for the strength of their carrying straps, if any.

Ease of use ratings are based on adjusting the binocular to fit the case, putting it in, taking it out, and the comfort of carrying it in the case. Shoulder straps are a bit easier to use than wrist straps or belt fixings.

14 Use with spectacles

r = fold-down rubber rims to eyepieces
p = push-pull rubber rims to eyepieces

With most binoculars, moving them back from the normal position of having the eyecaps touching you around the eyes, greatly reduces the field of view. Fold-down rubber eyecaps allow the eyepiece lens to be positioned only a few millimetres from your spectacles, but this may still be further from your eyes than normal. The optics of a few of the binoculars tested were designed to get around this problem. Our ratings are based on how much the field of view is reduced by spectacles 20mm from the eye. A ■ rating means you'd see less than half the normal field width.

COMPACT CAMERAS

Fixed Focus and Autofocus Cameras

From *Which?* December 1989 and July 1990

Compact 35mm cameras have many advantages. They are easy to use. The best of them can produce very good pictures. There's a large choice – from small and light to big and versatile. And you don't have to pay a fortune to buy a good one. Serious photographers usually prefer *SLR* cameras for the versatility made possible by interchangeable lenses, add on flash units and other accessories, and controls which let you make fine adjustments to exposure and depth of field. But for those who mainly want a camera that they can just 'point and shoot', a compact is one answer.

Compact choice

There are several categories of compact camera around.

Fixed-focus (£15 to £85) These are designed to take acceptably sharp pictures of all subjects which are more than about 1.5m away. They're not good for taking pictures in poor light (unless you use the built-in flash or a very fast film). Cheaper fixed-focus cameras have manual winding and rewinding, which can make loading them with film rather a fiddly manoeuvre.

Manual focus Most people don't want the inconvenience of adjusting the camera for each shot so there are few manual focus compacts left. But we've tested one expensive camera designed for those wanting a very small camera which is still versatile.

Autofocus Autofocus cameras are generally better than fixed-focus cameras for taking close-up pictures or for use in dull weather. They also tend to have more accurate exposure control systems so can be suitable for making slides as well as prints. All autofocus cameras have other automatic features to make them easy to use.

Single focal length compact cameras (£40 to £175) have quite wide angle lens so that you can photograph a house, say, without having to be too far away from it.

Dual focal length cameras (£50 to £240) give you the option of switching to a 'tele' lens. These dual focal length cameras are not only useful for making distant subjects appear closer, but pictures of people appear more natural when taken from further away with a tele lens.

Zoom lens cameras (£100 to £220) let you vary the focal length to match the size of your subject without having to move your position. Cameras with zoom lenses are becoming less expensive.

FACTS, FIGURES AND TEST RESULTS

This guide covers both the fixed-focus cameras and the autofocus cameras. Focal length and film speed range are manufacturers' specifications; all other figures are based on our tests.

1 Target price
It's worth shopping around and looking at ads in photographic magazines.

2 Weight and 3 Size
Some of the autofocus zooms were quite large and heavy, but most of the other

BUYING GUIDE

CHEAPER CAMERAS
If you have less than £70 to spend, you have to be satisfied with a not-very-versatile camera. You can consider a cheap autofocus with far fewer features than our standard autofocus, or one of the better fixed-focus cameras.

BEST BUYS None of the cheaper autofocus cameras tested so far has done as well in our tests as the fixed-focus **Samsung SF-200**, £50. It's poor for close-ups but has good exposure control. For a very cheap and basic camera capable of taking good pictures in the right conditions, we choose the **Fuji FZ-5**, £15

AUTOFOCUS – SINGLE FOCAL LENGTH

BEST BUYS The camera to beat as regards value for money is the **Ricoh FF-9**, £90 (superseded by Ricoh FF-9S). But you should also consider: **Canon Sureshot Supreme**, £115, relatively easy to use if you wear glasses; **Konica A4**, £105, very small and good for close-ups; **Konica MT100**, £70, less versatile but cheaper; and the **Olympus AF-1 Super**, £130, small and splashproof – a major advantage for taking on the beach since the proofing also protects against sand. In our original report we also recommended the **Olympus AF-1** as a Best Buy – now discontinued (see page 285)

AUTOFOCUS – DUAL FOCAL LENGTH

BEST BUYS The option of using a tele lens is well worth paying extra for. Consider: **Nikon TW20**, £120, with anti red-eye feature; **Nikon TW2**, £150, wider focal length range; **Olympus AF-1 Twin**, £140, splashproof and quite small. In our origianl report we also recommended the **Konica MR640** as a Best Buy – now discontinued (see page 285)

AUTOFOCUS – ZOOM

BEST BUYS The choice of good zoom cameras gets wider and wider. Consider the **Canon Sureshot Zoom XL**, £190 and **Konica Z-up 80RC**, £200. Both have plenty of facilities but are rather big and heavy; **Canon Sureshot Caption Zoom**, £165, and **Olympus AZ-200**, £200, have cord-less remote controls (the Olympus also has an anti red-eye flash feature). With fewer features the **Fuji DL-800 Zoom**, £130, **Nikon TW Zoom**, £180, and **Ricoh RZ-750**, £160, all did well in our tests. Last but not least, the **Fuji FZ-2000 Zoom**, £220, has an extended zoom range; it's small compared with an SLR with a similar lens but big for a 'compact'.

cameras would fit easily into a pocket or handbag. Weight includes batteries and film. For size, the more ▶▶▶ the larger the camera.

The Minox cameras are very small if the flash is detached.

4 Maximum aperture

The lower the figure for maximum aperture the faster the lens. Cameras with faster lenses tend to do well for versatility because if other things are equal, they will take pictures in less light and have a greater flash range.

Dual focal-length and zoom cameras have smaller maximum apertures at their telephoto settings; this reduces the range of their built-in flash units so you have to be particularly careful not to take flash pictures from too far away.

5 Focal length

The focal length of a lens determines the angle of view it takes in (for a particular film format). This did not vary much between cameras of fixed focal length but you can see that the 'tele' setting of the others varied. The larger the second figure for dual-focal length and zoom cameras, the better the camera will be for making distant subjects appear close.

6 Film speed range

This is important if you want to use all the films available. Very few cameras would set the correct exposure with the very fine grain Kodak Ektar 25 or Kodachrome 25 films. For everyday photography with ordinary print films you can get by with ISO 100 and ISO 400 film only, or just use ISO 200. If you use ISO 200 film in a camera marked 100, 400 it will give you one stop over-exposure (probably an advantage with print film but not for slides).

7 Shutter speed range

Shutter speeds slower than about 1/60 second are useful for taking pictures in dull conditions without flash (but for good results you'll probably need a tripod or steady support). Some cameras can go to shutter speeds of 1/250 or faster, but this is not much of an advantage even for action pictures, because you can't set the shutter speed yourself on any of these cameras; with programmed exposure control the camera will not set a fast shutter speed except in very bright light or when it is loaded with a very fast film. Only on the Minox manual focus could you control the shutter speed (by varying the aperture).

8 Exposure control

Exposure is set automatically on nearly all the autofocus cameras. Systems used by most of the fixed-focus cameras are less versatile and likely to be less accurate. These drawbacks are reflected in our overall ratings.

Ap = automatic with programmed exposure – aperture and shutter speed change with the level of light
As = aperture fixed (except for flash); shutter speed changes automatically
At = automatic changeover between two exposure settings
Aw = two apertures set to weather symbols; shutter speed changes automatically
F = shutter speed fixed, aperture changes with film speed or when flash is set
W = shutter speed fixed, you set apertures to weather symbols
AA = you set the aperture; shutter speed changes automatically
N = no control – aperture and shutter speed are fixed

9 Optical quality

This includes measurements for *sharpness* at maximum and reduced lens apertures, *vignetting* (which causes the corners of the picture to be darker than the centre) – small cameras of short focal length tend to be poor – and *flare* (how clearly pictures came out when a source of light such as a street lamp was included) – zoom cameras, with complicated lens systems, are often poor in this department.

10 Focus accuracy

It is no use having a lens capable of giving sharp pictures if the subject is not in focus. For autofocus cameras we took pictures of subjects at a large range of distances. For fixed-focus cameras we found out the distance at which the lens was exactly focused; knowing the aperture and focal length of the lens we were then able to calculate the sharpness of focus at all other distances. Our ratings take into account how out of focus the cameras were at all distances including infinity, though we bore in mind what the instructions said about the closest focus distance.

11 Close-up ability

We measured how close each camera could get to a subject and still take a sharp picture (some of the instructions, particularly for fixed-focus cameras, were too optimistic). However, this distance does not tell the whole story for cameras with varying focal lengths. Our rating is based on how many times larger the real object is than the image on the negative – the reproduction ratio (◪ = less than 10; ◩ = 10 to 20). For a head-and-shoulders portrait filling the picture you need a rating of ◩ or ◪ in this column; this rating is also important if you want detailed pictures of small things.

12 Exposure accuracy

Here again we took into account instructions on how close to or far from the subject you could be for flash pictures, and the accuracy of any low light warnings or automatic (sensor) flash operation. We gave more importance to accuracy with ISO 100 and 200 films than with high speed films. Exposure accuracy is much more important with slide film than with print film, so if you plan to take slides, choose a camera with at least a ◩ rating for daylight and flash.

13 Picture quality

Our overall rating for picture quality takes into account:

- all the four previous columns
- flash uniformity – how evenly flash lighting was spread out
- camera shake warning – how well the camera warned you to use flash or a tripod if the level of light was so low that the camera had set a shutter speed slower than 1/60 second
- viewfinder accuracy – how closely what you see matches what will be in your print or slide.

14 Versatility

A camera that has a high rating in the Table for picture quality should let you take excellent pictures if conditions are right. But how wide a range of conditions the camera can cope with depends on its versatility. Our ratings take account of how well the camera could cope with:

- poor light (for subjects not suitable for taking with flash)
- subjects which appear too small if taken with a lens of usual focal length
- subjects against a bright background (needing exposure adjustment)
- subjects needing the use of a very fast or very slow (less grainy) film

- very close subjects
- rainy conditions or underwater subjects
- subjects which are dark, away from the centre of the scene, or otherwise difficult to focus on
- close or further away subjects needing flash
- moving subjects (needing a fast shutter speed)
- subjects needing fill-in flash to light up shadows in daylight
- getting yourself in the picture
- taking flash pictures in quick succession
- subjects in dim light where you cannot use flash (needing a slow shutter speed, a tripod socket and maybe a cable release)
- a series of exposures taken quickly
- subjects needing a filter to get correct colour or other effects.

15 Convenience

These ratings take account of:

- how automatic loading, winding and rewinding the film are
- whether the flash comes on automatically
- whether you need to set exposure controls or the focal length of the lens
- the type of lens protection
- how often you have to change batteries
- whether film speed setting is automatic (the DX system)
- how good the instructions are
- how likely you are to release the shutter accidentally, or before the flash is charged up, or to think the film is loaded when it isn't.

Expensive auto everything zoom cameras tend to do best. However, individual opinions vary as to how a camera feels and handles, so it's worth trying several.

16 Advantages and disadvantages

We list each camera's advantages and disadvantages as compared with a 'standard' fixed focus or autofocus camera.

You can see at a glance which cameras have plenty of extra features and which are very basic – lacking many features of the 'standard' cameras. But, because the standards are different, *don't be tempted to compare fixed-focus with autofocus cameras*.

Construction

We tested the cameras for light leakage, and the wear and tear of 60 films (over 2,000 exposures). We then hit them with a spring-loaded hammer to simulate dropping. Any significant problems we had are noted in the 'disadvantages' column of the table.

Keys which apply to fixed-focus cameras only

Advantages

A = rewind starts automatically when the end of the film is reached
I = flash interlock
L = lithium-type battery
N = LCD display panel
S = sensor flash comes on automatically in low light
T = has a tripod socket
V = has fill in flash
X = film speed is set automatically using the DX coding system on the film cassette
h = has self timer
k = shutter speed setting shown in viewfinder

Possible advantage

U = buttons for close up and distance increase versatility but make camera less easy to use

Disadvantages

A = no lock against accidentally pressing shutter release

FIXED AND MANUAL FOCUS CAMERAS

	Target price (1)	Weight (2)	Size (3)	Maximum aperture (4)	Focal length (5)	Film speed range (6)	Shutter speed range (7)	Exposure control (8)
	£	g		f	mm	ISO	sec	
FIXED FOCUS								
1 **Canon Snappy EZ** (Japan)	40	265	▶▶▶	4.0	35	100–1600	1/100	F
2 **Chinon Auto GL** (Taiwan)[1]	35	320	▶▶▶	4.1	35	100,400	1/125	F
3 **Fuji DL-15** (Indonesia)	35	280	▶▶▶	4.0	35	100,400	1/125	F
▶ 4 **Fuji FZ-5** (Japan)	15	225	▶▶▶	8.6	35	100,400	1/125	N
5 **Halina Vision 400** (Hong Kong)	40	310	▶▶▶	4.1	36	100,400	1/125,1/250	F
6 **Halina Vision 350** (Hong Kong)	40	270	▶▶▶	8.3/8.9	38/58	100,400	1/100	F
7 **Hanimex 35ES** (Hong Kong)	20	225	▶▶	6.3	33	100–400	1/125	F
8 **Hanimex 35 DL** (China)	25	295	▶▶▶	7.2/8.9	34/43	100–400	1/100	F
9 **Hanimex 35KF** (Malaysia)	34	285	▶▶▶	5.4	35	100,400	1/125	F
10 **Jessops Quick Shot 2** (Hong Kong)	30	340	▶▶▶	3.6	35	100–1000	1/125	F
11 **Keystone Le Clic Tuff 35** (USA)	55	420	▶▶▶▶▶	7.0	38	100–1000	1/70	F
12 **Kodak S100 EF** (Hong Kong)	30	270	▶▶▶	4.6	35	100–400	1/150	F
13 **Kodak S300MD** (Brazil)	40	290	▶▶▶	4.3	35	100,400	1/100	F
14 **Konica EFP 3** (Japan)	20	270	▶▶▶	4.1	36	100,400	1/125	F
15 **Konica Pop-Super** (Japan)	50	235	▶▶	4.1	34	100–400	1/125	F
16 **Minolta FS 35** (Malaysia)	40	265	▶▶▶	4.3	35	100,400	1/125	F
17 **Minolta FS-E III** (Japan)	60	285	▶▶▶	4.4	35	100–400	1/20–1/125	Ap
18 **Minox 35 AL + FA35 flash** (W Ger)	85	210 + 80	▶	4.0	35	100–400	9–1/250	Aw
19 **Olympus AM-100** (Hong Kong)	70	250	▶▶	3.3	35	50–1000	1/30–1/250	Ap
20 **Olympus Trip MD** (Taiwan)	50	295	▶▶	4.2	35	100–1000	1/180	F
21 **Panasonic C310EF** (Japan)	25	270	▶▶▶	6.1	38	100,400	1/150	F
22 **Panasonic C340EF** (Japan)	60	225	▶▶	4.3	35	100,400	1/30–1/250	Ap
23 **Practica Sport MD** (Hong Kong)	35	345	▶▶▶	3.6	35	100–1000	1/125	F
24 **Practica Sport MD2** (Hong Kong)	30	340	▶▶▶	6.1	35	100–1000	1/100	F
▶ 25 **Samsung SF-200** (Korea)	50	290	▶▶▶	4.4	35	100–1000	1/30–1/1000	Ap
26 **Sirius M-22** (Taiwan)	30	310	▶▶▶	5.4	38	100–1000	1/125	F
27 **Vivitar PS:10** (China)	20	245	▶▶▶▶	5.9	38	100–1000	1/125	F
28 **Vivitar PS:120** (Korea)	30	275	▶▶▶	5.9	35	100,400	1/150	F
29 **Vivitar PS:130** (Korea)	40	275	▶▶▶	5.9	35	100,400	1/150	F
30 **Yashica MF-3 Super** (Brazil)	30	255	▶▶▶▶	3.6	38	100–1000	1/200	W
31 **Yashica Motor-J** (Hong Kong)	45	330	▶▶▶	3.4	32	100,400	1/150	F
32 **Yashica DF-10** (Japan)	60	340	▶▶▶	5.6/8.6	35/55	100,400	1/60,1/125	F
MANUAL FOCUS								
1 **Minox 35 GT-E (FC-E flash)** (W Germany)	200 + 60	220 + 100	▶	2.9	35	25–1600	30–1/500	AA

▶ Recommended in the Buying Guide ◀

KEY TO RATINGS best ◩ > ◪ > □ > ◪ > ■ **worst**

Optical quality 9	Focus accuracy 10	Close-up ability 11	12 Exposure accuracy: Daylight	Flash	Overall ratings: Picture quality 13	Versatility 14	Convenience 15	Compared with 'standard' camera: Advantages 16	Possible advantages 16	Disadvantages 16	
□	□	■	□	◩	□	◪	◩	P		BR	1
□	□	■	◪	◩	□	■	◩	TX	C	BJ	2
◩	□	◪	■	□	□	◪	◩			BK	3
◩	▨	◪	◪	◩	◩	■	□	P	C	BEFMQU	4 ◀
◩	□	■	◪	□	□	■	◩	ASVXg	C	BO	5
□	□	□	◪	◩	□	■	◩	SXg		BFJO	6
□	□	◪	◪	◩	□	■	□		C	BEJKMNU	7
□	□	◪	■	□	□	◪	◪	GPT	C	ACFJMNUW	8
□	◩	■	◪	◩	□	■	◩	X		BFQ	9
◩	◪	◪	■	◩	□	◪	◩	G	C	JWv	10
□	◩	◪	◪	◩	□	■	◩	Agy		BJKRaf	11
◩	◪	■	■	◩	□	■	□	g	C	BKMN	12
□	□	◪	□	□	□	■	□	g		JR	13
□	◩	■	◪	◩	□	◪	◪	P	Cf	ACKMRUW	14
□	◪	■	◪	◩	□	■	◩	ALPSX	C	FJOf	15
□	□	◪	◪	◩	□	■	◩	PX		BFQ	16
◩	□	■	◩	□	□	◪	◩	AISXh		BOWf	17
◩	◪	■	□	◩	□	□	□	FGTh	Cfr	EJMNRUWx	18
◩	■	◩	◪	◩	□	□	◩	ABLSX	Ud	JORf	19
□	■	■	■	◩	□	◪	◩	APT	r	Bv	20
□	◩	◪	□	□	□	■	□	Pg	C	BM	21
□	□	■	◩	▨	□	◪	◩	ABILPSTXgh		BO	22
□	□	■	□	◪	□	◪	◩	P		W	23
□	◩	◪	◪	□	□	◪	◩	P		J	24
◩	□	■	◩	◩	◩	◪	◩	AGPSX		NOf	25 ◀
◩	◪	◪	□	◩	□	◪	◩	PST	C	JO	26
◩	□	■	□	□	□	■	□			BFGJMU	27
□	◩	■	◪	▨	□	■	◩	X	C	BJ	28
□	◩	■	◪	▨	□	■	◩	SX	C	BJO	29
□	□	■	◪	▨	□	◪	□	P	Cf	ABCMNW	30
◩	◪	□	◪	□	□	■	◩	PX		GJ	31
◩	■	□	■	□	□	◪	◩	AGINTX		FJR	32
◩	□	□	□	◩	□	◩	◪	FLMOPThk	fr	MNQRWx	1

Our 'standard' fixed-focus camera has the following features

- motor wind and rewind – film winds to the next frame as soon as a picture is taken; when you have finished the film you move a control which starts the camera rewinding
- easy load system – you place film in the camera, pull the end across to a mark and close the camera back; indicator shows that the film is loaded correctly
- built-in electronic flash which you switch on in response to a 'low light' signal in the viewfinder
- a manual control to set the required film speed
- a window on the back to show what type and length of film is loaded
- two LR6 alkaline batteries to provide power
- a manually controlled lens cover which also locks the shutter release
- a viewfinder with a bright frame
- a 'flash ready' light in or near the viewfinder
- a wrist or neck strap.

The 'Advantages' and 'Disadvantages' columns in the Table show you how the cameras we tested compared with this 'standard'.

Disadvantages which apply to fixed-focus cameras only (cont.)

E = uses the small LR03 alkaline batteries which cost about as much as the larger LR6s, but last only about half as long

K = no low-light warning to tell you when to use flash

U = manual loading (you have to thread the film into or around the take-up spool)

Keys which apply to fixed-focus and autofocus cameras

Advantages

B = either ordinary alkaline-type batteries or a lithium battery can be used

D = can mark date and/or time on each picture

E = eye-piece can be adjusted for your eyesight

F = a separate flash unit can be attached

G = viewfinder easier than average to use when wearing glasses; bright frame easily seen

J = series exposures can be made

K = extra viewfinder usable with camera at waist level or overhead – useful for candid shots

M = manual focusing possible

O = automatic or press-button system to improve exposure for subjects taken against the light

P = carrying pouch included camera

Q = can give double flash to help avoid red-eye

R = infra-red cordless remote control

W = camera warns if you are too close to the subject to get sharp focus

Y = waterproof

Z = zone symbols in viewfinder to give you an idea of what the camera has focused on

a = will set zoom automatically for a half or whole person portrait

b = can imprint selected greetings on pictures

c = self timer can be set to take two or three pictures in succession

g = extended manufacturer's guarantee (5 years for Panasonic, Keystone and Kodak, 2 for Halina and Ricoh)

i = infinity setting (useful to prevent camera focusing on glass or bars in front of a subject)

Our 'standard' autofocus camera has the following features

- motor wind – film winds to the next frame as each picture is taken
- automatic motor rewind after the last picture is taken; you can start rewind earlier if you want to remove a film before the end
- easy load system – you place film in the camera, pull the end across to a mark and close the camera back
- built-in sensor electronic flash which comes on automatically when light is low. The flash can also be used to fill in shadows in daylight leaving the background properly exposed, and it can be switched off it not wanted
- a flash interlock to prevent you taking a flash picture before the flash is charged up
- viewfinder with a bright frame and a small area in the centre for aiming the autofocusing
- 'flash ready' light in or near the viewfinder
- you can hold the focus for off-centre subjects – usually by half pressure on shutter release
- automatic setting of the film speed using the DX coding system on the film cassette
- an LCD display panel to show the frame number and/or other settings
- a lithium-type battery which charges the flash quickly and should last several years (or over 400 flashes). Costs £5 to £10 to replace
- a tripod socket
- a manually controlled lens cover which also locks the shutter release
- a window on the back to show what type and length of film is loaded
- frame counter or separate indicator shows film is correctly loaded
- self-timer control which delays shutter release for about 10 seconds
- a neck or wrist strap.

The 'Advantages' and 'Disadvantages' columns in the Table show how the cameras compared with this 'standard'.

j = can be set to take at set intervals
m = can make multiple exposures on one frame
n = multiple flash for special effects
o = will automatically focus correctly even when subject is positioned slightly off centre
p = prewinds whole film when loaded, then winds back as you take pictures – your pictures are protected should the camera back be opened
s = spot metering possible
u = bulb setting for time exposures in low light
w = 'slow synchro' flash setting to help show up background if there is some ambient light
x = indicates when subject is out of flash range
y = splashproof – but not to be immersed

Possible advantages

C = available in two or more colours
d = date-marking version available
e = teleconverter to extend zoom range available
f = filters can be fitted
r = socket for remote control or cable release
s = alternative lens for soft-focus

Disadvantages

B = no bright frame or equivalent in viewfinder

AUTOFOCUS CAMERAS

	Target price (1)	Weight (2)	Size (3)	Maximum aperture (4)	Focal length (5)	Film speed range (6)	Shutter speed range (7)	Exposure control (8)	Optical quality (9)	Focus accuracy (10)	Close-up ability (11)
	£	g		f	mm	ISO	sec				
AUTOFOCUS – SINGLE FOCAL LENGTH											
1 Canon Sureshot EX (Taiwan)	65	325	▶▶▶	4.3	35	50–1600	1/50–1/300	Ap	◤	□	□
2 Canon Sureshot Ace (Taiwan)	100	350	▶▶▶	3.2	35	50–1600	1/50–1/300	Ap	◤	◼	□
▶ **3 Canon Sureshot Supreme** (Japan)	115	325	▶▶▶	2.8	38	50–1600	1/50–1/500	Ap	□	◼	◤
4 Chinon Belami AF (Japan)[1]	70	260	▶▶	3.6	35	100–1000	1/125	At	◤	□	◪
5 Fuji DL-60 (Japan)	60	320	▶▶▶	4.2	35	100,400	1/125	F	◤	◼	◪
6 Halina Vision 700 (Hong Kong)	70	330	▶▶▶	3.6	37	100–1000	1/60–1/250	Ap	◤	□	□
7 Hanimex 35KAF (Malaysia)	60	290	▶▶▶	3.9	35	100,400	1/125	F	□	◼	◪
8 Keystone Easyshot 2AF (USA)	50	340	▶▶▶▶	7.0	38	100–1000	1/125	F	□	□	□
9 Kodak S500AF (Brazil)	85	315	▶▶▶	3.2	35	64–1000	1/60–1/250	Ap	□	◤	◪
10 Kodak S1100XL (Japan)	120	335	▶▶▶▶	2.8	35	25–1000	1/30–1/250	Ap	□	◼	◤
▶ **11 Konica MT-100** (Japan)	70	265	▶▶	4.1	34	100–400	2–1/500	As	◼	◤	◪
▶ **12 Konica A4** (Japan)	105	230	▶	3.4	35	50–3200	1/2–1/500	Ap	◤	◤	◼
13 Minolta AF-E II (Japan)	70	315	▶▶▶	4.1	35	100–1000[3]	1/30–1/90	Ap	◤	□	□
14 Minolta AF-SP (Japan)	80	345	▶▶▶▶	4.1	35	100–400	1/30–1/100	Ap	◤	◪	□
15 Minox 35 AF + AF-F flash (W Germany)	175	210 + 70	▶▶	3.2	32	100–800	1/60–1/500	Ap	□	◤	□
16 Nikon RF2 (Japan)	90	315	▶▶▶	3.2	35	100–1000	1/30–1/200	Ap	◼	◤	◤
17 Olympus AF-10 (Japan)	90	225	▶▶	3.2	35	50–800	1/30–1/250	Ap	□	◤	◤
▶ **18 Olympus AF-1 Super** (Japan)	130	275	▶▶▶	2.6	35	50–3200	1/8–1/500	Ap	◤	□	◤
19 Opus Elite AF (Hong Kong)[2]	55	365	▶▶▶	4.0	35	100–1000	1/15–1/125	Ap	◤	◤	◪
20 Panasonic C420 AF (Korea)	50	300	▶▶▶	3.7	34	100,400	1/60	F	◤	◤	◪
21 Panasonic C520AF (Japan)	80	230	▶▶	3.1	35	50–1600	1/30–1/250	Ap	□	□	□
22 Pentax PC-303 (Japan)	60	255	▶▶	4.2	35	100–400	1/125	F	□	◼	◪
23 Pentax PC-505 (Japan)	90	290	▶▶▶	3.5	35	100–400	1/30–1/500	Ap	◤	◤	□
24 Practica Sport AFX (Taiwan)	50	275	▶▶▶	3.5	35	100,400	1/60,1/125	F	◤	□	□
25 Practica Sport AFQ (Japan)	60	315	▶▶▶▶	3.7	35	100–1000	1/2–1/400	As	◤	◤	◪
26 Ricoh S-30 (Taiwan)	50	300	▶▶▶	3.6	35	100–1000	1/200	F	◤	◼	□
▶ **27 Ricoh FF-9** (Taiwan)	90	280	▶▶	3.5	35	100–1600	1/4–1/250	Ap	◤	◤	□
28 Samsung AF-200 (Korea)	50	340	▶▶▶▶	4.8	35	100,400	1/2–1/200	Ap	◤	◤	■
29 Samsung AF-500 (Korea)	90	340	▶▶▶	2.6	35	50–1600	1/60–1/500	Ap	□	□	◤
30 Sirius A-10 (Korea)	40	325	▶▶▶	3.9	35	100–1000	1/8–1/150	Ap	◤	◪	◼
31 Vivitar PS:135 (Korea)	50	300	▶▶▶	3.8	34	100,400	1/60–1/250	At	◤	◤	◪
32 Vivitar PS:145 (Korea)	60	300	▶▶▶	3.8	34	100,400	1/250	F	◤	◤	◪
33 Yaschia AF-J2 (Hong Kong)	75	345	▶▶▶	3.0	32	100–1600	1/15–1/250	Ap	◤	□	□
34 Yashica T3 (Japan)	130	340	▶▶▶	2.8	35	64–1600	1–1/500	Ap	◤	◤	◤

▶ Recommended in the Buying Guide ◀

KEY TO RATINGS **best** ◼ > ◤ > □ > ◪ > ■ **worst**

[1] Available from Dixons
[2] Available from Supasnaps shops

12 Exposure accuracy: Daylight	Flash	Overall ratings: Picture quality 13	Versatility 14	Convenience 15	Compared with 'standard' camera: Advantages 16	Possible advantages 16	Disadvantages 16		
◤	◤	□	□	◤	JP	d	OVfn	1	
□	◤	◤	□	▨	KPRW	d	OVfn	2	
◤	▨	◤	◤	▨	GOPW	d		3	◀
□	□	◤	◢	◤			GIRSTVZn	4	
◢	◤	◤	■	◤			BGILOSTVZnv	5	
◤	◤	□	◢	◤	g	C	FILOSTn	6	
◢	◤	◤	■	◤	G		ILQSTVZn	7	
◢	□	□	■	◤	Pg		IJLQRSTVXfn	8	
□	□	◤	◢	◤	GWp		IJLOSTVf	9	
◤	◤	◤	□	▨	Zgo			10	
◤	▨	◤	□	◤	P	d	FGfn	11	◀
◤	□	◤	◤	▨	WZw		FJR	12	◀
□	◤	◤	◢	◤	B		GOSTVWfn	13	
◤	▨	□	□	◤	BPy	d	FGJOVWafn	14	
▨	□	◤	□	□	FG		HJMNQRanvx	15	
◤	◤	◤	□	◤	BGc	d	OVn	16	
□	▨	◤	□	◤	B	d	IORVn	17	
□	▨	◤	◤	◤	JOy	d	G	18	◀
◢	◤	□	◢	◤			IJLOSfn	19	
◢	◤	◤	◢	◤		C	ILQSVZn	20	
◤	□	□	□	◤	BP		OVfnv	21	
◢	◤	◤	■	□	P		BGILQRSTVXZn	22	
◤	◤	◤	◢	◤	P	d	ILOVZn	23	
◢	▨	□	◢	□	P	d	GIJLQSTVWn	24	
◢	◤	□	◢	◤	D		GIJLQRSTVWZn	25	
■	◤	□	◢	◤	BPg	d	FQSVnv	26	
◤	▨	◤	▨	▨	JOWgjm	Cdr		27	◀
□	◤	◤	◢	◤		d	FIJLNOVZn	28	
▨	◤	◤	□	◤	PZ		JLNOVZn	29	
□	◤	□	◢	◤	GP		ILQSTVZn	30	
◢	◤	◤	◢	◤		C	ILQSVZn	31	
◢	◤	◤	◢	◤		C	ILSVZn	32	
◤	▨	◤	□	◤	P	d	FILOVZnv	33	
◤	◤	◤	◤	▨	KPWy	d		34	

C = lens cap rather than integral lens cover

D = several of our samples broke down

F = flash range less than about 3m with ISO 100 film (applies to tele lens only on some cameras)

G = viewfinder difficult to use with glasses

H = no focus hold for off-centre subjects

I = no flash interlock (you might press the shutter release before flash is charged up)

J = slight light leaks; streaks or fogging may show on pictures if you leave the uncased camera in the bright sun

L = alkaline batteries, not lithium-type

M = has manual wind and rewind

N = no indicator that film is loaded correctly; there is a risk of getting through a whole film only to discover that the film never wound on

O = you cannot prevent flash firing in low light

Q = no sensor flash; you have to switch flash on when indicated by a light

R = no 'ready' signal in or near viewfinder or audible bleep when flash is charged – you may have to move your eye away from the subject

S = no self timer

T = no tripod socket

V = flash cannot usually be used to fill in shadows in daylight

W = no window at the back to show what type and length of film is loaded

X = no DX system; you must set film speed

Z = motor rewind does not start automatically

a = shutter lock must be set separately to lens cover (you can forget)

f = you can't rewind before end of film

n = no LCD display panel

v = vignetting is particularly severe – dark corners noticeable in many pictures

x = flash is not built in

AUTOFOCUS CAMERAS

	Target price (1)	Weight (2)	Size (3)	Maximum aperture (4)	Focal length (5)	Film speed range (6)	Shutter speed range (7)	Exposure control (8)
	£	g		f	mm	ISO	sec	
AUTOFOCUS – DUAL FOCAL LENGTH								
1 **Fuji DL-160 Tele** (Japan)	80	365	▶▶▶▶	4.7/7.1	35/55	100,400	1/100	F
2 **Fuji DL-400 Tele** (Japan)	130	375	▶▶▶▶	3.2/7.1	35/70	50–1600	1/10–1/250	Ap
3 **Leica AF-C1** (Japan)	240	405	▶▶▶▶	2.6/5.3	40/80	50–3200	1/8–1/250	Ap
4 **Minolta AF-Tele 60** (Japan)	110	335	▶▶▶▶	3.7/6.8	38/60	100,400	1/30–1/125	Ap
5 **Minolta AF-Tele Super** (Japan)	150	405	▶▶▶▶	2.6/5.6	38/80	50–3200	1/8–1/200	Ap
6 **Minolta Weathermatic 35 DL** (Japan)	130	465	▶▶▶▶▶	3.6/6.0	35/50	100–1000[1]	1/30–1/125	Ap
▶ 7 **Nikon TW20** (Japan)	120	335	▶▶▶	3.6/5.5	35/55	100–1000	1/4–1/250	Ap
▶ 8 **Nikon TW2** (Japan)	150	355	▶▶▶	3.1/6.7	35/70	50–1600	1/4–1/250	Ap
▶ 9 **Olympus AF-1 Twin** (Japan)	140	310	▶▶▶	3.0/6.3	35/70	50–3200	1/15–1/350	Ap
10 **Ricoh RT-550** (Japan)	140	355	▶▶▶▶	3.0/6.2	35/70	64–3200	1–1/500	Ap
11 **Sirius Twin 90** (Korea)	50	355	▶▶▶▶	3.3/5.5	35/55	100,400	1/30–1/60	Ap
12 **Vivitar TL 125** (Korea)	60	380	▶▶▶▶	4.7/7.2	35/55	100,400	1/30–1/200	Ap
13 **Yashica DF-100AF** (Hong Kong)	90	350	▶▶▶	5.0/8.4	35/55	100,400	1/60,1/125	N
AUTOFOCUS – ZOOM								
▶ 1 **Canon Sureshot Captain Zoom** (Japan)	165	440	▶▶▶▶	3.6–6.0	38–60	50–3200	2–1/500	Ap
2 **Canon Sureshot Zoom-S** (Japan)	150	425	▶▶▶▶	3.5–5.6	38–60	50–3200	2–1/500	Ap
▶ 3 **Canon Sureshot Zoom XL** (Japan)	190	620	▶▶▶▶▶	3.4–7.0	39–85	50–3200	2–1/250	Ap
4 **Fuji DL-350 Zoom** (Japan)	100	375	▶▶▶▶	3.9–4.8	38–55	50–1600	1/2–1/250	Ap
▶ 5 **Fuji DL-800 Zoom** (Japan)	130	505	▶▶▶▶▶	3.5–7.2	40–80	50–1600	1/8–1/250	Ap
▶ 6 **Fuji FZ-2000 Zoom** (Japan)	220	565	▶▶▶▶▶	3.6–9.0	40–105	50–1600	1/4–1/250	Ap
▶ 7 **Konica Z-up 80 RC** (Japan)	200	510	▶▶▶▶▶	3.6–6.8	40–80	50–3200	1–1/200	Ap
8 **Minolta AF-Zoom 65** (Japan)	135	405	▶▶▶▶	4.3–6.6	38–65	50–1600	1/4–1/250	Ap
9 **Minolta AF-Zoom 90** (Japan)	190	505	▶▶▶▶▶	3.4–7.2	38–90	50–3200	1/8–1/250	Ap
▶ 10 **Nikon TW Zoom** (Japan)	180	415	▶▶▶▶	3.1–6.5	35–80	64–1600	1–1/300	Ap
11 **Olympus AZ-1 Zoom** (Japan)	170	465	▶▶▶▶	3.5–6.7	35–70	50–800	3–1/250	Ap
▶ 12 **Olympus AZ-200 Superzoom** (Japan)	200	420	▶▶▶▶	4.3–5.5	38–80	50–3200	1–1/125	Ap
13 **Panasonic C-900 ZM** (Japan)	150	465	▶▶▶▶	3.6–7.0	35–70	50–1600	1/2–1/250	Ap
14 **Panasonic C-2000ZM** (Japan)	150	445	▶▶▶▶	3.4–7.0	38–80	50–1600	1/2–1/125	Ap
15 **Pentax Zoom 60** (Japan)	130	370	▶▶▶▶	4.4–7.1	38–60	50–1600	1/30–1/200	Ap
16 **Pentax Zoom 70-X** (Japan)	180	435	▶▶▶▶	3.2–5.9	35–70	50–1600	1/4–1/250	Ap
17 **Pentax Zoom 90** (Japan)	185	460	▶▶▶▶	3.3–7.3	38–90	50–1600	2–1/250	Ap
▶ 18 **Ricoh RZ-750 Zoom** (Japan)	160	415	▶▶▶▶	3.2–6.1	38–76	64–3200	3–1/125	Ap
19 **Samsung AF Zoom** (Korea)	150	430	▶▶▶▶	3.1–6.1	35–70	50–1600	1/4–1/250	Ap
20 **Vivitar 300Z** (Japan)	100	400	▶▶▶▶	4.0–6.1	38–60	50–1600	1/15–1/125	Ap
21 **Yashica Zoomtec** (Japan)	150	430	▶▶▶▶	3.4–7.0	38–80	50–1600	1/2–1/125	Ap

▶ Recommended in the Buying Guide ◀

KEY TO RATINGS best ◩ > ◩ > ☐ > ◪ > ■ **worst**

Optical quality 9	Focus accuracy 10	Close-up ability 11	12 Exposure accuracy: Daylight	Flash	Overall ratings: Picture quality 13	Versatility 14	Convenience 15	Compared with 'standard' camera: Advantages 16	Possible advantages 16	Disadvantages 16	
◤	□	□	■	◤	□	■	◤			FGILOSTVZn	1
◤	▨	◤	◤	◤	◤	◤	◤	Wip		RW	2
□	◤	▨	▨	◤	◤	◤	▨	OWx			3
◤	□	◤	◤	▨	□	□	◤	BP	d	FOVWfn	4
□	◤	▨	◤	◤	□	◤	▨	OWx	f		5
◤	◤	◤	◤	◤	◤	□	◤	BY		FJOSTVWafn	6
◤	▨	▨	▨	□	◤	◤	◤	OQc		FGn	7 ◀
◤	▨	▨	◤	□	◤	◤	▨	JOW	ds	J	8 ◀
□	▨	▨	◤	◤	◤	▨	◤	JOcwy		FGIJ	9 ◀
◤	□	◤	◤	◤	□	◤	◤	JOWcg		FJ	10
◤	◪	■	◪	◤	□	◪	◤	BP		FIJQSTZn	11
◤	◤	□	◤	□	◤	◪	◤			IJLQSTZn	12
◤	◤	◤	■	◤	□	◪	◤	GP	d	FJLQRV	13
□	◤	▨	◤	▨	◤	◤	▨	DGOPRWbo			1 ◀
□	◤	▨	◤	▨	◤	◤	▨	GOPWo			2
◤	▨	▨	□	◤	◤	▨	▨	JOPRWaiw	d		3 ◀
□	▨	◤	◤	◤	◤	□	◤	i		FJOVfn	4
◤	◤	▨	◤	▨	◤	◤	▨	GOWcip	d	W	5 ◀
□	▨	▨	◤	▨	◤	▨	◤	GJOWimw	d		6 ◀
◤	▨	▨	◤	◤	◤	▨	▨	DEGJOPRWZjmu	fr	J	7 ◀
□	◤	◤	◤	▨	◤	◤	▨	PWx		F	8
□	▨	▨	◤	◤	◤	▨	◤	Oao	ef	DFQ	9
◤	◤	▨	◤	◤	◤	▨	▨	JOWacx	d	J	10 ◀
◤	▨	▨	□	◤	◤	▨	◤	JOPWmw	df	DIJa	11
□	◤	▨	◤	▨	◤	▨	▨	GJOQRWanos	df	DIJ	12 ◀
◤	▨	◤	◤	◤	◤	◤	◤	Ggu	d		13
□	◤	▨	◤	▨	◤	◤	▨	GWiuw	r		14
◤	◤	◤	▨	◤	◤	□	▨	Gw	d	OSTf	15
◤	◤	▨	□	▨	◤	▨	◤	JOWcmuw	d		16
□	□	▨	◤	▨	□	▨	▨	JOPWcjmw	dr	G	17
□	◤	▨	◤	▨	◤	▨	▨	GJOWgjm	der		18 ◀
□	▨	▨	◤	▨	□	◤	◤	OWw	d	Gn	19
◤	▨	◤	◤	◤	◤	□	◤			JO	20
□	◤	▨	◤	▨	◤	◤	▨	GPWiuw	r		21

[1] Instructions say not to use slide films faster than ISO 400

SLIDE PROJECTORS

From *Which?* October 1989

A wide range of devices can be used for viewing your slides, from a simple hand viewer that you hold up to the light, costing under £1, to an audio-visual set-up with two powerful projectors for a lecture hall, costing well over £1,000. We have tested autofocus projectors with 150W lamps. These are the most popular and probably the most sensible choice for normal home use. If you often want to use a very large screen, it would be worth considering a 250W projector; some of these are listed in the similar models column of the Table.

For several brands you can buy models with infra-red remote controls. These are rather more convenient to use and store than the wired versions we tested, but currently cost about £40 more.

Two of the tested projectors had built-in back-projection screens for viewing your slides without having to set up a separate larger screen. However, the best performing of these was bulkier, heavier and more expensive than the equivalent model without this facility. You might do better to buy a separate viewer with medium-sized screen and magazine feed – about £50 – in addition to a projector.

You'll also need a projection screen; they cost £20 to £30.

Do you need a special lens?

Most projectors come with a standard lens with an aperture of f2.8 and focal length of 85mm. You may be quite satisfied with the picture this gives, but if you want to improve the quality of the image, consider buying a special lens.

High quality lenses (£40 to £110) may improve both brightness and sharpness. We were able to buy high quality lenses for all the projectors except the Hanimex and Reflecta AFM. Leitz Pradovit projectors are usually supplied with a high quality lens (or you can ask for a curved field lens instead). The high quality lenses produced a significant improvement in picture quality for the Braun, Kinderman and Zeiss projectors.

BUYING GUIDE

BEST BUYS The **Reflecta Diamator AF** (£80) offers the best combination of performance, convenience and price. Marginally better on performance and convenience (except for carrying around), but more expensive, is the **Liesegang 3000 AF-S** (£130).

Curved field lenses (£60 to £90) are designed to give a sharp picture when the heat of the projector causes the slide to bow. This bowing – particularly severe with unglazed slides in loose mounts – makes it impossible to get both the centre and edges of the picture in focus at the same time. We tested curved field

Slides on TV

For £1,265, the Tamron Fotovix IIx will project slides on to your TV – and even record them on video tape. You just plug it into your TV or VCR and put a slide underneath the lens. It then transmits the photographic image to the screen. It's flexible too. By means of a colour reversal switch it can project colour negatives – so you can use the negatives from print films as well as slides. There's also a zoom feature.

In our tests, the actual quality of the picture wasn't particularly good. The best images were directly from slides, but these weren't up to the standard of a good slide projector: some detail was lost and subtler shades of colour didn't show up. The quality of the image from colour negatives was less good than from slides. It could be improved by manual adjustment, but no instructions were given for this.

When slides or negatives were transferred on to video tape the quality was reduced still further. The Fotovix IIx doesn't have connections for S-VHS either, to take advantage of new video technology.

At the price we can't recommend the Fotovix IIx – it's very convenient, but the results don't justify the cost. If you still like the idea of having your slides on video tape, a number of photo processors offer this service starting at about £30 for 130 slides.

lenses for Braun, Kinderman, Leitz, Reflecta and Zeiss projectors. The Leitz was much the best at producing pictures which were sharp all over (particularly if you focused on a spot slightly away from the centre) and could be used with several different projectors – see Table. The Braun and Reflecta were a bit better than a normal lens.

FACTS, FIGURES AND TEST RESULTS

1 Brands

All the projectors tested have automatic slide feed from magazines into which you have previously loaded slides, a wired remote control for slide changing and a 150W halogen-type lamp. We did not include a Kodak Carousel projector because the cheapest autofocus model costs about £350.

2 Price

There can be big differences in what you pay for projectors and accessories, so it's worth checking advertisements in photographic magazines and phoning dealers, who often don't list all the projectors they stock.

3 Lens supplied

We bought the projectors with the lenses normally supplied; we list their specifications so that you can check in the shop that you are buying the same type. You can buy zoom lenses for some models. These can fill the screen from a range of distances without having to move projector or screen, but quality is unlikely to be as good as with a fixed focal length lens. You can also buy longer focal length lenses if you want to project from the back of a hall.

4 Similar models

We list alternative models which have similar optics and construction; footnotes show how they differ from tested models.

SLIDE PROJECTORS

Brands (1)	Price (2) £	Lens supplied[1] (3)	Similar models (4)	Types of slide magazine (5)	Weight (6) kg	Picture quality (7): Brightness	Sharpness	Evenness
1 **Braun Novamat 515 AF-S** (W Germany)	100	2.8/85	515 AF £85[3]	AEL	3.5	◤	◤	◤
2 **Braun Multimag 5015 AF-S** (W Germany)	140	2.8/85	5025 AF-S £160[4]	ABELP	4.8	□	◤	▩
3 **Enna Monitor AF** (W Germany)[10]	130	2.8/90		AEL	4.5	◤	◤	□
4 **Hanimex Autofocus** (China)	90	2.8/85		EH	4.0	□	■	□
5 **Jessop Showmaster AF** (W Germany)	70	2.8/85	A £55[7]; AFP £95[6]; AFP-IR £115[5,6]	BES	4.4	□	◤	□
6 **Kinderman Diafocus AF 8001** (W Germany)	80	2.8/85	A 8002 £70[7]; AF250 8004 £150[4]	AEL	4.1	◤	□	◤
7 **Kinderman Diafocus 1500L** (W Germany)	150	2.8/85	2500L £180[4]	AEL	4.3	◤	◤	▩
▶ 8 **Liesegang 3000 AF-S** (W Germany)	130	2.8/85	3500 AF-S £160[4]	AEL	4.3	◤	◤	▩
9 **Leitz Pradovit 153** (W Germany)	230	2.5/90	153IR £295[5,8]; 253IR £350[4,5,8]	AEL	4.6	▩	▩	▩
▶ 10 **Reflecta Diamator AF** (Portugal)	80	2.8/90	A £70[7]; AF-IR £130[5]	AELR	4.2	◤	◤	◤
11 **Reflecta Diamator AFM** (Portugal)	110	2.8/90		AE	7.9	◤	◤	◤
12 **Zeiss Ikon Ikolux Autofocus** (W Germany)	100	2.8/85	RF £80[7]	AEL	3.5	□	□	▩
13 **Zeiss Ikon Perkeo 315 AF** (W Germany)	130	2.8/85	315 IR £150[5]; 415 AFS £140[9]	EL	4.0	◤	□	□

▶ Recommended in the Buying Guide ◀

KEY TO RATINGS best ▩ > ◤ > □ > ◪ > ■ worst

[1] Figures are for aperture and focal length
[2] No problems likely when using a European Standard magazine
[3] No remote control focusing
[4] Has 250W lamp
[5] Has infra-red remote control
[6] Has timer, fade control and audio/visual socket
[7] No autofocus
[8] Has spare lamp for immediate changeover
[9] Has remote control focusing for fine adjustments
[10] Now replaced by similar AF-D (£140) – has advantage D but not T
[11] Manufacturer tells us modified to improve slide handling

5 Types of slide magazine

A = CS straight (Agfa), 40 or 100 slides
B = Paximat box-type, 36 or 50
E = European standard (Leitz), 36 or 50
H = Hanimex Rondex 120 circular
L = LKM straight, 60 or 80
P = Paximat circular, 100
R = Reflecta CS circular, 175
S = Showmaster circular, 100

All the projectors can take the European standard straight magazine. However, if you like to keep your slides already sorted into magazines, ready for projection, this type takes up a lot of storage space. The newer CS and LKM magazines hold up to twice the number of slides in the same space and have the added advantage that the slides will not easily fall out if you accidentally invert the magazine. On the other hand, for CS magazines you must use CS mounts (returned from the Agfa laboratory or available for d-i-y mounting) and neither type will take older slides which are thicker

	8 Working of autofocus	9 Handling poor slides	10 Clearing a jammed slide	11 Overall convenience	12 Advantages and disadvantages		
	▨	□	▨	□	F	hlv	1
	◩	◪[2]	◩	□	FP	s	2
	□	□	◪	◩	ABCFRTZ	abmst	3
	◪	◪[2]	□	□	PQT	dhms	4
	◩	■[11]	□	□	FKPTZ	cdhsv	5
	◩	◩	◪	□	CTZ	h	6
	◩	▨	■	□	AFLMTZ	h	7
	◩	▨	▨	◩	ACFP	hls	8 ◀
	◩	◩	■	□	ACFMTZ	—	9
	◩	▨	□	◩	AFQRT	dmsv	10 ◀
	◩	▨	□	□	BDT	dsv	11
	◩	◩	▨	□	CQ	hv	12
	◩	▨	■	◪	CPST	lv	13

than 2mm. Circular magazines can be awkward to store.

6 Weight

The Reflecta Diamator AFM was much larger than and twice as heavy as most of the other projectors because of the way it converted to back-projection on to its built-in screen.

7 Picture quality

Brightness We tested all the projectors with identical 150W lamps. The brightest projectors were those which lost least light in their optical systems. Choose a projector with a higher rating if you want to use it for lecturing or if you like to under-expose your slides so as to get more intense colours.

Sharpness Even when tested with a glass slide, all the projectors were noticeably less sharp in the corners, the Hanimex was quite blurred. For the more standard slides (without glass) corner sharpness would be worse, since the slides tend to curve slightly after a few seconds of projection due to heat from the lamp. You may be able to improve things by setting the focus to be sharpest slightly away from the centre, or you could try a curved-field lens.

But there is no point in worrying about a lens to make the whole picture sharp unless you take special care to align the projector perpendicular to the centre of the screen. An inexpensive projector stand is a better solution than telephone directories, but if you must tilt the front of the projector upwards you should tilt the screen forwards at the top.

Evenness Before measuring how evenly the light was distributed over the screen we checked that the lamps were correctly centred in their holders. Only the Braun Multimag and Enna projectors supplied a test slide and gave instructions for lamp centring.

8 Working of autofocus

With autofocus, you focus the first slide – usually by turning the lens in its mount – and the rest are corrected automatically even as they curve due to heat. Except for the Hanimex which focused less consistently, most worked well, although the Braun Novamat was the only one to focus correctly a mixture of glazed and unglazed slides.

9 Handling poor slides

Not all your slides may be thin and in good condition. We made up a set of 36 slides of various makes and materials (including cardboard), thick and thin, glazed and unglazed, and ran them through each projector. Several projectors coped with everything without trouble; others misfed and jammed – see rating.

10 Clearing a jammed slide

When a projector does jam, it's annoying – and the slide can be damaged by heat from the lamp or in the process of extracting it. Our ratings reflect how easy it was to unjam the projector and extract a slide without damage. In the case of a jam, you should immediately turn off the lamp; unplug the projector before trying to extract the slide.

Some projectors (none tested this time) can be set to change slides at timed intervals; it is unwise to leave these unattended in case a jam occurs.

11 Overall convenience

This rating is based on ease of:

- making fine adjustments of focus
- slide changing by remote control
- clearing a jammed slide
- carrying the projector
- fitting magazines
- correcting an inverted slide
- changing the lamp
- cleaning the optical system
- tilting and levelling to fit your screen
- projecting a single slide
- projecting a particular slide from its numbered position in the magazine.

We also looked at the instruction booklets (none was very clear and comprehensive) and checked whether there was a mains switch to turn off the fan without having to unplug the projector.

12 Advantages and disadvantages

All have a screw foot for raising the front of the projector.

Advantages

A = light-beam arrow in remote control, for pointing
B = can be converted for back projection on to its built-in screen
C = carrying case available as an extra
D = dimmer control – useful with back-projection screen
F = remote control focusing – for fine adjustments
K = slides remain cooler than average
L = spare lamp which can be switched into place immediately
M = screen is masked when a slide is missing from the magazine
P = small preview panel for checking a slide in the dark
Q = both fan and slide changing are quieter than average
R = packs up well for carrying
S = projecting a specific slide is easy with both types of magazine
T = socket for linking to tape recorder for sound commentary
Z = can be fitted with the Leitz Color Plan CF 2.5/90 curved field lens (£75)

Disadvantages

a = remote focus only after switching off autofocus at the projector
b = back-projection screen too bright when viewed straight on
c = remote focus changes autofocus setting
d = difficult to clean dust off optical system
h = no handle for carrying
l = hard to change lamp until it's cooled
m = mains switch does not turn off fan noise; you have to unplug
s = slide-changing arm sticks out in use – you need extra space
t = slides get hotter than average
v = no provision for sideways levelling
z = large – needs more storage space

ABOUT THE HOUSE AND GARDEN

Computers • Answering Machines
Fax Machines • Shavers • Smoke Alarms
Emergency Alarms • Drills • Hot Air Guns
Heated Propagators • Lawnmowers • Lawn Trimmers

COMPUTERS

PC/AT Compatibles

From *Which?* November 1989

What sort of computer?

The computer world is split between computers which work with the same programs as an IBM PC (IBM personal computer), and those which don't. The IBM PC was introduced in 1981 and has been both copied by other manufacturers, and developed by IBM and others over the years.

Because the copies are made by a variety of different manufacturers, they are often called IBM- (or PC-) compatible computers (or 'clones'). The important point is that these new computers can use the same programs as the original PCs, but they can do things faster and better.

As the computers have developed, so have the programs that they can use. There's now an impressive array of programs for the IBM PC and compatibles which can, for example, help trace your family tree or run machine tools. Computers which work like the IBM PC are by far the commonest type used by businesses. For this report, we've tested 13 IBM-compatibles. Leading non-compatibles such as the Apple Macintosh may have advantages – in ease of use, graphics or speed, say – which make them suitable for you.

Which type of IBM-compatible?

There are three distinct types of IBM compatible. What separates them is the silicon chip which does the computer processing. These chips are identified by numbers.

The first PCs had 8088 or 8086 processor chips. The next step up is the 80286 chip which can operate faster (and can do more things). IBM used this chip in their PC/AT computer (AT stands for advanced technology). The computers in this report are fitted with 80286 chips. Beyond this there are even faster machines which have 80386 chips.

To test the difference in performance of computers fitted with the three types of chip, we put machines with an 8086 and an 80836 chip through the same performance tests as we did the PC/AT (80286) computers. The Table shows the differences in performance that you might expect (the higher the number in the Table, the faster the chip performed, relative to the PC). Performance depends not only on the chip, but on the speed the computer runs at (the 'clock speed'), so computers fitted with the same chip won't necessarily perform identically.

	Chip	Typical cost £	Computer performance
PC	8086	920 to 2,000+	1
PC/AT	80286	1,200 to 4,000+	3.6
386	80386	2,100 to 7,000+	6

Prices include a monitor and a hard disk drive, but not a printer. Generally the level of equipment is higher with the faster chips – a 386 is likely to be fitted with a bigger and faster hard disk as standard.

BUYING GUIDE

For this report, we've tested 13 PC/AT compatible computers. These can work in the same way as the original IBM PC and use the same programs.

In a joint test with Belgian and Dutch consumer organisations, we tested some of the computers most readily available in each country. However, there is a vast number of other brands and models.

Prices will, of course, vary, depending on things like the monitor and video option that you choose. All the prices of the versions that we tested are in **bold** in the summaries.

Technological advances occur rapidly in the computer market and this may mean that some prices have fallen considerably since our tests – in some cases, up to £1,000 less. If you come across one of our tested computers at a greatly reduced price, use our ratings to check its performance. Where prices have increased, this may be because the specification has been changed such as more computer memory or a larger hard disk – which may make the computer better value for money.

FOR PERFORMANCE

BEST BUY

If performance is all-important to you, the **Compaq Deskpro 286e** £2,806 plus £81 for operating system performed extremely well but is expensive.

BUDGET BEST BUYS

BEST BUYS

If price is a major consideration, choose between the **Amstrad PC2286** £1,379 for mono, £1,609 for high resolution colour (includes 40Mb hard disk) and the **Tandon PCA sl** £1,321 (with Hercules-type display).

Of the other machines we tested, the **Dell system 200** £1,724 (plus £75 for MS-DOS) and the **Tulip AT Compact 2** £1,820 performed well at a fairly reasonable price.

OVERALL

BEST BUY

The **Commodore PC40 III** £1,899 performed well at a reasonable price and is our Best Buy overall.

Do I need a fast machine?

As you can see from the Table there's a big difference in the speeds that computers work. However, even the slowest of computers could be satisfactory if your requirements are undemanding.

A PC (8088 or 8086) is likely to be fast enough for word processing, and for small spreadsheets and databases. But, for example, the spreadsheet recalculation we used to measure computing performance took 27 seconds on a PC. The machine had to perform thousands of separate calculations, so 27 seconds may not seem that long to wait. However, it can get very tedious waiting for the computer to catch up. By comparison the PC/AT took just 7½ seconds to complete the same task.

If you want to make use of desk top publishing, or other programs which need a lot of computer power (a large database, say), you're likely to find that a PC isn't fast enough. You may even find that a PC/AT isn't fast enough either (though for home use that would be unlikely). If you can, it's worth seeing the programs you want to use demonstrated on PC, PC/AT and 386, to find out which type you need.

Can I use my home computer if I bring work home?

Although data can be sent along telephone lines using special equipment, the most likely way of bringing work home will be on a floppy disk. If you use an IBM-compatible at work, you should be able to work on one at home, too. But you'll need matching sized floppy disks. There are now 5¼in disks with 360Kb and 1.2Mb capacities, and 3½in with 720Kb and 1.44Mb capacities. The higher capacity drive in each size will usually work with lower capacity disks, but not vice versa. The 3½in disks are becoming more popular – one reason being that they are in hard plastic cases which offer more protection for the magnetic disk inside.

Once you've got the data home, you're likely to need the same programs you use at work. These can be expensive so you should check prices before you splash out on a computer.

Do computers go out of date?

Yes. What was a fast and fully featured computer five years ago won't run much of the advanced business software available now – either because there isn't enough computer memory, or because you need a hard disk or a better display, for example.

We can't guarantee that there won't be dramatic changes over the next year or so, but it's likely that the computers featured in this report will last a good few years before becoming outdated. A 386 machine will outlast a PC/AT – not just because it's faster, but also because the 386 chip has facilities (not found on the AT chip) which programmers will want to make more use of in the future.

What are the options?

These are some of the things you'll need to make decisions about:

Size of hard disk (storage) In general the bigger the better – it's surprising how quickly it fills up. We've tested computers with 20Mb hard disks. You can get hard disks which will store over 100Mb, but they are expensive. Most manufacturers offer a range of hard disks of different sizes for their computers.

Amount of memory (for running programs) For a PC/AT you should aim for a minimum of 640Kb. Some of the computers on test have more memory fitted as standard.

Type of display You need to decide whether you want a colour screen (useful with many different programs), and also the quality of video display you want. There are different standards of display; the highest quality displays can usually show all the lower quality ones, too. For highest quality colour choose VGA or EGA (though for some programs, EGA can't show quite such sharp pictures). Avoid CGA which is not good enough for many programs. You can also use these displays with monochrome monitors. The colours will appear as shades of grey – again the best display will be VGA. Hercules-type displays give high resolution text and graphics and this is the standard to go for if you just need black and white (or green or amber). Most of the computers in this report were tested with colour VGA displays.

Technotalk

This report uses certain technical terms to describe features and functions – here are some explantions:

Mouse This is a control – about the size of a bar of soap – which you push around the desk top to move a pointer on the screen.

Operating system (MS-DOS for the computers in this report) This is the program which tells the computer how it should work and allows you to tell it to, for example, load a program. You can't use a computer without an operating system. Usually this will come with the computer. We tell you with which of the computers MS-DOS is extra.

Spreadsheet A computer program which deals with numbers (usually in columns and rows) and allows you to add, subtract, etc. It may also enable you to draw graphs from the information you enter.

Database With this type of program a computer can be used like a card index – one which can be sorted through very fast.

Word processor These programs allow the computer to be used as a typewriter with a memory. You can go back and edit, check the spelling and combine documents for example.

Desk top publishing (DTP) A program for laying out text on a page, of a magazine, for example.

Hard disk This is a high capacity disk (usually built-in) on which you can keep programs and information.

Kb and Mb (or Meg) – kilobytes and megabytes. These are measures of the amount of information that can be stored either on a disk or in the computer's memory. A byte can store one character. A Kb is 1,024 bytes, and a Mb is 1,024 Kb.

Windows This is a program that allows you to use a mouse to tell the computer what to do.

Display standards VGA, EGA, CGA and Hercules-type are standard computer displays. They offer different quality pictures.

FACTS, FIGURES AND TEST RESULTS

Performance

This has been tested by seeing how long the computer takes to perform various tasks, and then giving a rating for:

- **computing** We looked at how long each computer took to recalculate a large spreadsheet. The Zenith took up to one and a half times longer than the others to complete our test. Pick a faster machine than the Zenith if you want to perform lots of calculations or computer-intensive work (eg desk top publishing)
- **video** The time a computer takes to display things on the screen can be important – eg for desk top publishing or working with graphics. The best performers generally took half as long as the worst
- **hard disk** How quickly the computer can get information from the hard disk. It's important to have a good performer if you're working with large programs or a large database, say.

Monitor

This rating is for picture quality. Our tests checked picture distortion, effects if you are displaying a white screen and so on. Our samples of the Hewlett Packard and Olivetti couldn't be turned up bright enough – you'd need to work in a darkened room. If reflections are going to be a problem, the Amstrad and Compaq suffered most. For all the screens which are bright enough, a screen filter would help.

Noise

Noise levels that are acceptable in an office could be very annoying in quieter surroundings. None of the computers we tested is silent – they all have cooling fans. Some make other noises, too. There is also noise from the disk drives when they are in use – this didn't affect our ratings. If you think you'll be bothered by noise, consider the computers with a ◤ rating. The Amstrad was particularly noisy.

Interference

Computers cause interference which can affect radios, TVs etc. Computers with a rating of □ or ◪ are likely to cause interference to a radio in the next room; the Amstrad (with a rating of ■) is likely to cause interference throughout your home and could affect neighbours, too. From 1992 new computers will have to comply with an EC standard which would require a ◢ rating in this table.

Manuals

We've looked at how useful the manuals provided are for beginners and experts. For experts the Compaq was best. Complete beginners are unlikely to find all the help they'd need even from the best beginners' manuals.

Cost of sample systems

Here we give prices for some of the monitor and video options available (the option tested is in **bold**). Where available we've tested computers with a 20Mb hard disk – in the summaries we tell you if this wasn't standard. You can usually pay extra to have extra disk drives or a bigger hard disk, say.

Where to buy

The computers in this report are available from a variety of sources – shops in the high street (eg Tandy), specialist dealers (eg Hewlett Packard), or only by mail order (Dell).

The price you pay can vary, too – though you may need to sacrifice the advantages of having a local dealer to sort out your problems if you choose the cheapest price. Look for discount prices in specialist magazines.

KEY TO RATINGS best ◢ > ◤ > □ > ◪ > ■ worst

AMSTRAD PC2286

Performance		**Monitor**	◤
computing	◤	**Noise**	■
video	◢	**Interference**	■
hard disk	[1]	**Manuals**	◤

Cost of sample systems: mono VGA £1,379, **12″ high resolution colour VGA £1,609,** 14″ high resolution colour VGA £1,724 (low resolution £1,494)
Prices include: 1Mb computer memory, 40Mb hard disk, mouse and Windows, 12 month on-site maintenance.
Verdict: Noisy. Tested model had a slow hard disk.
Budget Best Buy
[1] Early Amstrad PC2286 and PC2386 computers – including our sample – had faulty hard disk controllers which could cause the hard disk to fail. Amstrad say that they have modified faulty machines and that the replacement controller works more quickly.

COMMODORE PC40 III

Performance			
computing	◩	**Monitor**	□
video	□	**Noise**	◩
hard disk	▨	**Interference**	□
		Manuals	□

Cost of sample systems: mono VGA £1,699, **colour VGA £1,899**
Prices include: 1Mb computer memory, 40Mb hard disk, 12 month on-site maintenance.
Verdict: Fast hard disk, quiet. Best Buy

COMPAQ DESKPRO 286E

Performance			
computing	◩	**Monitor**	□
video	◩	**Noise**	□
hard disk	▨	**Interference**	◩
		Manuals	▨

Cost of sample systems: mono VGA £2,496, **colour VGA £2,806**
Prices include: 1Mb computer memory, 20Mb hard disk. MS-DOS £81 extra.
Verdict: Pricey. Fast hard disk. Best Buy for performance

DELL SYSTEM 200

Performance			
computing	◩	**Monitor**	◩
video	◩	**Noise** [2]	◪
hard disk	□	**Interference**	□
		Manuals	◩

Cost of sample systems: Hercules-type mono £1,379, mono VGA £1,551, **colour VGA £1,724**
Prices include: 640Kb computer memory, 20Mb hard disk. 12 month on-site maintenance. MS-DOS £75 extra.
Verdict: Rather noisy, but worth considering
[2] Makers say that current models are quieter

HEWLETT PACKARD VECTRA ES/12

Performance			
computing	◩	**Monitor**	□
video	◩	**Noise**	□
hard disk	◪	**Interference**	▨
		Manuals	□

Cost of sample systems: mono VGA £2,772, **colour VGA £2,890**
Prices include: 640Kb computer memory, 20Mb hard disk, 12 month on-site maintenance. MS-DOS £108 extra.
Verdict: Pricey. Passed interference test. Slow hard disk

HYUNDAI SUPER 286C

Performance			
computing	◩	**Monitor**	□
video	□	**Noise**	◪
hard disk	□	**Interference**	□
(tested with 20Mb hard disk)		**Manuals**	◩

Cost of sample systems: Hercules-type mono £1,542, **colour EGA £1,927,** mono VGA £1,812, colour VGA £2,065
Prices include: 640Kb computer memory, 30Mb hard disk (around £12 more than 20Mb option)
Verdict: Generally a poor performer

IBM MODEL 50

Performance			
computing	◩	**Monitor**	□
video	□	**Noise**	◩
hard disk	◩	**Interference**	▨
		Manuals	□

Cost of sample systems: mono VGA £2,377, **colour VGA £2,639**
Prices include: 1Mb computer memory, 20Mb hard disk. MS-DOS £75 extra.
Verdict: Pricey. Passed interference test

LASER 286/2

Performance		**Monitor**	□
computing	◩	(different monitor supplied in UK)	
video	□	**Noise**	□
hard disk	◪	**Interference**	□
		Manuals	◩

Cost of sample systems: Hercules-type mono £1,857, **colour EGA £2,283,** mono VGA £2,202, colour VGA £2,668
Prices include: 640K computer memory, 20Mb hard disk. 12 months on-site maintenance.
Verdict: Pricey. Generally a poor performer

OLIVETTI M290

Performance		**Monitor**	□
computing	◩	(now superseded)	
video	◩	**Noise**	◪
hard disk	■	**Interference**	■
		Manuals	◩

Cost of sample systems: mono VGA £2,830, **colour VGA £3,268**
Prices include: 1Mb computer memory, 20Mb hard disk.
Verdict: Good performance, but rather noisy and pricey. Passed interference test

TANDY 3000NL

Performance		**Monitor**	◩
computing	◩	**Noise**	◪
video	◪	**Interference**	□
hard disk	◪	**Manuals**	◩

Cost of sample systems: Hercules-type £1,954, **colour EGA £2,299**
Prices include: 512Kb computer memory (upgrade to 640Kb £148), 20Mb hard disk. Menu system with various programs (eg word processor). 12 month on-site maintenance.
Verdict: Generally poor performer

TANDON PCA SL

Performance		**Monitor**	□
computing	◩	**Noise**	◪
video	◩	**Interference**	◪
hard disk	◪	**Manuals**	◩

Cost of sample systems: Hercules-type £1,321, mono VGA £1,569, **colour VGA £1,868**
Prices include: 640Kb computer memory, 20Mb hard disk, Windows.
Verdict: Slow hard disk. Rather noisy. Budget Best Buy with Hercules-type display

TULIP AT COMPACT 2

Performance		**Monitor**	□
computing	◩	**Noise**	◪
video	◩	**Interference**	□
hard disk	◩	**Manuals**	□

Cost of sample systems: Hercules-type £1,395, mono VGA £1,590, **colour VGA £1,820**
Prices include: 1Mb computer memory, 20Mb hard disk, Windows, 6 month on-site maintenance.
Verdict: Smallest of the computers on test, good performance though rather noisy. Worth considering

ZENITH Z-286-25

Performance		**Monitor**	□
computing	□	**Noise**	◪
video	◪	**Interference**	■
hard disk	◪	**Manuals**	◩

Cost of sample systems: Hercules-type £1,783, colour EGA £2,069, mono VGA £1,783, **colour VGA £2,069**
Prices include: 512Kb computer memory (upgrade to 640Kb £408), 20Mb hard disk, Windows.
Verdict: Poor performer. Passed interference test

Warranties and servicing

Before you buy your computer, it's worth checking out what servicing is available. Due to increased competition there's a bigger range, and more choice, than ever before. Depending on what computer you buy, you may deal with the manufacturer direct, or you may have to rely on your dealer, or a third party maintenance company such as Granada or Dictaphone. Some High Street retailers, such as Dixons and Comet, now offer servicing deals comparable with more traditional ones.

Once you've bought your computer, you should automatically get a free warranty or guarantee for one year, which provides maintenance (including parts and labour). All the computers in this report had this. About half of the manufacturers we spoke to provide 'on-site' maintenance, which means that they'll come to your home or office to fix the computer. Otherwise you have to pack up the computer, and 'return it to base' – take it back to the manufacturer, perhaps through your dealer. If 'on-site' is an option, there may be an extra charge for it, but it may be worth paying for this if, for example, you don't want to subject your computer to a long journey which could perhaps cause more damage.

If you can't afford, or don't want, to have your computer out of action for any length of time, look for a warranty which promises to mend your computer within a certain period, or even lend you a similar model for the duration. A few companies offer this, with a response period ranging from one to 14 days.

After your free warranty period is up, you may well want further servicing protection. This is called a *maintenance contract* or *extended warranty*. Again, this type of contract could be with the manufacturer, if they offer one, a third party maintenance company recommended by the manufacturer with the dealer, or with an insurance company recommended to you by the manufacturer (with this type of cover, you'd have to organise getting the machine repaired and then invoice the insurers).

The details of these – and the cost – can vary enormously, so it's worth deciding what services you need, and how much you can afford to pay. As with the first-year warranty, look out for on-site maintenance, response time, and how long it lasts. We found costs ranging from £35 for a three-year contract to £310 for only one year. The cost may depend on the retail value of the computer you've bought and things like the type of monitor it has; each year, you may have to pay from about six per cent to 13 per cent of what the computer cost. And again you may have to pay extra for on-site maintenance.

If you're not an experienced computer user you may want *after sales support*, which is usually offered by dealers rather than manufacturers. It means they are obliged to help should you have any problems, say, with a computer program.

Most companies offer a telephone 'hotline' service, to answer queries as they arise. This is usually free, and for as long as you need it.

ANSWERING MACHINES

With or without Built-in Telephones

From *Which?* August 1990

You may want an answering machine because you work at home. Or you may simply want to keep track of your calls or avoid disturbances. You could pay anything between £50 and £250 for one of the machines in this report.

How many messages?

If you expect to receive a lot of messages regularly, you would be wise to go for an answering machine with separate tapes for your announcement and messages. Machines using one tape for both can be inconvenient, since they fast forward to a blank part of the tape before the caller can leave a message.

How convenient?

Most of the readers in our survey were happy with their answering machines. The biggest complaint was losing messages. Panasonics came out better than average for this.

A remote control lets you listen to messages from another phone, when you're away from home. It's a useful feature, but some people in our survey found it too complicated to use.

How reliable?

Three-quarters of the people in our survey had no problem with their machines during the first year. Panasonic machines proved more reliable than average.

BUYING GUIDE

MACHINES WITHOUT A TELEPHONE

BEST BUYS The **Phonelog Datam PM7200** (£130 plus £10 for optional bleeper), has most of the features you're likely to need. The **Panasonic Easa-Phone KX-T1445BE** (£95), was cheaper but still has convenient features. It doesn't record two-way conversations, but it has no time limit for messages when set to VOX operation.

BEST BUYS If you're simply after a cheap, basic machine, the **Answercall TAM90** (£70) and the **Teli Ansa TAM 1** (£70) were the best performers. And they had useful remote controls too.

For a model with a particularly useful paging facility, the **Answercall Challenger** (£250) would be the one to go for.

MACHINES WITH A TELEPHONE

BEST BUY At £100 the **Audioline 890** has useful features and no serious disadvantages. In our original report we also recommended the **British Telecom Rapport** and the **Dialatron 961** as Best Buys – now discontinued (see page 285).

Our survey
The information on the reliability of different brands comes from a survey of 1,475 members carried out in March 1990.

FACTS, FIGURES AND TEST RESULTS

NB: British Telecom have changed their models since our tests. We haven't included them in the Table, but see page 285.

1 Target price
For most machines it's worth shopping around. Find out if the price includes the remote control. Our prices include remote control where this came as standard.

2 Size
The more ▶▶▶s, the larger. Machines using micro cassettes are particularly small and compact but a small machine may be fiddly to operate. A machine which includes a telephone will save shelf or table space. Several models had provision for wall mounting.

3 Similar models
We list machines identical to the tested versions except as noted in the footnotes.

4 Recording system
Where two letters are shown, the first is for the outgoing (announcement) message, the second for incoming messages. On the others the same tape is used for both.

A = standard endless-loop announcement tape – alternative lengths can be bought

M = standard micro cassette tape – 10, 15 or 30 minutes each side

O = ordinary cassette tape – 30 or 45 minutes each side

Machines using ordinary cassettes will take any C-60 or C-90 tape. C-120 cassettes can cause snarl-ups with repeated use.

5 Maximum time for announcement
All the machines allow you at least 30 seconds – long enough for all but the most detailed announcement.

6 Maximum time for each message
Most machines limit the time for each message received; some give you a choice of two time limits. If the caller stops speaking before the limit is reached, the machines are designed to cut off after a period of silence – varying from four to ten seconds on the machines tested. This is convenient, although the Goodmans GTA 50 was much too sensitive to short pauses and could switch off before a caller had finished. A few other machines were also too sensitive. Two of the Panasonics can be set to voice operation (VOX) only, so that the caller can speak for as long as he or she wants – or the end of the tape is reached.

If the message time is limited, you should tell callers in your announcement how long they have got and how to tell when they are about to be cut off – usually a beep, but on a few machines there is no warning (R in *disadvantages* column of the Table). If you receive messages adding up to 30 minutes or more (45 minutes if you use a C-90 tape), your message tape will get full. Most machines warn the caller when this happens and after that either will not answer the call at all, give an alternative announcement, or the caller hears a series of beeps.

7 Features
Capital letters indicate features you're likely to find particularly useful:

ANSWERING MACHINES

	Target price (1)	Size (2)	Similar models (3)	Recording system (4)	Max time for announcement (5)	Max time for each message (6)	7 Features: Answering machine	7 Features: Telephone
	£				sec	sec		
MACHINES WITHOUT TELEPHONES								
▶ 1 **Answercall Challenger** (China)	250	▶▶▶		O/O	60	180	ADMNPRTWa	
2 **Answercall Code-A-Phone 900** (Korea)	50	▶		M	130	150	Ma	
▶ 3 **Answercall TAM90** (China)	70	▶		M	60	145	ACDMRWas	
4 **Betacom LR9000** (China)	60	▶		M	60	60	CDLMNRSmt	
5 **Commtel 628** (Hong Kong)	100	▶▶▶		A/O	39	150	ACEMNRTas	
6 **Goodmans GTA50** (China)	60	▶	GTA 60 £50[6]	M	150	150[3]	CDMNa	
▶ 7 **Panasonic Easa-Phone KX-T1445BE** (Japan)	95	▶▶	KX-T1440BE £80[1]	A/O	33	60/VOX	ACDEMNRa	
▶ 8 **Phonelog Datam PM7200** (Japan)	130	▶▶		A/O	30	300	ACDELMNRT	
9 **Sanyo TAS 270** (Japan)	135	▶▶		A/O	30	145	ADEMRa	
▶ 10 **Teli Ansa TAM 1**(Hong Kong)	70	▶		M	60	145	ACDMRWas	
MACHINES WITH TELEPHONES								
1 **Answercall Voyager** (China)	100	▶▶		M	60	180	CMRWa	# Xm10
▶ 2 **Audioline 890** (Hong Kong)	100	▶▶	Audioline 880 £70[7]	O	120	165[3]	CLMNRWa	# Xm10
3 **Binatone Telecorder 300R** (Taiwan)	100	▶▶		M	45	90	CDMNTWa	# Xm10
4 **Dialatron 1510-S** (Hong Kong)	90	▶▶		M	60	120	CDMNRWm	# Xm10
5 **Panasonic Easa-Phone KX-T2386DBE** (Japan)	100	▶▶		M	33	155	CDMNPWaf	# Xm15
6 **Panasonic Easa-phone KX-T2445BE** (Japan)	180	▶▶▶	KX-T2440BE £150[8]	A/O	30	60/VOX	ACDELMNRTWa	# HMXm32

▶ Recommended in the Buying Guide ◀

KEY TO RATINGS best ■ > ◪ > □ > ◪ > ■ worst

[1] No remote control facility
[2] Control to retain messages or reset to start of tape must be set before you go out
[3] Max time for messages less time taken for announcement
[4] Manufacturer claims microphone now improved
[5] Remote facilities possible only with optional bleeper (£15)
[6] Available only from Boots, excludes remote control
[7] No time/date stamp
[8] On-hook dialling only, no time/date stamp, no LCD display

Answering machine

A = can be set to announce only and not record

C = message counter – usually a flashing light which indicates number of messages received. The Dialatron, Answercall Voyager and Panasonic KX-T2445BE display the number and the Phonelog and Audioline tell you by voice

D = dictation facility – you can record memos on the message tape

E = fast erase – can erase messages on rewind

L = logs time and date of recorded messages

M = monitoring facility – you can listen to incoming message and decide whether to pick up the phone

N = auto-on – if you've forgotten to turn

Remote control	8 Sound quality: Announcement	Incoming message	9 Convenience: Recording announcement	Using machine for messages	Use by remote control	10 Disadvantages	
ABCFPRT	□	◩	□	□	◩	BG	1 ◄
[1]	□	□	□	◪	[1]	BFM	2
A(B)CFPRTV	□	◩	□	□	◪	BFMV	3 ◄
A(B)RV	□	□	◩	◩	■	GHNR	4
ABPR[2]	◩	◩	□	◪	◪	–	5
ABCRT	◪	◪	◩	□	□	IV	6
BMPR	◩	□	□	◩	□	GIV	7 ◄
A(B)CFPRT	◩	□	□	◩	◩	GV	8 ◄
ABCFPRT	□	◩	□	◩	◩	GMPR	9
A(B)CFPRTV	□	◩	□	□	◪	BFMV	10 ◄
(B)RTV	□	□	◩	□	□	BFHIL	1
BCRT	□	□	◩	□	◩	GI	2 ◄
ABCRT	◪[4]	◪	□	□	□	INR	3
BCRT	□	□	□	□	◪	G	4
(B)MPR[5]	◩	□	□	□	□	DGI	5
A(B)CFMPRT[5]	□	□	◩	□	□	G	6

machine on, it will switch on when you phone in and wait for ten or so rings

P = paging – will call you at another number to say there is a message

R = ringing time control – can usually be set to between two and four rings. Longer time useful if you are in the house and may want to answer

S = skips to next message at touch of a button

T = two-way record facility – you can record your conversations

W = machine can be wall-mounted

a = comes with mains adaptor incorporating a 13-amp plug

f = flex in and out of mains adaptor totals over 3½m; no plug supplied

m = plugs directly into the mains – no adaptor needed

s = separate message can be recorded for answer-only setting

t = time of message can be found out by listening to a series of beeps

Telephone

= last number redial

H = has on-hook dialling – you lift handset to speak

M = mute button

X = can be switched to tone dialling – useful for electronic exchanges such as System X and those used in most new offices

m10,m15,m32 = telephone has the number of memories indicated

The built-in telephones had many of the features of separate telephones. The tone dialling option (X) is particularly useful if you are, or are shortly to be, on an electronic exchange. All these phones allowed you to recall at least some of the numbers in their memories by pressing just one key.

Remote control

A = you can change announcement by remote control

B = bleeper supplied

(B) = bleeper optional

C = coded tones on remote control for security – prevents others with a similar machine having access to your messages

F = you can fast forward to next message

M = after hearing your messages you can record a marker beep or words so that next time you call in, you will know which messages are new

P = you can wind back to re-listen to part

of your messages, rather than returning to beginning

- R = you can retain messages after listening to them or reset tape to beginning
- T = from a tone dialling telephone you do not need the remote control
- V = you use a voice sequence to play messages – no remote control supplied

8 Sound quality

We rated the machines for how clearly understandable the announcements and recorded messages were. Machines rated ◩ were satisfactory. Machines rated ◪ might be difficult to understand, particularly if the connection is poor. In general, machines using micro cassettes sounded less good than those using full-sized cassettes.

9 Convenience

Like many appliances, answering machines are easy enough to use once you know how and have had a bit of practice. But the basic operations should be fairly easy to understand, in case someone who doesn't know the machine wants to use it. Instructions were sometimes not very clearly set out, although most machines had instructions permanently marked on them, and/or their remote controls.

Recording your announcement was simple enough on most machines if you followed the instructions carefully. All had built-in microphones and facilities for checking the recording. If you don't get it right first time, you can easily re-do it.

Using the machine for messages – setting it to answer when going out and listening to the messages when you come home – was made very simple with some machines, requiring you to press just one button.

Use by remote control from a telephone away from home was usually easy. Using the voice method rather than a bleeper could be slightly more difficult, but the convenience of not carrying a remote control might make it worthwhile.

10 Disadvantages

We have used the column to note particular drawbacks with some of the machines.

- B = no indication between incoming messages to separate them
- D = cover to cassette compartment easily broken
- F = no fast-forward tape control
- G = there can be gaps of four seconds or more between messages as you listen to them
- H = does not reset to answer after power failure
- I = if you answer the phone from another extension you cannot stop the announcement once it has started – you have to wait until it finishes
- L = after hearing messages by remote control they may be lost when you disconnect – a problem if, due to a poor line, you can't hear them distinctly even when repeated
- M = there is a gap of over five seconds in your messages when someone rings and does not leave a message
- N = no warning to caller that message tape is full
- P = difficult to retrieve messages if there has been a power failure
- R = no warning to caller when recording of message has stopped
- V = VOX system sensitive – machine may cut off if caller pauses for too long.

Electrical safety

All the machines passed our standard tests for electrical safety.

FAX MACHINES

Test Results on Eight Models

From *Which?* August 1990

A fax lets you receive written information – including handwriting, drawings and photographs – down a telephone line.

The machines are coming down in price; the ones in our test cost between £575 and £810 (inc VAT) and it's now possible to get a basic fax for £400 plus VAT.

It costs the same to send a fax as to make a phone call of the same length. Most faxes print on special heat-sensitive paper which comes in rolls and works out at about 3p for an A4 sheet (paper varies in sensitivity; make sure you get the right type for your machine). There are new machines costing over £2,000 which use plain paper.

Faxes can also make copies of documents, but they are slower and not as good as a plain paper photocopier.

If you've got a fax machine, you'll probably want a separate phone line, but you could get by with a fax/phone switch, or by getting people to phone you first.

Brands and reliability

In our survey the most-owned brands were: Canon, NEC, British Telecom, Sharp and Panasonic. (Amstrad was too new on the market.) A fifth of our members' fax machines had gone wrong in the last year, and we found no differences in reliability between brands.

Fax directories

Even if you have a separate line for your fax, think twice before having your fax number listed in a directory. There have been cases of users being charged for listings in bogus directories which never appear; but more important, your line may be tied up and your fax paper wasted by unsolicited fax 'junk mail'.

Do you need an extra phone line?

You've probably got only one telephone line – if you want to plug a fax machine into your phone line, you won't be able to use the fax and the phone at the same time. One solution to this problem is to rent another telephone line from British Telecom.

To install a second residential phone line, BT charge up to £133 (depending how much work the engineers need to do). The quarterly line rental is £17.65, and the call charges are the same as for ordinary lines. If the extra line is for business use, different charges apply – £145.75 and £28.55, respectively.

A second solution is to buy a phone/fax switching device for about £90. This plugs into the normal BT wall socket, and you plug in both the fax machine and a phone (or answering machine). When another fax machine calls, the switch recognises the high-pitched tones and directs the signal to your fax machine; if there's no fax signal the call is sent to the phone. But you still won't be able to use phone and fax machine at the same time.

Or you could ask your contacts to phone first before sending a fax. This low-tech solution seems to work well if you don't get too many fax messages, and your fax callers know to phone you first.

Fax machines can be set to manual answer. When the phone rings, you lift the handset, listen for the fax tone and press a button on the fax machine to receive the fax.

FACTS, FIGURES AND TEST RESULTS

1 Target price

In late June 1990 we carried out a telephone survey of office equipment dealers around the country. Quoted prices varied enormously – some dealers quoted twice the price of others – so it's essential to shop around in your area or even further afield. You may be able to beat the prices shown, especially if you are prepared to bargain. Our prices include VAT but most dealers quote prices without. Before you buy, make sure that the dealer can arrange servicing during and after the guarantee period.

2 Advantages

Most of the machines tested had all of the features of our 'standard' fax. However, all machines had certain additional facilities. These are indicated by the **bold** letters and are described opposite. Capital letters show the features which you're likely to find most useful.

Our survey

In March 1990, we sent a questionnaire to 3,042 members who worked at home for at least two days a week; 2,060 responded. We filtered out housewives and people who, for instance, occasionally take work home at night – leaving 1,475 questionnaires.

A standard fax machine

A standard fax has these features:

- Dialling keypad on the machine
- Extra space needed for loading or retrieving documents
- Display to show the number dialled and other information
- Last number redial button (except where no keypad is provided)
- Can be set to transmit in *standard*, *fine* or *half-tone* mode
- Voice contact can be requested after the fax is finished by pressing a button
- A4 documents can be fed in one at a time
- Can be programmed to print automatically: your name, fax number, the date, time and page number, on each fax sent
- Loudspeaker to monitor dialling and ringing tones
- Takes a roll of thermal fax paper at least 210mm (A4) wide and 30m long
- Paper must be torn off manually against a cutter bar as faxes are received
- Can be used for copying documents
- Will redial automatically at least twice more if your number is engaged
- Has a 'polling' facility to send a fax in response to a signal from another machine
- Normally prints an acknowledgement that the fax has been sent without error and received
- Shows amount of paper remaining
- Can be set to print out, on request, a list of faxes sent or received
- Compatible with Group 3 and the older Group 2 machines.

BUYING GUIDE

BEST BUY The **Amstrad FX9600T** (£630) stands out as being considerably cheaper than any other machine having all the most useful features. It performed well in most of our tests. If you have a personal computer, or intend to get one, the Amstrad's computer interface should enable you to send a fax without first having to print it out and feed it into the machine – a useful feature.

For a machine that's easy to use (once you have set it up), relatively cheap to run (has a fast transmission speed) and has good facilities, the **Ferranti Rhapsody FAX305** (£720) would be worth considering (however, it might not work well unless you have a separate line or a fax/phone switch).

A = alphabetical dialling – you key in just the name of your correspondents to dial 15 preset numbers
C = can be connected to a computer to send faxes without first printing them; the fax machine can also be used as a computer printer, or, with the right connectors, to scan documents for feeding into the computer
D = delayed dialling – can be set to send a fax at a programmed time
F = document feeder for sending five or more sheets automatically
(F) = feeder is an optional extra
L = longer 50m paper roll can be fitted
M = can be set to print a confirmation mark on each sheet transmitted.
N = some or all of the memories can store a telephone number as well; this will be dialled if no document is loaded
R = low REN number. If the REN numbers marked on all your telephone equipment add up to more than four you're likely to have problems with ringing – unless you have more than one line or a fax/ phone switch
S = has *modified read* or proprietary system for fast communication with a compatible machine
T = telephone handset incorporated
U = automatic cutter separates pages as faxes are received
W = 'broadcast' facility – will send up to 3 pages to up to 16 different numbers automatically
a = automatic dialling – you don't need to wait by machine to press 'transmit' button when the connection is made
d = document carrier supplied – for faxing small or flimsy papers
f = free service at your home for faults in first year (6 months for Ferranti)
p = can be set to require a pass code for sending a fax
s = has superfine mode; useful only for sending faxes to a compatible machine of same brand
t = telephone handset provided – plugs in separately (any other phone would do)
y = display tells you status of fax, eg when machine is transmitting

3 Disadvantages

Similarly, most machines lack at least one of the facilities of our standard fax:

K = no keypad – you must use a separate telephone for dialling
M = no monitoring loudspeaker

N = no polling facility
P = has no half-tone mode for sending photographs
R = no automatic redial if number engaged
j = cannot list faxes sent and received
n = no preset numbers that can be dialled by pressing just *one* key
w = no low paper indicator (but paper is marked when roll is nearly finished)
y = cannot communicate with Group 2 machines

4 Preset numbers possible

The STT fax machine had no dialling facilities and had to be used in conjunction with a separate telephone – not a disadvantage if you buy a good phone with memories and on-hook dialling. All the others could be programmed with the numbers you most often use. Once this is done it should seldom be necessary to dial a complete number again. Batteries protect the programming in the event of a power failure.

5 Reception quality

We found that nearly all the machines were capable of acceptable quality print-out if the sending machine was a good one and the connection was good. The print of the STT was very faint but improved somewhat when we bought a new roll of fax paper.

6 Transmission quality

Standard mode We sent copies of test charts from each machine to a good quality receiving fax machine. None of the results was as good as you get from a normal photocopier – text was usually acceptable but quite a bit of detail was lost. Adjusting the contrast control, which some machines had, usually gave some improvement when the original was light.

Fine mode Transmitting in fine mode – which takes about twice as long and so costs more in telephone charges – produced only a slight improvement with most machines. Generally fine mode is useful only for small print or detailed drawings.

FAX MACHINES

		Target price (incl VAT) 1	Similar models	Advantages 2	Disadvantages 3	Preset numbers possible 4	Reception quality 5	Standard
		£						
►	**1 Amstrad FX9600T** (Hong Kong)	630	FX9600AT £750[5]	**CFMNRTUf**	NRwy	50	◩	□[1]
	2 Betacom Murata F-20 (Japan)	575	Murata M-1 £460[6]	**Day**	MPw	50	◩	◪
	3 British Telecom CF10 fax (Japan)	685	CF20 £920[8]	**ADFLp**	MPn	15	◩	□
	4 Canon FAX-120 (Japan)	750		**(F)NSTWay**	P	26	◩	□
►	**5 Ferranti Rhapsody FAX305** (Japan)	720		**DFLSUadfy**	—	30	◩	□
	6 Funai PFX6800 (Japan)	690		**Nft**	NRw	60	◩	□
	7 Panasonic Panafax UF-120 (Japan)	720	UF-140 £920[4]	**Safs**	j	10	◩	□
	8 STT 520 (Japan)	810		**CFLRU**	KMPRy	—	□[7]	□

► Recommended in the Buying Guide ◄

KEY TO RATINGS best ■ > ◩ > □ > ◪ > ■ **worst**

Photos We tried transmitting both black and white and coloured photographs (which are received in black and white), using the half-tone mode on the machines which had this. Machines without a half-tone mode, and some of those which had one, reproduced pictures which were too dark. Before actually sending a photo it's worth experimenting by making copies of it using the fax machine as a photocopier.

7 Reception with a poor line

If the signal coming through is weak, due maybe to a long telephone line from the exchange, machines will compensate by printing more slowly than normal. This should reduce the chances of errors. Similarly, continuous background mush is unlikely to give trouble. However, if the line suffers from intermittent noises or clicks, you may get garbled messages.

8 Reception speed

The speed at which a fax comes over is governed by the slower of the sending or receiving machines. From a fast transmission there was not much to choose between the reception speeds.

9 Transmission speed

This is what costs you money because the time taken to send a fax governs the charge that goes on your telephone bill. Sending in fine mode takes about twice as long. With machines having *modified read*, or proprietary systems (which take effect automatically when communicating with other machines of the same make), the times were reduced. Times would be extended if the connecting telephone line was poor.

Fax speed depends on the density of information on a page. This is why the usual cover sheet confirming the destination comes over quickly and doesn't add much to the cost. Machines getting a ◩ in this column would take about one minute to send a double-spaced typed page of A4.

10 Setting up

Even when the instructions were good, it was usually a complicated procedure to set the machine up so that it imprinted the correct time and your identification on each page sent, and then to programme the pre-set numbers. If you are not good at this sort of button pushing, ask the shop to set the machine up for you; it should need doing only once.

11 Instructions

Some of the manuals were well set out and easy to follow; a few were confusing.

6 Transmission quality

Fine	Photos	7 Reception with a poor line	8 Reception speed	9 Transmission speed	10 Setting up	11 Instructions	12 Normal use	
□	□[2]	□	□	□	□	■	□	1 ◀
◩	■	□	□	□	◪	◪	□	2
◩	■	□	□	◩	◪	◩	□	3
◩	■	□	□[3]	◩[3]	◪	◩	◩	4
◩	◪	□	□[3]	◩[3]	◪	□	◩	5 ◀
◩	◪	□	□	◩	◪	◩	□	6
◩	□	□	□[3]	◩[3]	□	◩	◩	7
◩	◪	□	□	◩	◪	□	◩	8

[1] Results are worse unless contrast control is adjusted
[2] Better than average when sending from a coloured picture
[3] Faster when in contact with a compatible machine – see advantage S
[4] Has extra advantages **DFNy** and not disadvantage **j**
[5] Has built-in telephone answering machine and fax/phone switch
[6] Lacks advantages **Dy**; has extra disadvantages **NR** and has no preset numbers at all
[7] Results were worse (very faint) on fax paper originally supplied

12 Normal use

We assessed the machines for how well the controls were laid out and labelled, how easy it was to use the controls to send or receive a fax, and the ease of loading documents for sending and taking out faxes received. We experienced no serious difficulties.

Durability and faults

All the fax machines were generally satisfactory, although the feeder tray of the Betacom could be quite easily damaged. We had a few problems with the on/off switch on the Amstrad.

With all machines there's a slight chance of fax paper jamming as it gets near the end of the roll, and this could cause the loss of messages without the sender knowing. So it's good practice to change the roll as soon as the warning marker shows.

Power consumption and electrical safety

You will probably want to leave your fax permanently connected and turned on. In standby condition most machines consumed about 10W and so, unless used a great deal, shouldn't add more than about £7 to your annual electricity bill. The Amstrad might cost about £12.

We checked the machines for electrical safety and found them all to be satisfactory.

Please see page 287 for how to subscribe to ***Which?****.*

See page 8 for how to use ***Which? Buying Guide****.*

SHAVERS

For Men and Women

From *Which?* December 1989

British men are a pretty traditional bunch, when it comes to shaving; two out of three use a blade and soap, rather than an electric shaver. *Which?* readers are more Continental in their tastes; around half use an electric shaver, about the same proportion as in the rest of Europe.

For women, shaving is by far the most popular method of removing body hair. 85 per cent of the *Which?* women readers who removed body hair told us that they used a shaver.

At one time both men and women had to choose between an electric shaver that ran off the mains electricity or one that took batteries. In recent years, shavers powered by a built-in rechargeable bat tery instead of, or in addition to, mains electricity have grown in popularity. Today, 40 per cent or so of electric shavers sold run off the mains, 35 per cent are rechargeable and 25 per cent use batteries.

Usually, mains and rechargeable shavers have the same shaving head (foils or cutters), so the difference between the two is really whether you want to be plugged in or not. Battery shavers have different shaving heads.

Men's beard trimmers

Despite the fact that most electric shavers incorporate a trimmer for long hairs, moustaches and so on, they can be difficult to use on thicker and longer beards where you need evenness and consistency of trim. Beard trimmers, which have a range of trim depth settings, should do this job better.

To find out how well beard trimmers work we bought nine – four powered either by mains electricity or rechargeable batteries, and five powered by batteries. We found bearded volunteers who were willing to try them out for us and tell us how well they got on.

Wet shaving

With more men shaving with blades than with any other system, it's not surprising that the choice of razors and blades is considerable. Because of this wide choice, and because blades are often interchangeable with other makes of razor, we've concentrated on the different types of razor available. We tested:

- swivel head versus fixed head razors. They're similar in price; the razor costs about £1.10 to £1.70; blades are about £1.15 to £1.60 (for a pack of five)
- blades with lubricated strips versus non-lubricated ones. Blades cost around £1.25 to £1.55 for packs of five (lubricated generally cost a few pence more)
- twin-bladed versus traditional double-edged razors. Dougle-edged razors (made only by Wilkinson Sword) cost £2.49 with five blades. Blades are 79p for a pack of five. Twin bladed prices are similar to swivel-head, above
- a variety of disposable razors. A pack of ten disposables costs about 65p to 72p for single-bladed, 90p to £1.70 for twin-bladed.

Our users had to rate each blade for smoothness, evenness and comfort, from when the blade was new, until they considered the blade could not provide an acceptable shave. From these user trials, our conclusions were:

- twin-bladed razors were significantly better than double-edged ones.
- twin-bladed were significantly better than single-bladed disposable razors
- swivel heads were not significantly better than fixed head non-disposable razors
- blades with lubricated strips were not significantly better than non-lubricated ones.

BUYING GUIDE

Shavers that run from the mains, and rechargeables, use very little electricity. Battery shavers are much more expensive to use. Batteries use raw material heavily. Their disposal has serious environmental drawbacks.

MEN'S ELECTRIC SHAVERS

Mains/Rechargeables

Mains/rechargeables are more expensive than mains-only shavers. If you don't want to pay for the extra convenience of a rechargeable battery, try the equivalent mains-only version if there is one (see Similar Models).

BEST BUYS

Braun System 1-2-3 3512 (£52.50) was best, but pricey. **Braun Universal 2505** (£39.95) was almost as good, and cheaper (superseded by 2515 – cosmetic differences)

Mains only

BEST BUYS

Braun Linear 235 (£21.25) was the best all round and cheap (superseded by 245 – cosmetic differences). **Boots Visage** (£22.75) was almost as good

Battery

Consider one of these only as a second shaver for occasional or emergency use.

None was oustanding; **Boots Visage** (*£14.95*) did best

BEARD TRIMMERS

There was little to choose between the nine trimmers. Battery beard trimmers are more expensive to run than mains/rechargeable ones. However, because they're likely to be used less often, battery beard trimmers are at less of a disadvantage than battery shavers.

Mains/rechargeable

GOOD VALUE

Panasonic ER202B (*£29.95*), **Braun Exact Universal** (£33.45), **Philips Zoom HS075** (£24.45)

Battery

BEST BUYS

Wahl Groomsman II 9910 (*£17.95*) – best all round
Carmen Man 3027 (*£14.95*) – almost as good

Women's shavers

A majority of women in our survey said they preferred shaving to other methods of removing body hair, because it is smoother, quicker, easier, cheaper, less messy, odourless and there is less risk of allergies.

The survey showed that about 30 per cent of women who shave use electric shavers and over 60 per cent use a blade type razor (wet or dry). For this report we asked women to try out 13 different women's electric shavers.

BUYING GUIDE

WOMEN'S ELECTRIC SHAVERS

As the ratings in the Table show there isn't much to choose between the different types of women's shavers in efficiency and convenience. Women's shavers are likely to be used less often than men's, so running costs are unlikely to be important. Battery models and those needing replacement blades will cost slightly more to use than the others.

Mains/rechargeables

BEST BUY **Philips Ladyshave HP2631** (£24.75)

Battery

BEST BUYS **Philips Ladyshave HP2602** (£12.75) was the best all round for shaving dry. For shaving wet, **Carmen Lady 3219** (*£9.95*), and **Remington Lady Lektro Blade LVB-1** (£9.45) both did well

Survey results in this report are based on a survey among random samples of over 2,000 men and 1,500 women *Which?* subscribers.

FACTS, FIGURES AND TEST RESULTS

MEN'S ELECTRIC SHAVERS

The Panasonic ES303 (and the dry battery ES804B wet/dry) can be used as an ordinary electric shaver on a dry face or on a face covered in shaving foam. A similar model we tested before was less efficient to use wet than dry; this time we tested it only dry.

We checked them in our lab (all passed our electrical safety tests) and asked people to try them out.

1 Price

We give target prices, likely to be beaten only by special offers. For models we didn't find as widely available, we give manufacturers' guide prices in *italics*.

2 Cost of replacement parts

Foils can last as little as two or three months but may last for years, depending on use, but most manufacturers quote about 12 months as an average figure. Panasonic claim 18 to 24 months for their foils, Hitachi five years. Our tests found little differences on resistance to wear. In our survey, Braun foils lasted for a shorter period than other brands. Cutters should not need replacing more than every two or three years, assuming daily use.

MEN'S SHAVERS

	Price (1)	Cutter type	Cost of replacement parts (2): Foils	Cost of replacement parts (2): Cutters	General quality (3)	Shaving: Tricky bits (4)	Shaving: Irritation (5)	Shaving: Convenience (6)	Shaving: Noise/vibration (7)
	£		£	£					
MAINS/RECHARGEABLE									
1 **Boots Sprint** (Austria)	*29.95*	foil	4.95	3.95	□	◩	◩	□	□
2 **Boots Visage** (Austria)	*31.95*	foil	5.50	3.95	□	◩	□	◩	◩
3 **Braun Linear Univ 266** (W Germany)	33.45	foil	5.00	4.50	□	□	◩	◩	◩
► 4 **Braun System 1-2-3 3512** (W Germany)	52.50	foil	5.50	4.50	◩	◼	■	◩	◼
► 5 **Braun Universal 2505** (W Germany)[1]	39.95	foil	5.00	4.50	◩	◩	◼	◩	◩
6 **Hitachi RM 9400 Phase 2** (Japan)	35.00	foil	6.95	4.95	□	◩	◩	◩	◩
7 **Philips Philishave Tracer HS350A/B** (Netherlands)[2]	31.50	rotary (2 head)	n/a	5.99	□	□	◩	◩	◩
8 **Philips Philishave HS900** (Netherlands)	63.50	rotary (3 head)	n/a	6.99	□	□	■	◩	◼
9 **Remington Micro Screen ULT-3** (USA)	49.45	foil	4.50	5.50	◩	◩	◼	◩	◩
10 **Remington Micro Screen XLR1100** (USA)	27.75	foil	4.50	5.50	◩	◩	◩	◪	□
MAINS ONLY									
► 11 **Boots Visage** (Austria)	22.75	foil	5.50	3.95	◩	◩	◩	◩	□
► 12 **Braun Linear 235** (W Germany)[3]	21.25	foil	5.00	4.50	◩	◩	◩	◩	◩
13 **Panasonic ES385BK** (Japan)	*24.95*	foil	6.00	6.00	□	◩	□	◩	□
14 **Payer Porsche 32** (Austria)	*57.50*	foil	8.00	7.00	◩	◩	◩	◩	□
15 **Philips Philishave HS550** (Netherlands)	27.45	rotary (3 head)	n/a	5.99	□	□	◩	◩	◼
16 **Remington Micro Screen ULT-4** (USA)	*29.95*	foil	4.50	5.50	◩	□	◩	□	◩
17 **Remington Lektro PM650** (USA)	16.45	bar	n/a	5.75	□	◪	□	◪	□
BATTERY									
► 18 **Boots Visage** (Austria)	*14.95*	foil	5.50	3.95	◩	◩	◩	□	□
19 **Braun 100** (W Germany)	13.25	foil	4.50	4.50	□	◩	◩	◩	□
20 **Hitachi BM5200** (Japan)	9.95	foil	4.70	4.95	□	□	◩	◩	□
21 **Panasonic ES815B** (Japan)	*9.95*	foil	4.73	4.73	□	□	◩	◩	□
22 **Panasonic ES804B wet/dry** (Japan)	*12.95*	foil	4.73	4.73	□	□	◩	◩	◩
23 **Payer Porsche 27/2** (Austria)	29.00	foil	5.00	5.99	□	□	□	□	□
24 **Philips Philishave HS155** (Netherlands)[4]	14.75	rotary (2 head)	n/a	5.99	□	◩	◩	◩	◩
25 **Remington Micro Screen XLR500** (USA)	*12.95*	foil	4.50	4.50	□	◩	◩	□	□
RECHARGEABLE BATTERY									
26 **Panasonic ES303 wet/dry** (Japan)	*44.95*	foil	6.00	6.00	◩	◩	◩	◩	□

[1] Superseded by 2515
[2] Superseded by HS355A/B
[3] Superseded by 245
[4] Superseded by HS165

► Recommended in the Buying Guide ◄

8 Controls, features and accessories	9 Recharge time	10 Discharge time	11 Batteries	
	hours	min		
abcdhioz AC	8	58	–	**1**
abcdhimo A	8	54	–	**2**
abcdilopwz AC	5	23	–	**3**
abcdhimoz AC	5	22	–	**4** ◀
abcdimoz AC	5	44	–	**5** ◀
abcdiop AC	5	60	–	**6**
abcdiopz AC	2	70	–	**7**
abcdhioxyz AC	1	112	–	**8**
abcdhimo ABC	16	23	–	**9**
bcdiop AC	24	30	–	**10**
bcdhimo	–	–	–	**11** ◀
bcdhiop	–	–	–	**12** ◀
abcdhimo	–	–	–	**13**
bcdhimo	–	–	–	**14**
abcdhio	–	–	–	**15**
bcdhio B	–	–	–	**16**
bchi	–	–	–	**17**
bcio	–	–	Size C-2*	**18** ◀
bcilo	–	–	Size AA-3*	**19**
bclmo	–	–	Size AA-2	**20**
bcmo	–	–	Size AA-2	**21**
bcmo	–	–	Size AA-2	**22**
bco	–	–	Size AA-2*	**23**
bciop	–	–	Size AA-3	**24**
bchio	–	–	Size AA-4	**25**
abcdhilmors A	8	31 + 22 reserve	–	**26**

KEY TO RATINGS best ◩ > ◪ > □ > ◪ > ■ worst

3 Shaving – general quality
How close, even and fast a shave each shaver gave on the main facial hair.

4 Shaving – tricky bits
How well the shavers coped with moustaches, sideburns, long hairs, awkward parts of the face.

5 Shaving – irritation
The higher the rating, the less evidence of hairs being pulled, faces being nicked, and soreness after shaving.

6 Convenience
How easy our users found it to understand instructions, use, handle and clean the shavers.

7 Noise and vibration
The ratings are based on our users' findings in the trials. No shaver was particularly noisy.

8 Controls, features and accessories
Necessary

b = brush for cleaning
c = cover for shaving head
d = dual voltage – essential in some countries when travelling abroad
o = on/off switch
C = overcharge protection – to avoid damage to rechargeable battery

Useful

a = automatic voltage selector – useful safety feature when abroad
h = hard case – good for storage
i = integral trimmer – good for shaving longer hairs and neat edges
l = lock off – guards against accidental switching on
p = pouch or soft storage case
r = reserve power – an emergency

measure when battery needs a recharge
y = charge alarm – clear indication that battery needs a recharge
z = quick recharge available for single shave if the battery is flat
A = indicator lamp on when recharging

Not very useful
m = mirror
s = storage stand
w = wall bracket
x = comfort control (adjusts the angle of cutters to suit different skins)
B = beard lifter – stretches skin and lifts hair (not outstanding in our tests)

9 Recharge time
The time given in instruction books to charge the battery fully from flat.

10 Discharge time
The average we found in the laboratory, based on fully discharging each battery three times.

11 Batteries
Lists the batteries needed for the shavers.
* = batteries supplied with the shaver.

SIMILAR MODELS Listed below in *italics* are models (plus makers' guide prices) similar to those in the tables.
Braun Linear 266 – *Linear 265* (£28.95) powered by rechargeable battery only, no quick charge facility. **Braun Linear 235 – *Linear 230*** (£19.95) no storage case. **Braun System 1-2-3 3512 – *3012*** (£37.95) powered by mains only; ***3510*** (£49.95) has different storage case; ***3010*** (£34.95) is the same as 3510 but powered by mains only. **Braun 2515 – *2015*** (£24.95) powered by mains only. **Braun 100 – *Pocket Battery*** same but without integral trimmer (£9.95). **Braun Lady Style** (mains and battery model) – rechargeable battery model (£24.95). **Carmen Smoothie SN457 – *Close Encounters SN471*** (£9.99) no alternative foil head. **Hitachi RM 9400 Phase 2 – *9500*** (£49.99) has different cutting control. **Hitachi BM5200 – *BM5300*** (£12.99) has retractable trimmer. **Panasonic ES386HK – *ES387*** (£29.95) has deluxe hard case. **Panasonic ES303 wet/dry – *ES301 wet/dry*** (£29.95) has different foil and no reserve battery. **Philishave HS550 – *HS540*** (£29.99) has pouch instead of hard storage case. **Philishave HS155 – *HS135*** (£13.99) no integral trimmer. **Remington ULT-3 – *ULT-1*** (£59.95) has extra quick charge facility and shaver stand; ***ULT-5*** (£34.95) cosmetic differences only; ***ULT-9*** (£34.50) powered by rechargeable battery only. **Remington ULT-4 – *ULT-2*** (£32.99) cosmetic differences only. **Remington XLR1100 – *XLR800*** (£19.95) powered by mains only, hard case; ***XLR1000*** (£22.95) powered by mains only, hard case. **Remington Lecktro PM650 – *PM750*** (£17.95) has dual voltage facility. **Remington LVB-1 – *LVB-3*** (£16.95) powered by rechargeable battery; ***MVB-1*** (£9.95) is men's version of **LVB-1** with double blade instead of single blade; ***MVB-3*** (£16.95) is a rechargeable version of MVB-1.

MEN'S BEARD TRIMMERS

1 Price
As for shavers, ordinary numbers are target prices; *italic* numbers are manufacturer's own likely High Street prices.

2 Number of trim depth settings
For different beards or amounts of trim.

3 Trimming – general quality
The ratings are based on how quick, even

and accurate the trim, including how effective the different trimming depth settings were on beards and moustaches.

4 Trimming – irritation

Pulling of hair, nicking or general soreness after trimming were included in the ratings.

5 Convenience

The ratings show how easy it was to understand instructions and use the shavers, taking into account using controls, features, general handling and cleaning.

6 Noise and vibration

The higher the rating, the quieter and smoother the trimmer; based on user's observations.

7 Controls, features and accessories

Most of these were the same as on shavers.

Three accessories unique to trimmers were:

D = comb – useful but not essential

E = scissors – useful but not essential

F = small bottle of oil – necessary for lubricating blades of trimmer.

8 Recharge time

The time to recharge fully a flat battery.

9 Discharge time

The number of minutes' use from full charge to flat battery.

10 Batteries

Lists the batteries needed to run the trimmers.

★ = batteries provided.

WOMEN'S ELECTRIC SHAVERS

We asked 36 women each to try out four different shavers. Those shavers that could be used wet or dry were tested both ways; D = dry shave, W = wet shave. The one mains/rechargeable battery shaver was also tested both ways – using the mains and its rechargeable battery for power.

BEARD TRIMMERS

	Price (1)	No of trim depth settings (2)	Trimming: General quality (3)	Trimming: Irritation (4)	Convenience (5)	Noise/vibration (6)	Controls, features and accessories (7)	Recharge time (8)	Discharge time (9)	Batteries (10)	
	£							hours	min		
MAINS/RECHARGEABLE											
► **Braun Exact Universal** (Japan)	33.45	4[5]	◩	◩	◩	◩	abdop AC	8	38	—	◄
► **Panasonic ER202B** (Japan)	29.95	9	◩	◩	▨	◩	abdop AF	8	30	—	◄
► **Philips Zoom HS075** (USA)	24.45	6	◩	◩	◩	□	blos ACDF	8	35	—	◄
Remington HC200 Hair Set (Hong Kong)	24.75	3	□	◩	□	□	bo CDEF	16	30	—	
BATTERY											
Boots Visage (W Germany)	15.95	4	◪	◩	□	□	bco DF	—	—	Size C-1★	
► **Carmen Man 3027** (Hong Kong)	14.95	3	◩	◩	◩	□	bcos DF	—	—	Size AA-3	◄
Philips Zoom HS050 (USA)	14.75	6	◩	□	◩	◪	blo DF	—	—	Size AA-2	
Remington MB-1 (Taiwan)	14.75	3	□	◩	◩	□	bos DF	—	—	Size AA-3	
► **Wahl Groomsman II 9910** (USA)[6]	17.95	5	◩	◩	◩	□	bcos DF	—	—	Size AA-3★	◄

[5] New models have five depth settings [6] For availability contact Wahl Europe Ltd (0227 740066)

► Recommended in the Buying Guide ◄

KEY TO RATINGS **best** ▨ > ◩ > □ > ◪ > ■ **worst**

1 Price
As for men's shavers, ordinary numbers are target prices; *italic* prices are those given to us by manufacturers as likely High Street prices.

2 Cost of replacement foil
As for men's shavers; but, in general, since women shave less often than men, replacement intervals are likely to be long and the cost very low.

3 Shaving – general quality
Ratings show how close, even and fast each shaver shaved, on legs and underarms.

4 Shaving – irritation
The higher the rating, the less evidence of any pulling, nicking or soreness after shaving.

WOMEN'S SHAVERS

	Price (1)	Cutter type	Cost of replacement foil (2)	Shaving: General quality (3)	Shaving: Irritation (4)	Convenience (5)	Noise/vibration (6)	Controls, features and accessories (7)	Batteries (8)	
	£		£							
MAINS/RECHARGEABLE										
▶ **Philips Ladyshave HP2631** (Austria)	24.75	foil	6.25	◩	◩	◩	◩	abdhilmo	–	◀
MAINS ONLY										
Boots Ladyshave (Austria)[7]	*15.95*	foil	6.95	□	□	◩	□	bcdhio	–	
Braun Lady Style (W Germany)	19.90	foil	5.95	□	◩	◩	◩	abcdhio	–	
Philips Ladyshave Classic HP2612 (Austria)	18.75	foil	6.25	□	◩	◩	□	bdhimo	–	
BATTERY – USED DRY										
Boots Ladyshave (Austria)[7]	*11.75*	foil	6.95	◩	□	◩	□	bcio	Size AA-2*	
Braun Ladystyle (W Germany)	12.00	foil	5.95	□	◩	◩	◩	bcilo	Size AAA-4	
Carmen Smoothie SN457 (Japan)[7]	*12.95*	foil/circular cutter	[8]	□	◩	□	◩	bciop	Size C-1	
▶ **Philips Ladyshave HP2602** (Austria)	12.75	foil	6.25	◩	◩	◩	□	bcio	Size AA-2	◀
Philips Ladyshave HP2703 (Austria)	*11.99*	bar	4.95	□	□	□	□	o	Size AA-2	
Remington Lady LR7000 (Korea)	*8.95*	bar	3.95	◪	◩	◩	□	bop	Size C-1	
BATTERY – USED WET OR DRY										
Clairol BeautyLine LS2 (Japan)	11.75	oscillating cutter	4.20	◪D ◪W	◩D ◩W	□D ◩W	◩D ◩W	bho	Size AA-1	
▶ **Carmen Lady 3219** (Hong Kong)	*9.95*	oscillating blade	[9]	□D ◩W	◩D ◩W	◩D ◩W	◩D ◩W	o	Size AA-1	◀
▶ **Remington Lady Lektro Blade LVB-1** (China)	9.45	oscillating blade	5 blades for 2.25	◩D ◩W	□D ◩W	□D ◩W	□D ◩W	co	Size AA-1*	◀

[7] Manufacturer tells us this model has been modified
[8] Parts not available
[9] Uses razor blades for fixed head non-disposable shavers (Gillette II type)

▶ Recommended in the Buying Guide ◀

KEY TO RATINGS best ◼ > ◩ > □ > ◪ > ■ worst

5 Convenience
The ratings show how easy our testers found the instructions to follow, and the shavers to use, handle and clean.

6 Noise and vibration
The higher the rating, the quieter and smoother the shaver was to use.

7 Controls, features and accessories
(See Key for Men's shavers.)

8 Batteries
Lists the batteries needed to power the shavers.
★ = batteries provided.

SMOKE ALARMS

Essential Home Safety Devices

From *Which?* June 1990

Every year about 700 people die in household fires. If *you* have a fire – especially at night – a smoke alarm can give you precious extra minutes to escape. Smoke alarms (sometimes called smoke detectors) are cheap to buy and fairly simple to fit: we think every home should have (at least) one.

The way they work

Smoke alarms come in two basic types. The most common is the *ionisation* type: this contains a tiny radioactive source which ionises air inside the alarm, producing electrically charged particles (ions) and allowing a small current to flow from a battery. When smoke enters the detector, it reduces the current flow and triggers the alarm. You can buy one for as little as £5.

The alternative *photoelectric* type looks much the same from the outside, but depends on smoke scattering a light beam inside the detector to set off the alarm. This type usually costs around £20 and isn't so widely available.

Some research has suggested that ionisation alarms are slightly better at detecting hot, blazing fires than the photoelectric type, which tends to be more sensitive to smoke from slowly smouldering fires. Some alarms incorporate *both* types of detector.

But our tests using different types of fire don't show significant differences, and there's little reason in principle to go for one type rather than another.

Fitting a smoke alarm

All alarms come with fitting instructions and putting them up is easy. Fitting an alarm in every room (except kitchen and bathroom) where there is a potential fire hazard is worth doing – particularly where there are young children or elderly or disabled people in the house.

The centre of the hall ceiling is a good place to fit an alarm. Smoke from downstairs fires should be detected here before it reaches upstairs. Don't fit alarms near walls or corners – the smoke may not reach them so soon, or at all.

Test your alarm every week with the test button or other facility. This checks the battery and the electronics. An occasional test with smoke from a snuffed candle or a cigarette is also worthwhile. Replace the battery (or batteries) routinely once a year.

Half the people with smoke alarms in our survey had fitted only one alarm, but we think even a small house will probably need two alarms. If the first is in the hall, then a second on the landing ceiling is probably a good idea. If this makes it hard to reach, choose a type with a special test feature (see Table). In a larger house you'll need more than two for satisfactory protection. Choose interconnecting models so they'll all sound if one is triggered by a fire. The wiring this involves isn't difficult, though making a tidy job of it may be. Closing doors last thing at night may delay detection by a unit for a few minutes but is important because

BUYING GUIDE

Differences in performance between most of the smoke alarms we've tested were slight. Models shown in the Table passed all our tests.

Which you choose may depend on the features you want, such as a silence button, escape light, torch test or auto test, or interconnect facilities.

If you come across a smoke alarm we haven't listed, look for the British Standard BS5446 Kitemark before buying (though versions with a 'silence' button won't be kitemarked until the BS has been amended to cover this feature).

We recommend that if you buy a Plasplugs SA110 alarm you check that you get the latest version with slots on the sides of the casing. This problem does not apply to Plasplugs SA111 and SA112 models.

you'll have a better chance of escaping once alerted.

Smoke kills

The statistics for house fire deaths show that many more people are killed by smoke than by flames. Burning upholstered furniture can be particularly dangerous if it's filled with polyurethane foam: this can burn rapidly, producing large quantities of dense toxic smoke and so much heat that everything else in the room ignites.

The fire hazard presented by a piece of upholstered furniture depends on how easily the fabric cover will ignite and on

Plasplugs SA110

When we tested Plasplugs alarms previously, they were satisfactory, but letters from some worried members prompted us to investigate further. We bought ten more samples, all from different shops, and compared them in our lab. We found that although all ten looked identical from the outside, two of them contained quite different internal parts from the ones we'd previously tested. One of them failed part of the British Standard test, and the other was rather insensitive to smoke.

We then bought three new samples at random (all had identical packaging) and found a mixture of different internal parts and some different external casings. Some of the casings had slots at the sides. Our tests show that these slots critically affect how the smoke reaches the detector inside. Further fire tests have confirmed that these slots increase the sensitivity of the detector whichever type of parts are used. Plasplugs say that all current SA110 production has these slots.

If you buy a Plasplugs SA110 alarm, make sure you get the latest version with the slots. This means opening the packaging in the shop – there's no means of telling from the carton which type is inside. If you've already got a Plasplugs alarm that doesn't have the slots, check the inside. If the internal parts are marked with the numbers 78101 and 5001, Plasplugs have agreed to supply a modified cover. Write to Customer Service Dept, Plasplugs Limited, Westmore Road, Burton-on-Trent, Staffs DE14 1SD. Plasplugs have insisted that you send 95p for postage and packing.

how rapidly the fabric and its fitting will burn. Government regulations mean that from 1 March 1989 all new foam-filled furniture sold in shops must have been made using special 'Combustion Modified' foam which prevents fire spreading so rapidly. And from 1 March 1990, there have been stringent requirements for the covering fabric as well: it must resist ignition tests with both a smouldering cigarette and a match-like flame, unless a fire-resistant interliner between the fabric and the filling is used instead.

Second-hand furniture can be sold in shops only if it passes the smouldering cigarette test. From 1 March 1993 it will have to meet the same requirements for fillings and coverings as new furniture. Antique and period furniture made before 1950 is exempt, but there are controls on loose covers, stretch covers and re-upholstery fabrics. All *mattresses and divans* must pass the match test.

Our survey
Questionnaires were sent to 2,000 *Which?* members chosen at random in November 1989, of whom 1,250 responded.

Too much of a good thing

Our survey showed that nearly 50 per cent of our members have at least one smoke alarm. The survey also showed that it's fairly common for alarms to be triggered accidentally. Many people said their alarms were occasionally set off by fumes from frying or burnt toast; fumes from d-i-y jobs – such as using a blow-lamp – were another common cause of accidental operation.

It's obviously difficult for manufacturers to design a detector which will *never* give a false alarm but still respond quickly to a real fire. But an alarm shouldn't go off if someone walks past with a cigarette, for example. To reduce the possibility of false alarms, some installation instructions advise fixing the unit at least ten yards from the kitchen, but that could be quite tricky in a small house or flat.

Some alarms are now available with a temporary 'silence' button (see Features); this may solve the problem but won't be very convenient for regular use if your alarm's mounted on a fairly high ceiling. Some people, on the other hand, were worried that their detector wasn't sensitive *enough.*

Very few of the people with more than one alarm had them interconnected so that all would sound together. But over 80 per cent said they tested their alarms regularly, half of these at least once a month.

Overall, members who took part in our survey were satisfied with their smoke alarms, though two per cent said there had been an occasion – such as a lot of smoke from a cooking mishap – when they felt their alarm should have gone off but didn't. However, none of the people in our survey had been unfortunate enough to have a serious fire.

Radioactivity

Radiation hazards are an emotive subject. Judging from letters we receive, many people are confused by sometimes conflicting statements about what's safe and what isn't.

Mildly radioactive material can be hazardous if it gets into the body by swallowing, inhalation or through a skin wound; the more powerful kinds of radiation can penetrate the body from a distance. Either way, increasing radiation doses (from whatever source) can increase the risk of cancer.

Ionisation smoke alarms contain a very small amount of a radioactive isotope, Americium-241. This is shielded, and the radiation dose you'd receive simply from fitting smoke alarms in your home is far less than normal levels of natural background radiation. There *would* be a significant hazard if the isotope's sealed cover (*not* just the outer casing of the alarm) could be broken open and the contents swallowed, but the cover's designed to make this extremely difficult to do. From April 1990, regulations under the Consumer Protection Act mean that all ionisation alarms sold have to be type-approved by the National Radiological Protection Board (NRPB) and marked accordingly.

There's some disagreement about whether it would be safer to return faulty or unwanted smoke alarms to the manufacturer for disposal rather than get rid of them in ordinary household refuse. With many millions of smoke alarms now installed, we'd like to see more research into this aspect.

Photoelectric smoke alarms don't contain any radioactive material. But there are few makes in the shops, and they cost more.

FACTS AND FIGURES

The Table lists all the alarms we've tested which passed our tests, together with others which are very similar but are sold under a different brand name or have slightly different features.

SMOKE ALARMS

	Price	Features
	£	
IONISATION TYPES		
Addis AS01129	11	–
Addis AS01178	13	AD
Addis AS01179	15	AC
Addis AS01199	17	AF
Black & Decker A9430[1]	10	A
Black & Decker A9431 [1]	13	AD
Black & Decker A9432 [1]	15	AF
BRK 83R	10	A
BRK 83RI/2	22[2]	AE
BRK 1201	19	AF
Dicon 300	6	A
Dicon 300i	12	AE
Dicon 300AP	11	AD
Dicon 350	14	AF
Dicon SA4	5	A
Ever Ready 999	10	A
Family Gard 888	5	A
First Alert SA76RD-UK	10	A
First Alert SA83RI-UK	22[2]	AE
First Alert SA90TT	10	AB
First Alert SA120C-UK	19	AF
First Alert SA150TT	19	ABF
Homeguard F102	10	A
Homeguard F103	13	AE
Homeguard F104	16	AF
Homewatch 168101	8	A
Pifco 1389	10	A
Pifco 1390	16	AF
Plasplugs SA110[3]	8	A
Plasplugs SA111	15	AF
Plasplugs SA112	11	AD
Polycell 637	13	D
Superswitch 1351	12	AE
Superswitch 1353	25	AF
Superswitch 1355	9	A
Wickes	20[4]	A[4]
PHOTOELECTRIC TYPES		
BRK 2001 I	20	AE
First Alert SA2001 I	20	AE
Superswitch 1352	20	AE
COMBINED TYPES		
BRK SA3001	30	A
First Alert SA3001	30	A

[1] New range only available in time for limited tests but carries BS Kitemark
[2] Pack of two
[3] Latest version only
[4] Pack of three, of which one has feature F

Features

All the models we've tested use a small nine-volt battery which should last about a year. All have a bleep warning that the battery is running down, and a button to test the alarm; most alarms also have:

A = a small *flashing indicator* to show that all is well.

If reaching the test button would be difficult you can buy alarms which approach the problem in one of two ways:

B = *torch test* facility which you can test by waving a torch beam across the casing to trigger the alarm, or

C = *automatic test*: a built-in timer starts when you fit the alarm battery; every seven days afterwards at the same time of day the alarm will sound for three seconds. The idea is that you choose a time when someone's at home and awake to hear it.

D = *silence button* to reduce the problem of false alarms – see 'Too much of a good thing'. You press a button to desensitise the detector for about 15 minutes: during this time it bleeps or flashes periodically, then automatically returns to normal.

In a large house you'll need several alarms and it's important that any of them could be heard even if you're asleep. To deal with this, some smoke alarms have:

E = *interconnect* feature so that if one alarm is triggered by smoke, all the alarms will sound

F = built-in *escape light* – powered by a separate battery – which comes on when the alarm sounds; this may help you find your way to safety if the electricity supply has failed.

Performance tests

Our tests – to British Standard 5446 – included:

- speed of response to different types of fire: smouldering and fast-burning wood, liquid fuel and burning polyurethane foam. One sample of the First Alert SA3001 combination type failed the smouldering wood test, though a fresh sample was satisfactory
- sensitivity to strong draughts
- whether humidity or (for photoelectric types) very bright light caused faulty operation
- oversensitivity to smoke
- directional dependence – the detector should work equally well regardless of the direction of smoke flow towards it
- loudness of the alarm
- effectiveness of the warning that the battery's running down
- whether the 'silence' feature supposed to prevent false alarms safely returned to normal sensitivity after 15 minutes as the amendment to the British Standard specifies
- effectiveness of the torch test and automatic test features. Both types worked satisfactorily, though we think the torch test system is preferable.

EMERGENCY ALARMS

Alarms for Elderly People

From *Which?* November 1989

An alarm system can be valuable to anyone worried about what would happen if they, or someone they care for, became ill or had an accident with nobody around to help. An alarm can give peace of mind as well as practical aid in an emergency.

When we last reported on alarms, half the models tested were electrically potentially dangerous, or would not work in a power cut. All the alarms in this report passed our electrical safety tests and have battery back-up.

Where to get an alarm

Only the Carephone Plus can be bought in shops. Other alarms are available from organisations which supply alarms and monitor calls from them. Alternatively, you can buy an alarm from a manufacturer and arrange monitoring separately. We explain the options below. Costs exclude VAT unless we say otherwise.

Local authorities Over 200 alarm schemes are run by local authority housing or social service departments. Some have mobile wardens who respond to calls; others will contact friends and relatives whom you have nominated – and whom you are happy to give your front door key to. In certain areas, schemes include regular telephoning or visits to check on how you are. The authority will supply, install and may maintain the alarm equipment.

There are no set rules about who qualifies for an alarm. Some schemes are for council tenants only, some take into account such things as your age, health and whether you live alone. Others provide an alarm to any elderly or disabled person who wants one. Local authorities sometimes have long waiting lists.

Charges vary; alarms are provided free by some local authorities, although this may be limited to council tenants and people receiving Income Support or other benefits. Where charges are made they are usually between £1.50 and £3 a week, which covers renting the equipment and monitoring. Some authorities sell alarms.

If your own local authority doesn't have an alarm service, another authority might be prepared to link an alarm you have bought independently to their emergency centre. You will need to know which brands of equipment they can accept calls from before buying the alarm. Some authorities will rent out alarms as well as monitor them outside their area. The telephone alarms use the ordinary telephone network, so it doesn't matter if you live a long way from the centre, though emergency calls will cost more, and you are unlikely to get a mobile warden service.

Charges made for local authority monitoring-only services usually vary from less than 30p to £1.75 a week. Occasionally an extra one-off connection charge is made.

Commercial firms The Table shows which manufacturers sell direct to the public. A few run their own emergency centre; others will put you in touch with organisations which supply their alarms and run emergency centres. Centres run by alarm manufacturers and commercial firms will usually contact your nominated helpers in an emergency (or the emergency services if necessary); few have mobile wardens.

Monitoring charges vary – around £1 a week is typical, sometimes with an extra connection charge. With many firms you have to sign on for a minimum period – usually from three months to a year.

Charities A few charities sell or rent alarm units and arrange for monitoring. Apart from these, you might be able to get help with the costs of having an alarm from a national or local charity – you can find addresses at your local library or Citizens Advice Bureau.

Help the Aged run a national alarms scheme. They supply some brands of alarm and arrange for them to be monitored by local authority emergency centres. They advise on funding and will try to raise money to cover the cost of an alarm and a year's monitoring if you need it. For an information pack contact: Community Alarms Department, Help the Aged, 16–18 St James's Walk, London EC1R 0BE, ☎ 071-253 0253.

Housing associations Some housing associations supply and monitor alarms for non-tenants. Depending on the association, you will either buy, rent or wait for an alarm to be donated. Monitoring costs of £1 a week (including VAT) are typical. Some associations contact nominated helpers; a couple have mobile wardens covering certain areas.

Getting plugged in Whoever supplies your alarm will probably programme it with all the information it needs, and install it for you. This involves simply plugging the alarm unit into a modern British Telecom (BT) standard socket, and to a nearby power socket. If you don't already have a telephone, BT charges £133 to install a line. If you do, but it has an old-style connection, they charge £28.75 to replace it with a modern plug-in socket. Radio alarms need a power socket only. Some alarm units are supplied with their back-up batteries disconnected; reconnection with some involves unscrewing the casing.

The Carephone Plus is sold in shops with detailed instructions of how to programme and install it – and how to record your own emergency message.

British Telecom can provide fast telephone line repair services: contact your local BT sales office for options and charges. They also have a (free) 'protected service scheme' so that people at risk without a phone will not have their line automatically disconnected for not paying their bill: application forms are available from the address on your phone bill.

How alarms work

1 You set off the alarm You have a portable trigger – most brands are worn like a pendant. You press or pull the trigger in

More information

This report has been prepared by our sister organisation, the Research Institute for Consumer Affairs. RICA has compiled a list of organisations which have emergency centres and local authorities which provide a service outside their own area. It gives telephone numbers and brief details of charges. To get a copy send £1.50 to: RICA, 2 Marylebone Road, London NW1 4DX.

BUYING GUIDE

If you can get an alarm cheaply or free through your local authority, this is likely to be your best bet. If you're buying one independently, you need to decide which type of alarm would suit you best. Do you want:

- **an alarm which calls an emergency centre or calls helpers direct?** If you use an emergency centre you will probably have to pay monitoring fees, but someone will always be there to answer your calls. Get details of costs and services from any centre you are considering.
- **an alarm with a speech link?** The big advantage of a speech link is that in an emergency you can talk to whoever answers your call without having to get to the phone. And they can find out exactly what help you need.
- **an alarm with a built-in phone?** An alarm unit with its own phone means you get a telephone extension as well as an alarm, or it could save you renting or buying your main phone
- **an alarm to buy or rent?** If you want an alarm for more than two years it is likely to be cheaper to buy. Renting is convenient if you want the alarm for a short time only, but check what the minimum rental period is.

We give manufacturers' prices: what you pay will depend on where you get the equipment.

GOOD VALUE If you want a system with a speech link and a built-in telephone, **Lifeline II** £230 performed well as an alarm and as a telephone, and it can dial helpers' ordinary telephones. The **Homelink III** £220, **Independence Phone II** £290 and **Vitalcall 2** £229 are worth considering, but their telephones eventually stop working if the units are unplugged and run out of battery power. Homelink III and Vitalcall 2 can call helpers direct.

GOOD VALUE The following speech systems without telephones performed well and are reasonably priced: **Homelink II** £220 and **Vital-link** £209 – Vital-link can call helpers direct.

GOOD VALUE If you want a non-speech system consider the **Aid-Call** £195 initial fee plus £35 a quarter for rental and monitoring – it has to be rented – and the non-speech version of **Homelink II** £180.

an emergency and it sends a radio signal to the alarm unit.

You can also set off the alarm by pushing a button on the alarm unit itself. And you can have other buttons or pull cords fixed around the house. Some alarms can be extended to work automatically if sensors detect a low room temperature, smoke, an intruder or even if you have not moved around for a while.

2 The alarm unit calls for help Some alarm units have a telephone handset (see Table) and look like push-button telephones. The rest are like boxes with one or two buttons and small lights. All the alarm units automatically contact an emergency centre or people whom you have nominated as helpers, such as friends or relatives.

3 Your call gets through The staff at the centre will usually try to speak to you through the alarm's speech link or by telephone. If you need help or if they get no reply, they will arrange for someone to visit. (You will have given them details about things like your health and people to contact.) Alarms which call friends directly can be programmed to dial more than one number, to increase the chance of finding someone at home.

4 Someone arrives to help Your problem might be able to be dealt with over the telephone. If not, someone will arrive to help you. This could be a friend or relative, a mobile warden from the emergency centre, or the centre may have called a doctor or ambulance for you.

FACTS, FIGURES AND TEST RESULTS

1 Types

All the alarms tested work by telephone, except for the Selcare Solitaire which contacts the emergency centre by radio. All send an alarm signal to their emergency centre that identifies who has made the call – apart from the Carephone Plus which sends a recorded message.

Built-in telephone Alarms which have their own telephone handset can also be used as an ordinary phone. Of those we tested, all but the Carephone Plus had a two-way speech link as well. With the Carephone, whoever answers its emergency call hears a recorded message, asking for help. They can then hear you speaking – even if you are some distance from the unit – but you cannot hear them.

Speech link Most alarm units now have a built-in loudspeaker and microphone. These let you explain to the person answering your call what help you need even if you're lying on the floor some distance away from the alarm unit. If you have fair hearing, you should be able to hear the person answering your call from the room *next* to where the unit is.

No speech With these alarms, emergency centres receive alarm calls as identifiable signals, without a speech function. If the caller has an ordinary telephone, the operator will try to contact them to find out what is wrong. If this is not possible, help will be sent anyway.

2 Price

We give the manufacturer's price for an alarm unit with one portable trigger, excluding VAT. But remember that what you pay depends on where you get your alarm from.

Under the Chronically Sick and Disabled Persons Act, some people do not have to pay VAT on alarms equipment or services. You do not have to be *registered* as disabled to qualify. More information is available from your local VAT office – under Customs and Excise in the phone book.

3 Available from

Manufacturers told us where you can obtain their alarms:

C = charities
H = housing associations
L = local authorities
M = direct from manufacturer
O = other commercial firms
S = telephone shops

To buy or rent direct from a manufacturer,

or for further information on availability, use the telephone numbers listed.

4 Can call helpers direct

In the Table we tell you which alarms can be programmed to dial ordinary telephones (rather than an emergency centre only). All of these could be programmed to call *both* friends and an emergency centre. Carephone Plus helpers hear a recorded message. With the other brands, the helper hears a series of tones. Each helper needs a small, hand-held *responder unit* (you buy them from the alarm manufacturer) which is held next to their phone and lets the caller and helper speak to each other.

5 Using the alarm

Alarm button All the alarms tested have an emergency button on the main unit, which can be used instead of a remote trigger. Our ratings take into account size, the force needed to press them, and labelling.

Attempts to call If the alarm call does not get through (because the line is engaged, for example), the unit will try again. We give the maximum number of tries each brand will make, assuming it is programmed to dial all the numbers it can. The more tries a unit makes, the better. All the units tested can be set off again with the portable trigger – without having to reset the unit.

F = keeps dialling until it is answered
M = tries for 30 minutes

Cancel button If the alarm is set off by mistake it is useful to be able to stop the call going out (you can with most brands).

Reassurance signals The brands vary in how well informed they keep you about the progress of an alarm call – through a variety of bleeps and buzzes and small indicator lights.

B = light shows unit has received signal
I = sound shows unit has received signal
J = light shows centre has received call
K = sound or speech shows centre or helper has received call
T = warning of faulty telephone line
W = unit stores emergency calls throughout telephone line failure and sends signals to centre when line is restored

Be careful not to leave separate extension telephones off the hook. Depending on how they are wired, this can stop an alarm call going out. Leaving the *built-in* telephone off the hook did not stop an alarm on the brands tested.

6 Power failure

Battery power All the alarms work on mains electricity and all those tested have back-up batteries which take over automatically in a power cut, if a fuse blows or if the unit is unplugged by mistake. We tell you how long the units can work, and still send an alarm call, on battery power. Most have batteries that automatically recharge when mains power is restored. The Carephone Plus and Telecare have dry cell batteries that need to be changed: you would be wise to check them every three months.

Failure indicators All the alarms which contact an emergency centre automatically tell it of a mains failure or when their battery power is running low; some brands do both. In the Table we show which ones also tell *you* – with a light or sound or both.

A = audible indication of mains failure
N = visible indication of mains failure
Q = audible indication of low battery
U = visible indication of low battery
() = optional indicator

7 Portable trigger

Type tested It is important that you wear or carry the portable trigger at all times.

Triggers which cannot be worn are too easy to forget.

P = worn around neck like a pendant
P/C = can be worn as a pendant or clipped to clothing or wrist strap
W = worn like a wristwatch

All the triggers stood up well to knocks and bumps and steamy conditions. They varied in how well they dealt with very wet conditions: when having a shower it's best to take them off and put them within reach.

Range The more ★s, the further the trigger can be from the unit and still set it off. All the triggers we tested worked from anywhere in a three-bedroom house, even when we simulated a fall on the trigger (which reduces the range). Most pendant triggers have their aerial in the neckcord; carrying these by wrapping the neckcord around the pendant is likely to reduce their range. We have found large differences between samples of the same brand. When you have an alarm installed make sure the trigger is tested at the furthest point from the unit that you are likely to use it.

Low battery warning All the portable triggers have batteries which need replacing. They last from six months to five years depending on brand. They can be fiddly to change. We tell you which ones

EMERGENCY ALARMS

	Price exc VAT (2)	Available from (3)	Can call helpers direct (4)	(5) Using the alarm: Alarm button	Attempts to call	Cancel button	Reassurance signals	(6) Power failure: Battery power	Failure indicators	(7) Portable trigger: Type tested	Range: worn normally	Range: fall on trigger
	£							hours				
(1) BUILT-IN TELEPHONE												
1 Carephone Plus	180	CHLOS	√	★★	6	√	BI	23	ANQU	P	★★★	★★
▶ **2 Homelink III**[10]	220	CHLO	x[9]	★★	14	√	BIKT	11	N	P	★★★	★★★
▶ **3 Independence Phone II**	290	CLO	x	★★★	F	√	BIKTW	12	(A)N(Q)U	P	★★	★★
▶ **4 Lifeline II**[2]	230	CHLO	√	★★★	20	√	BIKT	13	NU	P/C	★★	★★
▶ **5 Vitalcall 2**	229[3]	CLO	√	★★★	24	√	BIK	8	AN	P	★★	★
(1) SPEECH LINK												
▶ **6 Homelink II**[4]	220	CHLO	x	★★★	20	√	BIKT	19	N	P	★★★	★★★
7 KRS Companion	350	LM	x	★★★	40	√	BK	6	NU	P	[7]	[7]
8 Selcare Solitaire[5]	755	L	x	★★★	M	√	BIK	[6]	ANQU	P	★★	★
9 Talisman	250	CHLO	x	★★★	F	√	BIKW	4	AU	P	★★	★★
10 Telecare HTS 785	[1]	L	x	★★★	12	x	BIK	50	U	P	★★	★
11 Unidial II	250	CHLO	√	★★★	F	√	BIKW	4	AU	P	★★	★★
▶ **12 Vital-link**	209[3]	LO	√	★★★	24	√	BIK	8	AN	P	★★	★★
(1) NO SPEECH												
▶ **13 Aid-Call**	195[8]	CLM	x	[7]	10	√	BIJK	22	NQ	P	★★★	★★★
										W	★★	★★
14 Britannia Distress Call	332	M	x	★★★	20	√	BIJK	14	NU	P	★★	★
15 Response	275	M	x	[11]	8	x	IKTW	57	N	P	★★	★★

▶ Recommended in the Buying Guide ◀

warn you that their battery is getting low (usually by a light which doesn't come on when you press the trigger). Some triggers automatically warn the emergency centre instead or as well. A low battery reduces the trigger's range.

E = indicator on trigger to show low battery

G = emergency centre alerted when you use trigger with a low battery

Ease of use The more ⋆s the easier to use. Some have a button to press; with others you push or pull on the pendant. Our ratings take into account the size and type of button, the force needed and how long pressure needs to be maintained. If your hands are stiff or weak, triggers that you can operate with the whole hand – ones with a large protruding button, for example – are likely to be best. Try out the trigger for comfort; its size, weight and how easy it is to wear are important.

Low battery warning	Ease of use	8 Other triggers available	Performance drawbacks	Features	Convenience drawbacks	9 Built-in telephone
E	⋆⋆	JKLN	mqz	FM	ko	1
G	⋆⋆⋆	fjln	t	DFS	f	2 ◀
G	⋆⋆⋆	FHJjKLN	t	DFS	cw	3 ◀
EG	⋆⋆⋆	dFHJjKLN	r	FMRSV	cp	4 ◀
G	⋆⋆⋆	FHJKL	t	DF	—	5 ◀
G	⋆⋆⋆	JKLN				6 ◀
[7]	[7]	FHJKLN				7
—	⋆⋆⋆	FHJKLN				8
G	⋆⋆⋆	fhjkln				9
—	⋆⋆⋆	FHJKLN				10
G	⋆⋆⋆	fhjkln				11
G	⋆⋆⋆	FHJKL				12 ◀
E —	⋆⋆ ⋆⋆	dfhjKl				13 ◀
-	⋆⋆⋆	dFHJKLN				14
G	⋆⋆⋆	fhjkln				15

8 Other triggers available

We list some of the types of trigger that manufacturers tell us you can have installed with each alarm unit. Most need to be wired in; these are shown as capital letters in the Table. Some work by radio instead (like pendant triggers); these are shown as small letters. Radio triggers are more expensive to buy – typically around £50 each compared with around £10 for wired triggers (though installation costs will be higher for wired triggers).

d = portable trigger which is not attached to your body or clothing

F/f = pull cord which should reach to the floor

H/h = wall pushbutton fixed in places where you spend a lot of time

J/j = alarm set off by smoke detectors

K/k = room temperature sensors can be set to operate the alarm when the temperature falls below a certain level

L/l = intruder sensors are usually fitted to windows or doors to set off the alarm if anyone tries to break in

[1] No price available from manufacturer
[2] The similar Piper Solo II, £200, has no built-in phone. These models have been superseded by Lifeline II Plus and Solo 2 Plus with some extra features
[3] Can be rented from Aid-Call, for same charges as Aid-Call unit
[4] Non-speech version available, £180
[5] Works by radio
[6] No accurate measurement; satisfactory duration
[7] Changed since our tests
[8] Available for rent only; £195 initial fee, plus £35 a quarter, including monitoring, or £375 fee plus £65 a year; or £19 a month
[9] Manufacturer tells us unit can now be programmed to dial helpers direct
[10] Also sold by Shorrock (manufacturer of **3** and **8**) as Sentinel
[11] Different types of buttons can be attached to unit

N/n = inactivity monitors set off the alarm if you do *not* do something, such as pushing a button on the unit once a day or walking across a pressure mat

9 Built-in telephone

Performance drawbacks All the alarm units with their own telephone handset performed satisfactorily as telephones, but see Table for drawbacks. We measured the quality of the sound you hear through the earpiece. Only the Lifeline II had a volume control, and it was effective. Three people who are very hard of hearing found the special 'T' setting on their hearing aid useful with all the telephones, particularly with the Lifeline II. But the response an individual user will get from any of the telephones with the 'T' setting will depend on their hearing difficulty and their aid. (Many people who wear a hearing aid can use telephones without using the 'T' setting.)

m = memory of all numbers and messages lost when battery back-up exhausted
q = rings quietly
r = rings quietly if poor line and extension phones are fitted
t = telephone stops working if mains and battery power exhausted
z = alarm function can be switched off with a button next to alarm button – the two could be confused

Features The units have many facilities in common with ordinary modern telephones and all have last number redial:

D = can dial any number without lifting handset
F = fast-dial buttons for frequently used numbers
M = raised identification dot on a central key
R = remote answering using portable or fixed trigger(s)
S = hands-free speaking
V = volume control for handset

Convenience drawbacks The units were assessed for ease of dialling, using the handset, size of the keys, the force needed to press them, the weight and balance of the handset and how loudly the phone rang. The assessments took into account problems such as stiff hands and general weakness.

c = only slight click in earpiece when keys pressed
f = fairly small keys
k = keys close together
o = unit unstable when set up at an angle
p = underside of handset close to keypad
w = handset slightly heavy

Manufacturers

The numbers refer to the order of the alarms in the Table. Contact the manufacturer if you need more information on availability.

Britannia Distress Call is now supplied by **ADT** (same number).

1 Answercall Ltd ☎ 081-804 1235

2,6 Homelink Telecom Ltd ☎ (0594) 543343

3,8 Shorrock Community Care Division ☎ (0942) 811717

4 Tunstall Telecom Ltd ☎ (0977) 661234

5,12 Modern Vitalcall ☎ (0527) 67607

7 KRS Electronics ☎ (0274) 584115

9 Cass Electronics Ltd ☎ (0784) 436266

10 ANT Telecommunications Ltd ☎ (0753) 820242

11 Davis Security Communications Ltd ☎ (0742) 431577

13 Aid-Call ☎ (0647) 40804 and 071-352 2822

14 Britannia Monitoring Services Ltd ☎ (0276) 692737

15 Wessex Alarms ☎ (0747) 52878

The following brands came on to the market too late to be included in our tests:

Homecall II, a speech system, no built-in telephone. Information from **Oakland Communications** ☎ 081-843 2345
Patron, a speech system, no built-in telephone. Information from **Watchbase Communications** ☎ (0564) 794044.

ALARMS CHECKLIST

These are the key questions to consider when choosing an alarm system:

- Does the alarm unit have an alarm button that is easy to use?
- Does it have a cancel button?
- Does it make more than five attempts to call for help after you have pushed the button once?
- If it makes fewer than 10 attempts, can you restart it using the portable trigger if the call doesn't get through?
- Does it give clear signals to show that an alarm call is getting through?
- Does it have battery back-up that lasts at least eight hours?
- Does it warn both the emergency centre and you if mains power fails or back-up battery power runs low?
- Is the speech link (and the telephone if it has one) loud enough for you?
- Is the portable trigger easy for you to use?
- Is it comfortable to wear?
- Is the range long enough for your home and garden?

DRILLS

Hammer, Electro-pneumatic and Cordless Drills

From *Which?* February 1990

Different drills are suitable for different jobs. To help you choose the drill that's right for you, we report on 49 hammer, electro-pneumatic and cordless drills.

Hammer drills

An electric hammer drill is one of the most versatile d-i-y tools. It will drill holes in wood and metal, and with the hammer action engaged it should cope with concrete and brickwork, too.

Hammer action works by making the drill bit vibrate forwards and backwards, pounding the material at the tip of the drill, so it's important to use masonry drill bits with specially hardened tips.

If you want to do more than just drill holes, you can get a wide range of attachments like saws and sanders. All the hammer drills we tested had conventional chucks, mostly suitable for drill bits from 1.5 to 13mm in diameter.

Take particular care when using a mains-powered drill outdoors, and always use a residual current device to minimise the risk of an electric shock. Protect your eyes with goggles when drilling, too.

Power The power you need to make a hole depends on the material you're drilling into and the size of the hole. Most hammer drills are rated at 500 watts or more. But that's the input power; in our Table (see overleaf) we also give the more important maximum output power of each drill.

Speed Control of speed is very important for some jobs. In general, higher speeds are best for soft materials, lower speeds for tough materials. But even when drilling at high speed, it's often useful to be able to start the drill slowly and build up to full speed.

Most of the hammer drills we tested had a variable speed control – the more firmly you press on the trigger, the faster the drill goes. With some, this was combined with a speed pre-select control – a way of limiting the movement of the trigger, so you won't exceed the maximum speed you want.

Some of the drills also had two-speed gearboxes. This means that the torque of the drill – the twisting force – is greater at the lower speed, which is ideal for masonry.

Reverse Many of the hammer drills we tested could be reversed. This is useful for undoing screws, and possibly for freeing a drill bit which has jammed.

Feedback An ordinary drill will tend to slow down as the load increases. A **constant speed control** tries to combat this by increasing the power to the motor to match the load. A **variable torque control** limits the twisting force at the chuck to a pre-set level – this is very useful for delicate jobs like screwdriving. An **overload cut-out** prevents the motor burning out by disconnecting the power when there's a danger of overloading it. A **clutch** does the same sort of job, by disconnecting the drive to the chuck.

BUYING GUIDE

HAMMER DRILLS

A hammer drill is a versatile tool which can cope with most household jobs.

BEST BUYS

One-gear drill, with reasonable performance: **Black & Decker BD143V**, £40. If you're going to do a lot of masonry drilling, it's worth paying more for the **AEG SB2 500**, *£84* or **Peugeot PC508E**, *£76*. For a drill with constant speed and variable torque controls, but poor hammer drilling, **Black & Decker BD155RT**, £60, is worth considering

BEST BUY

Two-gear drill: **Hitachi FDV 16VA**, *£108* or the similar **FDV 16V**, *£104*, without reverse

ELECTRO-PNEUMATIC DRILLS

Electro-pneumatic drills are good tools for masonry work. But they're less versatile than hammer drills.

BEST BUY

Wickes, £75, without reverse or variable speed control, but good performance

CORDLESS DRILLS

Cordless drills are not tough enough for many jobs. But they're handy for light tasks – drilling in wood and screwdriving, for example – and safer to use outdoors.

BEST BUYS

Bosch PBM 7.2VE, £70 Two gears, good performance, particularly for screwdriving.

Best of the single gear drills, and with hammer action: **Hitachi FDV 10D**, £70

Electro-pneumatic drills

These look like hammer drills, but in an electro-pneumatic drill the hammer action is provided by a piston driven by air pressure. This is more effective than mechanical hammer action, and electro pneumatic drills tend to out-perform ordinary hammer drills in tough masonry jobs. Because less of the vibration gets transmitted back, they can be more comfortable to use, too. But they're bulky, heavy and relatively expensive.

Most of the electro-pneumatic drills we tested had SDS Plus toolholders rather than conventional chucks. These toolholders take special drill bits which are about two or three times the price of ordinary masonry drill bits, from about £2.50 to £6, depending on size. The advantage is that they don't rely on how securely you've tightened the chuck to stop the drill bit slipping. You can still fit a conventional chuck, about £10, but you'll also need an SDS adaptor, another £10 or so.

Power The electro-pneumatic drills we tested had about the same maximum output power as the conventional hammer drills, but generally did better for hammer drilling.

Speed Electro-pneumatic drills have maximum speeds similar to two-speed hammer drills on their lower speeds. This is ideal for masonry but not so suitable for

HAMMER DRILLS

		Price (1)	Accessories (2)	Flex length (3)	Weight	Chuck capacity (4)	(5) Maximum diameter hole: Concrete	Wood	Steel	Rated input power (7)	Maximum output power (8)	Maximum stated speed (9)	Variable speed control (10)	Reverse (11)	Feedback (12)
		£		m	kg	mm	mm	mm	mm	W	W	rev/min			
	ONE-GEAR HAMMER DRILLS														
	1 AEG SBE 10RLN (W Germany)	82	CDH	2.5	1.9	1.5 to 13	10	25	10	450	250	2600	PT	yes	no
►	**2 AEG SB2 500** (W Germany)	84	DH	2.5	1.8	1.5 to 13	15	25	10	500	350	2300/2900	E	no	no
	3 Black & Decker BD142 (UK)	37	—	1.9	1.9	1.5 to 13	13	25	13	500	275	2600/3000	E	no	no
►	**4 Black & Decker BD143V** (UK)	40	—	1.9	1.9	1.5 to 13	13	25	13	500	275	3000	PT	no	no
	5 Black & Decker BD154R (UK)	50	BH	1.9	2.0	1.5 to 13	13	25	13	550	275	3000	PT	yes	no
►	**6 Black & Decker BD155RT** (UK)	60	BDH	1.9	2.1	1.5 to 13	13	25	13	550	275	3000	PT	yes	CV
	7 Black & Decker BD163V (UK)	43	DH	1.9	2.0	1.5 to 13	13	25	13	550	300	3000	PT	no	no
	8 Black & Decker BD552 (UK)	30	H	1.3	1.5	1 to 10	10	20	10	400	225	2600/3100	E	no	no
	9 Black & Decker Proline PL15 (Italy)	60	DH	2.0	1.8	1 to 13	18	32	13	450	300	2750	T	yes	no
	10 Bosch CSB 500RE (Switzerland)	62	DH	2.5	2.1	1.5 to 13	15	25	10	500	263	3000	PT	yes	no
	11 Bosch PSB 400RE (Switzerland)	46	—	2.5	1.7	1 to 10	10	20	8	400	250	2600	T	yes	no
	12 Bosch PSB 400 (Switzerland)	32	—	2.4	1.7	1 to 10	10	20	8	400	200	2600	—	no	no
	13 Hitachi FV 12VA (Japan)	52	H	2.5	1.9	1.5 to 13	12	25	10	420	250	2800	PT	yes	no
	14 Kango 2388 (UK)	110	—	2.9	2.1	1.5 to 13	10	22	13	400	225	2500	PT	yes	no
	15 Kress 520 EHD (W Germany)	100	C	3.9	2.0	1.5 to 13	13	30	10	520	325	3000	T	yes	no
	16 Makita M802 (Japan)	73	H	2.1	1.9	1.5 to 13	13	18	13	430	250	2700	PT	yes	no
►	**17 Peugeot PC 580E** (France)	76	—	1.4	2.1	1.5 to 13	13	30	13	580	325	2600	PT	no	no
	18 Peugeot PC 550RCP (France)	88	—	1.4	2.2	1.5 to 13	13	30	13	550	275	2600	PT	yes	V
	19 Skil 6434 (Netherlands)	55	H	2.6	1.7	1.5 to 13	13	40	13	520	275	2900	PT	yes	no
	TWO-GEAR HAMMER DRILLS														
	1 Black & Decker Proline PL20 (Italy)	70	DH	2.3	2.2	1.5 to 13	27	35	13	600	325	1050/2500	T	no	no
	2 Black & Decker SR 910RT (W Germany)	89	DH	4.9	2.3	1.5 to 13	16	30	13	650	275	1100/2700	PT	yes	COV
	3 Bosch CSB 7002RE (Switzerland)	93	DH	2.5	2.7	1.5 to 13	20	40	13	700	313	1000/3000	PT	yes	no
►	**4 Hitachi FDV 16VA** (Japan)	108	DH	2.6	2.5	1.5 to 13	16	35	13	600	375	1300/2800	PT	yes	no
►	**5 Hitachi FDV 16V** (Japan)	104	DH	2.6	2.5	1.5 to 13	16	35	13	600	375	1300/2800	PT	no	no
	6 Kango 2345 (UK)	130	H	2.9	1.9	2 to 13	16	22	13	475	225	1050/2300	PT	yes	no
	7 Metabo SbE500/2SR + L (W Germany)	172	DH	2.5	2.6	1.5 to 13	16	30	13	500	275	950/2400	PT	yes	S
	8 Perles XSR2100 (Yugoslavia)	113	CH	2.7	2.2	1 to 13	16	20	13	500	200	480/1200	PT	yes	no

ELECTRO-PNEUMATIC DRILLS

		Price	Accessories	Flex length	Weight	Chuck capacity	Concrete	Wood	Steel	Rated input power	Maximum output power	Maximum stated speed	Variable speed control	Reverse	Feedback
	1 Bosch PBH 200RE (W Germany)	121	ADH	2.5	2.1	SDS	20	30	13	420	300	1400	PT	yes	S
	2 Kango 285 (UK)	145	CDH	3.8	2.4	SDS	16	25	10	425	250	930	T	no	no
	3 Kress HM 10E (W Germany)	115	CDH	1.9	2.3	SDS	20	40	13	500	—	1200	PT	yes	no
	4 Skil 6850 EMH (Netherlands)	80	DH	2.6	2.4	1.5 to 13	16	30	13	500	—	1500	T	yes	no
►	**5 Wickes** (W Germany) [1]	75	ACDH	2.0	2.3	SDS	20	40	13	500	350	1200	—	no	no

► Recommended in the Buying Guide ◄

KEY TO RATINGS best ◩ > ◪ > □ > ◪ > ■ worst

13 Performance: Hammer drilling	Drilling in wood	Drilling in steel	Screwdriving in wood	Screwdriving in steel	15 Endurance	16 Convenience	17 Noise	
◪	◩	◩	□	□	◩[2]	◩	◪	1
◩	▩	◩	◪	◪	◩	◩	■	2 ◀
◪	▩	◩	◪	◪	▩	□	◪	3
◪	▩	◩	□	□	▩	□	◪	4 ◀
■	◩	□	◩	◪	▩	□	◪	5
■	▩	◩	◩	□	▩	◩	◪	6 ◀
◪	◩	□	◩	◪	▩	□	◪	7
◪	□	□	◪	◪	▩	□	◪	8
◪	▩	◩	□	□	◩	◩	◪	9
■	▩	◩	◩	□	□	◩	◪	10
■	◩	□	◩	◪	◩	□	◪	11
■	▩	◩	◪	◪	◩	□	◪	12
■	▩	◩	□	□	□	◩	◪	13
■	◩	□	◩	□	▩	□	◪	14
◪	▩	◩	□	□	▩	◩	◪	15
■	◩	□	◩	◪	▩	□	■	16
□	▩	◩	◩	◩	▩	□	■	17 ◀
◪	▩	◩	◩	◩	▩	□	■	18
◪	▩	◩	◩	◩	◩	◩	◪	19
◪	▩	◩	□	□	□	□	■	1
■	▩	◩	▩	▩	◩	◩	◪	2
◪	▩	◩	◩	◩	□	◩	◪	3
□	▩	◩	◩	◩	▩	◩	◪	4 ◀
□	▩	◩	◩	◩	▩	◩	◪	5 ◀
■	▩	◩	◩	◩	▩	□	◪	6
◪	▩	◩	◩	◩	▩	◩	◪	7
◪	▩	◩	◩	◩	▩	□	◪	8
□	◩	□	◩	◩	▩	◩	◪	1
■	□	□	◪	◪	▩	□	■	2
◩	◪	□	◩	◩	▩	◩	■	3
◪	◩	□	◩	◩	▩	◩	◪	4
◩	□	◪	□	□	▩	◩	■	5 ◀

other materials, and the ordinary hammer drills were better than the electro-pneumatics for drilling in wood and steel. Most of the models we looked at had reverse.

Cordless drills

The main advantages of cordless drills are that they're light, easy to handle, less noisy than big mains-powered drills, and there's no trailing flex to worry about. Although more powerful cordless drills are coming on to the market, at present most don't have the power of larger, mains-powered drills, though that can be an advantage for delicate jobs. Because cordless drills work at low voltages, they're much safer to use outdoors.

Power Power for cordless drills comes from rechargeable nickel cadmium batteries. Some are contained within the drill, others come as a separate pack which you can detach from the drill for charging. This has the advantage that you can have a back-up pack standing by when the first is discharged.

Speed Cordless drills generally run at much lower speeds than mains-powered drills. Many also have a lower second speed. This is partly to get enough torque to drive the drill bit from the relatively small motor, and it makes them suitable for screwdriving, though only at the expense of drilling performance. All the models we tested had reverse.

Feedback Only one of the cordless drills we tested had a variable speed control. Three had variable torque controls – useful for small screws and soft materials – and two had overload cut-outs.

Charging time All the cordless drills we tested came with mains-powered chargers. But there was a wide variation in the time it took to recharge the batteries, from as little as one hour to as much as 16. We measured how well each drill would perform on a short, 'emergency' charge of 15 minutes.

FACTS, FIGURES AND TEST RESULTS

1 Price

We give target prices in the Tables. Our price survey showed that only models from Black & Decker and Bosch were widely available in d-i-y stores and hardware shops. For those models which are harder to find, we give manufacturers' list prices (including VAT) in *italics*. This is the most you should have to pay; most shops will charge less. Phone makers for details of stockists in your area.

AEG ☎ 0753 872224; **Black & Decker** ☎ 0753 74277; **Bosch** ☎ 0895 838402; **Hitachi** ☎ 0908 660663; **Kango** ☎ 0733 371707; **Kress** ☎ 0756 798625; **Makita** ☎ 0582 455777; **Metabo** ☎ 0703 266355; **Perles** ☎ 081-668 7141; **Peugeot** ☎ 021-552 4580; **Skil** ☎ 0753 869525; **Wickes** ☎ 081-863 5696

CORDLESS DRILLS

	Price (1)	Voltage	Accessories (2)	Weight	Chuck capacity (4)	(5) Maximum diameter hole: Wood	Steel	Stated charging time (6)	Maximum stated speed (9)	Variable speed control (10)	Reverse (11)	Feedback (12)
	£	v		kg	mm	mm	mm	hr	rev/min			
ONE-GEAR CORDLESS DRILLS												
1 **Black & Decker BD405R** (UK)	35	[4]	B	0.8	1 to 10	10	8	16	400	no	yes	no
2 **Bosch PBM4.8V** (Switzerland)	42	4.8	B	0.9	1 to 10	12	8	12	500	no	yes	no
▶ 3 **Hitachi FDV 10D** (Japan)[3]	70	7.2		1.4	1.5 to 10	13	6.5	3	720	no	yes	no
4 **Hitachi FDW 10DA** (Japan)	*87*	7.2		1.0	1.5 to 10	10	6.5	3	600	T	yes	no
5 **Hitachi FDW 10D** (Japan)	50	7.2		1.0	1.5 to 10	10	6.5	3	600	no	yes	no
6 **Makita M003** (Japan)	80	7.2	B	1.0	1.5 to 10	10	10	3	600	no	yes	O
7 **Peugeot 6CP** (France)	*110*	7.2	C	1.2	1.5 to 10	20	8	1	600	no	yes	no
8 **Wickes 7.2V** (W Germany)[1]	50	7.2	C	1.2	1 to 10	10	8	3	330	no	yes	no
TWO-GEAR CORDLESS DRILLS												
1 **AEG ABS 10RL** (Japan)	129	7.2	BC	1.5	1 to 10	15	10	1	300/600	no	yes	V
2 **Black & Decker 9013** (USA)	45	7.2	B	0.9	1.5 to 10	13	8	3	300/600	no	yes	no
3 **Black & Decker SC522R** (UK)	58	[4]	B	1.2	1 to 10	13	10	16	300/600	no	yes	no
▶ 4 **Bosch PBM 7.2VE** (Switzerland)	70	7.2	B	1.3	1 to 10	15	10	3	300/650	T	yes	no
5 **Kango 1640** (Japan)	*154*	7.2	B	1.2	1.5 to 10	15	10	1	230/700	no	yes	V
6 **Makita 6012 DWK** (Japan)	117	7.2	BC	1.3	1.5 to 10	15	10	1	250/600	no	yes	O
7 **Peugeot 7CD** (France)[5]	*75*	7.2		1.2	1.5 to 10	20	8	4	300/600	no	yes	no
8 **Skil 2140 H** (Netherlands)	*40*	4.8		0.8	1.5 to 10	10	6	4	180/360	no	yes	no
9 **Skil 2503 H** (USA)	*58*	7.2		1.2	1.5 to 10	18	10	1	300/600	no	yes	V

▶ Recommended in the Buying Guide ◀

KEY TO RATINGS **best** ◩ > ◤ > □ > ◪ > ■ **worst**

2 Accessories

We list the accessories supplied with the tools we bought for testing.

A = drill bits
B = screwdriver bits
C = carrying case
D = depth stop
H = second handle

3 Flex length

For mains-powered drills only.

4 Chuck capacity

The size range of bits which will fit the chuck supplied with the tool. Most of the electro-pneumatic drills had SDS Plus toolholders rather than chucks.

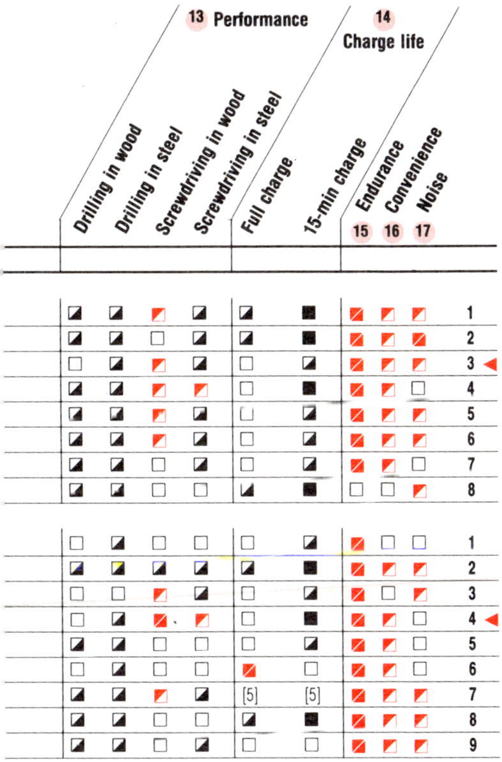

5 Maximum diameter hole

The largest holes that the manufacturer says the drill can make in various materials.

6 Stated charging time

The time the manufacturer gives to recharge fully a completely discharged battery, using the charger supplied.

7 Rated input power

The amount of power that the drill draws from the mains, according to the manufacturer.

8 Maximum output power

The maximum output power that each drill could sustain for at least 100 seconds – a better indication than rated input power of what you actually get out of the drill. The higher the maximum output power, the tougher the tasks that the drill should be able to perform.

9 Maximum stated speed

Manufacturers' figures for 'no load' speeds.

10 Variable speed control

E = electronic switch gives high or low speed
P = pre-select
T = trigger pressure controls speed

11 Reverse

Needed for undoing screws.

12 Feedback

C = constant speed control
O = overload cut-out
S = clutch
V = variable torque control

[1] Available from Wickes stores
[2] We found internal cable wear – Manufacturer tells us drill is now modified
[3] With hammer facility
[4] Voltage not stated
[5] Charger unit changed since our tests

13 Performance
The drilling ratings are based on tests using a variety of diameter bits. The hammer drilling ratings are based on tests drilling into granite.

14 Charge life
The ratings are based on the numbers of holes and the number of screws that each tool could achieve before the batteries were flat, from batteries which were fully charged, and batteries charged for 15 minutes. A rating of □ means that the drill would drive about 50 5 × 60mm screws into softwood, on a full charge.

15 Endurance
Our tests simulated years of routine work for each type of tool. For the hammer and electro-pneumatic drills, we tested the endurance of both the motor and the hammer mechanism.

16 Convenience
Drills were assessed by a panel which included men, women, right- and left-handed users.

17 Noise
Electric drills are noisy, especially when used with the hammer action – around 100 decibels is common. Cordless drills are quieter.

Electrical safety
The chuck key on the Skil 6434 hammer drill, when fitted in a recess provided for that purpose in the handle, could come into contact with one of the mains supply cables. The manufacturers assure us that they've modified this model to make it safe. If you've got one, don't store the chuck key in the recess on the handle. All the other drills were satisfactory.

Drill bits

The type of drill bit you need depends on the material you're dealing with.

Steel and other metals HSS (high speed steel) twist drill bits are the usual choice for steel or other metals. They cost from around 50p for a 3mm bit to about £3 for a 12 mm bit.

Cutting holes in thin metal – to mount a radio aerial on a car, for example – can be a problem. There are special conical cutting tools for this purpose. They cost £10 or more, depending on size.

Wood HSS twist drill bits work reasonably well in wood, but make sure the waste material is cleared to prevent the drill jamming.

Most traditional wood-boring tools are designed to work at low speeds. But there are special tools for wood designed specifically to work with power drills. Often called flat boring bits, or flat drill bits, they're shaped rather like a spade, with a slim shank and a large, flat cutting head. Typical prices are around £2 each.

If the hole you want to make goes right through the wood, and it's not too thick, there are also hole saws. These are useful for larger holes. They're usually sold in sets, from around £6.

Masonry Masonry drill bits have a small piece of very hard material at the tip – usually tungsten carbide. This can withstand the hammering of a powerful electric drill and the hard, brittle nature of masonry materials. Standard length masonry drill bits cost from £1 to £2, depending on size, and there are also long masonry bits which tend to cost more.

HOT AIR GUNS

Electric and Gas-powered

From *Which?* July 1990

Electric hot air guns have ousted the traditional blowlamp as the preferred tool for stripping paint from woodwork. They're easier to use, no inflammable liquid is involved, they can't blow out in the wind and they're less likely to scorch the wood. But there's a major disadvantage – they have to be connected to the electricity supply. And that means that when you're up a ladder stripping paint from window-frames, or down the garden working in the shed, you'll need an extension lead.

So flame-powered strippers are making something of a comeback, in the form of hot air guns powered by gas. But instead of the flame playing directly on the paint, it's used to create a blast of hot air. In some guns, the gas is stored in a small cartridge which forms part of the gun. In others, a separate gas cylinder is connected to the gun by a flexible hose. We found little to choose between gas and electric models in performance but, apart from trailing leads, the electrics were generally easier to use.

Different standards?

Our tests were carried out with other European consumer organisations. We were surprised to find that samples of the Black & Decker, Bosch and Steinel models bought on the Continent had a tough rubber sheathed flex, but samples of the same model bought in the UK had a less heat resistant PVC flex. European standards do not appear to permit PVC flexes for hot air guns. We think all guns for sale in the UK should be fitted with rubber sheathed flexes.

Bubble and scrape

Hot air guns work by softening paint, causing it to bubble up and separate from the surface underneath so you can scrape it away. Because the heat from a hot air gun is less fierce than from a blowlamp or blowtorch, hot air guns are a good deal easier to use, though they don't cover the surface as quickly.

The normal way of working is to hold the hot air gun in your less favoured hand (left hand for right-handers and right hand for left-handers), so you can manipulate the scraper or shavehook with your stronger one.

Co-ordinating the heating of the paint with removing it using the scraper or shavehook needs a little practice. For the most efficient progress, you should be heating the next section while scraping away the one you've just covered. It's best to work on only a fairly small section at a time, aiming for continuous progress over the area to be stripped.

Take care not to burn the hand holding the scraper or shavehook with the hot air. Most right-handers will find it safest to work from right to left and left-handers from left to right on horizontal surfaces, and all users should work from bottom to top on vertical surfaces. Wear heat-resistant gloves, and collect the scrapings in a paint kettle or metal bucket.

Stripping successfully

If you find that the paint is difficult to scrape away then it could be that you're not heating it enough. The amount of heat you need depends on the temperature you're working in and how much paint you have to remove. Or it could be that it's not the type of paint which responds readily to heat. Most gloss paints do, but emulsions don't soften when heated.

Take extra care around windows. Using a special window nozzle, you can remove paint with a hot air gun right up to the window glass – something that's virtually impossible with the naked flame of a blow-lamp without breaking the glass.

Don't use a hot air gun to remove paint which may contain lead, particularly indoors where ventilation is limited. Few modern paints have lead in them, but it used to be a common ingredient. If you suspect that at least some of the layers you're going to scrape away could contain lead, use a chemical stripper instead.

Watch what you're doing when you have to lift the hot air gun away from the work: to concentrate on scraping a stubborn bit of paint, for example. That's when accidents can occur.

BUYING GUIDE

BEST BUY For a basic electric gun: **Black & Decker BD 1602**, £22, was easy to use, easy to find in the shops and has a good range of accessories available.

Others to consider: the **Bosch PHG 560 E**, £44, one airflow setting but variable heat. It had fair performance and a range of accessories; the **Wickes Electronic**, £33, (exclusive to Wickes) was good value for a gun with a variable heat control. Though it has no accessories, its flex is rubber sheathed.

If a gas-powered gun suits you best, and particularly if you already have a suitable gas cylinder (for camping or caravanning, for example) the **BEST BUY** **Camping Gaz DT 780 R**, £36, offers very good paint-stripping performance at a price which competes directly with electric hot air guns.

Other uses for a hot air gun

- Quick drying: used with care, a hot air gun can speed the drying of paints, varnishes, fillers and some adhesives.
- De-frosting: on a low setting, a hot air gun can be very useful for defrosting frozen plumbing.
- Soldering: a hot air gun can be used both for directly heating solder-type plumbing fittings, using a reflector nozzle (see 'Nozzles available'), and for soldering using a special soldering nozzle.
- Hot-melt adhesives: a hot air gun can be used to separate joints made with hot-melt adhesives (the sort which comes as sticks to be used with a glue gun) without scorching the wood, and to help remove sticky labels. It can also be used to warm pieces of wood before glueing them together. This is particularly useful for large joints: without warming the hot-melt adhesives might cool and start to set before the joint is made.

• Pipe bending: a hot air gun can be used to bend and shape plastic pipes, though you must take care not to let the pipe collapse as it is bent.
• Heat shrinking plastic: heat shrink sleeving is available for insulating electrical fittings and components, and heat-shrinkable plastic sheet for packaging or 'cocooning' larger items. A hot air gun is ideal for shrinking these materials.
• Roof repairs: a hot air gun can be used to melt the sticky coating on the undersides of roof repair strips and flashings.
• Other possible uses:
Waxing furniture or skis
Loosening screws, nuts and bolts
Lighting charcoal for barbecues
Darkening or scorching wood surfaces.

Safety measures
With temperatures at the nozzle as high as 500 degrees Celsius, hot air guns can cause nasty burns:

Don't point them at anyone
Don't put your hand over the nozzle
Don't put them down where the nozzle will touch anything
Don't use them as hairdriers

When you're working above ground level with an electric hot air gun, drape the flex over your shoulder, or tape it to the ladder, so you don't have to support its weight with the hand holding the gun. Take care not to crush the flex underfoot when working on a ladder. When working outdoors, always use a residual current device (RCD) to safeguard against the risk of electrocution.

If you're working with a gas-powered gun which uses a separate cylinder of bottled gas, make sure that the cylinder is safely supported when you're working above ground level.

Protect yourself with gloves, goggles and boots – watch out for smouldering slivers of old paint. Keep children and pets away from where you're working.

FACTS, FIGURES AND TEST RESULTS

1 Type
We've divided our Table into electric and gas guns.

2 Target price
Prices in ordinary type are those we found in our shopping survey. Those in *italics* are manufacturers' prices. Black & Decker and Bosch hot air guns were easy to find in the shops. For other brands you may have to go to specialist tool shops or builders' merchants. For hard-to-find models, contact manufacturers for stockists in your area:
Camping Gaz ☎ (0753) 691707
Kress ☎ (0756) 798625
Metabo ☎ (0703) 200355
Peugeot ☎ 021-552 4580
Sievert ☎ 081-769 0015
Stayer ☎ (0483) 740700
Steinel ☎ (0733) 238265

3 Power
For electric guns, we give the maximum amount of power drawn from the mains, in Watts. For gas guns, we give the equivalent based on the amount of gas consumed.

4 Weight
For electric guns the weight includes the flex. For gas-powered guns, the weight

HOT AIR GUNS

	Target price (2)	Power (3)	Weight (4)	Number of heat/airflow settings (5)	Temp range (6)	Features (7)	Nozzles available (8)	Instructions (9)	Performance (10)	Convenience (11)	Noise (12)	Safety (13)	
	£	W			Deg C								
(1) ELECTRIC HOT AIR GUNS													
1 **Black & Decker BD 1600** (UK)	19	1345	W	1/1	390	FH	CRSW	□	□	□	◤	□	
► 2 **Black & Decker BD 1602** (UK)	22	1650	W	2/2	180–330	FH	CRSW	◤	□	◤	◤	□	◄
3 **Black & Decker BD 1610 E** (UK)	33	1575	WW	V/1	60–320	FH	CRSW	◤	□	□	◤	□	
4 **Black & Decker PL 70** (UK)	40	1875	WWW	2/2	290–440	FH	CRSW	◤	□	◤	◤	□	
5 **Bosch PHG 490** (W Germany)	22	1490	WW	2/2	270–400	F	—	◤	□	◤	◤	□	
6 **Bosch PHG 520** (W Germany)	26	1480	WW	2/2	230–350	FPS	CRSW	□	□	◤	◤	□	
► 7 **Bosch PHG 560 E** (W Germany)	44	1610	WWW	V/1	70–360	FHPS	CRSW	◤	□	◤	◤	□	◄
8 **Bosch PHG 600 CE** (W Germany)	50	1905	WWW	V/2	90–490	FHPS	CRSW	◤	▨	◤	◤	□	
9 **Kress 1600 EHB** (W Germany)	83	1475	WWW	V/1	90–415	F	**SW**	□	◤	□	▨	◤	
10 **Metabo HG 1500/2** (W Germany)	67	1400	WW	2/2	310–390	FHPS	RSW	□	□	◤	▨	◤	
11 **Peugeot DT 1500** (W Germany)	47	1410	WW	2/2	340–420	FHPS	**RSW**	◪	◤	□	▨	◤	
12 **Peugeot DT 2600 E** (W Germany)	74	2210	WW	V/2	70–440	FHPS	RSW	□	▨	□	◤	◤	
13 **Stayer SU 500** (Italy)	76	1660	WW	2/2	250–370	F	CRSW	□	□	□	◤	◤	
14 **Steinel HL 1400 M** (W Germany)	24	1385	WW	1/1	410	FHP	CRSW	◪	◤	◤	◤	□	
15 **Steinel HL 1500 S** (W Germany)	30	1465	WW	2/2	250–370	FHP	CRSW	□	□	◤	◤	□	
16 **Steinel HL 1600 ME** (W Germany)	40	1560	WW	V/1	70–420	FHP	CRSW	□	◤	◤	◤	□	
17 **Steinel HL 1800 E** (W Germany)	60	1980	WWW	V/2	130–420	FHP	CRSW	□	▨	◤	◤	□	
18 **Steinel HF 2000 S** (W Germany)	22	1880	WW	2/2	260–410	F	—	□	□	□	◤	□	
19 **Steinel HL 25 Jubilee** (W Germany)	20	1475	WW	2/2	255–280	F	CRSW	□	□	□	◤	□	
► 20 **Wickes Electronic** (W Germany)	33	1475	WW	V/1	80–490	F	—	□	◤	□	▨	◤	◄
(1) GAS-POWERED HOT AIR GUNS													
1 **Camping Gaz DT 750** (France)[1]	20	875	WWW	V/—	up to 350	FIPS	—	□	□	◪	◤	◤	
► 2 **Camping Gaz DT 780 R** (France)[2]	36	965	WW	V/—	up to 430	IP	—	□	▨	□	□	◤	◄
3 **Sievert Hot Air Burner 2956** (Sweden)[2]	35	1345	WW	V/—	up to 460	H	—	◪	◤	◪	□	□	
4 **Sievert Siever-Matic 3534** (Sweden)[2]	59	1375	WW	V/—	up to 515	FHI	—	◪	▨	□	□	◤	
5 **Taymar HG 750** (UK)[1]	21	607	WW	V/—	up to 390	FI	RSW	◤	□	□	◤	□	

► Recommended in the Buying Guide ◄

KEY TO RATINGS best ▨ > ◤ > □ > ◪ > ■ worst

[1] Gun incorporates gas cartridge [2] Connected by hose to gas cylinder

includes a full canister of gas or 2.5 metres of hose, as appropriate:

W = less than 0.6kg
WW = between 0.6 and 0.75kg
WWW = over 0.75kg

5 Number of heat/airflow settings

Variable heat and airflow settings expand the range of jobs you can tackle with a hot air gun

V = variable

6 Temperature range

We measured this at the surface of the area being treated, rather than at the nozzle of the gun, to give a more accurate guide to the temperature the gun could achieve in use.

7 Features

F = free-standing position. Most guns incorporate a stand or flat base so you can rest them on a work surface without scorching.

H = hanging loop. This can be useful when working on a ladder, and for storage.
I = built-in ignition device (gas guns only).
P = removable nozzle protector. Some of the guns had a shroud around the nozzle which could be removed to help you get into confined spaces.
S = safety handle. Some guns had handles with guards to prevent accidental operation of the on/off switch.

8 Nozzles available

Those in **bold** type were supplied with the guns and are included in the price. others are available as extras at between £2 and £6.

C = concentrator nozzle. This narrows down the stream of air; useful for stripping paint on narrow ledges and in crevices and corners.
R = reflector nozzle. Designed to spread the heat around the back of plumbing fittings when soldering.
S = spreader nozzle. This guides the air into a fan shape useful for stripping paint from larger areas.
W = window nozzle. This has a shield to prevent hot air cracking the glass when stripping window frames.

9 Instructions

All the hot air guns came with instructions. Our rating takes into account their clarity, completeness, and whether they gave satisfactory advice about safety.

10 Performance

Our ratings are based on a series of tests, stripping layers of both old and fresh paint.

11 Convenience

We asked a panel of users (including a left-hander) to assess the hot air guns for convenience in use. All the guns had pistol-grip handles; the best were comfortable and well-balanced. Electric guns rated □ were either slightly front heavy or were uncomfortable to hold according to our users.

On the whole, the gas-powered guns didn't fare so well. The Camping Gaz DT 750 was front-heavy, had an uncomfortable handle and some of the controls were awkward to use. The Sievert Hot Air Burner 2956 had a rather fiddly gas valve and lacked a built-in igniter.

12 Noise

Electric hot air guns are less noisy than most power tools, though the noise could still be irritating when using the guns for long periods. Of the gas-powered guns, the Camping Gaz DT 780R and the two Sievert guns made loud roaring noises.

13 Safety

We've downrated, from ◩ to □, the Black & Decker, Bosch and Steinel hot air guns because the versions on sale in the UK weren't fitted with rubber sheathed flexes. The relevant European standard suggests that appliances like hot air guns should be fitted with this type of flex to avoid problems if it came into contact with hot parts of the appliance. Steinel have told us they have now fitted rubber flexes to all their UK models. Black & Decker and Bosch have no plans to change existing models. Two new Black & Decker models – the BD1666 and BD1680 – which weren't on the market in time for our tests, both have rubber sheathed flexes.

Of the gas-powered hot air guns, the Sievert Hot Air Burner 2956 and Taymar HG 750 were downrated because parts of the guns which might easily be touched became very hot in normal use. Taymar tell us the HG 750 has been modified since our samples were bought.

Endurance

We put each hot air gun through a test simulating years of normal use. All the electric guns were still in working order at the end of the test, though the Bosch PHG 520 and Steinel HL25 Jubilee had become somewhat noisier on their low power settings. Of the gas-powered guns, the spark ignition on the Sievert Siever-Matic 3534 became rather erratic towards the end of the test.

---

*If you're new to **Which?**, we hope you'll find enough in **Which? Buying Guide** to consider subscribing to the magazine itself – see the advertisement on page 287 for how to get three trial issues completely free.*

*The ratings given in the Tables are based on **Which?**'s latest tests of each product. The date of the original report is noted just below the main heading.*

See page 8 for an explanation of Best Buy.

HEATED PROPAGATORS

With and without Thermostats

From *Gardening from Which?* February 1990

For early crops and bedding displays and greater success with seeds and cuttings, it is worth investing in a heated propagator. They can cost from as little as £11 for a simple tray, lid and heating element, to over £50 for a more powerful thermostatically-controlled model.

Which is the best propagator for you depends on when and where you want to use it. Our tests have shown that, in general, window-sill propagators and ordinary propagators without thermostats are suitable for use indoors or in a heated greenhouse in early spring, but they will not be effective in an unheated greenhouse until late spring. More powerful propagators with thermostats, on the other hand, should give good results in an unheated greenhouse from early spring through to autumn.

Window-sill propagators

If you do not have a greenhouse, you may want to raise a few seedlings on a window-sill. If you are prepared to maintain a room temperature of 18°C (64°F) or more, you could use an unheated propagator. But since heated rooms can cool down at night, a heated window-sill propagator may be a worthwhile investment. All those we tested were narrow enough to fit on a window-sill 18–20cm (7–8in) wide.

From our tests, the Erin 466P and Ward would need a background temperature of around 10°C (50°F) or more in order to maintain a reasonable compost temperature. Both would be suitable for a cool room.

BUYING GUIDE

WINDOW-SILL TYPE

BEST BUYS

For a cold room or greenhouse in early spring, the **Erin 465P** (£11.89 or less) is the Best Buy. For a cool room (around 10°C), the **Ward** (£18.99 or less) is worth considering. For a warm room or for striking cuttings in the summer, the **Erin 466P** with thermostat (£20.79 or less) is best.

WITHOUT THERMOSTAT

BEST BUYS

For a cheap propagator to germinate a few seeds, the **Jemp Fastgrow** (£10.95 or less) is worth considering. If you want a more robust propagator, there is very little to choose between the **Sankey 14in** (£22.62 or less) and **Ward 14in** (£22.99 or less).

WITH THERMOSTAT

BEST BUYS

We pick the **Sankey Plantmaster** (£55.99 or less) and **Ward Thermostatically Controlled** (£52.49 or less) as joint Best Buys.

The Erin 465P is worth considering for a greenhouse with a background temperature of 5°C (41°F) or less, but could make the compost too warm in the house especially if it is heated.

Only the Erin 466P had a thermostat. Although germination was slightly slower at low temperatures in our trial, the thermostat could be a useful feature to prevent the compost from getting too warm on sunny days or in a room which is heated for part of the day.

To get the best from a window-sill propagator:

- place it on a well lit window-sill that does not receive direct sunlight (which will cause the temperature inside the propagator to rise rapidly on bright, sunny days)
- bring it into the room when you draw the curtains at night – especially on very cold nights.

Propagators without thermostats

These are roughly the same size as a standard seed tray. The limitations, as with window-sill propagators, are that the compost can get too warm if the propagator is kept indoors in a room which is heated during the day or in a greenhouse on a sunny day. Conversely, they are not powerful enough to use in a greenhouse early in the season unless you provide background heat.

Propagators with thermostats

These have relatively powerful heaters and are able to cope with low background temperatures in a greenhouse in early spring. Both the ones we tested maintained temperatures of over 20°C (68°F) with a background temperature of 5°C (41°F).

Thermostats stop these propagators from getting too hot, so they can be used in rooms which are heated for short periods during the day, or for cuttings later in the season, when average temperatures are much warmer.

The Sankey and Ward both have fixed temperature thermostats which cut off the heater at around 20°C (68°F) – a suitable temperature for germinating most common types of seed.

To be safe:

- use a residual current device (RCD)
- if you accidentally damage the base of an electric propagator, disconnect it immediately and do not use it again
- disconnect before moving or cleaning it. Never immerse in water
- do not let water collect around the outside of a propagator.

Running costs

Propagators cost around 1p per Watt (W) of heater per week to run if left on continuously – less if they have a thermostat. In order to use a propagator in a greenhouse in early spring, you will need to provide background heating of 5–7°C (41–45°F). On cold nights, cover the propagator with bubble polythene, to help retain heat.

FACTS, FIGURES AND TEST RESULTS

1 Price

The recommended retail price. Propagators are often discounted at chainstores.

2 Compost temperature

The range of the compost temperatures in the propagators was monitored over a 48 hour period. With the window-sill

HEATED PROPAGATORS

	Price (1)	Heater	Length	Width	Compost temperature (2)	Seed germination (3)	Electrical safety (4)	Extras	
	£	W	cm	cm					
WINDOW-SILL PROPAGATORS									
► **Erin 465P**	11.89	14	58	21	24°C to 28°C	◩	[1]	24 × 6cm square pots [2]	◄
► **Erin 466P** (with thermostat)	20.79	18	50	21	17°C to 19°C	◪	√	24 × 6cm square pots [2]	◄
► **Ward**	18.99	14	50	16	17°C to 21°C	□	√	2 half trays with lids 12 × 8cm pots with saucers	◄
PROPAGATORS WITHOUT THERMOSTATS									
Humex Louvaire R033	19.95	12	37	23	13°C to 25°C	—	√	4 quarter trays	
► **Jemp Fastgrow**	10.95	12	36	23	22°C to 31°C	—	√	—	◄
► **Sankey 14inch**	22.62	12	36	21	16°C to 28°C	—	√	2 half trays, plug	◄
► **Ward 14inch**	22.99	12	36	21	16°C to 27°C	—	√	4 quarter trays	◄
PROPAGATORS WITH THERMOSTATS									
► **Sankey Plantmaster**	55.99	40	57	38	21°C to 23°C	—	√	6 half trays, 20 pots, capillary matting, plug	◄
► **Ward Thermostatically Controlled**	52.49	65	61	33	22°C	—	√	2 half trays, 3 quarter trays	◄

► Recommended in the Buying Guide ◄

KEY TO RATINGS best ▨ > ◩ > □ > ◪ > ■ **worst**

[1] Easy to pull apart but no exposed live parts. More recent samples (with yellow and red outer packaging) were satisfactory.

[2] Refills available as 499P Plant Starters and Propagator Refills.

propagators, the compost temperature range is based on background room temperatures of 8°C to 12°C. For the other propagators, the background temperature of the room ranged from 5°C to 14°C.

3 Seed germination

We used the window-sill propagators to raise tomato seedlings in an unheated greenhouse in early and late spring. The average background temperature at 6am (the coolest time of day) was 8°C (46°F) in early spring and 12°C (54°F) in late spring. All produced good results with a background temperature of 12°C but germination was sometimes slower at 8°C. Seedling emergence at 8°C:

◩ = 80% after six days
□ = 80% after nine days
◪ = 80% after 12 days
— = not tested

4 Electrical safety

√ = satisfactory in our tests

LAWNMOWERS

Cylinder, Hover and Rotary

From *Which?* and *Gardening from Which?* April 1990

Buying a mower for the first time or replacing an old one can be a daunting business. With new models coming on to the market every year priced at anything between £35 and £1,000, it pays to choose wisely. These are some of the questions you should be asking before you decide which mower to buy.

What size is the lawn?

Small lawns under 50sqm It's worth thinking about a hand-pushed mower especially if there are a lot of obstacles in your lawn like trees, beds or play equipment – or if you value the exercise aspect of gardening! Otherwise one of the small electric mowers recommended for medium lawns is likely to be suitable.

Medium lawns, 50 to 250sq m Choose a mower with a cutting width of 300mm. Most of these are electric, but if your garden is long you'll find a small petrol mower easier than coping with lengths of cable.

Large lawns, over 250sq m For lawns up to about 500sq m a cutting width of 350 to 400mm is adequate; larger than this a 500mm cutting width will save you time.

Which power supply is best?

Electric lawnmowers are cheaper, lighter, cleaner and easier to keep in good working order. But coping with the electric cable can be a nuisance, and the power will drop off noticeably if you use an extension lead more than 30m long.

Petrol lawnmowers can be used far from a power source, and virtually all self-propelled mowers are petrol-powered. The main drawbacks are the need to buy and store petrol, and to actively maintain the petrol engine. Many petrol engines also have a rope-pull start, which can be hard work. Electric starters are available on many larger models, but add around £80 to the price.

Which type of mower?

The precise model you choose is likely to have more effect on performance than the type of cutting system. Nevertheless the three types – cylinder, rotary and hover – do have their pros and cons.

Cylinder mowers are the traditional kind with four or six blades which turn at the front of the mower and cut against a fixed blade. Cylinder mowers can cut very close and are the only way to maintain *very* short, fine turf. However, they do need a level surface to perform well, and often can't cope with long grass.

Wheeled rotary mowers usually have a single blade rotating at high speed under a protective skirt. The best rotary mowers can cope with short or long grass and uneven surfaces and still produce a reasonable finish. However, many electric-powered models have safety drawbacks so you must choose carefully. Some rotary mowers now have plastic blades, and the best of these cut as well as metal blades.

Hover mowers also have a rotary blade,

but are designed to produce a cushion of air to lift the mower so wheels aren't needed. They're manoeuvrable but hovers generally cope poorly with long grass.

Get mowing!

It's tempting to put off the first mow of the year for as long as possible, but this can be a false economy of effort because the weeds get a head start on the grass which means more weeding later. Think about the first cut as soon as the milder weather has encouraged the grass to grow.

Research by *Gardening from Which?* shows that the type of mower you use is less important than how often and on what setting it is used. Whatever mower you choose, the task will be easier with a well-maintained machine that has sharp blades; but you shouldn't mow the lawn if there's a frost or if the grass is wet.

How often?

For a typical family lawn in normal weather conditions, mowing once a week should be sufficient. During dry spells, when growth slows down, once a fortnight should be adequate. Regular mowing encourages grass to form side-shoots – so it looks thicker and healthier. Leaving too long a gap between cuts means the lawn looks discoloured after mowing and becomes patchy and uneven as the new grass grows.

How short?

A common mistake is to close shave the lawn in the hope that it will take longer to grow again. A healthy lawn grows 2.5cm (1in) a week. Family lawns containing ryegrass should not be cut shorter than 2.5cm (1in) whilst fine quality lawns should be cut to 12–18mm (½–¾in). In any case don't cut shorter than 12mm (½in) – this is the domain of the professional greenkeeper and a lawn this short takes hours of intensive work. Cutting too short weakens the grass and allows weeds and moss to grow. It also makes the lawn vulnerable to hot, dry spells when the grass can easily become scorched.

BUYING GUIDE

SMALL AND MEDIUM-SIZED LAWNS

BEST BUYS **Black & Decker GB200C** (£70), cylinder mower, good for short and medium length grass and collects clippings. **Qualcast Hover-safe 30** (£60), hover mower reasonable on all types of grass, but does not collect clippings. **Qualcast Suffolk Punch 35** (£290), cylinder mower with finely adjustable height settings.

LARGE LAWNS

BEST BUYS **Flymo Chevron 420 S** (£208), electric rotary. **Honda HREL 171 PDE** (£242), electric rotary. **Mountfield Empress 16** (£249), electric rotary. **Mountfield Empress 16in HP** (£299, self-propelled version £80 more), petrol rotary. All will collect clippings. **Allen E40** (£150), electric hover. **Flymo Pilot L38** (£270), petrol hover. Both good for lawns with slopes, soft patches or overhanging shrubs.

Clippings: to collect or not to collect?

If you mow frequently, leaving the clippings on the lawn is a good idea. Apart from saving time, nutrients from the clippings actually do the lawn good. *Gardening from Which?* trials showed that leaving the clippings did not result in an increase in weeds or a build up of thatch – the fibrous layer that *can* build up between leaves and soil.

But you should collect the clippings from the first mow in spring or if the grass is particularly long. And if the grass is very wet, the clippings may lie like a blanket causing the grass underneath to turn yellow.

Edging your bets

If you have a large or informal garden, untrimmed lawn edges won't look amiss but in a small formal area they can look untidy. Cylinder mowers and rotary mowers with a roller or inset wheels will cut right up to the edge. Hover mowers and most rotaries will leave a fringe of upright grass. You might also need to trim round trees or along walls.

Safety

Our first concern is for safety, particularly from mechanical hazards. Most serious lawnmower accidents involve hands or feet coming into contact with the cutting blade, especially on rotary or hover mowers. Good design can greatly reduce the risk of injury. In particular we look for:

Blade enclosure This must be continuous around the blades in order to prevent accidental contact with the user's feet.

Lock-off switch If a lawnmower can be turned on in a single simple operation it is all too easy to knock the switch accidentally into the on position. It could also be operated easily by an inquisitive child. A lock-off switch is safer because it requires two separate operations to turn it on.

Dead-man's handle This switches the motor off when it is released, so the mower will stop when you move away from the operating position.

Blade stopping times It should not be possible to stop the mower, turn it over and still touch a moving blade. Some mowers have a blade brake that stops the blade quickly when you release the control lever. With models which have had blade brakes fitted since our test, make sure you get a 1990 version – earlier models won't have the brakes. We think the blade should stop completely within three seconds, though the proposed European Standard for lawnmowers allows a stopping time of five seconds.

Clutch-release On self-propelled mowers, a clutch-release stops the mower moving forward when you release the handle.

We commend the recent trend of providing plastic blades. These are standard on Qualcast Mow 'n' Trim, Rota-Safe and Hover-safe. Some other mowers have plastic blades as a free option and we have tested their performance alongside the metal blades.

Residual current devices (RCDs) are not provided with electric mowers. If you accidentally cut a mower cable, an RCD will cut off the power in a split second, eliminating the risk of electrocution. If you use an electric mower, we strongly recommend that you buy one.

— = not tested

▶ Recommended in the Buying Guide ◀

KEY TO RATINGS best ◩ > ◪ > □ > ◩ > ■ **worst**

LAWNMOWERS: PERFORMANCE

	Price (2)	Performance (3): Short grass	Medium grass	Long grass	Very long grass	Damp grass	Convenience (4)	Safety (5)	
	£								
(1) ELECTRIC CYLINDER									
► **Black & Decker GB200C** (UK)	70	◤	◤	◪	—	□	◤	satisfactory	◄
Black & Decker GB201P (UK)	80	◤	□	◪	—	□	◤	satisfactory	
Qualcast Concorde E30 De Luxe (UK)	75	□	◪	◪	—	□	◤	satisfactory	
Qualcast Concorde XR35 (UK)	120	□	◪	□	—	□	◤	satisfactory	
(1) PETROL CYLINDER									
► **Qualcast Suffolk Punch 35** (UK)	290	●	□	◪	—	◤	□	satisfactory	◄
(1) ELECTRIC HOVER									
► **Allen E40** (UK)	150	●	◤	◪	■	□	□	satisfactory	◄
Black & Decker GX303C (UK)	70	◤	◤	◪	—	□	◤	D	
Black & Decker GX303C (plastic blades) (UK)	70	□	◪	■	—	—	—	satisfactory	
Flymo Sprinter E25 Twin (UK)	81	□	□	□	—	□	□	C	
Flymo Sprinter E25 Twin (plastic blades) (UK)	81	◪	□	□	—	—	—	satisfactory	
Flymo Sprinter E30 Twin (UK)	88	□	◤	□	—	□	□	C	
Flymo Sprinter E30 Twin (plastic blades) (UK)	88	◪	◤	□	—	—	—	satisfactory	
Flymo Sprinter E38 Twin (UK)	121	◪	□	□	■	□	□	B	
Flymo Sprinter E38 Twin (plastic blades) (UK)	121	◪	◪	—	—	—	—	satisfactory	
Flymo Sprintmaster XE25 Twin (UK)	121	□	□	□	—	□	◤	B	
Flymo Sprintmaster XE25 Twin (plastic blades) (UK)	121	□	□	□	—	—	—	B	
Flymo Sprintmaster XE30 Twin (UK)	135	◤	◤	◪	—	□	◤	B	
Flymo Sprintmaster XE38 Twin (UK)	174	□	◤	□	■	□	◤	B	
Flymo Sprintmaster XE38 Twin (plastic blades) (UK)	174	□	◪	—	—	—	—	satisfactory	
Qualcast Hover-Safe 25 (UK)	50	◪	□	□	—	□	◤	satisfactory	
► **Qualcast Hover-Safe 30** (UK)	60	□	◤	□	—	□	◤	satisfactory	◄
(1) PETROL HOVER									
► **Flymo Pilot L38** (UK)	270	◤	◤	□	■	□	□	satisfactory	◄
(1) ELECTRIC ROTARY									
Al-Ko Aero 340A (Austria)	160	◪	◤	◪	—	◤	◤	satisfactory	
Al-Ko Sapphire 34EW (Austria)	160	◪	◤	□	■	□	◤	satisfactory	
Black & Decker GR200C (UK)	80	◪	□	□	—	□	◤	satisfactory	
Black & Decker GR410C (Belgium)	120	◪	◪	□	—	□	◤	C,E	
Black & Decker GR421C (Belgium)	155	◤	◤	◤	□	◪	◤	satisfactory	
Flymo Chevron 300T (UK)	135	□	□	□	—	□	◤	C	
Flymo Chevron 300T (plastic blades) (UK)	135	□	□	◪	—	—	—	satisfactory	
Flymo Chevron 350S (UK)	175	◤	◤	□	—	□	◤	C,F	
► **Flymo Chevron 420S** (UK)	208	◤	●	◤	□	□	◤	satisfactory	◄
► **Honda HREL 171PDE** (France)	242	◤	●	◤	□	□	◤	satisfactory	◄
► **Mountfield Empress 16** (UK)	249	◤	◤	◤	□	◤	◤	satisfactory	◄
Mountfield Princess (UK)	155	□	◤	◤	—	□	◤	satisfactory	
Qualcast Mow'n'Trim (UK)	45	□	□	◪	—	□	◤	satisfactory	
Qualcast Rota-Safe (UK)	40	□	□	◪	—	□	□	satisfactory	
Qualcast Turbo S3000 (UK)	100	□	◪	□	—	◪	◤	satisfactory	
Wolf E30 Cub (W Germany)	149	□	◤	□	—	□	◤	C	
Wolf E42 Consul (UK)	249	◤	●	◤	□	◤	□	B	
(1) PETROL ROTARY									
Al-Ko Pearl 42 BWT (Austria)	278	◤	◤	◤	◤	◤	□	satisfactory	
Flymo Chevron 420GL (UK)	300	□	◤	◤	◤	□	□	satisfactory	
Hayter Harrier 41 (UK)	300	◪	□	◤	□	□	◤	satisfactory	
Honda HR173 QDE (France)	397	◤	◤	◤	◤	◤	□	satisfactory	
Mountfield Emblem 15in (UK)	239	◤	□	◤	◤	□	◤	satisfactory	
► **Mountfield Empress 16in HP** (UK)	299	◤	◤	◤	◤	◤	□	satisfactory	◄
► **Mountfield Empress 16in SP** (UK)	379	◤	◤	◤	◤	□	◤	satisfactory	◄
Wolf P42R Consul (UK)	279	◤	◤	◤	—	◤	◤	satisfactory	

FACTS, FIGURES AND TEST RESULTS

1 Type
We've split the mowers up into six different categories.

2 Price
The recommended retail price.

3 Performance
With each mower we assess the closeness, cleanness and evenness of cut on different types of grass as follows:
Short grass represents a fine lawn cut every week to around 20mm (¾ inch) high.
Medium grass is more typical of slightly coarser grass used in family lawns and cut to around 40mm (1½ inch) high.
Long grass is what you might find after returning from your summer holiday.
Very long grass is what you might find on areas of grass that have not been cut for most of the season. We test only larger mowers on very long grass.
Damp grass highlights any tendency for the mower to clog up with clippings. We use medium length grass after a heavy dew or light shower to test mower performance on damp grass.

4 Convenience
Features which make a mower convenient to use are important. For example, do the handles fold up conveniently for storage? How many cutting height settings are there and how easy is it to adjust the height? Can the cable be removed? Is it easy to store?

The mowers are used by two experienced testers on a lawn with a number of typical obstacles such as trees, paths and walls near to the grass. Each mower is then rated for eight aspects of use, including operating position, use of the grasscatcher and adjusting the mower before use. All these are combined into a convenience rating.

5 Safety
See the Features Table for what safety features each mower has; here we tell you how they performed in our tests.

B = blade stopping time too long
C = blade stopping time too long when tested (over 5 secs). Now fitted with a blade brake
D = handle can swing into an almost vertical position – possible to pull mower back onto feet in our tests
E = supply cord scraped on metal deflector plates – Black & Decker say this has been rectified
F = motor overheated in our tests – Flymo say they have fitted a thermal cut-out

Models with long blade stopping times are satisfactory if fitted with a plastic blade.

KEY TO FEATURES

Grass collection
BR = rear bag BXF = front box
BXR = rear box

Cutting positions
The number of levels at which the cutting height can be set FV = fully variable

Handle type
HB = handle bar PT = pram type
SS = single stem

Safety features
B = blade brake C = clutch-release
D = dead-man's handle
L = lock-off switch P = plastic blade
PO = plastic blade optional

Other features
A = adjustable handle height
R = rear roller

LAWNMOWERS: FEATURES

	Power	Cutting width	Self-propelled?	Grass collection	Weight	Cutting height	Cutting positions	Handle type	Safety features	Other features	
		mm			kg	mm					
1 ELECTRIC CYLINDER											
► **Black & Decker GB200C**	380W	300	N	BXF	7.2	10–20	3	SS	L	A,R	◄
Black & Decker GB201P	380W	300	N	BXF	7.6	10–20	3	PT	L	A,R	
Qualcast Concorde E30 De Luxe	280W	300	N	BXF	9.5	13–29	3	PT	L	A,R	
Qualcast Concorde XR35	325W	350	N	BXR	10	11–24	6	PT	L	A,R	
1 PETROL CYLINDER											
► **Qualcast Suffolk Punch 35**	114cc	350	Y	BXF	29	3–30	FV	HB	C	A,R	◄
1 ELECTRIC HOVER											
► **Allen E40**	1000W	400	N	none	10	12–36	3	PT	B	A	◄
Black & Decker GX303C	1150W	300	N	none	7	4–16	3	PT	B,L,PO	A	
Flymo Sprinter E25 Twin	900W	250	N	none	6	20–40	4	PT	B,D,L,PO	A	
Flymo Sprinter E30 Twin	950W	300	N	none	7	20–40	4	PT	B,D,L,PO	A	
Flymo Sprinter E38 Twin	1150W	380	N	none	8	20–40	4	PT	D,L,PO	A	
Flymo Sprintmaster XE25 Twin	900W	250	N	BXR	8	20–40	4	PT	D,L,PO	A	
Flymo Sprintmaster XE30 Twin	1150W	300	N	BXR	8.8	20–40	4	PT	D,L,PO	A	
Flymo Sprintmaster XE38 Twin	1400W	380	N	BXR	13.7	20–45	5	PT	D,L,PO	A	
Qualcast Hover-Safe 25	800W	250	N	none	5.9	22–30	2	PT	L,P	A	
► **Qualcast Hover-Safe 30**	1000W	300	N	none	7.6	22–30	2	PT	L,P	A	◄
1 PETROL HOVER											
► **Flymo Pilot L38**	98cc	380	N	none	14	10–34	4	PT		A	◄
1 ELECTRIC ROTARY											
Al-Ko Aero 340A	1100W	340	N	BXR	20	18–50	4	PT	B,L		
Al-Ko Sapphire 34EW	1100W	340	N	BXR	16	17–50	3	PT	B,L	R	
Black & Decker GR200C	1100W	300	N	BR	5.7	15–38	4	PT	L	A	
Black & Decker GR410C	900W	330	N	BR	16.9	20–50	3	PT	B,L	A	
Black & Decker GR421C	1500W	410	N	BR	20.9	20–50	4	PT	B,L	A	
Flymo Chevron 300T	900W	300	N	BXR	10.5	20–60	5	PT	B,D,L,PO	R	
Flymo Chevron 350S	1150W	350	N	BR	16	20–80	5	PT	B,D,L	A,R	
► **Flymo Chevron 420S**	1500W	420	N	BR	22	16–65	7	PT	B,D,L	A,R	◄
► **Honda HREL 171PDE**	1300W	420	N	BR	22	13–76	7	PT	I		◄
► **Mountfield Empress 16**	1050W	405	N	BR	22	12–56	FV	PT	B	A,R	◄
Mountfield Princess	1000W	355	N	BR	17.5	12–50	FV	PT	B	R	
Qualcast Mow'n'Trim	475W	300	N	none	6.3	22–37	2	PT	B,L	A,R	
Qualcast Rota-Safe	475W	300	N	none	5.6	22–37	3	SS	B,L	A,R	
Qualcast Turbo S3000	900W	300	N	BXR	12	19–37	3	PT	B,L	R	
Wolf E30 Cub	800W	300	N	BXR	14	19–55	4	PT	B,D,L		
Wolf E42 Consul	1800W	400	N	BXR	28	10–50	5	PT	D,L	R	
1 PETROL ROTARY											
Al-Ko Pearl 42BWT	3.5hp	420	N	BXR	33	20–50	6	PT		R	
Flymo Chevron 420 GL	3.5hp	420	N	BR	28	16-65	7	PT		A,R	
Hayter Harrier 41	3hp	410	N	BR	29	13–57	5	PT		R	
Honda HR 173QDE	2.4hp	420	N	BR	22.5	13–51	7	PT	B	R	
Mountfield Emblem 15in	3hp	380	N	BR	21.6	16–64	7	PT		A	
► **Mountfield Empress 16in HP**	3.5hp	405	N	BR	23.2	12–56	FV	PT		A,R	◄
► **Mountfield Empress 16in SP**	3.5hp	405	Y	BR	28.4	12–56	FV	PT	C	A,R	◄
Wolf P42R Consul	3.5hp	400	N	BXR	31	10–50	7	PT		R	

► Recommended in the Buying Guide ◄

LAWN TRIMMERS

Electric Nylon-line Trimmers

From *Gardening from Which?* June 1990

Small electric trimmers cut grass and other vegetation by means of a nylon line which spins around at high speed. They can cope with fairly soft growth but not with large areas of brambles and dense undergrowth (for this you will probably need a brushcutter). With use, the nylon line will gradually wear down and it can break when it hits something hard. However, line wear or breakage is not a major inconvenience if the line can be replaced quickly. Each trimmer has a spool of nylon line which can be fed out either manually or automatically. With a manual feed you have to stop and unplug the machine and pull out more line by hand. This method is very inconvenient so we do not recommend trimmers with manual feeds.

The alternatives are auto feeds, where the line can be advanced automatically, and bump feeds, where you bounce the trimmer on the ground to advance the line. There are also foot-operated feeds and push button feeds. With these you often have to stop the trimmer to advance the line so they may not be quite so convenient.

There were no major problems renewing the lines of most of the trimmers. The exception was the Black & Decker GL210C. Its line tended to disappear into the spool and had to be rethreaded, which proved fiddly and time consuming.

When all the line is used up, you usually need to buy a replacement spool (usually around £4). However, with Black & Decker trimmers you can buy the line separately which works out cheaper than buying a new spool every time. We had problems changing the spool on the Black & Decker GL220CM.

BUYING GUIDE

All of the trimmers tested coped with light trimming tasks satisfactorily. However, we recommend the following as they performed well, were convenient to use, had automatic feeds and passed our safety test. Choose the cheapest one you can find locally which is comfortable to hold and has features that you could find useful.

BASIC TRIMMERS

Suitable for light tasks. Can cope reasonably well with tougher tasks.

BEST BUYS **Flymo Multritrim 250** (£40). **Gardena Turbotrimmer 190** (£39)

TRIMMERS FOR TOUGH TASKS

Will cope with both light and tough tasks well.

BEST BUYS **Black & Decker GL630C** (£48). **Gardena Turbotrimmer 200** (£55). **Gardena Turbotrimmer 300** (£70). **Skil 538H** (£51). **Skil 539H** (£57)

Handles

Some trimmers have adjustable handles. For example, the Flymo Minitrim and Bosch PRT 23 had telescopic handles which could be adjusted to match your height. The Flymo Multitrim 250, Gardena Turbotrimmer 300 and Wolf RQ400 had single handles that could be adjusted to various angles.

Some trimmers have a second handle, which is an advantage on the heavier trimmers or if you want to use the trimmer for tougher tasks.

Sledges and frames

A sledge can be rested on the ground during use to make trimming less tiring. We found the sledge on the Bosch PRT 280 useful when trimming level ground and when sliding the trimmer under shrubs. The sledge on the Gardena Turbotrimmer 300 was useful when trimming on level ground, though it tended to catch on long grass.

Some trimmers have wire frames which allow them to stand up when not in use. We found little real advantage in this feature.

Rotating heads

With some trimmers you can rotate the cutting edge for cutting vertical lawn edges. We found this a more useful feature on the Flymo Multitrim and Wolf RQ400 than on the Gardena Turbotrimmer 300.

Any trimmer can be used to trim lawn edges but none of those we have tested could give such a neat finish as you would get with edging shears.

Safety

The main danger from trimmers is that a broken line or flying debris could hit your eyes, so it is a sensible precaution to wear goggles (Kite mark BS 2092) when using them. Of the trimmers tested, safety goggles were only supplied with the Flymo Multitrim.

When using a trimmer or handling cut vegetation, it is also advisable to cover up your arms and legs as the plant sap can cause quite a severe skin rash.

The instructions and warnings supplied with all the trimmers we tested were satisfactory. Make sure you read them carefully before using your trimmer.

Electrical safety

All the electric trimmers on the market have a deadman's handle which turns off the motor when you release the switch. Some models also have a lock-off switch which prevents accidental starting.

The Peugeot CB300NA had no coupler on the short supply lead. If a female coupler was fitted to the trimmer supply lead and a male coupler fitted to the extension cable, the prongs on the male coupler would be live and could prove fatal. Peugeot tell us they will fit couplers. Before buying a trimmer with a short supply lead, check that it is fitted with the correct coupler.

NYLON-LINE TRIMMERS

		Price (1)	Power	Cutting width	Weight	Line feed	Lock-off switch?	Second handle?	Extra features (2)	Light tasks (3 Performance)	Tough tasks (3 Performance)	Electrical safety (3 Performance)	
		£	W	mm	kg								
	Black & Decker GL210C (UK)	25	230	230	1.2	bump	no	no		◤	□	satisfactory	
	Black & Decker GL220CM (UK)[1]	30	230	250	1.3	bump	no	no		□	□	satisfactory	
►	**Black & Decker GL630C** (UK)	48	550	300	2.5	push	no	yes	C,R,W	◤	◤	satisfactory	◄
	Bosch PRT 23 (W Germany)	26	200	230	1.5	manual	yes	yes	C,T	□	□	satisfactory	
	Bosch PRT 280 (W Germany)	50	280	300	2.6	push	yes	yes	C,N,S	◤	□	satisfactory	
	Flymo Minitrim (UK)	28	250	200	1.8	auto	yes	no	T	◤	◪	satisfactory	
►	**Flymo Multitrim 250** (UK)	40	350	250	2.9	auto	yes	yes	G,R,V	◤	□	satisfactory	◄
►	**Gardena Turbotrimmer 190** (W Germany)	39	190	220	1.6	bump	no	no	C	◤	□	satisfactory	◄
►	**Gardena Turbotrimmer 200** (W Germany)	55	190	250	1.9	foot	no	no	C,S	◤	◤	satisfactory	◄
►	**Gardena Turbotrimmer 300** (W Germany)	70	270	250	2.3	foot	no	no	C,R,S,V	◤	◤	satisfactory	◄
	Peugeot CB300 NA (France)	64	300	250	1.6	bump	no	yes		◤	□	unsatisfactory[2]	
	Skil 536H (Netherlands)	47	175	250	1.3	bump	no	no		□	◪	satisfactory	
►	**Skil 538H** (Netherlands)	51	200	250	1.5	bump	no	yes		◤	◤	satisfactory	◄
►	**Skil 539H** (Netherlands)	57	200	250	1.7	bump	no	yes	S,W	◤	◤	satisfactory	◄
	Wolf RQ202 (W Germany)	50	220	230	2	manual	no	no		◤	◤	satisfactory	
	Wolf RQ205 (W Germany)	60	250	230	2.3	manual	no	yes		◤	□	satisfactory	
	Wolf RQ400 (W Germany)	90	350	300	2.8	auto	no	yes	R,V,W	◤	□	satisfactory	

► Recommended in the Buying Guide ◄

KEY TO RATINGS best ◩ > ◤ > □ > ◪ > ■ **worst**

[1] Only available through Argos and mail order catalogues [2] No cable coupler fitted – see 'Electrical safety'

FACTS, FIGURES AND TEST RESULTS

1 Price

Prices for Black & Decker (except GL220CM), Bosch and Flymo trimmers are typical selling prices. Others are manufacturers' suggested selling prices.

2 Extra features

C = cable restraint, prevents plug and socket separating

G = safety glasses supplied

N = two nylon cutting lines supplied for quicker trimming

R = rotating head for lawn edging

S = sledge for resting trimmer on ground in use

T = telescopic first handle, adjusts to height of user

V = variable handle angle

W = wire frame

3 Performance

The trimmers were tested for a series of light tasks such as trimming lawn edges and cutting back grass growing beneath a wall and around posts. They were also tested to see how they coped with tougher tasks such as cutting moist dense grass, long grass (up to 30cm/12in high) and rough vegetation (such as very long coarse grass with ferns).

ON THE ROAD

Family Estate Cars
Small Family Cars • Tyres

ESTATE CARS

Seven Cars for Family and Luggage

From *Which?* November 1989

A good estate car has to be versatile. Can it carry five adults and all the paraphernalia needed for a holiday? Does it drive as easily as the saloon version? Is there enough space in the back to carry that antique chest of drawers home from the auctioneers? Can it be driven down to the shops, parked and loaded with the minimum of fuss? Will the dog like it?

We've tested seven estates priced between £11,845 and £15,150. None of them can answer 'Yes' to all our questions. But some get closer than others.

What's inside

All our test cars have space to seat four or five adults. Rear-facing seats are standard on the Mazda, optional on the Volvo and the Montego (£245), while the Renault has the option of a factory-fitted third row of forward-facing seats (£400).

With all the rear seats folded, the luggage space that's available in these estates makes them among the roomiest on the market. Power-assisted steering is standard on the Carlton, Mazda, Peugeot, Volkswagen and the Volvo, optional on the others. You can adjust the headlight beam from inside the car – which avoids dazzling other drivers when fully laden – on the Peugeot, Renault and Vauxhall. The Volvo has a ride height adjuster as an option (£375) for use when the car is loaded. The Montego has it as an option (£305 or £450 including rear-facing seats). Some of the models we've looked at can be bought in cheaper trim versions. The Peugeot GRD and the GLD, for example, have the same engine. For about nine hundred pounds less, the latter comes without electric door mirrors and central locking, and looks a good buy.

Diesel or petrol?

For this report we've concentrated on diesel versions (two of them turbocharged), and included two petrol-engined estates not available in diesel form.

Diesel cars don't give the performance of petrol-engined ones, but our drivers did not feel at a disadvantage with them on the road. And there's a plus side.

On a day to day basis, diesels should be cheaper to run than their petrol equivalents – at the pump, diesel is around 7p per gallon cheaper than unleaded. And fuel consumption, particularly in urban driving, is better. So the outstandingly frugal diesel Montego, which managed an overall consumption figure of 45mpg, would save you £££ in fuel, over the thirsty petrol-engined Volvo's 25mpg.

Diesel versions can cost considerably more than petrol ones, so you'll need to balance this against day-to-day savings. Depreciation, another factor in the equation, now seems less important; some diesel models hold their value better than their petrol equivalents; and, while service intervals may be more frequent on diesels, insurance costs can be cheaper. If you value economy more than sparkling performance, a diesel engine would be a good choice.

Are you sitting safely?

During our safety inspections we found problems on two of our cars that make them potentially dangerous.

On our **Renault 21 Savanna**, the latches which hold the middle row of seats in place didn't engage properly. This is an extremely serious safety problem, because the seat belt buckles and central lap belt are attached to the seat and not directly to the floor. If the latches failed in a crash, even passengers wearing their seat belts could move forward with the weight of the seat behind them in a frontal impact.

When we told Renault of the problem, they examined our test car, but could not find the same fault on cars from their production line in France. They said that the fault on our test car must be an isolated incident.

The **Mazda 626** has two rear-facing seats that can be used by small adults or children. These seats don't have their own head restraints; passengers in them are meant to be restrained by the back of the head restraints fitted to the normal forward facing rear seat. But the restraints do not align properly with rear-facing passengers. Correct support of the head in rearward-facing seats is essential to avoid neck injury in frontal impacts. We've written to the Department of Transport about this and recommend that you don't buy the Mazda for use as a seven-seater.

We also found a problem with the **Volvo 240**. The folding rear-facing seat did not always latch securely to the floor. The seat belt attaches to the seat itself rather than directly to the floor of the car. If the seat is not secure, passengers would not be restrained correctly in a rear impact.

Volvo say that, if fitting instructions are properly carried out by their dealers, the seat should be secure. They say they

BUYING GUIDE

All the seven estates we tested had something to recommend then.

For luggage, the Carlton has the largest available boot space with the rear seats folded. Almost as large and easy to load were the Montego, Renault and Volvo.

The Mazda, Peugeot and Carlton will all seat five adults reasonably comfortably. Some of the cars have rear-facing seats to carry extra passengers. We have reservations about these.

For a refined diesel engine the Peugeot has the edge; but the Montego's overall fuel consumption (over 45mpg) is outstanding for a large car. The Peugeot and Passat were also over 40mpg.

There were marked differences between the cars for secondary safety. The Mazda, Montego, Peugeot and Renault rated 5. The Passat and the Volvo both scored a commendable 7. But if secondary safety is your major concern, the **Vauxhall Carlton** was one of the highest rated cars we've ever looked at and is a clear Best Buy.

Overall we liked the **Peugeot 405 GRD** because of the refinement of its diesel engine and its steering and road-holding.

have changed their instructions to ensure fitting is done correctly and that dealers will check free any cars brought into them. We welcome this, but think the design of the seat is wrong and should be modified.

Safety ratings
Ratings given in this report are for the cars used as five-seater saloons with luggage space. It does not cover using any extra seats in the rear. The higher the rating the better the car will protect you in a crash. Points in each car entry are listed in order of importance.

MONTEGO 2.0 DLX TURBO [1]

The engine needs refinement and the steering is heavy; but very economical and has good luggage space

Engine/transmission – best at speed
Quite lively acceleration from a willing, if unrefined, diesel when turbo comes in. But less good at lower revs, where drivers found noticeable vibration. Fairly positive gear change. Relaxed on motorways.
Brakes – satisfactory
Fairly heavy effort needed to brake at higher speeds.
Steering – an effort at low speed
The non-assisted steering (power-assisted steering was £285 extra) was fairly heavy on the move and heavy at low speed. Accurate with reasonable road feel.
Road-holding – good
Confident when cornered. Gripped satisfactorily in all conditions.
Controls – few problems
All major controls were well positioned. Some minor controls slightly obscured by steering wheel, but displays were clear. Manual sunroof was stiff to open, the radio/cassette was a stretch, and hands could hit door pocket when using the window winder.
Visibility – some blemishes
Windscreen wiper pattern left some areas of screen unwiped. Visors left small gaps, but screen had tinted strip.
Space – easy access
Good legroom front and rear, but front headroom was restricted by the sunroof. The rear seat width was not adequate for three adults in comfort. Central locking not fitted. Lock plungers were hard to grasp – annoying when unlocking from inside.
Seats – adequate
Well-controlled on good surfaces, but worse on bumpier roads. Larger bumps made suspension bottom out noisily. Rear passengers complained of restless ride.
Noise – not quiet
Had pronounced diesel rattle in most situations; wind noise and interior rattles.
Heating – straightforward
Easy to use, but heat was not that well distributed.
Ventilation – acceptable
Not linked to heater and could be fan assisted.
Luggage – plus point
Cavernous luggage space, and still large even when unconverted. Rear seat folding straightforward: roller blind parcel shelf kept prying eyes away. Flat floor and high tailgate made loading easy.
Security – poor
We gained entry in seven seconds. Steering column lock was secure.
Attention – simple
Routine maintenance was easy to check.

[1] Tested as 2.0 TD DL

Wear and tear
Insufficient data. Our car came with 12 minor defects, the worst of which was an oil leak from the turbo oil drain tube.
Secondary safety – Rating 5
For All seat belt buckles are designed to resist inadvertent release. Nearside facia is free from structures likely to cause high loads on legs of belted front seat passengers. Adjustable upper anchorage on front seat belts should improve fit of belt for shorter people, although taller people may have problems if belts are used in lowest position. Refer to user handbook. Design of front door and sill may stiffen vehicle somewhat in a side impact.
Against Steering wheel design offers belted driver little protection in head or face contact. Column lock and bracketry are in driver's knee impact area. Steering wheel does not offer good load spreading for a chest impact. Front seat lap belt angle is undesirably shallow with seat adjusted right forward. This decreases the chance of lap belt remaining safely positioned on the pelvis. Rear seat belts are inconvenient to use in conjunction with folding rear seat; some slack may be concealed. Fuel filler vulnerable to damage, if bodywork is distorted in an accident, increasing risk of fuel spillage. Fuel line from diesel pump is vulnerable to damage in a frontal impact. Child restraint information in handbook suggested that four point mounted child seats – a good safety feature – cannot be used. In our view, if fitted with care, they can be.

Rear-facing seats can be fitted in the Montego as an option. If they are, the head restraints, which have to be removed to fold the seat, should be repositioned before use, as described in the handbook.

PEUGEOT 405 GRD

A good all-round package. A refined diesel engine, reasonable space, good economy, and pleasant to drive

Engine transmission – capable and willing
Responsive, quite lively diesel power unit that pulled smoothly and easily even in higher gears. Particularly willing for a diesel engine. Relaxed motorway cruiser with power to spare. Some drivers found the gear change a little clunky.
Brakes – no problem
Very light efforts needed, although they became heavier with repeated use in our brake fade test. They were progressive with good feel, but the handbrake was sometimes heavy.
Steering – well-balanced
Power-assisted steering was light without taking away too much feel of the road.
Road-holding – reassuring
Cornered confidently even at higher speeds. Gripped well on all surfaces, wet or dry, and always felt secure.
Controls – mostly good
Comfortable driving position with controls well placed. Minor controls were easy to use. Displays were clear although the warning lights were scattered. The only drawbacks our drivers found were the radio/cassette, where the security flap made inserting a tape awkward, and a window winder which was obstructed by the door pocket which could scrape unwary hands.
Visibility – no problems
The electrically operated door mirrors were a plus. The wipers with their integral screen washers gave acceptable coverage, though the interior visors left some gaps.

Space – adequate
No problems with access, but the doors needed a hefty shove to close. There was enough width for three adults on the rear seat. Leg- and headroom throughout were acceptable. Our drivers liked the remote control key and central locking.
Seats – well-shaped
Gave good support; firm and comfortable for most even on longer journeys.
Ride – firm but absorbent
Well-controlled. Suspension absorbed both uneven roads and single bumps well. Slight jitteriness for rear passengers on poorer surfaces.
Noise – subdued
Commendably quiet for a diesel car. Few other problems apart from some tyre noise on coarse surfaces.
Heating – sufficient
Heating system was easy to control and had adequate output and distribution.
Ventilation – efficient
Easy to use, linked to heater, but still acceptable.
Luggage – useful load carrier
Low sill and flat area for luggage made loading and unloading easy. Rear parcel shelf was sometimes awkward to remove, but seat folded easily.
Security – poor
We gained entry in five seconds. Steering column lock was secure.
Attention – easy
Routine checks were simple to carry out, although replacing the plastic oil filler cap could be messy.
Wear and tear
Insufficient data on this model. This car came with a high number of minor defects – 21 in all. Although none of them was serious on its own, collectively they were annoying. Six of the defects were paintwork imperfections.

Secondary safety – Rating 5
For Adjustable upper anchorage on front seat belts should improve seat belt fit for shorter occupants.
Against Column lock, adjuster, bracketry and switch mounting bracket all in driver's knee impact area. Steering wheel offers belted driver only mediocre protection in head or face contact, and does not offer good load spreading for a chest impact. Front head restraints contain only a shaped wire which will not load the head reliably, and may concentrate bending on the neck. The restraints are also not locked securely against vertical movement, and could ride down in a crash, particularly if set too low initially. The rear seat hinges could release due to bodyshell or seat back distortion, allowing luggage to load the occupants. The fuel line is vulnerable to damage in frontal impact.

RENAULT 21 GTD SAVANNA

Good ride and quite spacious, but spoilt by heavy steering and noise

Engine/transmission – felt like a diesel
Reasonably willing engine with fair acceleration. Good on motorways. Vibrations were felt particularly at lower speeds. Gear selection is a touch notchy.
Brakes – some niggles
Light efforts required, although they became heavier with repeated use in our brake fade tests. Some drivers found them over-sensitive.
Steering – fairly heavy
Precise and accurate, but it took some effort to move the unassisted wheel when on the move or manoeuvring at low speed

(power-assisted steering is now standard). Some kick-back also noted.

Road-holding – good
Sure-footed in corners and nicely predictable. Loads and crosswinds made little difference.

Controls – several complaints
Some found the hard steering wheel uncomfortable. The pedals were set too high, and too close together. The minor controls were not well laid out. They were either obscured by the steering wheel or out of easy reach of the driver. The radio/cassette was also a stretch, and the window winders were awkward.

Visibility – some problems
Wipers gave good coverage, except at the top of the screen. Visors left gaps around interior mirror.

Space – best in front
Getting in and out was easy in front, but slightly less so in rear. Three adults could just fit in the second row of seats, although leg- and headroom were limited and they were uncomfortably close to the sides of the car. The third row of seats was suitable only for children. No central locking. Separate door and ignition keys were found irritating.

Seats – acceptable
Soft but satisfactory. Some drivers said the seat material stuck to clothes.

Ride – one of the better aspects
Capable ride in front on a variety of surfaces and did not deteriorate when fully laden.

Noise – not a quiet car
Engine noise, especially under acceleration, was very noticeable. Better on motorways but here road and tyre noise took over. Some boominess at lower revs.

Heating – satisfactory
Reasonable output of heat but distribution could make it stuffy in back.

Ventilation – not ideal
Acceptable flow of air, but was closely linked to heater.

Luggage – spacious
After folding, a slightly complicated procedure for the rearmost seat, the space available for luggage was cavernous. The flat floor and the high opening tailgate made loading easy.

Security – poor
We gained entry in five seconds. Steering column lock was secure.

Attention – mainly easy
Routine checks were simple, but the dipstick, towards the rear of the engine, was a stretch.

Wear and tear
Insufficient data. The car came with only three minor defects on delivery.

Secondary safety – Rating 5 (See 'Are you sitting safely?')

For Driver's knee impact area free from stiff structures other than the steering column and lock. Middle row seat belts remain convenient to use even when rear seat is folded up and down again. Steering system has specific anti-intrusion feature which should help limit steering wheel movement.

Against Steering wheel design offers belted driver little protection in head or face contact, and does not offer good load spreading for a chest impact. The front seat head restraints do not adjust high enough for taller people and have poor vertical location. Seat belts on the second row of seats are not convenient to use when folding seat is converted.

Changes
Since we tested this model Renault have introduced a new version of the GTD Savanna. This will have an 1870cc diesel unit, which is likely to alter the performance of the car, plus power assisted

steering as standard. The dashboard has also been re-designed. Our findings apply to the pre-September 1989 cars.

VAUXHALL CARLTON 2.3 LD

Good load carrier, with notable safety rating let down by an unrefined diesel engine

Engine/transmission – slow off the mark
Drivers found starting slow from cold, and said car felt sluggish, although acceleration was fair. Once at required speed, cruised easily on motorways. Reasonable gear change and clutch.

Brakes – sometimes grabby
Moderate efforts needed, but was not always easy to achieve smooth braking.

Steering – good
Effective power assistance made this one of car's plus features. Precise and very light, but retained good road feel.

Road-holding – capable
Stuck to road well in dry and bumpy conditions. Slight deterioration of grip in wet, but no dramas when cornering.

Controls – mixed verdicts
Comfortable driving position for most, although some found pedals offset too far to right. Handbrake in awkward position for some. There was a confusing selection of switches, knobs and blanks on dashboard. The displays were uncluttered. Sunroof was easy to open.

Visibility – no major obstructions
Wipers left small uncleared space on driver's side.

Space – mostly good
Easy access front and rear. Some drivers found left leg cramped by transmission tunnel and clutch footrest. Ample legroom and width for three in rear. Central locking fitted.

Seats – mostly good
Seats were firm and comfortable, although passenger in middle of rear was less comfortable because of 50/50 split of seat.

Ride – good in front, worse in rear
Smooth ride in front even when fully laden, but rear passengers found it restless.

Noise – unimpressive
Prominent diesel rattle when motorway cruising. Other sources are better suppressed. Some drivers reported wind noise from open sunroof at 50mph.

Heating – generally good
Heating system worked well although some found it difficult to control.

Ventilation – good
Generous ventilation. Cool air possible even though linked to heater.

Luggage – cavernous capacity
Loading and seat folding were both simple operations. Even when unconverted, the boot was large. The flexible luggage cover kept prying eyes away.

Security – good
We failed to gain entry to the Carlton through the doors. The deadlock system on this model defeated our expert. He did however gain entry to the car via the tailgate. This took around 30 seconds. Steering column lock was secure.

Attention – simple
Routine checks all easy to carry out.

Wear and tear
Insufficient data on this model. The car came with six minor defects on delivery. More seriously, when running, the steering idler arm fell from its mounting bracket because a vital retaining washer had been left off the car. Vauxhall checked their assembly procedures and

say the fault was an isolated incident.

Secondary safety – Rating 8

The Carlton, together with the Saab 9000i and BMW 520i, scores higher than any other car we have tested for secondary safety.

For Steering wheel offers belted driver good protection in face or head contact. Apart from the steering column and ignition lock for the driver, both sides of the facia are free from structures likely to cause injury. Rear seat belts have adjustable upper anchorage position – which may give better restraint for children, while the adjustable upper anchorage on the front seat belts should improve fit for shorter people. Taller people may have problems if belt is used in its lowest position. The handbook could be clearer on this point. Steering column contains specific anti-intrusion feature which should help to minimise steering wheel movement.

Against Steering wheel does not offer good load spreading for a chest impact. The axial compression column contains basic telescoping steering shaft that has been cited as causing column malfunction during driver impacts with the steering wheel in other models.

VOLKSWAGEN PASSAT CL TD

A firm ride, good space and steering, but a slightly reluctant turbo diesel that needs to be pushed

Engine/transmission – some turbo lag

The turbo-charged engine needed to be worked to get the best from it, which didn't always make for smooth driving. It was sluggish at lower speeds with noticeable lag. Good motorway cruiser. Positive, though slightly notchy, gear change.

Brakes – acceptable

Fairly light effort. There was some pedal travel before they began to bite.

Steering – responsive

Accurate, precise steering. The power assistance made it light, but still allowed enough road feel.

Road-holding – confident

Cornered tidily and gripped well in all conditions. There was little difference when fully laden or in crosswinds.

Controls – pedal problems

The positioning of the pedals came in for some criticism. They were too close to some drivers and the difference in height between the brake and accelerator was awkward. Some found the handbrake set too far back. Minor controls were laid out logically, although some warning lights on switches were hard to see.

Visibility – adequate

Sloping bonnet made judgement when parking difficult. Otherwise there were few problems apart from the visors which left gaps around interior mirror.

Space – better in front

Acceptable head- and legroom in front. Rear legroom was best in group, but the seat width was tight for three. Central locking fitted

Seats – firm

Comfortable for most although some found them rather firm.

Ride – some jostling

Well-controlled on good surfaces, but poorer surfaces were felt.

Noise – acceptably suppressed

Some under hard acceleration. Fairly quiet on motorway, but some road noise.

Heating – good

Good heating output and distribution which was easily controlled.

Ventilation – not ideal
Too closely linked to heater, but satisfactory with heater off.
Luggage – useful space
Seat folding could have been easier but once accomplished the luggage area is large, and even unconverted it's big. Rear seats do not split, which made it less versatile for load carrying.
Security – good
We did manage to break into the Passat, but it took our expert around one minute. This is considerably longer than almost any other car we've tested, and would deter many a less determined assault on the mechanism. Steering column lock was secure.
Attention – simple
All the routine checks were easy to carry out.
Wear and tear
No data available on this model. It came with three minor defects on delivery.
Secondary safety – Rating 7
The Passat is above average for this group.
For The steering wheel is considerately designed for belted driver's head impact. The recessed spokes and the column end are covered with energy absorbing foam. The driver's knee area is relatively free from stiff structures apart from the steering column and lock. The fuel filler is not rigidly attached to the exterior bodywork, reducing the risk of fuel leakage due to panel distortion. Adjustable upper anchorage on front seat belts should improve fit for shorter people. Taller people may have problems if belt is used in lowest position. Users are advised to follow the instructions in the handbook carefully. The steering column contains a specific anti-intrusion measure which should help minimise steering wheel movement. Special anchorage points are provided on the load space floor for four point mounting child restraints.
Against The steering wheel does not offer good load spreading for a chest impact. The rear seat belts are inconvenient to use when the rear seat is folded down and up again, as the buckles do not reposition themselves automatically. Unshielded starter solenoid terminal could allow electrical shorting in frontal impacts.

MAZDA 626 2.0 GLX

An estate car that does most things in a competent and efficient manner but none of them outstandingly

Engine/transmission – fairly flexible
Willing two litre petrol engine with lively performance. An able motorway cruiser. Some harshness under hard acceleration.
Brakes – acceptable
Light efforts required for brakes which had progressive feel.
Steering – satisfactory
At first drivers thought it too light, but, once used to it, found it accurate. Satisfactory road feel.
Road-holding – acceptable
Good in dry, slightly less good in wet. Some twitchiness at rear when going round corners. Stable in straight lines and crosswinds.
Controls – generally good
Driving position was good (steering wheel rake was adjustable) and so were the controls on the stalks. But some displays and minor controls were obscured by the steering wheel, and the radio cassette was a stretch for the driver.

Visibility – judgement sometimes hard
Drivers did not find it easy to see the full extent of the bonnet. But the interior and door mirrors gave a good field of vision. The rear wiper covered only a narrow portion of the screen, and the visors left gaps.

Space – good for five
No real access problems, except to luggage area seats, where legroom is cramped (see 'Are you sitting safely?'). The leg- and headroom were acceptable in the front and there was room for three in the back with good headroom. Central locking, except for tailgate, which had own control inside car.

Seats – good
The front and rear seats were good. They adjusted easily, and were firm and comfortable.

Ride – unexceptional
Not outstanding in this department. Some complaints of jitteriness, but felt better when fully laden.

Noise – disappointing
Some noise, mainly engine and exhaust under hard acceleration, better on motorways. Some annoying rattles from dashboard area.

Heating – adequate
Heating system did job efficiently, with reasonable output and distribution, but some drivers found controls needed frequent adjustment to maintain temperature.

Ventilation – satisfactory
Ventilation was acceptable with a reasonable, easily distributed flow.

Luggage – good
Loading and unloading was made easy by the low sill, flat floor and a high opening tailgate. The rear seats folded easily, and in unconverted form it still had a large boot.

Security – poor
We gained entry in five seconds. The steering column lock was secure.

Attention – not difficult
It was easy to get at for all routine maintenance checks.

Wear and tear
Insufficient data for this model but Mazdas have proved reliable in our surveys. The car had nine defects when delivered. The worst of these was an excess amount of travel on the footbrake, which was cured by bleeding the system.

Secondary safety – Rating 5 (See 'Are you sitting safely?')

For All seat belt buckles are designed to resist inadvertent release. The steering column has a specific anti-intrusion feature which should help minimise steering wheel movement. Head restraints are fitted to outside seats in middle row as standard.

Against Steering wheel design offers the belted driver little protection in head or face contact. The column lock, adjuster and support bracketry are in driver's knee impact area. The steering wheel does not offer good load spread for a chest impact. The hinges on folding middle row of seats are liable to release, if seat back or bodyshell distorts in an accident, which could allow additional loading from seat back and luggage on occupants. The fuel filler is vulnerable to damage if body work is distorted in an accident, increasing the chance of a fuel spillage. The adjustable upper anchorage on the front seat belts does not go high enough for taller occupants. No mention of child restraints in the handbook.

*See page 8 for how to use **Which? Buying Guide**.*

VOLVO 240 GL

Spacious, but falling behind in other areas, especially road-holding, when compared with its more modern competition

Engine/transmission – lacked refinement
Willing, if not always smooth, engine with lively acceleration. Gear changing was on the heavy side, as was the clutch. Gears were also notchy.

Brakes – good
Moderate effort needed – braking was both progressive and reassuring.

Steering – uninspired
Power assisted and required little effort, but some found it lacked road feel.

Road-holding – showing its age
Tendency to roll made corners less than enjoyable. Gripped well in dry, but some wheel spin in wet when accelerating hard. Twitchy in crosswinds.

FAMILY ESTATE CARS

	Engine/ transmission	Brakes	Steering	Road-holding	Controls	Visibility	Space	Seats
DIESEL ENGINES								
Montego 2.0 DLX Turbo	●	○	○	★	○	○	○	○
Peugeot 405 GRD	★	○	★	★	○	○	○	★
Renault 21 GTD Savanna	○	○	○	★	●	○	○	○
Vauxhall Carlton 2.3 LD	○	○	★	○	○	○	○	○
Volkswagen Passat CL TD	○	○	★	★	○	○	○	○
PETROL ENGINES								
Mazda 626 2.0 GLX	○	○	○	○	○	○	★	★
Volvo 240 GL	○	○	○	○	○	○	○	○

	Price[1]	Engine capacity	Engine power	Kerb weight	Number of doors	Length	Width	Luggage capacity[2]	Sill height	Max height of load space	Length of load space	Width at wheel arches	Fuel tank
	£	cc	bhp	kg		m	m	litres	cm	cm	cm	cm	litres
DIESEL ENGINES													
Montego 2.0 DLX Turbo	12,500	1994	81	1180	5	4.47	1.94	465/850	57	82	168	92	50
Peugeot 405 GRD	13,165	1905	70	1120	5	4.40	1.71	410/775	56	86	158	112	70
Renault 21 GTD Savanna	11,845	2068	67	1103	5	4.64	1.71	505/875[3]	57	90	173	114	66
Vauxhall Carlton 2.3 LD	15,150	2260	72	1354	5	4.73	1.93	475/885	62	76	188	111	70
Volkswagen Passat CL TD	13,060	1588	60	1190	5	4.57	1.99	410/770	60	81	169	92	70
PETROL ENGINES													
Mazda 626 2.0 GLX	12,749	1998	110	1225	5	4.59	1.69	415/700	59	77	163	98	60
Volvo 240 GL	13,950	1986	118	1349	5	4.79	1.71	495/865	64/68[5]	83	187	102	60

[1] Manufacturers' list prices for September 1990
[2] First figure is normal boot space with 4/5 passengers. Second is with rear seats down
[3] Boot capacity with third row of seats folded
[4] Over revs in 4th
[5] Adjustable ride height. 1990 model has automatic system
[6] 1990 models are 4 E unless fitted with catalytic converter. These are unleaded
[7] U = runs on unleaded petrol
L = runs on leaded petrol
E = runs on either leaded or unleaded without adjustment

Controls – fair
Upright driving position liked, but the offset pedals were not. Drivers also disliked the handbrake. Minor controls scattered across dashboard, and some were hidden by steering wheel as were some of the warning lights.

Visibility – several problems
The view to the rear was obstructed by the large headrests. Slightly compensated by the door mirror on driver's side, which gave wider than usual field of vision. Wipers left large area uncovered. Visors left gaps.

Space – some access criticisms
Heavy doors were not always easy to open, and the doorway width was narrow. The highish sill took some stepping over. But head- and legroom for driver and passengers were good. Rear seat width made it a two to three seater only. Central locking fitted.

Ride	Noise	Heating	Ventilation	Luggage	Security	Attention	Wear/tear	Secondary safety
○	○	○	○	★	●	○	[1]	5
○	○	○	○	★	●	○	[1]	5
○	○	○	○	★	●	○	[1]	5
○	○	○	★	★	★	○	[1]	8
○	○	★	○	★	★	○	[1]	7
○	○	○	○	★	●	○	[1]	5
○	○	○	★	★	●	○	[1]	7

Insufficient data from our reliability survey

Fuel grade[7]	Consumption: Overall	Consumption: Steady 70mph in 5th	Consumption: Simulated city	Consumption: Oil	Insurance group	Time to cover ¼mile	Acceleration: Time to reach 60mph	Acceleration: 30 to 50mph in 4th	Acceleration: 60 to 70mph in 4th	Acceleration: 60 to 70mph in 5th	Maximum speed: 4th gear	Maximum speed: 5th gear	Stopping distance from 60mph
star	mpg	mpg	mpg	mpp		sec	sec	sec	sec	sec	mph	mph	ft
Diesel	45.3	48.2	26.1	4800	5	20.1	14.9	13.4	7.2	10.9	91.2	95.5	136
Diesel	42.3	43.3	24.6	2100	4	21.0	16.9	9.9	7.2	11.5	72.5	94.4	135
Diesel	39.4	43.9	21.1	1000	5	21.5	18.7	12.1	9.0	11.9	91.5	94.6	148
Diesel	35.7	39.0	18.4	1700	6	21.4	18.0	13.0	8.2	10.6	92.1	99.1	137
Diesel	42.8	49.5	24.4	1400	5	20.2	15.2	14.8	6.7	8.0	95.4	104.9	150
4 E	26.6	33.2	14.4	None	6	19.1	12.7	9.5	5.4	7.4	[4]	110.9	137
4 L[6]	24.8	30.1	14.1	3200	7	18.6	12.0	11.1	6.3	9.5	106.7	104.3	136

RATINGS ★ = commendable, ○ = adequate, maybe a mixture of good and bad, ● = poor overall or serious shortcomings that we think you shouldn't have to live with.

The higher the score given for secondary safety the better your chances of surviving an accident without serious injury.

Seats – adequate
Firm with good support, but some drivers reported lateral movement.
Ride – rarely restful
Acceptable on good surfaces but disappointing on poorer ones where every bump and irregularity was felt.
Noise – some complaints
Some intrusive engine noise under hard acceleration, and wind noise at speed.
Heating – adequate
Satisfactory heating output and distribution, but was difficult to control.
Ventilation – good
Adequate supply of temperature-adjustable fresh air.
Luggage – good capacity
Folding the seats was slightly complicated, the head restraints had to be removed. The rear sill was higher than others in the group, and the tailgate opened lower but loading presented no major problems.
Security – poor
We gained entry in seven seconds. The steering column lock was secure.
Attention – easy
No problems with simple maintenance.
Wear and tear
No data for this model. The car had six minor defects on delivery, incorrect front wheel alignment being the worst.
Secondary safety – Rating 7 (see 'Are you sitting safely?')
The Volvo is above average in this group.

For Fixed height head restraints on front and outboard middle row seats. The steering column has a specific anti-intrusion measure which should help minimise steering wheel movement. There are beams in the front and rear doors to increase resistance to glancing impacts. Front doors also have substantial foam arm rests to help protect pelvis from side loads. The fuel filler is designed to tolerate moderate distortion. The substantial locks on either side of the folding rear seat back reduce the risks of occupants being loaded by luggage in the rear. Tailgate latches and hinges are unusually strong.

Against Column lock and box section in facia are in driver's knee impact area. The steering wheel offers a belted driver only moderate protection against head or face contact. The steering column design aimed at limiting loads on a driver's chest in a frontal impact is liable to be somewhat compromised by bodyshell intrusion before the driver hits it in more severe accidents. The lap section of the standard seat belts on the additional seat tend to lie high on the abdomen – important for small children who may use this seat. They should use booster cushions.

*Please see page 287 for how to subscribe to **Which?**.*

SMALL FAMILY CARS

The Rover 200, plus our Buying Guide

From *Which?* July 1990

The new Rover 200 is the British manufacturer's latest entry into the smaller family hatchback market. It competes on size with the Ford Escort and Vauxhall Astra, but most of the models in the Rover range are aimed at the more luxurious end of the market; prices range from £9,335 to £13,950.

This is another collaborative venture with Honda – the Honda Concerto is basically the same car, built alongside the 200 at Rover's Longbridge factory. In the cheaper 200s there's an all-new Rover 1.4 litre engine, with 16 valves and fuel injection, coupled to a Peugeot five-speed gearbox built under licence in the UK. The top model gets a 1.6 litre engine, manufactured by Honda in Swindon, plus the choice of a Japanese-built Honda manual or automatic gearbox.

BUYING GUIDE

SMALL FAMILY CARS

The majority of small family cars are sold as hatchbacks, though almost every manufacturer now offers a traditional saloon derived from the hatchback, a few also offer estates. These are the smallest cars most would consider as suitable for a family of four.

If it proves to be reliable, the Rover 200 will rate amongst the best small family hatchbacks. But until then, there are two other cars in this category which fit the bill and offer an impressive record of reliability.

BEST BUY

Toyota Corolla (£8,399 to £12,244). In a class where standards of many cars are mediocre, the Corolla stands out by offering excellent reliability, good bodywork, a comfortable interior and an easy drive. Space is a bit tight in the back of the three-door, however, and the choice of models is limited

BEST BUY

Nissan Sunny (£7,350 to £12,499). The latest Sunny impresses with its all-round competence and reliability. Versions sold before the latest revisions in March 1989 aren't nearly so good. Pre-September 1986 Sunnys make reasonably pleasant and reliable used buys

WORTH CONSIDERING

Mazda 323. If you are looking for a cheap car, a pre-1987 Mazda 323 looks a good bet. The reliability is among the best, and just as importantly, the oldest models resist rust well. Not an outstanding car in other respects, but no major weaknesses either.

The 200 range includes three-, four- and five-door models; the Rover 400 is the saloon version of the car tested for this report.

Our tests showed the 200 to be a big step forward over its predecessor and one of the best cars in its class. It is refined, generally comfortable, easy and enjoyable to drive – though the 1.4 was noisy at times. Our biggest concern is whether this new car will better the poor reliability showing of many past Rover and Austin cars. The old 200 was the best yet, particularly when fitted with a Honda engine, but until the new car has established a record we have to reserve a wholehearted recommendation.

ROVER 214Si: DETAILS AND TEST RESULTS

Good to drive, comfortable, but noisy at times. A promising newcomer

Engine/transmission – refined
Willing, flexible engine provided lively performance and easy motorway cruising. Fully loaded, the car struggled a bit starting off on a 1 in 4 hill. Engine generally smooth, though some vibrations at higher revs. Firm but smooth gear change; clutch on the heavy side.
Brakes – good
Light and progressive, with good feel.
Steering – mostly good
Steering a little heavy for some when parking and prone to tugging in your hands when accelerating hard. But drivers liked the road feel and accuracy.
Road-holding – inspired confidence
Handled reassuringly even at higher speeds. Gripped well on dry, wet and bumpy roads.
Controls – very good
Very good driving position, with adjustable steering wheel and all major controls well placed. Most switches and buttons well placed but a few awkward to reach, with their warning lights hidden. Displays otherwise excellent.
Visibility – few problems
All-round visibility satisfactory, though difficulty in seeing ends of car caused some problems parking. Good mirrors, visors; wiper coverage could be better.
Space and access – generous in front
Easy access to both front and rear. Ample room in the front, but rear legroom slightly restricted with front seat right back. Shoulder room tight for three adults in the rear.
Seats – mostly good
Most drivers found the seats firm and comfortable, but a few would have liked more lumbar support. Rear seat generally liked, though backrest lacked sideways support.
Ride – acceptable
Firm, well-controlled ride, mostly smooth but occasionally restless, more so in the back. Very little body roll on corners.
Noise – a weak point
Engine sounded busy when driven quickly. Uncomfortable boom at motorway speeds and there were some problems with tyre noise too.
Heating – good
The heater output was good and generally well distributed, though driver's left foot could get overheated.
Ventilation – very good
Plenty of fresh air available with or without the heater in use.
Luggage – practical
High-opening tailgate and reasonably low sill made loading the roomy boot

easy. The 60/40 divided rear seat was straightforward to fold, giving a large flat load area.

Security – poor

We gained entry in five seconds. Steering column lock secure.

Attention – easy

All the routine checks were easy to carry out.

Wear and tear

This model is too new for us to have reliability data. The previous Rover 200, also built in co-operation with Honda, has been reliable when fitted with a Honda engine, less so with a Rover engine. The 214 tested here has an all-new Rover engine, the more expensive 216 is Honda-powered.

ROVER 214Si

CAR RATINGS

Engine/transmission	★
Brakes	★
Steering	○
Road-holding	★
Controls	★
Visibility	○
Space	○
Seats	○
Ride	○
Noise	●
Heating	○
Ventilation	★
Luggage	○
Security	●
Attention	★
Wear/tear	[1]
Secondary safety	6

[1] Insufficient data from our reliability survey

KEY TO RATINGS

★ = commendable.

○ = adequate, maybe a mixture of good and bad.

● = poor overall or serious shortcomings that we think you shouldn't have to live with.

The higher the score given for secondary safety the better your chances of surviving an accident without serious injury.

CAR FACTS

Engine capacity cc	1396
Engine power bph	95
Kerb weight kg	1040
Number of doors	5
Length m	4.22
Width m	1.94
Luggage capacity [1] litres	315/704
Sill height cm	65
Max height of load space cm	87
Length of load space cm	142
Width at wheel arches cm	87
Fuel tank litres	55
Fuel grade star	4E [3]
CONSUMPTION	
Overall mpg	33.1
Steady at 70mph in 5th mpg	38.9
Simulated city mpg	13.5
Oil mpp	None
Insurance group	4
ACCELERATION	
Time to cover ¼ mile sec	19.3
Time to reach 60mph sec	13.0
30 to 50mph in 4th sec	10.5
60 to 70mph in 4th sec	5.9
60 to 70mph in 5th sec	9.9
MAXIMUM SPEED	
4th gear mph	[2]
5th gear mph	104
Stopping distance from 60mph m	45.1

[1] First figure is normal boot space. Second is with rear seats down
[2] Over-revs in 4th
[3] E = runs on either leaded or unleaded without adjustment

Secondary safety – Rating 6

For Steering wheel designed to reduce the risk of head and facial injury if struck by a belted driver. All safety belt buckles designed to resist inadvertent release. Left facia free from structures likely to cause high loads on legs of belted front seat passangers. Adjustable upper anchorage on front safety belts should improve fit for shorter people.

Against Column lock, adjuster, brackety and stiff tubular members placed in driver's knee impact area. Filler pipe rigidly attached to wing panel and could be stressed in an accident. Adjustable upper anchorage on front seat belts is unusually low and cannot be adjusted to the ideal position for taller occupants. Rear safety belts are a little inconvenient to use when the rear seat is folded down and up again. Inadequate advice on child restraints in handbook.

MODELS AND PRICES

	3-dr	4-dr	5-dr	engine	power	auto	power assisted steering	anti-lock brakes	catalytic converter
	£	£	£	cc	bhp	£	£	£	£
214 S 16v	9335	9635		1396	95			895	295
214 Si 16v	9690		9990	1396	95		330	895	295
214 SLi 16v			10795	1396	95		330	895	295
214 GSi 16v			11900	1396	95		330	895	295
216 GSi 16v			12550	1590	116	769	330	895	
216 GTi 16v	12760		13950	1590	130		std	895	
414 Si 16v		10260		1396	95		330	895	295
414 SLi 16v		11075		1396	95		330	895	295
416 GSi 16v		12995		1590	116	769	330	895	
416 GTi 16v		14995		1590	130		std	895	

5-speed gearbox standard on all models. std = standard. Prices are list prices for September 1990.

TYRES

Cheap Tyres for Family Cars

From *Which?* April 1990

We tested cheap tyres suitable for use on small to medium family cars. We found:

- all the tyres performed satisfactorily on dry roads
- some had weaknesses in the wet which would make them unsuitable for driving conditions in this country
- others were let down by their performance on snow and ice
- some tyres could last you three times as long as others.

The choice

Some high performance cars need a tyre with a higher speed rating than the ones we tested and they could easily cost around £80 each. Brand name tyres from the major tyre manufacturers for family cars can cost around £35 each. Some well-known manufacturers sell their cheaper tyres under a different name. Of the tyres we tested, Dayton is made by Firestone, Courier by Pirelli, Kelly by Goodyear, and India by Dunlop. Prices vary from £15 to £35; availability tends to vary, too.

Retread tyres

Retreads, sometimes known as remoulds, are used tyres which are given a new life by means of a new tread. They cost about half as much as an equivalent new tyre. Retread tyres have to meet British safety standards, which at present specify that they must be suitable for speeds of up to 70mph, although many retreads are manufactured and tested to higher standards and speeds. For example, any tyre made or sold by a member of the Retread Manufacturers Association and marked accordingly is suitable for speeds up to 95mph. Soon, new UK regulations will require retreads to be marked with a speed rating and load capacity in the same way as new tyres are now.

At the moment, all radial type car tyres in this country must meet current Economic Commission for Europe (ECE) regulation standards and are 'E' marked to this effect on the tyre wall, so you know when buying any new or retread radial tyre that it meets basic safety standards.

Part-worn dangers

You may see very cheap tyres, called 'part-worns' on sale. **Don't buy them.** Investigations have shown that as many as half of them could be unsafe.

Part-worn tyres are second-hand tyres that may have been taken off accident-damaged cars, or that have been repaired in some way, or that have been imported from countries which have a higher tread depth requirement than our own.

Many of these tyres could be damaged internally, and there is no way to tell.

For the last 11 years, some Trading Standards Departments have been highlighting the problems of unsafe used tyres. These are their findings:

- checks on 169 tyres by West Yorkshire Trading Standards Department over six

BUYING GUIDE

BEST BUY For good all-round performance and exceptional durability, we recommend the **Kelly Steelmark II**. This tyre should be available from around £20

The **Nokia Rollster TS** performed exceptionally well on wet roads, but didn't last as long as the Kelly. It might be difficult to find, but should cost between £16 and £28. The **Vredestein Sprint** is also a good all-rounder, which should be fairly easy to find, and will cost around £20.

years found 40 per cent of them were unsafe

- a survey by West Midlands Metropolitan County Council revealed that half of used tyres on sale from dealers they visited in the area were defective
- as a result of the concern expressed by local Trading Standards Departments and by tyre manufacturers at the large number of defective tyres on sale, the Local Authorities Co-ordinating Body on Trading Standards, in conjunction with the British Rubber Manufacturers Association, carried out a national survey to determine the scale of the problem. They found a third of secondhand tyres were 'unfit for service'
- among the defects they found were nails embedded in the tread rubber, severe perishing of the rubber, and even one tyre fitted with an inner tube that was the wrong size and had a hole in it
- meanwhile, West Yorkshire Trading Standards Department have continued to test used tyres and have consistently found that, despite their constant monitoring and enforcement, there are still many substandard used tyres on sale in their area.

Trading Standards people have brought these worrying findings to the Government's attention. But the Department of Transport (DTp) has repeatedly asserted that there is no evidence that secondhand tyres are generally unsafe. They've refused to investigate. The most they've done is issue posters and a press release urging people to take care when buying used tyres.

If you set out to buy used tyres you will be unable to tell whether they have been internally damaged unless you are a tyre expert. We would strongly advise you against buying used tyres in any circumstances.

Looking after your tyres

Tyres play a crucial role in your road safety, however good a driver you are, and this safety is dependent on their condition.

Don't mix tyres

It is illegal and dangerous to mix radials and crossplies on the same axle, or to have radials on the front and crossplies on the rear, except in the case of the emergency use of a spare. You should never mix tyres of different sizes or types, since their different characteristics could cause problems. You shouldn't change your tyre type or size (eg fitting low-profile, wider tyres) without advice from the manufacturer on whether the tyres that you are planning to fit are suitable for your car.

Check your valves

The seals inside and around valves will

deteriorate with time, making them less airtight, so it's a good idea to have your valve changed when you buy a new tyre.

Check your balancing
You should get your wheel balance checked whenever you have a tyre fitted, in order to prevent uneven wear and ensure smooth running. If you find that your car vibrates at speed, this could mean that your tyres are unbalanced or that your wheels are misaligned.

Check your tyre pressure
Maintaining the correct pressure in your tyres is vital for safe, comfortable and economical driving.

Under-inflation causes rapid and irregular wear, increases fuel consumption and can lead to internal heat build up within the tyre. Over-inflation leads to reduced tyre life and grip since less of the tyre is in contact with the road. It can cause a hard ride and makes the tyre more susceptible to damage. Tyre pressures should be checked once a fortnight and before long journeys, when the tyres are cold. Your handbook will tell you the correct pressure. If it is not clearly displayed in your car, and you have trouble remembering it, put a sticker on your dashboard or in the glovebox.

Take care in the wet
Generally grip decreases as the amount of water on the road increases, so you should always slow down, whatever the condition of your tyres. The deeper your tread, the better in wet conditions.

Look out for damage
Driving on under- or over-inflated tyres can make them more vulnerable to damage. Knocks on kerbs and potholes can also cause damage. It's a good idea to check your tyres yourself regularly for visible external damage. If you spot any lumps or bulges, get the tyre examined by a specialist.

Tread depth
Safer tyres mean safer driving – yet many people are driving on over-worn tyres. In 1988, almost a quarter of MOT failures were due, in part at least, to worn or damaged tyres. The minimum legal tread depth in this country is at present 1mm across three-quarters of the total tread width of the tyre, and visible tread over the remaining quarter. In 1992 the minimum requirement for the whole of the European Community will be 1.6mm across the central three-quarters of the tread. The UK Government has tried to resist any change, arguing that this will cost British motorists an extra £70 million a year. But for many years, *Which?* has argued that the safety benefit greatly outweighs the relatively low cost to the individual motorist – so we welcome this long overdue change – but we'd prefer a regulation that covered the *whole* of the tread, not just three-quarters. Bear in mind, too, that damaged or over-worn tyres could compromise an insurance claim.

FACTS, FIGURES AND TEST RESULTS

We put 17 brands of cheaper tyre (our target price was around £20) through a rigorous testing procedure. In conjunction with other European consumer organisations, over 1,000 tyres were put through their paces in all weathers in Germany and Switzerland.

We assessed tyre performance in the wet and dry, on snow and on ice. We also looked at how tyres affected comfort in the car, and how long you can expect the tyres to last. Any one make of tyre is usually sold in varying sizes to suit cars of different weights and performance levels. We chose to test the 155 and 165×13, suitable for small to medium family cars. Our findings should hold for different-sized tyres of the same make, as long as you follow the car maker's recommendations on which size of tyre is suitable for your car.

Speed rating

The maximum speed of which the tyre is capable is indicated by a code letter on the tyre. S = 113mph; T = 118mph. Other letters refer to higher or lower maximum speeds. You should always by tyres suitable for the maximum potential speed of your car, even if you never drive at top speed.

Price range

We checked prices of 155 and 165×13 tyres in 90 outlets throughout the country, including specialist fast-fit centres and independent outlets. We give you the range of prices we found for the 155 size; 165s should cost you about £2 more. You can look up the dealers in your area in *Yellow Pages*. Prices include fitting, but you may have to pay an extra £1.50 for each new valve, and about £3 per wheel for balancing.

Availability

Tyres rated as **widespread** were easy to find in all areas, so shopping around should be worthwhile. Tyres rated as **fairly widespread** should be available in all areas, although your choice of outlet may be limited. Tyres rated as **limited** may be difficult to find; tyres rated **very limited**, very difficult.

On dry roads

Before testing started, all the tyres were run in for at least 250 miles on a dry surface. The tyres were fitted to VW Golfs driven by test drivers. They tested for precision and response at various speeds. At top speed, the drivers evaluated road-holding ability in a curve, and when changing direction. All the tyres performed at least adequately in the dry.

On wet roads

Wet road grip is probably the most crucial element of a tyre's performance, especially with the sort of weather we get in this country. A particular danger is aquaplaning, where tyres lose their grip on the road entirely, ending up by skimming across the surface of the road. Our testers measured the speed at which the tyre started aquaplaning in 4mm and 11mm of water.

Our testers looked at the tyres' braking ability and handling on wet asphalt and concrete. The **Nokia Rollster TS** and **Viking VSS** performed best.

On snow

It is comforting to know that your tyres could deal with snow if the need arose. We tested braking performance from 19mph and traction on compacted snow, and carried out timed trials on the Albula Pass in the Swiss Alps. None of the tyres did as well as the Goodyear Vector, an 'all season' tyre tested previously, so if you live in an area where you experience a lot of snow we would still recommend that you buy this tyre.

On ice
Black ice is a danger often experienced by motorists in the winter. We took the cars to an ice-rink to test braking performance, traction and steering on a circular course. Not surprisingly, no tyre did particularly well on ice, although some did better than others.

Comfort
We drove the cars at various speeds, over a specially designed bumpy surface. We also tested for vibration, caused by a lack of uniformity in the construction of the tyre, and for noise level, both inside and outside the car. Many of the tyres did well in this respect, but the **Stomil**, **Tigar** and **India** were much worse than the others, let down by excessive vibration.

Tyre life
Each make of tyre was fitted to three different types of family car, and tread wear was measured when new, and after 6,000 and also 16,000 miles. Tyres were examined for weak spots and defects.

The life rating gives you an idea of how many miles each tyre lasted. A tyre rated ■ lasted up to 21,000 miles; ◪ up to 26,000 miles; □ up to 33,500 miles; ◤ up to 41,500 miles, and ▧ over 41,500 miles. The **Kelly** and the **Courier** did best.

High speed durability
The tyres were tested to the European Standard for load/speed performance. They were run at gradually increasing speeds up to their maximum permitted limit. All the tyres passed this test.

COURIER R 874
Made in UK

Speed rating	S
Price range	£19 to £26
Availability	Widespread
On dry roads	□
On wet roads	□
On snow	□
On ice	◪
Comfort	□
Life	◤

FEDERAL 715
Made in Taiwan

Speed rating	S
Price range	£16 to £26
Availability	Limited
On dry roads	◤
On wet roads	◪
On snow	◪
On ice	◪
Comfort	◤
Life	□

HAN KOOK R810
Made in South Korea

Speed rating	S
Price range	£16 to £23
Availability	Fairly widespread
On dry roads	□
On wet roads	◪
On snow	□
On ice	□
Comfort	◤
Life	◪

DAYTON
Made in Spain, Portugal

Speed rating	S
Price range	£19 to £25
Availability	Limited
On dry roads	□
On wet roads	◤
On snow	□
On ice	□
Comfort	◤
Life	□

FIRESTONE F 560
Made in Europe

Speed rating	T
Price range	£19 to £35
Availability	Widespread
On dry roads	□
On wet roads	◤
On snow	◪
On ice	◪
Comfort	◤
Life	◪

INDIA GT
Made in UK

Speed rating	S
Price range	£18 to £26
Availability	Widespread
On dry roads	◤
On wet roads	◤
On snow	◪
On ice	◪
Comfort	◪
Life	■

KELLY STEELMARK II
Made in UK

Speed rating	S
Price range	£19 to £26
Availability	Fairly widespread
On dry roads	◩
On wet roads	◩
On snow	□
On ice	□
Comfort	◩
Life	▧

MARSHAL 777
Made in South Korea

Speed rating	S
Price range	£17 to £22
Availability	Limited
On dry roads	◩
On wet roads	□
On snow	◪
On ice	◪
Comfort	□
Life	□

NOKIA ROLLSTER TS
Made in Finland

Speed rating	T
Price range	£16 to £28
Availability	Limited
On dry roads	◩
On wet roads	▧
On snow	□
On ice	□
Comfort	◩
Life	□

PNEUMANT P 46
Made in East Germany

Speed rating	S
Price range	£15 to £22
Availability	Widespread
On dry roads	□
On wet roads	◩
On snow	□
On ice	□
Comfort	◩
Life	◪

SAVA BEST
Made in Yugoslavia

Speed rating	S
Price range	£16 to £24
Availability	Limited
On dry roads	□
On wet roads	□
On snow	■
On ice	◪
Comfort	□
Life	□

SEMPERIT M 601
Made in Austria, Eire

Speed rating	T
Price range	£20 to £35
Availability	Fairly widespread
On dry roads	◩
On wet roads	◩
On snow	◪
On ice	◪
Comfort	◩
Life	□

STOMIL D 124
Made in Poland

Speed rating	S
Price range	£16 to £22
Availability	Fairly widespread
On dry roads	◩
On wet roads	◩
On snow	◪
On ice	□
Comfort	◪
Life	□

TIGAR TG 615
Made in Yugoslavia

Speed rating	T
Price range	£16 to £24
Availability	Fairly widespread
On dry roads	◩
On wet roads	□
On snow	□
On ice	□
Comfort	◪
Life	□

TOYO 300
Made in Japan

Speed rating	S
Price range	£22 to £25
Availability	Limited
On dry roads	◩
On wet roads	◩
On snow	□
On ice	□
Comfort	◩
Life	□

VIKING VSS
Made in Norway

Speed rating	T
Price range	£19 to £24
Availability	Very limited
On dry roads	◩
On wet roads	▧
On snow	□
On ice	□
Comfort	◩
Life	◪

VREDESTEIN SPIRIT
Made in Netherlands

Speed rating	S
Price range	£19 to £32
Availability	Fairly widespread
On dry roads	◩
On wet roads	◩
On snow	□
On ice	□
Comfort	◩
Life	□

Our tests were carried out in conjunction with consumer organisations in Belgium, the Netherlands, Sweden and West Germany and touring clubs in the Netherlands and Switzerland.

DISCONTINUED MODELS

Listed on this page are those discontinued models which we haven't included in the Tables in the book. The models may still be in some shops, or of interest to you if you're buying second-hand. Models flagged as 'Best Buy', 'Recommended' or 'Worth Considering' appeared in the 'Buying Guides' when the reports were first published. For full details, please consult the relevant issue of *Which?*. Back copies can be bought by subscribers to *Which?* (details overleaf) and are available at most public libraries.

IN THE KITCHEN

COOKERS (October 1989)
Moffat Program
Valor Vision
(both gas slot-in)

MICROWAVE OVENS (April 1990)
Goldstar ER 654PE
Hitachi MR7950 (**Best Buy**)

TOASTERS (November 1989)
Dateline DLN 3078
Morphy Richards 44104
Tefal 8444
(all two-slice/long slot)

COFFEE MAKERS (December 1989)
Morphy Richards American 4 cup
Rowenta FK35.2
Rowenta Fresco FK75
(all filter machines)

WALTER FILTERS (August 1990)
Scandinavia Direct Aquastream 3000
(on-tap filter)

CLEANING AND LAUNDRY

DISHWASHERS (November 1989)
ASEA Cylinda 1400
Candy 652W
(both full-size)

Bendix Table Top Compact 78868 (compact) (**Recommended**)

WASHING MACHINES (January 1990)
Ariston AW820
Ariston AW1150
ASEA Cylinda 1200
Bauknecht WA825
Creda Micron 17221
Indesit 823 (**Best Buy**)
Miele W701
Philips De Luxe AWB929
Philips AWB947/2
Philips Elite AWB949
Philips Series 90 1200 Electronic AWB989/2
Zanussi FJ1023
Zanussi FL815
Zanussi FL1022B/W
(all front-loading)

Miele W794 (top-loading)

Bendix Super Compact 71968A
(compact/front-loading)

Washer-Driers
Ariston CD852
Ariston CD1151
Indesit 1001
Servis Companion 9090
(all condenser driers)

Fagor F9800WD
Hoover A8548/50 (**Worth Considering**)
(both air-vented driers)

VACUUM CLEANERS (May 1990)
Electrolux Electronic 616 (upright cleaner with hose attached) (**Best Buy**)

Hoover Turbopower Autoflex U2336 (upright cleaner with separate hose)

Hand-held Cleaners (August 1990)
Black & Decker XL2 H650

SOUND AND VISION

CD PLAYERS (April 1990)
Kenwood DP2010

PERSONAL STEREOS (June 1990)
Aiwa HS T170 (cassette player) (**Best Buy**)

Sony WM BF 62
Sony WM BF 57
(both cassette/radio players)

CAR STEREOS (July 1990)
Clarion 918HP

SATELLITE TV (December 1989)
Alba SAT300
Maspro SRE 90R
(both Astra receivers)

(*Continued on page 288*)

Books from Which?

The Good Bed and Breakfast Guide £9.95

This book guides you across the length and breadth of Britain and the Channel Islands, with entries catering for every taste, from popular holiday resorts to quieter rural locations. The authors have visited every B & B in the guide to bring you reliable, firsthand descriptions. A handy index system and maps will help you pinpoint your chosen destination. Whether you're planning a weekend break or a summer holiday, this is your essential guide.

The Holiday Which? Guide to Weekend Breaks in Europe £10.95

This new book contains all the information you'll need to make the most of your next long weekend or spur-of-the-moment trip to one of Europe's beautiful cities. For each city featured you'll find plenty of details on the kinds of activities that will make your stay as fun-packed or leisurely as you want it to be, plus travel information and a shortlist of the best hotels to stay in, at all price levels. Make the most of your break by consulting ***The Holiday Which? Guide to Weekend Breaks in Europe*** first.

You and the Environment £8.95

With growing concern about and awareness of the state of the environment today, ***You and the Environment*** arrives at the right time to sort out any confusion about what you can do to help. Full of balanced advice and practical hints on how to go 'green' you'll discover what environment damaging materials and household appliances are in use in your home, garden and garage; what alternatives are available and what can be achieved through using them. Taking responsibility for the world in which we live starts with you – the individual – and the practical steps outlined in ***You and the Environment***.

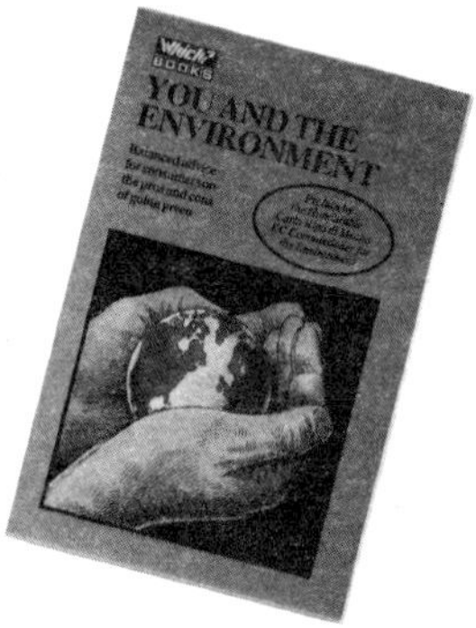

Our books are also available from most bookshops.

Gardening without Chemicals £12.95

This brand new book is packed with practical 'green' advice on ways to get the best out of your garden without resorting to chemicals. Armed with this information you'll be able to deal with all manner of gardening problems, identifying and coping with them without buying insecticides and weedkillers. From choosing trouble-free plants to controlling pests, ***Gardening without Chemicals*** is an essential reference book for everyone who gardens.

Here are just a few of the books published by Consumers' Association. For a complete list or to order any of the above, please write to Dept BG/AD, Consumers' Association, Castlemead, Gascoyne Way, Hertford X, SG14 1LH.
Cheques should be made payable to Consumers' Association.